Breaking the Silence

Breaking the Silence

Mental Health Professionals Disclose
Their Personal and Family Experiences
of Mental Illness

Edited by
Stephen P. Hinshaw

OXFORD
UNIVERSITY PRESS
2008

OXFORD
UNIVERSITY PRESS

Oxford University Press, Inc., publishes works that further
Oxford University's objective of excellence
in research, scholarship, and education.

Oxford   New York
Auckland   Cape Town   Dares Salaam   Hong Kong   Karachi
Kuala Lumpur   Madrid   Melbourne   Mexico City   Nairobi
New Delhi   Shanghai   Taipei   Toronto

With offices in
Argentina   Austria   Brazil   Chile   Czech Republic   France   Greece
Guatemala   Hungary   Italy   Japan   Poland   Portugal   Singapore
South Korea   Switzerland   Thailand   Turkey   Ukraine   Vietnam

Published by Oxford University Press, Inc.
198 Madison Avenue, New York, New York 10016

www.oup.com

Oxford is a registered trademark of Oxford University Press

Library of Congress Cataloging-in-Publication Data
Breaking the silence : mental health professionals disclose their personal and family
experiences of mental illness / edited by Stephen P. Hinshaw.
   p. ; cm.
Includes bibliographical references and index.
ISBN 978-0-19-532026-8
1. Mental health personnel—Mental health. 2. Mental health personnel—Family
relationships. 3. Mental health personnel—Biography. 4. Mentally ill—Family
relationships.
[DNLM: 1. Mental Disorders—Personal Narratives. 2. Family Relations—Personal
Narratives. WM 40 B828 2008] I. Hinshaw, Stephen P.
RC451.4.P79B74 2008
616.890092—dc22   2007012827

9 8 7 6 5 4 3 2 1
Printed in the United States of America
on acid-free paper

Contents

Contributors

Jarralynne Agee, PsyD

Organizational Psychologist, Lecturer, Department of Psychology and African American Studies, 615 C University Hall, University of California, Berkeley, CA 94720

Marc S. Atkins, PhD

Professor of Psychology and Psychiatry, Director of Psychology Training, Department of Psychiatry, University of Illinois at Chicago, Institute for Juvenile Research (M/C 747) 1747 W. Roosevelt Rd., Room 155, Chicago, IL 60608

Theodore P. Beauchaine, PhD

Robert Bolles and Yasuko Endo Endowed Associate Professor, Department of Psychology, University of Washington, Seattle, WA 98195–1525

Jessica L. Borelli, MS

Clinical Psychology Graduate Student, Department of Psychology, Yale University, Box 208205, New Haven, CT 06520

Kay S. Browne, MD

Behavioral Pediatrician, Diagnostic Center of Northern California, 39100 Gallaudet Drive, Fremont, CA 94538

Stephen P. Hinshaw

Professor and Chair, Department of Psychology, Tolman Hall #1650, University of California, Berkeley, CA 94720–1650

Esme A. Londahl-Shaller, PhD

Staff Psychologist, The Children's Center, Langley Porter Psychiatric Hospital and Clinics, University of California, 401 Pernassus Avenue, San Francisco, CA 94143

Jeffrey Liew, PhD

Assistant Professor, College of Education and Human Development, Department of Educational Psychology, Texas A&M University, 4225 TAMU, College Station, TX 77843–4225

Janet Lucas, PhD

Deceased

Laura B. Mason, PhD

Associate Clinical Professor and Coordinator, Psychology Clinic, Department of Psychology, University of California, Berkeley, Tolman Hall #1650, University of California, Berkeley, CA 94720–1650

Peter E. Nathan, PhD

University of Iowa Foundation Distinguished Professor of Psychology and Public Health, Department of Psychology, E119 Seashore Hall, University of Iowa, Iowa City, IA 52242

Elizabeth B. Owens, PhD

Research Psychologist, Institute of Human Development, University of California, Berkeley, Tolman Hall #1690, University of California, Berkeley, CA 94720–1690

Tara S. Peris, PhD

Postdoctoral Fellow, Semel Institute for Neuroscience and Human Behavior, University of California, Los Angeles, 300 Medical Plaza, Suite 1315, Los Angeles, CA 90095

Ruth C. White, PhD, MPH, MSW

Assistant Professor, Social Work, Department of Anthropology, Sociology, and Social Work, Seattle University, 901 12th Avenue, PO Box 222000, Seattle, WA 98122–1090

Carolyn Zahn-Waxler, PhD

Senior Scientist, Department of Psychology, University of Wisconsin, 1202 West Johnson St., Madison, WI 53706–1611

Breaking the Silence

Introduction

Stephen P. Hinshaw

In the chapters that follow, you will find 14 narrative journeys, written by students, clinicians, teachers, and scientists from the mental health professions, broadly construed. The subject matter of each chapter is the author's family or personal experience of mental illness.

You must, of course, judge for yourself, but my guess is that you will have a wide range of emotional responses when reading these contributions. You will hear, for example, about the suicide of a psychologist's mother when he was still an infant, along with the reverberations of that act over the ensuing decades. Other chapters also bear witness to the lasting effects of parental mental illness—schizophrenia, depression, bipolar disorder—on several contributors' identities and career choices, with pointed discussion of their own perceived vulnerability to mental disturbance. You will read, too, about the effects of severe abuse on personal development, as well as the major consequences of serious emotional disturbance in the brothers or sisters of several authors. You will share a medical doctor's experience of having her young adult son begin a long journey of psychotic and withdrawn behavior, followed by his gradual recovery. Still other material involves the accounts of contributors who have worked through the process of self-recognition of mental illness in their own lives.

The range of experiences described in these chapters is wide, and each narrative displays an astonishing degree of openness. My own responses include shock and outrage at the still-taboo nature of mental illness in today's world, deep sadness over many of the devastating experiences portrayed, tenderness and admiration for the responses often displayed by the authors and their family members, and hope regarding the future potential for mental illness to evoke a different set of reactions and outcomes. I have found all of these accounts to be riveting, and I believe that you will, too.

As editor of this volume, I have had the unique opportunity to read and edit these contributions, often being one of the first individuals to see the initial drafts. I must tell you at the outset that this has been one of the most gratifying challenges of my entire professional life. What a rare gift, to have become a part of the creative process in the formation of this volume!

At certain points in each contribution, there are passages that knife through everyday perceptions and mundane concerns, taking aim straight at the heart of the effects of mental illness on individuals and families. Some of these passages include the stark, sudden realization that mental illness is present, as when 8-year-old Jeff Liew finds his mother in the basement of their San Francisco apartment, moments before nearly hanging herself…or Ruth White comes to the clear understanding that she can no longer contemplate hurting, even killing, herself and her young daughter…or Marc Atkins realizes that the voice he hears across the college courtyard emanates not from someone else but from his own mind…or Laura Mason understands that her oldest sister will never be the same again and, subsequently, that her other sisters have major forms of mental disorder, shattering the family.

In other instances the recognition and realization are more gradual. Note, for instance, the process whereby Liz Owens experiences the seemingly endless series of drug-induced, self-destructive episodes of her beloved sister, interspersed with rare moments of deep contact, which quickly vanish when mental illness takes its toll once again. For Jessie Borelli, it is the repeated discovery that there are no rules for consistently engaging with her seriously emotionally disturbed brother, as unpredictability and potential violence lie just underneath the surface.

In the case of several other authors—Jarralynne Agee, Ted Beauchaine, Esme Londahl-Shaller, and Carolyn Zahn-Waxler—poignant moments surround the recognition that a parent is suffering from a mental illness too severe to conquer through love and support alone. For these authors, continued instances of irrational and unpredictable behavior throughout childhood have served to shape views of their families, themselves, and the world at large.

Janet Lucas's discovery was that, in the face of almost unspeakable abuse and neglect from her seriously disturbed parents, she had to feign competence and normality to survive in the world. These devastating words are not easy to hear, especially given that, several months after completing her contribution, Lucas took her own life. With hindsight, it is chilling to read her words that convey the hopelessness she felt with respect to ever feeling truly connected with the rest of the world.

In the case of Kay Browne, it is the realization that her beloved, athletic son, inexplicably home from college, was not experiencing the same reality as the rest of the world—and that her prior medical training had not even begun to prepare her for what lay ahead. And pointedly, Peter Nathan conveys the moment when, as an early adolescent, he could no longer believe that his mother passed away from "natural causes," as his father had alleged, but had instead killed herself barely a year after his own birth.

All of these moments, and all of these portrayals of emotional awareness, penetrate the fog of denial and misunderstanding that so often enshrouds mental illness. Painful as many of these words and images are, they signal the realities encountered each and every day by individuals and family members contending with mental disorder. Reading the contributions in this volume has, in fact, brought me back into close touch with my own personal and family experiences—of my father's lifelong bipolar disorder, misdiagnosed for 40 years as schizophrenia; of the professionally dictated silence about it that pervaded my childhood; of my mother's heroism in dealing with the situation, largely alone—rekindling a deep empathy for all individuals and family members who suffer from mental illness. Each contributor's articulateness, perseverance, and sheer determination to put intensely personal words on paper deserve the accolades of us all.

In its many forms and with its many consequences, mental illness covers a vast territory. Every chance that we get to experience the reality rather than the stereotypes of mental disorder is an opportunity not to be missed. Such portrayals are, after all, the sum and substance of the mental health professions, serving as the raw material for clinical intervention and research investigation. Sometimes mystifying and terrifying, sometimes tragic and inexplicable, sometimes uplifting and triumphant—but always fascinating, poignant, and human—each chapter tells a unique story.

WHY THIS BOOK?

It is a truism that many individuals who enter the mental health professions do so at least in part because of a desire to examine their own (or their family's) psychological issues, vulnerability, and pain. If this is, in fact, the case—that there are often deep personal and family roots that underlie the decision to engage in these disciplines—wouldn't there be a host of volumes like this one, in which people in mental health professions eagerly convey their stories?

Sadly, the actual situation is far different. Indeed, there is a strong current in medicine and mental health that pushes those in the field away from even mentioning such issues, much less exploring them in depth. It is as though such topics and experiences are completely out of bounds; silence remains the order of the day.[1]

Why would personal disclosure of the kinds of harrowing, moving, sometimes tragic, and deeply human events that motivate interest in the mental health field be viewed as almost unthinkable, even forbidden? In my view, there are two main roots of this situation. First, people with mental illness still undergo a huge amount of stigma, so that having a mental disorder in oneself or one's family is among the last things that most individuals would ever want to disclose, regardless of their line of work. Second, the mental health professions themselves convey stigmatizing attitudes, so those who work in the field are subject to a particularly strong code of silence. Let me elaborate on both of these interlinked themes.

At a general level, punitive responses toward mentally disturbed behavior have been strongly present throughout history, evidenced by rejection, overt discrimination, and distressingly poor access to treatment (if any intervention indeed existed). Although there are many roots of such prejudice and rejection, they are likely to have been influenced by ignorance, reductionistic views of causation (ranging from demonic possession to hereditary flaw), and biased accounts in popular lore and public media. Even today, despite our apparently more open and progressive era, serious forms of mental illness are akin to the leprosy of earlier eras, eliciting extremely high levels of shame and disgrace.[2]

Such stigma has deep roots. All societies have in-groups and out-groups, and strong motivation exists to identify with in-group members and to castigate those outside the mainstream. In its various forms, mentally disturbed behavior signals nonconformity, unpredictability, irrationality, and loss of control, qualities that threaten social perceivers both directly and symbolically. There may well be naturally selected origins of the tendency to stigmatize persons displaying mentally disturbed behavior, related to deep human propensities to avoid contagion and exploitation.[3] The history of social responses to mental illness is replete with rejection, punishment, and isolation, with periodic instances of compassion and enlightenment overshadowed by the long legacy of harsh stigmatization.

I hasten to point out that real signs of progress have occurred in recent years. Mental illness is now much more openly discussed than was the norm in the past, scientific knowledge of mental disorders is skyrocketing, and evidence-based treatments for many forms of mental illness now exist. Even if cures are not yet a reality, the potential for intervention strategies to yield symptomatic improvement, enhancement of life functioning, and significant rehabilitation is real.[4]

At the same time, however, distressing evidence exists that the stigmatization of serious forms of mental disorder has actually *grown* across the past 50 years.[5] In other words, our enhanced knowledge base regarding causes and treatments has failed to overcome pervasive practices of distancing from and openly rejecting people with major forms of mental illness. Furthermore, as social norms change in the future and it becomes less acceptable to show open rejection of mental illness, covertly expressed and implicit forms of bias and prejudice will be likely to escalate, similar to the ways that hidden stigma dominates with respect to racial bias in today's world.

On top of this discouraging state of affairs, it is upsetting and perhaps even shocking to realize that an important source of stigma comes from mental health professionals themselves. After all, shouldn't those entrusted with the care and treatment, as well as the scientific investigation, of people with mental illness be expected to show acceptance and compassion? Certainly, there are many professionals in the various disciplines related to mental health who display just these qualities, whether they are performing treatment, effecting prevention, delivering services, or conducting research.

Yet several factors make the reality of the situation more ominous. For one thing, the mental health professions are low on the status hierarchy of those who work in health care. In the words of Goffman—one of the twentieth century's seminal thinkers about stigma—those who perform such work receive "courtesy stigma," in that they are denigrated simply for their association with mental illness.[6] In addition, pay scales are relatively low, work can be quite stressful (with a clientele that can pose real challenges), and prestige is lacking. It would not be surprising if tensions and frustration got displaced onto the very individuals who require service and research investigation.

In addition, the tradition in medicine, psychiatry, and clinical psychology is that the healer is healthy, correct, and knowledgeable, whereas the patient is sick, flawed, and ignorant. That is, there is a huge status differential between those who give and those who receive care, with a resultant tendency for those in professional and scientific roles to hold to an "us versus them" attitude. Given the general degradation of mental illness in the wider culture, professionals may well seek to avoid being tainted by those believed to be inferior, either directly or by association.

In addition, psychological and psychiatric models of mental illness throughout the majority of the twentieth century held that the core cause of mental illness was faulty parenting, as well as personal weakness and deep character flaws within the afflicted person. In other words the field's basic causal models were inherently stigmatizing toward recipients of care—and particularly toward their relatives. In recent years, etiological models have shifted to genetic and biochemical perspectives. But even here, espousal of explicitly biogenetic theories of mental illness can be quite stigmatizing, fostering a view of individuals (and their relatives) as deviant at their very core. Indeed, if genetic perspectives on causation are promoted in reductionistic fashion, punitive attitudes and stigma may actually *increase*, fueled by a view of the subhuman status of those with mental illness.[7]

For all of these reasons, the mental health professions have a checkered history in terms of attitudes toward clinical clientele and research participants. Indeed, in systematic surveys, people with mental illness and their family members report that many of the messages they receive from mental health professionals are unhelpful, pejorative, and even ridiculing, with the frequent communication of low expectations for positive change.[8]

If negative views toward mental illness are present in the mental health professions, think of the bind for those people who work in the field and whose lives are touched by mental illness. In the first place, disclosing personal and family struggles is likely to be perceived as failing to keep appropriate boundaries, potentially tainting the dispassionate stance needed for effective treatment or potentially biasing an objective attitude toward research. At a deeper level, such disclosure is akin to admitting a terrible personal weakness, incompatible with serious, careful work. Furthermore, admission of mental illness in oneself or one's family is clearly a signal of lowered status. The premium is therefore placed on keeping distance from any signs of mental disorder—and on suppressing any disclosure of the deep personal and family issues that may well have been central in promoting initial interest in such work.

In this discussion, I am not contending that mental illness is uniformly uplifting and inspiring or that relevant disclosures should take place in cavalier fashion. Indeed, despite the sometimes-held view that mental disorders are linked with creativity and even genius, mental illness is far more likely to be seriously handicapping.[9] Individuals in the throes of psychosis would be hard pressed, for example, to provide adequate clinical services or perform rational research, much less take adequate care of themselves. In short, mental illness is not inherently adaptive or noble.

But is it the case that healers and investigators must be free of any sign of mental illness and show no history of mentally disordered functioning in order to be effective? For one thing, such a requirement would greatly limit the potential population of professionals, given the high lifetime prevalence rates of mental disorders in the population.[10] In addition, and crucially, personal or family experiences may well provide a unique kind of empathy, sensitivity, and even resilience. Those who know the pain of mental disorders may be uniquely motivated to help clients, work with families, or perform important research on basic mechanisms of pathology or on the effects of clinical services.

With respect to treatment, many sources of empathy and identification may facilitate good clinical contact, but a key wellspring may be the ability to recognize the pain that individuals and families experience when mental illness strikes—so long as overidentification can be avoided. As for research, most often emphasized is the "confirmation" phase of the scientific enterprise, which mandates objective testing of hypotheses and which doubtless requires dispassionate inquiry and rational control. Yet the "discovery" phases of research, linked to the creative process of generating ideas and hypotheses worthy of study, may well receive inspiration from rich personal and family experiences. Scientists with deep motivation to pursue questions of genuine clinical interest are bound to be those who can carry the spark and drive to persevere through the lengthy process of investigation.

In short, the stance of silence and shame for clinicians, teachers, and scientists serves to cut off much of the lifeblood of the field, short-circuiting needed discussion and insight. It may also act to maintain stigma: if we can't even admit to the sources of our own interest and inspiration, how can we accept parallel experiences in those we aim to help or investigate? A vicious cycle is likely to ensue, as crucial issues seldom get discussed or studied, mental illness is further silenced and stigmatized, distance between health-care providers and recipients of treatment grows, ignorance and fear escalate, media images remain derogatory, and discrimination continues. At the same time, funding levels for mental health research and care continue to remain low, and the lack of parity of health insurance coverage makes obtaining adequate treatment difficult, if not impossible.

It is time to stop this cycle. Multiple strategies are needed to overcome stigma, ranging from the elimination of discriminatory laws and the fostering of equitable health care policies to the alteration of pervasive media stereotypes.[11] A particularly helpful avenue for promoting change entails disclosure of the truth—that is, allowing the actual stories of those with mental illness, including those who work in the field, to emerge. Openness on the part of professionals and scientists may well usher in a new era, fostering appreciation of the realities of mental disorder and real concern for those with mental illness. As barriers are surmounted, mutual respect can grow, from professionals to patients/participants and vice versa; all can rise with the tide.

Several pioneers deserve accolades for paving the way. In the early 1960s Kaplan edited a remarkable volume, *The Inner World of Mental Illness*, which provided a compendium of first-person accounts of severely disturbed behavior that has served as an inspiration for numerous professionals in the field. Although several of the excerpts in the volume emanated from medical and mental health professionals, its focus was on portrayals of severe mental illness from a variety of sources. Next, in 1985, Rippere and Williams edited a daring compilation of personal accounts of depression from mental health workers in the United Kingdom, but this work did not readily spread to the United States. Gottesman's *Schizophrenia Genesis* contains lucid, compelling first-person accounts from individuals with this devastating disorder, but once again, the emphasis is not on providers or scientists.[12]

Norman Endler's *Holiday of Darkness*, a gripping account of serious depression, was written from the perspective of an eminent research psychologist. In the mid-1990s, Kay Redfield Jamison published her groundbreaking autobiography, *An Unquiet Mind*, an open and at times devastating account of her lifelong bipolar disorder, which began at age 16 and as a result of which she very nearly took her own life. As a practicing clinical psychologist (as well as author and scholar), she undertook particular risks in making such disclosure, given that it presented challenges to her ability to continue practice. Still, it heralded an atmosphere of openness rather than silence and shame.[13]

My own disclosure of serious family mental illness, *The Years of Silence Are Past: My Father's Life With Bipolar Disorder*, chronicled my father's 40-year struggle with misdiagnosed bipolar disorder and his major psychiatric hospitalizations. In it, I emphasized the silence I experienced as a child (his doctors told him never to discuss mental illness with me or my sister), as well as his gradual disclosures of his life story to me as I attained young adulthood and the effects of both on my professional and personal development. As I discuss in the concluding chapter to the present volume, the act of writing this book forever changed my entire professional identity.[14]

The field of neurology is, in some ways, a step ahead. I recommend a remarkable volume that appeared in the late 1990s: *Injured Brains of Medical Minds*, edited by Narinder Kapur. In this book, a large number of medical and health professionals courageously describe their own experiences with amnesia; memory, language, and perceptual disorders; Parkinson's disease; head injuries and brain tumors; stroke; and epilepsy.[15] This welcome book is accompanied by a growing tradition of case studies and clinical reports far more humanly portrayed than the dry and depersonalized accounts that previously dominated the field. Oliver Sacks is a noteworthy provider of such intriguing depictions of a range of neurological and psychiatric conditions.[16] A key consequence has been the humanizing of individuals formerly viewed as patients, labels, or mere "cases."

Finally, there are now a host of personal stories and narratives of mental illness in the media, ranging from books to magazine pieces and television programs.[17] But disclosures from mental health professionals and scientists per se have been slower to emerge. Even when such narratives have appeared, responses from people in the field have been far from universally positive.[18]

Overall, in regard to the question that constitutes the heading for this section of the Introduction—why this book?—the answer is that there remains a great need for those who work in the mental health fields to tell their own stories, to demystify the entire topic of mental illness, to shed light where darkness has for too long reigned, and to humanize the experiences of mental disorder. There is a parallel need for students, trainees, coworkers, patients, and the public at large to learn of the personal and family realities that have inspired many in the mental health professions to take on the clinical and scientific roles they have embraced. The hope is that this volume's contributions will portend a set of broad and deep discussions within the mental health professions—and across the culture at large—about the presence of mental illness throughout the health care and scientific professions and society as a whole.

HOW DID THIS BOOK GET STARTED?

Rather than emanating from a grand master plan, this book had its origins in personal contacts, individual-level communication, and in some instances quite fortuitous circumstances. Let me give you a brief sense of this process.

This volume got its real start through my writing of the previously noted account of my father, *The Years of Silence Are Past*. The act of disclosing my family's—and my own—experiences opened me up to the power of narrative in starting to comprehend difficult, even tragic life circumstances and in beginning to understand that mental illness can be associated with compassion, strength, and courage. It also alerted me to the harsh reality of stigma in relation to mental illness, prompting my subsequent writing of *The Mark of Shame: Stigma of Mental Illness and an Agenda for Change.* These experiences illuminated, for me, the particular burdens carried by family members of those who are afflicted. My mother, for example, suffered through years of almost impossible behavior patterns on the part of my father while receiving virtually no support from mental health professionals; how she kept our family together is difficult to comprehend. Yet the countless parallel stories of caregivers and relatives that exist are seldom heard.

During book readings, public talks, academic lectures, and course offerings related to my family narrative and the impact of mental illness and its stigmatization on families and society, I have encountered, with regularity, individuals who desperately want to talk about their own experiences. As a clinical psychologist, academic investigator, and professor, I have "known," through clinical experience and the research literature, of the high prevalence of mental illness and its substantial impairments. Yet on hearing countless people ask (almost beg) for contact, on reading the numerous letters and e-mails I received in conjunction with the book on my father, and on investigating just how pervasive the stigmatization of mental illness really is, I became aware at a deeper level of the need to reach out to the mental health professions.

That is, I began to contemplate a book of personal and family disclosures, written by those whose work relates to mental health in one way or another. At first slowly, I began talking with such talented individuals as former Berkeley undergraduates Jessie Borelli, Esme Londahl-Shaller, Jeff Liew, and Tara Peris, learning of their incredible family stories. I subsequently began to ask if each would contemplate writing a chapter for a still-unformed volume dedicated to such narrative disclosures. All contributed compelling narratives, and these were among the first completed entries for this book. All are wonderful, revealing deep sensitivities through intensive, often painful disclosures. Each of these contributors is destined for a stellar career, which should become apparent on reading their pointed and stirring words.

Picking up steam, I made more contacts. Over lunch or during discussions with friends and colleagues, I probed when I heard that someone I knew (or someone they knew) might have a story to tell. Gradually, after several promising leads and a few false starts, additional contributions came together.

For example, I work regularly with UC Berkeley Psychology Clinic Coordinator Laura Mason, and I had spoken with her on several occasions about the pain of mental illness in families. Given her role as a deeply compassionate therapist and educator of our Berkeley graduate students, I was not surprised at her interest in my emerging work in this area. Still, after she read *The Years of Silence Are Past*, I was floored when she revealed to me the stories of her three older sisters, each of whom suffers from devastating mental illness. Her decision to write about her family and about her own personal trajectory is a gift to the entire field.

Around the same time, my colleague Ted Beauchaine and I discussed the "genetic legacy" (a term I had used in *The Years of Silence Are Past*) of having parents with schizophrenia and bipolar disorder, respectively. After a period of reflection, he decided to produce a contribution; as with all of the others in this volume, it is searing in its honesty. Another colleague, Marc Atkins, began to talk to me about college experiences that he had never quite come to terms with. Following considerable thought, he realized that he would like to explore those experiences on paper. The integration of his late-adolescent symptoms of mental illness with his growing interest in children and in positive mental health serves as the subject matter for this deeply personal chapter.

More recent contacts began to mount, some by chance but also because I was increasingly ready to move ahead with the project. Jarralynne Agee, who teaches a course a cross-listed course in Psychology and African-American Studies at Berkeley, began to speak with me about her mother and her family's extremely difficult early years. After she was interviewed for inclusion in another book, she realized that a narrative she could herself create might be of real value. Her contribution is sobering, poignant, and inspirational.

Liz Owens, a skilled developmental psychopathologist with whom I work on my own research team, wondered whether telling the tragic story of her beloved sister's early demise from mental illness and drug abuse would be important to others—and to herself. Its power is a testament to Liz's love and courage.

Kay Browne, a behavioral pediatrician with whom I had collaborated over a decade ago and with whom I had several discussions at the onset of her college-age son's descent into psychosis during the 1990s, realized that she had many themes to cover in writing about her experiences as a parent, advocate, and professional. Her harrowing, moving, and informative contribution adds an incisive perspective to the assembled narratives. Although it is, of course, impossible to compare pain across people, the recognition that a son or daughter is battling a serious mental disorder must be near the top of any list of wrenching experiences.

Still other contacts were the result, it seems, of pure luck, but luck sometimes benefits from preparation and readiness. Ruth White, a UC Berkeley School of Social Welfare PhD who is now a faculty member at Seattle University, happened one day to read a nationwide alumni mailer from the Berkeley Development Office. One of the "Five Big Ideas at Berkeley" in this publication, selected from hundreds that had been proposed, was a piece that I had written on psychology's role in combating both mental illness and the stigma that surrounds it. On seeing this article, Ruth—whom I have never met in person—contacted me; we instantly began an e-mail discussion of our own personal experiences. Within a short time, given my instincts about her integrity, energy, and honesty, I invited her contribute to the book. Her jumpy, poignant chapter, interlaced with journal entries from much of her adult life, was completed within a few weeks; it discloses her awareness of and ambivalence about the need to obtain treatment for her increasingly severe bipolar disorder.

Janet Lucas, a gifted scholar and teacher of English and Lacanian theory, happened to have seen my image on the Berkeley Psychology Department homepage and then found links to my work on narrative and stigma. Contemplating a sabbatical summer in Berkeley (which unfortunately did not materialize), she sent me a dense, rich treatise on child abuse and the creation of false and true selves, with significant autobiographical component. I encouraged her to edit it for the present volume's specifications, and the result of our joint editorial work is found in these grueling yet enlightening pages.

However, I learned several months later that Lucas had died suddenly late in the summer of 2006. My almost-certain hypothesis is that the many burdens she had carried throughout her life led her to end it. The tragedy of recurrent mood disturbance, compounded in her case by a legacy of horrifying abuse, is inescapable.

Peter Nathan, a professor of psychology at the University of Iowa and a member of the Psychology Board at Oxford University Press, had the opportunity to read the book proposal for this very volume after I had submitted it to Oxford. Following the proposal's acceptance, he humbly contacted me, explained the situation, stated that he was intrigued by the idea, and respectfully asked if he could write a chapter about the lasting effects of his mother's suicide, which occurred when he was a year old. I was astounded, having had no idea of this history, and readily agreed. His wonderful contribution followed over the next months. Its title, "Reverberations," would have been an apt name for the entire volume.

Another senior investigator with a distinguished research record, Carolyn Zahn-Waxler, heard of my book on stigma, *The Mark of Shame*, and we subsequently communicated about it. Our e-discussions advanced to consideration of her own family experiences, and she ended up writing a stirring chapter about her mother, her father, herself, and her daughter—illustrating vividly the intergenerational patterns involved with mood disturbance within a family system—with the hope that it will itself expand into a book-length narrative in the near future.

I feel a deep connection with each contributor, in some cases supplemented by a rich friendship and in others solely through correspondence about the writing that now appears in this volume. I hope that you begin to feel such connection yourself as you read these contributions, given that one of the core aims of this book is to promote close linkages to the realities of mental disturbance in individuals and families. With material like this, there is no doubting the honesty, the reality, and the deep humanity of the material presented in each and every case.

Indeed, fostering a sense of the underlying *humanity* of individuals with mental illness is perhaps the key goal for the entire volume. Through presenting these narratives, the contributors and I hope to push beyond stereotypes, distortions, and silence to foster comprehension of mental illness in all its pain, reality, strength, and hope. I hope that you gain from joining in this process.

CORE THEMES

A number of issues and themes emerge from the chapters that follow; I cannot claim to have a handle on all (or even most) of them. But I present several of what I believe to be the main currents underlying these personal and family stories, toward the end of providing at least a preliminary framework for this rich material.

Confusion

The symptoms of mental illness are confusing for sufferers and family members alike. For individuals who become afflicted, problems can include diffusion of identity, exaggerations and distortions of preexisting characteristics, intense and inappropriate emotional responses, and a profound disorganization of mental life and behavior. Those who experience such conditions may not know that mental illness is descending on them; instead, they may incorporate the symptoms into their own paranoid, depressive, or grandiose worldviews. Even when self-recognition occurs, admitting to a mental disorder is extremely difficult, given the levels of stigma that still exist. As a result, seeking treatment may often be delayed. In short, the process is inherently confusing.

On the other hand, close contacts and relatives usually experience a different type of confusion, as they typically have far quicker awareness that things are different. For children, siblings, and parents alike, a clear sense emerges that stable family patterns are disintegrating and that they themselves may have to play extraordinary roles of caretaking for years to come. Mental illness is disorienting and befuddling for family members, and it can take lengthy periods of adjustment to incorporate a changed view of the loved one into a newfound sense of family. Getting a handle on the processes related to such altered perceptions is a prevalent theme throughout many chapters in this volume.

As just one example, Tara Peris had to deal with the disappearance of her mother—already displaying signs of an increasingly severe, yet still subtle, psychotic disorder—when she was a 12 years old, subsequently needing to figure out how to relate to the world (and to herself) in the face of this absence. Years later, the potential for a reunion appeared for an instant but then vanished. Not surprisingly, heartbreak, shock, anger, and a host of confusing emotions reemerged. Almost every other contribution in this volume expresses the confusion and bewilderment that so frequently accompany mental illness.

Searing Pain

There is no escaping the pain and devastation that pertain to mental disorders. Mental illness robs individuals of life opportunities and, in some cases, the will to live. Despair, hopelessness, and a sense of ultimate futility are frequent accompaniments to serious mental disturbance, bringing on severe levels of pain for the afflicted individual. Janet Lucas's narrative is telling in this regard: that she could ultimately not bear the pain related to the overwhelming legacy of her abuse and depression is a sobering reminder of the lethal power of mental disorder.

The pain of mental illness spreads quickly to those who are close to the afflicted individual. Family members, in particular, often experience emotions that are nearly unbearable. Witness the opening sentence of the chapter by Laura Mason, regarding the severe mental disturbances faced by all three of her sisters: "My experience of mental illness in my family of origin is a story of loss and what has been, for me, an unspeakable grief."

There is something about the identity diffusion, untapped potential, extreme disorganization, and lack of hope often present in those with mental disorder that taps a profound sense of loss in family members and close contacts. Responses include shame, survivor guilt (why my relative and not me?), sympathy, pity, frustration, and despair. Although the promise of recovery—or some degree of acceptance of the individual in his or her changed state—can provide an antidote, the pain linked to a family member's mental illness can be unrelenting. Overall, no contribution in this volume is without disclosure of levels of pain that may be among the most intense each writer has ever experienced.

Aloneness and Isolation

One of the most debilitating aspects of mental illness, both in those who experience it and in those close to the individual, is the isolation that often ensues. The strangeness and poignancy of many symptoms, along with decreased motivation for social contact, are among the most pernicious features of many mental disorders. Indeed, some forms of mental illness lead to intense self-absorption and preoccupation, resulting in evaporation of social connectedness. Frequently apparent in the narratives in this book is the sense that no one can understand and no one can help, that mental illness takes away the possibility of true communication and contact.

The sense of isolation and aloneness readily spreads to family members. Indeed, it is relatives who must often deal with not only the person's condition but also their own stigmatization, social shunning, embarrassment, guilt, and blame, incurred at the hands of relatives, contacts, and even the mental health profession. When family members are left to cope as best they can without adequate resources, either financial or psychological, the entire family system becomes further isolated. Think of Kay Browne, who was without adequate support in her fight to find the right services for her son's psychosis, struggling to find professionals and contacts who might really understand the situation.

We can only hope that the tide is turning and that the kinds of experiences depicted in these contributions—which range in time from early in the twentieth century to the past few years—will be different in the future. That is, recognition of mental illness may be quicker, with shame minimized, communication enhanced, and treatments instituted with faster turnaround.[19] The battle remains a long and hard one, however, given the isolation and stigma that are still attached to mental illness.

Vulnerability

Mental disorders promote intense feelings of vulnerability. Ruth White, Marc Atkins, and Jeff Liew give vivid portrayals of the personal vulnerability they have each experienced as they have wondered whether psychiatric symptomatology would recur. Ruth's vulnerability lay in her reluctance to come to terms with a diagnosis of bipolar disorder; Marc's took the form of the question of whether his college-age experiences were signs of an inevitable, lifelong mental disorder, a view promoted by his psychiatrist at the time; Jeff's reluctance to obtain treatment was exacerbated by the shame and stigma he experienced firsthand as a child when friends and neighbors derided his mother for her depression and suicide attempt.

Some of the sense of vulnerability is quite basic, as relatives wonder about their own risk for becoming mentally ill. This fear has been a main theme in my own life, particularly when I was in college and attempted to synthesize my father's disclosures to me about his own severe mental disorder.[20] In addition to wondering about one's own vulnerability to mental illness, knowing that a loved one is suffering (or causing others to suffer)—and at the same time not being able to really help—can lead to frustration, discouragement, and another kind of vulnerability. That is, relatives actively wonder when the next episode will ensue and what on earth might be done to prevent or stop it. Jessie Borelli has dealt with vulnerable feelings regarding her brother Daniel for many years, still wondering what the ultimate prognosis will be and how her next set of interactions with him will transpire. Carolyn Zahn-Waxler explores in depth her own vulnerability, emanating from the ripple effects of her mother's mood disturbance (and her father's anxiety and alcoholism), with implications for her own relationship with her adopted daughter. And the sense of vulnerability is extreme in Janet Lucas's devastating portrayal of the abuse and neglect she received as a child, leading to a lifelong sense that she had to compensate (indeed, overcompensate) to maintain a semblance of normality and humanity.

Everyday Lives and Experiences

Sometimes mental illness leads to extreme, nearly unthinkable actions and emotions. Far more often, it is enacted through the experiences of everyday life, as individuals struggle with difficult symptoms and attempt to cope, work, stay connected to their families, and simply live their lives. These routine actions can certainly be put to a severe test by manifestations of psychopathology, but the struggles encountered are on the same continuum as those of everyone else.

In other words, despite prevalent stereotypes of superhuman or subhuman qualities, mental illness is deeply embedded in the kinds of life experiences that we all share. Telling the truth about mental disorder involves bringing to life realities of struggling, coping, caregiving, and navigating the world, without promoting the false view that mental illness is somehow lived on a different plane. If we can understand that life goes on despite the pain and struggle often engendered by mental illness, we will have gone a long way to demystify it.

Esme Londahl-Shaller's tender, humorous, yet concerned portrayal of her father, with his foibles and his positive qualities, is a clear example of a depiction that emphasizes the day-to-day existence of a father and daugther. In addition, after a series of short-lived jobs following his psychotic-level mental illness that began during his second year of college, Kay Browne's son, Nathan, must now cope with work and with navigating his environment as everyday challenges. His struggle is compounded by medication side effects (including weight gain), which add to the burden of his residual symptoms. Jeff Liew's mother, after years of depression and then bipolar episodes, had to deal with the cancer of her husband, allowing the rest of the family to care for him. It may be instructive to look for additional daily challenges and coping strategies in the lives of each individual and each family represented in this volume.

Strength and Courage

Mental illness is often portrayed as unrelenting, hopeless, and utterly crushing of the spirit. There is no doubting the extreme impairments that mental illness can produce, but often left out of many depictions are the following facts: the symptoms of mental disorders wax and wane over time; periods of normality are often interspersed with those laden with problematic functioning; behaviors and emotions do change with situation and context; and individuals and family members may well show unexpected courage, strength, and even resilience in the face of mental illness.

Clear examples of this crucial point can be found in the narratives herein. For example, the early, tragic suicide of Peter Nathan's mother did not stop him from becoming an eminent psychologist—and, in fact, reverberations of that act may well have spurred his deep interest in the entire topic of psychology (as noted in the following section, "Shaping of Identity and Career"). In addition, whether as siblings, parents, or offspring, many of the contributors have benefited from the experience of mental illness through developing enhanced empathy, interest, or sensitivity in themselves. As a young teen, Laura Mason spent hours on end with her severely disturbed sister; these experiences served as a model for her ability to stay with and facilitate contact with noncommunicative, troubled patients years later. Jeff Liew's ability to manage both positive and negative images of his mother served him well as he fought for his own identity as a young adult. Jarralynne Agee's struggle to understand her mother's serious depression (coupled with serious poverty) enabled her to empathize with the most disturbed of the patients she saw as a trainee. Ruth White and Marc Atkins have used their own experiences related to mental illness as a major impetus to assist others.

In all, these examples highlight the ways in which encountering serious mental disorder can often fuel intense empathy, commitment, and passion. Mental illness is so often portrayed as inevitably frustrating, demoralizing, and chronic that we may forget—or never hear at all—that working through its symptoms and impairments can be inspirational to individuals and family members alike.

Shaping of Identity and Career

Personal and family experiences of mental illness are often related to an underlying desire to deal with conflict and pain, to give something back in the form of service and teaching, and/or to understand mental disorders or their treatments from a scientific perspective. In my brief "instructions" to the contributors of this volume, I asked each to address, in some way or another, the influence of personal and family experiences on identity formation and choice of profession.

In some contributions, this linkage is unmistakable—Laura Mason's dedication to training budding clinicians and to providing therapy for a wide range of clients is undoubtedly linked to her experience of the plight of her sisters. Carolyn Zahn-Waxler's long-standing interest in the development of empathy and the transmission of pathology and coping within families must have direct origins in her experience of her mother's depression. Still, career paths are likely to be multiply determined. What was it precisely about Liz Owens's witnessing, both close at hand and at a distance, her sister's deep emotional troubles that provided motivation for Liz to pursue the study of children at risk and the characteristics that shape resilient functioning? Or consider Ted Beauchaine, whose mother's progressive schizophrenia undoubtedly molded his interest in pursuing study of the origins and nature of mental illness. But how did this family experience translate into his sophisticated quantitative and developmental approaches to doing so?

In other cases, the path was more circuitous. Marc Atkins went from his vulnerable college days to the study of child development, poverty, and educational settings as a way of promoting positive mental health from a different angle, without directly confronting serious disturbance in adults. Janet Lucas became an expert in highly esoteric fields of postmodern scholarship through the need to prove herself as a competent, supremely intelligent individual rather than a tainted victim of rampant abuse. Peter Nathan became interested in psychology and the study of alcoholism largely through courses and research experiences he obtained as a student—yet at a deeper level, there must have been a profound interest in human behavior, both normal and atypical, prompted by the early loss of his mother.

Stigma and Treatment

Evidence of the continuing degradation and stigmatization of mental illness is apparent in all of the chapters. Although not the major theme of any particular narrative, levels of stigma depicted herein range from subtle to blatant.

One ramification of stigma is that mental illness may not even be recognized as such in many individuals and families—and they may have no access to care even if recognition is present. Thus some individuals in the following narratives never got help at all—for example, the mothers of Jarralynne Agee (because of poverty) and Tara Peris (because of lack of recognition of her often-hidden symptoms). As a boy, Peter Nathan was never seen in treatment, despite the early loss of his mother and his depressive temperament. His father's ways of dealing with his own loss of his wife and the era in which the family lived prevented any preventive care from occurring. Laura Mason's middle sister, whose behavior became increasingly bizarre, never really recognized a mental disturbance in herself.

Other individuals initially resisted and then relented to treatment, in part because of the stigma associated with labeling and diagnosis. Like so many individuals with bipolar disorder, Ruth White did not want to admit that she had this condition or that she needed mood-stabilizing medications. Finally, however, she has reached a degree of stability with treatment that she had not experienced for years. Jeff Liew's mother met with a counselor who had little cultural competence in reaching out to Chinese-speaking individuals and families. Liz Owens's sister was in and out of treatment, including residential facilities, for years. Yet even when intervention was good, aftercare in the community rarely occurred, prompting severe relapse. And despite helpful care, some contributors experienced stigma from providers (e.g., Marc Atkins's psychiatrist predicted a lifetime of schizophrenia; Janet Lucas's pharmacists looked askance at her prescriptions for multiple antidepressants).

Parents are particularly likely to feel blamed by the community and even by mental health professionals; Kay Browne's contribution provides particularly pointed evidence along these lines. Siblings have felt potentially cursed or betrayed by the serious problems of their brothers or sisters, with little available in the way of direct avenues for communication or understanding. The accounts of Jessie Borelli, Liz Owens, and Laura Mason are particularly gripping in depicting such isolation. Offspring have experienced a combination of anxiety, confusion, and mystification, largely related to the role of stigma and shame in stifling needed interchange about what was wrong with their parents (see, for example, the chapters by Ted Beauchaine and Carolyn Zahn-Waxler).

For many contributors, the decision to write about their experiences was marked by conflict over what their families, employers, or friends might think— in other words, by the rampant stigma that sill exists. Indeed, a number of potential contributors I was in touch with ultimately chose not to write for this volume. And for many of those who did contribute, the decision was not easy. In all, mental illness is still the subject of ridicule, banishment, and degradation, revealing the long road ahead in the fight against stigma.

Stigmatization transcends culture. In his contribution, Jeff Liew directly tackles the shame and stigma of admitting mental illness in Chinese-American culture. Indeed, for him the stigma had become so internalized that he fought against getting any help for himself for long periods, despite the presence of panic attacks and a suffocating sense of inadequacy. He now takes an activist stance, contending that active efforts must be undertaken to overcome stigma.

In all, at both implicit and explicit levels, the present narratives add to the evidence for continuing stigmatization of mental illness into the twenty-first century. One of my hopes for this volume is that it will provide a beacon of clear communication, which is essential in the battle against silence and stigma.

CHAPTER ORGANIZATION AND SUMMARY

With these themes in mind, I invite you to become immersed in the personal and family narratives that follow. My hope is that you will be intrigued, sensitized, and energized at the same time that you gain education about the realities, rather than the stereotypes, of mental illness. Perhaps reading these accounts will motivate you to learn more and even to contribute in some way to the fight against mental illness and the stigma that pulls down all aspects of mental health care, both here and around the world.

Some compendia of personal accounts include lengthy annotations for each contribution. I have chosen not to write such accompaniments to each chapter, as I believe that each account is sufficiently strong and self-explanatory that it does not need a specific road map. Indeed, the goal of this work is not to provide diagnostic tips or "teaching points" about symptoms, treatments, and the like. This volume is not a textbook but rather serves as compilation of intensely personal narratives, with the hope that story talks for itself. (Note: In order not to interrupt the flow of each chapter, I asked those authors who wished to include references to scholarly literature to do so in endnote style and to keep these to a minimum.)

Deciding on the ordering of the chapters has been a puzzle. At one level, it might have been logical to include a set of chapters on the experience of having a parent with mental illness, then another related to having an afflicted sibling, still another of being a parent, and finally a set of those dealing with personal experiences of mental disorder. Yet the contributions herein resist such simple categorization: some that begin with portrayals of parents or of offspring also contain a considerable amount of material on personal experiences; the chapters most connected with sibling issues have clear implications for personal adjustment and identity; and those narratives that deal most directly with personal experiences of mental illness convey great understanding of family dynamics.

What I have chosen instead is an impressionistic ordering, with longer contributions intermixed with those that are somewhat shorter and with younger authors interspersed with those having more life experience. First, Laura Mason's wrenching narrative about her three sisters and her own life's journey in the wake of this decades-long family tragedy starts the volume. It is followed by Ruth White's edgy and chilling contribution on her own bipolar disorder, which incorporates her views on the positive aspects of mania, her initial resistance to receiving treatment, and her gradual acceptance of intervention. Next is the harrowing, self-deprecating, yet devastatingly lucid chapter of Tara Peris on her mother's slow demise and disappearance, followed by the narrative of Liz Owens, which vividly and poignantly conveys her sister's chronic eating pathology and substance abuse, which led to her untimely death.

Jeff Liew's story about his mother's near-suicide and his own resistance to treatment during early adulthood provides a harrowing life-span narrative. It is followed by Kay Browne's agonizing account of her son's psychotic illness and her lack of preparation for this event, despite years of medical training. At this point, Marc Atkins tells the pointed story of his college-age activism, confusion, and mental disorder, as well as his newfound calling in work with children in community settings. This chapter is followed by Ted Beauchaine's deeply honest account of his mother's progressive schizophrenic illness.

Jarralynne Agee's pointed chapter on her mother's dual experience of depression and severe poverty is next, preceding Jessie Borelli's thorough and wrenching story of her brother's severe emotional disturbance, with its ripple effects on her entire family. Peter Nathan then describes, with eloquence, what he has learned about his mother's suicide when he was an infant and the continuing effects of this event throughout his and his family's life. Esme Londahl-Shaller then writes endearingly and honestly about her father's lifelong bipolar disorder, conveying both humor and wisdom.

The searing account of Janet Lucas follows, dealing with her severe abuse as a child and her isolation and depression as an adult. Finally, Carolyn Zahn-Waxler describes, with lucidity, her mother's depression, her own development, and implications for her own parenting. I conclude with a final chapter in which I respond briefly to these narratives, raise several cross-cutting themes, and provide my own personal view of the value of narrative works that deal with personal and family experiences.

So, I invite you to read, admire, identify, and empathize. I also invite you to become angry, to wonder at what might have been, and to deepen your appreciation of mental illness in the lives of individuals and families. Throughout, I ask that you consider the essential humanity depicted in each contribution.

Indeed, when we confront the realities of mental illness rather than stereotypical, media-portrayed images of inevitable violence and despair, all of us will gain. We may then begin to comprehend, more than ever, the deep variability in our species and the need to provide compassionate and science-driven treatments to those who need them. We are all human—none more so than those of us in the mental health professions—and it is through the telling of life stories that our humanity comes to the fore, deepening appreciation of our own contributions to the field and presaging a new spirit of openness and acceptance.

Welcome.

NOTES

1. In medicine, for example, there are strong proscriptions against disclosing personal weakness. Partly as a result, rates of suicide and substance abuse are

alarmingly high in the medical professions. See Myers, M., & Fine, C. (2003). Suicide in physicians: Toward prevention. *Medscape General Medicine, 5.* Retrieved from http://www.medscape.com/viewarticle1462619. Note that in the United Kingdom, two decades ago, Rippere and Williams compiled an edited book of the experiences of depression from those in the mental health fields: see Rippere, V., & Williams, B. (Eds.) (1985). *Wounded healers: Mental health workers' experiences of depression.* Chichester, UK: Wiley.

2. For extensive discussion of the stigmatization of mental illness, see my recent book: Hinshaw, S. P. (2007). *The mark of shame: Stigma of mental illness and an agenda for change.* New York: Oxford University Press. In this work, I cover historical, sociological, social psychological, evolutionary, and empirical evidence for the longstanding stigmatization of people with mental disorders. A key point is that despite deeply seated human tendencies to stigmatize those with mental illness, it is equally clear that such biases can be overcome, meaning that stigma is not inevitable.

3. Kurzban, R., & Leary, M. R. (2001). Evolutionary origins of stigmatization: The functions of social exclusion. *Psychological Bulletin, 127,* 187–208.

4. Nathan, P. E., & Gorman, J. (Eds.). (2007). *A guide to treatments that work* (3rd ed.). New York: Oxford University Press.

5. Phelan, J. C., Link, B. G., Stueve, A., & Pescosolido, B. A. (2000). Public conceptions of mental illness in the 1950 and 1996: What is mental illness and is it to be feared? *Journal of Health and Social Behavior, 41,* 188–207. For a review, see Hinshaw (2007).

6. Goffman, E. (1963). *Stigma: Notes on the management of spoiled identity.* Englewood Cliffs, NJ: Prentice Hall.

7. Mehta, S., & Farina, A. (1997). Is being "sick" really better? Effect of the disease view of mental disorder on stigma. *Journal of Social and Clinical Psychology, 16,* 405–419. Helping the public to understand that mental disorder entails both biological/genetic predisposition *and* life stress/psychosocial risk—and that even extremely heritable conditions can be amenable to nongenetic/nonbiological forms of treatment—is a major task ahead.

8. See, for example, the systematic national survey of Wahl, O. F. (1999). *Telling is risky business: Mental health consumers confront stigma.* New Brunswick, NJ: Rutgers University Press.

9. Kramer, P. (2005). *Against depression.* New York: Viking.

10. See Kessler, R. C., Berglund, P., Demler, O., Jin, R., & Walters, E. E. (2005). Lifetime prevalence and age-of-onset distributions of *DSM-IV* disorders in the National Comorbidity Survey replication. *Archives of General Psychiatry, 62,* 593–602; and Kessler, R. C., Chiu, W. T., Demler, O., & Walters, E. E. (2005). Prevalence, severity, and comorbidity of 12-month *DSM-IV* disorders in the National Comorbidity Survey replication. *Archives of General Psychiatry, 62,* 617–627.

11. Hinshaw (2007).

12. See Kaplan, B. (Ed.) (1964). *The inner world of mental illness: A series of first-person accounts of what it was like.* New York: Harper & Row. See also Rippere & Williams (1985) and Gottesman, I. I. (1991). *Schizophrenia genesis: The origins of madness.* New York: W. H. Freeman.

13. First, see Endler, N. S. (1990). *Holiday of darkness: A psychologist's personal journey in and out of his depression.* Toronto: Wall & Thompson. Second, see Jamison, K. R. (1995). *An unquiet mind: A memoir of moods and madness.* New York: Free Press.

Also, for a compilation of historical, literary, and personal perspectives on suicide, see Alvarez, A. (1972). *The savage god: A study of suicide.* New York: Random House.

14. Hinshaw, S. P. (2002). *The years of silence are past: My father's life with bipolar disorder.* New York: Cambridge University Press.

15. Kapur, N. (Ed.) (1997). *Injured brains of medical minds: Views from within.* Oxford, UK: Oxford University Press.

16. See, for example, Sacks, O. (1996). *An anthropologist on Mars: Seven paradoxical tales.* New York: Vintage. For a review of the trend toward greater humanization of neurological patients and conditions in case reports and write-ups, see Harrington, A. (2005). The inner lives of disordered brains. *Cerebrum: The Dana Forum on Brain Sciences, 7(2),* 23–36.

17. Even media celebrities have begun to disclose experiences of mental illness. Consider, for example, Shields, B. (2005). *Down came the rain.* New York: Hyperion, in which actress Brooke Shields disclosed her severe postpartum depression. In Pauley, J. (2004). *Skywriting: A life out of the blue.* New York: Random House, television personality Jane Pauley discusses her own bipolar disorder. In addition, Kitty Dukakis openly discusses her depression and substance abuse and the electroconvulsive therapy that greatly helped her in Dukakis, K., & Tye, L. (2006). *Shock: The healing power of electroconvulsive therapy.* New York: Penguin.

18. For an example of negative responses to professional disclosure, see Jamison, K. R. (1998). Stigma of manic depression: A psychologist's experience. *Lancet, 352,* 1053. Here, she reports that, following the publication of *An Unquiet Mind,* the most vehement reactions to her self-disclosures emanated from colleagues in the psychiatric and psychological professions.

19. In the national survey of Kessler and colleagues, it was found that, on average, the delay in the United States from recognition of symptoms of mental illness to first receipt of treatment was measurable in years and even, for some conditions, decades. See Wang, P. S., Berglund, P., Olfson, M., Pincus, H. A., Wells, K. B., & Kessler, R. C. (2005). Failure and delay in initial treatment contact in the National Comorbidity Survey replication. *Archives of General Psychiatry, 62,* 603–613.

20. See Hinshaw (2002).

1 My Story Is One of Loss

Laura B. Mason

My experience of mental illness in my family of origin is a story of loss, and what has been, for me, an unspeakable grief. When any loss or trauma cannot be spoken—either shared with another person or felt and "spoken" within oneself—there is a kind of loneliness that is hopeless and despairing. The facts of mental illness in my family, including the diagnostic information, the appointments with psychiatrists, the bizarre behavior that broke through periodically, and the rushed hospitalizations, were all out in the open. But we never found a way to talk about what was happening, to create what William Beardslee would call a "shared narrative" that could help us stay connected through these devastating illnesses.[1] My sisters' conditions have shaped my life, my choice of profession, and my sense of what it means to be human, yet these influences have operated in some private inner space. This narrative is an effort to open that private space, to share these experiences more fully with myself and with others.

I am the youngest of four daughters and the only one of us whose adult life has not been laid waste by severe mental illness. All of us now are middle-aged, our lives having taken whatever shape they will. The acute breakdowns, hospitalizations, and suicide attempts happened long ago. It has been well over 20 years since all of us were together with our parents, although amazingly all of us are still alive. I am now a practicing clinician and clinical professor, guiding young graduate students through their first clinical experiences. More profound an achievement is that I am married (for the third time) and the mother of two children. My sisters' stories are, of course, theirs to narrate, but here is mine.

When Steve Hinshaw first mentioned this book to me and asked if I might contribute, I had to ask myself, "Why is this aspect of my history and my identity NOT something I am open and public about?" I think of myself as an emotionally open and expressive person. I am quite willing to share all kinds of stories about my past; I am very self-disclosing when I teach; and even as a clinician I disclose many aspects of who I am. But this, this family story, is really private, I think. Or, I reason that it wouldn't be fair of me to write about members of my family. It's one thing to share my history, but not theirs. Or I think of "recovery" therapists, clinicians whose professional identities include being a "survivor" of some group or experience. I don't want to be thought of as an "adult sibling of mentally ill sisters." And I think of the people I work with: "I don't want to burden my clients with all this information about me."

One day at lunch with Steve, he asked me point blank, "So why is it, do you think, that you haven't talked about your sisters' mental illness, let's say, in a discussion with students or colleagues about personal experiences that influenced your choice of clinical psychology as a profession?" For me, the answer always begins with how overwhelmed and burdened my listeners might feel; my narrative is just too much. "But do you actually believe that would be the response?" Steve probed further. At that point in the conversation, fear took over, and thinking became difficult for me. My family did not respond to mental illness with silence and euphemisms; in our case, chaotic and disorienting behavior swept through the household like wildfire. Using another metaphor, torrents of emotion—shrill and fierce and tearful—were like destructive flood waters that spilled over the riverbanks. As Steve and I talked, it became clear to me that *I* am the person who is overwhelmed and burdened when I consider telling my story.

In working on this narrative, I have unpacked and explored many of these contradictory, confusing thoughts, feelings, and objections. My internal relationship to my sisters and our parents has become more textured and softer. The "simple" truth is that my story is hard to share because it's hard for me to bear. My much-loved big sister shattered into bits and pieces. She turned into someone frightening and unrecognizable, and she never came back to being the big sister I had grown up loving so much. It was as if she had died, although still physically alive. In some kind of internal collapse of emotion, I felt that any grieving was destructive, as if acknowledging the loss meant that I was trying to get rid of the person who was still there. Years later, my next-oldest sister disintegrated. Her breakdown was slow, steady, and bizarre, a creeping undertow that has never let her go. I had never been that close to her, and by the time of her decompensation, I was living far away from our parents and grateful to be so far away. And finally, in my early 30s, my third sister's depression erupted with a violent suicide attempt, which seemed to come out of nowhere, leaving her and me shaken. Twenty years and several hospitalizations later, her life is still dominated by despair.

So how can I tell my story? Let me try to do my best.

EARLY YEARS

When I was a very little girl, maybe around 4, I felt so lucky to be one of the Mason girls. There were four of us. Most families had three kids at the most, and we were ALL girls, which seemed so unlikely. My father—who was raised on a ranch on the sparsely populated high desert of Montana—took us camping in the summer, and my mother, noisy and busy and big like her hometown of Brooklyn, took us to New York City for spring vacation. When my parents first married, they lived outside of New York City, where my three sisters were born in the mid-1940s. In the early 1950s, my father's work took the family to Chicago, where I was born. My sisters, who were many years older than I and clustered closely together in age, were often the smartest pupils in their classes. We ate dinner at a round oak table with a lazy Susan, and there was lots of lively conversation. We fought loudly, and laughed loudly, and did lots of interesting things.

My sisters, then, had each experienced a big rupture in their elementary school years, when the family was uprooted. My own childhood, by contrast, has a seamless sense of place. The rambling old house on the South Side of Chicago was the only home I knew in my growing-up years, and although the neighborhood changed dramatically, it was always, to me, my familiar turf. My favorite sister, the oldest, Adelaine, took me special places and hugged me too tight. She was 9 years older than I, and I remember very early feeling that she was different. She had bright red hair, and whenever I saw another person with red hair, I would run home and tell her. I think I wanted to reassure both of us that there were other people like her in the world. When I was very little, she had been a baseball fan, but by the time I was 6, she was enormously fat and didn't go out in the street to bat a ball around anymore. She didn't have any friends of her own, although she was often included in things with my other sisters and their friends. She had lots and lots of interests—language and music and art and math. She was *so* smart, and she would play the piano sometimes and sing, but somehow it seemed that she was different and sad and not right.

I remember one winter night, in her senior year of high school, when Addie didn't come home for dinner. It was alarming to me: she never went anywhere, or with anyone, so where could she be? Finally when she came home, she was laughing, and her eyes were so bright. She was giddy and giggly. She'd been visiting a new friend, and they'd talked and talked and lost track of the time. Something about this didn't feel right to me. Addie didn't have friends, and her lively chatter was rushed. She laughed too loudly, and I couldn't tell what was funny. But I was relieved that she was back home and safe, and I recall feeling with shame that maybe she was even normal after all. I was embarrassed by her; she always seemed lonely and huge, though I would never have articulated that. I just knew that I felt anxious about her, even when I was a little girl. Clearly, I was watching her, noting the signs and shapes and textures of her life.

My second oldest sister, Anne, was an exceptional student. She had skipped a grade, so that she and Addie were graduating at the same time from high school. Anne was the class valedictorian, a sharp and witty girl, very sophisticated. When I think about her now, the most striking thing to me is how empty and discon-nected I feel. I always felt, as the littlest sister, that there was no way I could capture her interest. My most vivid recollection of her comes from around the time I was 8, and she would have been 16. Walking by her bedroom one afternoon, I saw her sitting still on her bed, with a sketch pad and fancy mechanical pencil. She looked very serious, which to me meant that she was doing something very important. "What are you doing?" I bounded into her room. "I'm drawing snowflakes," was the reply. "Can I see?" I was eager to be close to such a sophisticated and impressive person. Anne showed me the page, full of intricate, lacy designs. How could she see those patterns in the simple dots of snow? She seemed so far beyond me, so advanced. I always thought of her as the refined, polished sister, the only one of us who was small boned and elegant. She had style, she understood art, she was so responsible that, when she was 18 and I was 10 (and after Addie's first psychotic break), my parents named her my guardian. Anne went to college on the East Coast, whereas Addie went to a small liberal arts college in the Midwest.

Around Christmas of their freshman year, my parents got a phone call that Addie needed to return home. I would have been 9 at this time, just about to turn 10, and I remember how rushed and sudden everything seemed. I recall that my mother's face looked dark and closed. Something too terrible to talk about had happened. "What is it?" I had to ask. "Adelaine's sick, she's had something called a nervous breakdown." My mother explained to me that this was something that happened when people study too hard and they can't sleep.

This answer must not have satisfied me. Addie was admitted to a nearby hospital, but I was told that I couldn't visit her—my favorite sister!—because it might upset me. I stole into my parents' bedroom and found the cache of letters Adelaine had written to our parents during her first semester away from home. Here I read about Addie's belief that people were talking about her, that other students spied on her when she went to the bathroom, that when she passed gas she was sending messages to professors and to our father. I never told my parents about reading these letters. I knew that something was terribly wrong with Adelaine, that whatever was wrong with her was kind of exciting and definitely gross, and that whatever it was, I was not supposed to know.

> *It's hard to write about this. I'm confused about who I am writing this for—myself? An unknown audience? Writing about my sister and my family is very upsetting, and unsettling, and I question my motives and everything about myself. I wish that I came from another family; I wish that I hadn't had to raise myself so completely on my own.*

I don't remember too much about Adelaine's first breakdown or her return from the hospital. When she was better, Addie transferred to a state college. "She needs to be at a school where there's not so much pressure," my parents said. Something about this was a loss of face, but I wasn't sure why.

When she came home for spring vacation that year, everyone was very happy because Addie had made friends. My mother said, "There are such nice people at this school, they seem to have taken Addie under their wings, and encouraged her to lose weight and curl her hair." I guessed they were transforming my strange sister into somebody normal, somebody who went on dates and wore pastel skirts.

The next years swirl together and apart in my mind. I know that for 18 months or so we all thought that Addie was fine. I'm sure that I wanted this to be true, but there are so many troubled memories. What I can say, without regard to accuracy in the time line, is that Addie did well for some time at the state college and even fell in love. She might be engaged! Then, I thought, maybe we could relax at last. But once again, Addie fell apart, my parents rushed to the school to bring her home, and—that was it. Her decompensation never let up afterward.

Once I asked my mother what could have happened to make Addie so fragile and sick. My mother told me then that Addie's psychiatrist thought that maybe when our family moved from New York to the Midwest when Addie was 8, Addie never recovered, like a plant with weak roots that couldn't be transplanted.

I remember, too, that once again Addie was sent to a hospital and that I was not allowed to visit. When she came home, her speech seemed strange, as if she spoke with an accent. I have a vivid memory of sitting at our big, round dining room table, looking at Addie, with her coppery hair curled carefully in the style her state-college friends had taught her. She was wearing a pinkish blouse with a little Peter Pan collar, again so stylish, but in my mind's eye, I see all of this with some kind of edge or fracture. Addie doesn't look right, the collar is too loose around her neck, and her hair is curled in some freakish, uneven way. I didn't know it at that time, of course, but things would not ever settle down again. Ever.

Anne stayed at college on the East Coast, and when my third sister, Teresa, finished high school, she joined Anne at the same college. Neither of them came home very often; we couldn't afford the air fare except in summertime. Each time Addie had a breakdown, the expectations and hopes we had for her diminished. Although she had been a wonderful student, it seemed that going to school was "too much."

Some time later, Addie is back at home. She has been diagnosed as schizophrenic by this time. My mother blames herself, and so does Addie's psychiatrist, it seems. I hear my mother's anguished cries to my father, "What could I have done so wrong? Why does [her psychiatrist] accuse me of being cold? I just loved her, I did the best I could." She retreats from Addie and me in a way that frightens me. My mother is now out of my reach, and I am acutely aware that she can't sleep and that I must be quiet at all hours of the day and night in case she has managed to catch a few moments' rest. Sometimes, though, my mother bursts out with vicious and bitter tirades, insisting that Addie's illness is my father's fault because he doesn't talk enough. There are hints that my father's mother, Grandma Emeline, had some kind of mental illness.

GROWING UP TOO FAST

By now, I'm in sixth grade. Addie stays up all night and thumps around in her bedroom, which is next to mine. I scream at her a lot, I can't sleep. She's faking being crazy to get attention, I think, as she laughs hysterically and sits in the dark and cries. I am angry with her often: she is ruining everything, and Anne and Teresa aren't home to buffer me in any way. I hate them, too. My friends and I are crazy about boys, and my grades begin to fall.

My teachers pull me into the hallway for a talk. Have I done something wrong? I know I talk too much, I confess to them; I know that I'm becoming too social. No, they want to know if I'm OK, I seem different—is everything OK at home? I burst into tears and tell them about my mentally ill sister. They comfort me.

I feel dishonest, as though I have used Addie to get out of trouble. At the time, though, I think that I just don't like school, and Addie makes a good excuse.

It's funny how now, looking back on that incident, I wish that my teachers *had* called my parents and said something to them. I think, in retrospect, that I was more correct than I realized—I *was* upset about Addie, but I didn't know it, and I didn't even know how to experience it directly.

As Addie became acutely psychotic over and over, with sedated periods back at home, my family completely fractured. My two middle sisters stayed away. My father never said a word but silently took Addie to doctor's appointments, visited each day when she was hospitalized, made sure she had a book to read or a record to listen to. My mother raged and wept, screamed, working for years longer than she had planned to so that all the hospital and psychiatrist bills could be paid.

Something impossible to comprehend was happening, and we couldn't reason with Addie or comfort each other. I blamed my parents for Addie's mental illness. Once I pored through boxes of artwork my mother had saved from when Addie and Anne were little. Addie's drawings were bleak—trees without leaves, black and brown branches. Didn't my mother notice that the sun and green grass were missing? Why hadn't my parents DONE something? Maybe if they had taken her to see a psychologist when she was 4, or certainly when she was 11 and grotesquely obese, with no friends, things might have been different. Now that I have become a clinical psychologist and studied psychopathology,

I know that I was not alone in blaming my parents. Indeed, the entire field and profession of clinical psychology held parents and child rearing accountable for most mental illness at that time. There can't be anything worse than being told that your child has an incurable disease, except perhaps being told that it is your fault. The atmosphere of blame was, and still is, so strong. In high school in the late 1960s, I read articles about schizophrenogenic mothers and emotionally absent fathers and saw my parents in every description.

I developed theories of my own about the additional destructive influence of having Anne and Teresa so close in age to Addie: the bitter competitiveness among the three of them for academic achievement and our parents' affection had been ferocious. I remember that Addie once told me, "Anne is Mommy's favorite, and Teresa is Daddy's favorite, so you and I have to be each other's favorites." This frightened me, and I reassured myself by deciding that I was each parent's *second favorite*, so I wasn't as vulnerable as Addie. (Vulnerable to what? I ask myself now.) There was always something treacherous between Addie and Anne, something that in my mind came from their being only 11 months apart, as if there was not enough room for the two of them, not enough sunshine or water for two seedlings to flourish.

It's now ninth grade, and I skip school. My boyfriend and I will meet at my house, make out, maybe smoke a joint. On my way home, I see my mother rushing back to the house: Why isn't she at work? In an instant, I know the answer—Addie! My mother isn't even angry that I'm not at school; she doesn't notice at all. We have to call dad and arrange for him to pick Addie up. She had just started an entry-level clerical job, and she is creating a scene, insisting that her office manager is in love with her. There is a certain look on my mother's face: something closes, her eyes cast down. I am outside of that look and of wherever she goes internally at times like this. All I know is that I am outside and alone and growing up with no help.

My parents can't help it. They have four daughters to raise, and their life's dream is to be able to pay for all of us to go to college. But one of those daughters is mentally ill, in and out of psychiatric hospitals, now diagnosed manic-depressive. My mother can't take it, not one more time; we have to find another place for Addie to live when they let her out of the hospital. Addie moves into a boarding house nearby, works as a filing clerk, and sits in the dark when she gets back to her room at night. I am 13 years old, and I visit her regularly. I pass by her place often when I am out with friends after school, and I remember turning into her building, telling my friends, "I'll catch up with you later," and bracing myself for my time with her.

I always find her sitting, crying quietly in her room, hands folded in her lap, staring off into some place I cannot see. I sit very still beside her as the room darkens. Addie and I are together in the dusky twilight, the furniture in the room reduced to dark shapes and shadows. When I am with her, I hardly move or speak; I just want to be there so she is not alone, so that I don't lose her forever. Sometimes she tells me that our mother hates her because daddy loves her. Sometimes she tells me that mother hates me. She gives me a spending allowance, because our parents are selfish and don't love me enough. I take the money and buy meals for my friends and me. It's the late '60s, and we buy nickel bags of weed and sit in the local deli. We have the munchies, and with money from Addie, I can pay for all of us to gorge. We order French fries, then hot fudge sundaes, giggling hysterically and amazed at how much we can eat.

For years I feel guilty about this money from Addie. I make this guilt disappear by telling myself that I deserve the money because at least I spend time with my sister, which is more than anybody else in the family does. But I know this doesn't feel quite right, and I know this because I don't tell anybody about the money. I develop a private strand in my mind where I feel ashamed and confused and sneaky. It reminds me of the way I felt as a sixth grader when I told my worried teachers that maybe the reason I seemed upset or different at school was because one of my sisters was having a nervous breakdown.

This whole private narrative becomes a very important, but completely disconnected, part of my personality for the next 20 years. In this mental space, I am a bad person because I have used my sister's illness for personal gain (my special allowance; an excuse with a teacher), but I am a good person because at least I have spent time with her. The rest of my family has broken into bits. Anne and Teresa still almost never come home to visit, even for major holidays or over summer vacations. My parents, my mother in particular, never recovers from the interpretation that bad mothering has caused this devastating illness in her oldest child. She screams at my father that she needs help, too, but she is unable to make an appointment with a psychiatrist, insisting angrily that until my father goes with her, she won't go. The money that my parents saved so carefully for college is disappearing in medical bills for Addie.

I am now a high school sophomore. Addie has had another breakdown, cannot hold any kind of job, and is no longer giving me a special allowance. I have accelerated into an adolescent nightmare of my own, desperately in love with an older boy, and—*things rush into my mind as I recall those years*—the neighborhood deteriorates, becomes dangerous, but my parents don't seem to notice or care that I am going to high school in a ghetto. Or that I am running around with an older group of kids, coming home drunk or stoned, lying, not coming home at all, stealing their money, stealing my mother's diet pills. Addie is in and out of crises and hospitalizations; once she runs across the street naked in the middle of the night and tells the superintendent of the apartment building across the street that my father is trying to kill her. I tell my friends these stories as we get high.

One evening I am smoking in the bathroom at home, and I hear my parents come home. I throw my cigarette into the trash and air out the room. Minutes later, as I sit with my parents in the dining room, my mother smells smoke. The bathroom has caught on fire from the ashes I tossed in the garbage can.

Once, when I was 15, my boyfriend arranged for me to see a psychiatrist, because he knew about my sister and he thought I might need someone to talk to. I remember sitting in that appointment, sobbing violently with no words for the first few minutes. I said to this older man sitting across from me, "I don't know why I'm crying like this." "Perhaps you have something to cry about," was his kind response. But by the end of the appointment I had charmed him, and we agreed I did not need to see a psychiatrist. I wish now that I had not been so competent and skillful with my deceit. I wish, too, that this kind older man had not had the bias that I would need to see him only if there were something "wrong" with me.

I was definitely the kind of young person who survived by maintaining a competent and successful façade with adults. My family was in pieces, each of us disoriented and frightened; but no matter what, my grades were high. I always finished my homework, and I maintained solid relationships with many teachers. It is as if I was living two lives (and, in fact, I was). I had two teachers whom I found inspiring—one a history teacher, the other an English teacher—and I worked with all my heart for both of them. I would have died before I'd let either of them know about my home life or my after-school life. Both of them pulled me aside, expressing high hopes and praise. They wished that I would continue to take school seriously.

I was exhilarated by this attention, and somehow my teachers and I came up with the idea that perhaps I could go to college early and get out of this neighborhood that was increasingly overtaken by gang violence. With their help I found out about programs that accept "early entrants" to college. I took the SATs, wrote my college application, and applied to college at 15. My parents were so caught up in Addie's crises and the broken pieces of their lives that they didn't get involved in this process at all. My teachers were encouraging, and the spring of my sophomore year of high school I was accepted to a private liberal arts college for the following fall. My boyfriend, meanwhile, had ended up in a juvenile detention facility, and, strangely, I felt comforted by knowing at all times exactly where he was.

LEAVING HOME

This was 1967. I had already become sexually active, smoked marijuana, and managed to get myself on birth control pills by pretending to a local doctor that I was my older sister Teresa. The college I attended was a quaint, tiny, private school located in rural Illinois. The town is so small they didn't even have sidewalks or a movie theater. Within 4 weeks, I have slept with a senior and am stunned to realize that this does not mean we are a couple. Everyone is sleeping with everyone else, smoking weed, listening to the Beatles, the Stones, and the Doors; I barely manage to hang onto myself at all. Again, I am living two lives, or perhaps now I have split into even three selves.

The first self is my student self: I work hard, do all my readings at this demanding institution, learn to write serious academic papers, and major in literature. This enthusiastic student/scholar part of me is a crucial part of my life, which remains true to this day. I form strong relationships with professors and advisers, showing up for office hours and reading everything recommended. I was hungry for attachments that facilitated my development, and academia was one place where I found them.

My second self is a social one. A college freshman and only 15, I try to fit in socially, which leads me to adopt a kind of feverish and wacky persona to hide my immaturity. I want so desperately to belong to someone, and one person alone. By the winter vacation of that freshman year, I am engaged to a man 8 years my senior. He is about to graduate from the college and will teach elementary school as a way of avoiding the draft. The home he and I create together becomes an off-campus haven for our group of friends, and I find a role for myself as a somewhat hyper, friendly-as-a-puppy person whose house is always open.

And third, I construct a persona in relation to my parents and sisters. I write long letters to my parents about how grateful I am to them that I have been able to grow up in such an interesting, unique way. I don't realize it at the time, but now I know that I wanted so much to convince them, and myself, that nothing that had happened with Addie was their fault. I believe/hope at the time that if I can turn out to be normal, at least from the outside, then this is proof that my parents are not to blame. I want to give them this gift, and it does not occur to me that I am making up a story or leaving out some of my own feelings in this process.

During that year, Addie disappears for several days, and my parents are frantic with worry. She resurfaces, married to a very poor black man with dreadlocks. This man has a gift for language; today he would probably be a rapper. He and my mother argue. He says, "Don't nobody talk to me that way, this is my wife, and I am Toine." My mother's reply: "I don't give a damn who you think you are, this is my house, and this is my daughter, and I will not support the two of you." Screaming furiously, my mother kicks them out. In the midst of all this, I come home from my freshman year and plan my wedding. Although my parents tell me that I cannot get married until I am eighteen, my father signs the papers necessary for the judge to perform the wedding ceremony.

When I look back on it now, of course, I cannot imagine what in the world I was thinking of, to get married at the age of 16. How could my parents have let me do such a thing? But at the time, I claimed that many girls get married after their freshman year in college. If I were mature enough to go to college, then

I must be mature enough for marriage, too. There was something safe in that decision, strange as it sounds now. The man I married was very kind, very solid. The years he and I were together were a safe place to hold still. We lived on a farm. For the first time in my life, I had a dog, as well as kittens. I had a vegetable garden and learned how to make jam and put up preserves. My former husband taught fourth grade, and I fixed him breakfast, packed his lunch, and finished my sophomore year of college. We had friends over constantly for barbecues and bonfires and all-night games of hearts listening to Bob Dylan.

Around that time, in 1969, Anne was awarded a Fulbright to study abroad. At first she wrote home about the research in art history she was doing, but then long months went by with no word from her. Then my parents received strange letters from her, beautifully written but absolutely bizarre, about special diets, shaving her entire body, and finding truth in her reading of Marx, Reich, and Mao. I had become interested in social sciences during my first 2 years of college and had read enough sociology and psychology to offer my perspective to my parents: I reassured them that Anne must be having some kind of reaction to Addie's illness and to the years of stress and disorganization our family had weathered. It seemed natural that Anne would have some rebellious or outrageous phase; she had always been so steady and competent.

My first husband and I moved from rural Illinois to rural Oregon, and I completed my junior year of college at the University of Oregon in Eugene. At the age of 19, I was on the verge of graduating from college. Life outside the classroom had a magnetic pull for me, though. These were the (literally) intoxicating 1970s, when so many people my age were "tuning in, turning on, and dropping out" of conventional society. I dropped out of school with only one semester left toward finishing an undergraduate degree in sociology. In keeping with my personal need to present a stable image to my parents and sisters, I lied and told them all I had finished my degree.

In some ways, the life I was caught up in wasn't that different from Anne's at that time. The general atmosphere of those days, the late 1960s and the early 1970s, was full of experimentation and invention. Anne's life on a commune, exploring the possibilities of nonmonogamous collective living, was exciting and daring, as was my life with its organic garden and its marches. I was a revolutionary hippie and getting a divorce at 19; she lived on a "free love" commune in Austria. She defaulted on college loans from my parents; I lied and told my parents I had finished college.

ON MY OWN

Through the 1970s, my family limped along in pieces, each daughter connected to our parents and none of us connected to one another. None of us visited our parents at the same time, and neither Teresa nor I visited our parents more than once every other year or so. Teresa had married her college sweetheart and begun graduate school in biophysics. Addie was relatively stable, living in Chicago near my parents' home. She worked in an insurance company at some kind of tedious technical job that required almost no interpersonal interaction. I knew that she had serious crushes on coworkers and an active fantasy life, but as long as she took her medication faithfully, she didn't have acute psychotic breaks.

Anne stayed in Austria for the next 10 years without visiting the family once. After a while, though, her correspondence grew more frightening and extreme. She sent us all photos of the entire commune, everyone naked with shaved heads, demonstrating their ritual sexual practices. Alarmed, my parents urged her to come home. Anne refused, relinquished her Fulbright funding, and defaulted on thousands of dollars of college loans my parents had cosigned. We hardly heard from her, and when we did, her letters were incoherent and disturbing. Finally, she was deported from Austria during a roundup of noncitizens there. When she returned to my parents' home in Chicago, she was a completely changed person: unkempt, withdrawn, and hostile. She lived in my parents' basement for months and claimed they owed her financial support.

My own life during those years makes for a very "interesting" story if I tell it in a particular entertaining way. But a more authentic version is that I spent the decade of my 20s, from 1972 to 1982, presenting a false self to my parents and sisters and struggling with my own identity in ways that are painful to remember. My first husband and I had grown apart by the time I was 19; I was most interested in the political counterculture, whereas he was more attracted to the spiritual self-discovery movement. We agreed to divorce, but remained friendly. Like many middle-class young white people in the 1970s, I explored ways of life quite different from the world in which I had grown up: I worked on assembly lines and in warehouses, I drove a freight truck across the United States and back, I operated a forklift, I tried various drugs and substances, I waited on tables, I dropped out of school and went back to school, I lived in sordid neighborhoods in Chicago and Oakland and on an organic tree farm in Oregon. I was quick and friendly, and my intuitive response to all the subcultures I explored was to adapt, using camouflage to survive. As a precocious college student, I had been literary, political, an idealistic hippie child. As a young factory worker, I listened to country music in Oregon and to soul music in Oakland and Chicago. I marveled at the utter boredom this kind of work life forced on people; I joined my new friends in drinking too much and hanging out as wasted as possible on weekends.

Once I went to a doctor, complaining of gastrointestinal pain. I told this kind physician in Portland, Oregon, that I was from Los Angeles and that my father was a doctor, too. I explained to the doctor that I was working and going to college, that I wanted to make it on my own without my parents' help. He did a thorough history and asked me about all kinds of symptoms. He ordered some blood and urine tests, and then he sat me down. "You know what I think, young lady?" he asked. "I think you need to go back home to your family and let your parents take care of you. Everything you've told me sounds like you're under a lot of stress, and I think you're depressed." Like so many experiences that I have written about for this chapter, I felt bad for lying to this doctor—yet today, as I write this, I feel bad, too, for the young woman that I was.

This doctor was right, of course. I was a distressed, lost, unhappy kid, and I needed my parents to look after me. But my parents could not do that; I felt they were too overwhelmed keeping Addie stable and worrying about Anne. I thought that I would just add to their burden, so I went on in my own way. I thought that the only way for me to survive was by not needing any help.

I tried harder than ever to be fun, enthusiastic, and pleasing. When I met my second husband, a professional musician, I incorporated into our relationship the kind of false self that I was presenting to my parents in those days. I wanted everything to be OK, so I would tell everyone, including myself, that this was so. My second husband was (and still is) a tremendously talented musician, and I saw my role as moving the drudgery of life out of his way so that he could work on his art. We had a romantic relationship that was based more on illusions than on authentic knowledge of each other. Occasionally my cheerful façade cracked, and a swirling sense of pressure broke through. I couldn't express this distress in words; it expressed itself in a physical way that left me short tempered and cranky.

Once, early in my second marriage, my husband and I tried some kind of hallucinogenic drug. I didn't sleep for 3 days, and toward the end of that time, I thought I heard voices. Just whispers or muffled sounds—just out of reach. I remember thinking, in a way that etched itself into my mind, "I have created a psychotic state with these drugs. This must be what Addie or Anne experience." That thought jolted me; I had to consider why I would create such an experience. What kind of danger was I in? What kind of self-destructive current could be operating in me? I shook these thoughts and questions off as quickly as I could.

My second husband and I wanted to buy our own home, and we went to a financial planner. During the course of that meeting, discussing our goals and lifestyle and tolerance for risks, I burst into tears. The man interviewing us was sensitive and thoughtful; like the well-meaning physician years earlier in Oregon, he suggested that perhaps I was unhappy in some way and would benefit more from psychotherapy than from financial planning. Without any hesitation, I responded favorably. I hadn't realized that I was looking for such a suggestion, but I recognized immediately this time that I wanted help.

PUTTING THE PIECES TOGETHER

It's striking to me now, as I write this narrative 30 years later, that my entrée into my own psychotherapy did not come from my own request or even my own awareness of what I needed. Of course, that was in 1976, and psychotherapy was not so much a part of our culture as it is today. The stigma attached to seeing a psychotherapist was quite strong, and I didn't tell anyone for many months that I was in therapy. I had expected to uncover all kinds of ugly truths about myself once I began psychotherapy, that I was damaged and damaging.

Instead, I was encouraged to think about my own feelings and desires. What was I interested in? What had happened to the young adolescent who loved ancient history and literature? What had I been through, all those years living and working in so many different situations? I went back to school to finally finish my undergraduate degree, discovering anthropology and rediscovering psychology. My own positive growth experience led me to consider working as a psychologist myself.

I began to do volunteer work to see whether working as a psychologist would suit me. I studied family systems theory, reading books by R. D. Laing and studies of family communication by Margaret Singer. My heart pounded as I read these accounts of family dynamics in which one person was driven crazy by the family system and in which contact with their parents made young people with psychosis worse. Had I grown up and developed my sense of self within some sick system that had made two of my sisters ill? According to these theories, the identified patient in a family is the person carrying the family's illness. Filled with anxiety and dread, I concluded that I had been raised in a severely disturbed system and must be carrying part of that insanity in everything I do. The way I related to people must cause mental illness, and I had all kinds of memories to make me believe this.

For example, there was the time that I lost my temper when Addie kept me up night after night, when I was in eighth grade and so excited about going to high school. Addie never washed; the whole upstairs of our house stank, and I had run into her room and ripped the sheets off her bed and screamed at her. I had grabbed her arms in mine and squeezed until she cried. When my mother tried to break us apart, I had hit my own mother. And what about taking Addie's money when I was in ninth grade—even though I could "justify" it because she had given me the money freely and I had been good to her? Or the way that I had presented myself to my parents and teachers as such a stable and enthusiastic adolescent (even though my illicit behavior was not that different from that of many young people in the late 1960s and early 1970s)? But, really, the problem wasn't that I had done "bad" things; it was that I had no way to understand why I was doing these things and no way to be bad openly. Through my first psychotherapy, I began to make sense of these upsetting secrets and to dispel my fears that I carried an unhealthy way of interacting into every relationship.

I got into graduate school in clinical psychology. Still, I was terribly anxious when I began clinical work. My first clinical placement was at a school for severely disturbed children. I had not considered working with children, ever, and I was utterly distressed to be assigned to work with a 9-year-old boy who was diagnosed as schizoaffective. He was violent, oppositional, and easily frustrated, but he had a curious love of and talent for drawing. I spent several days working in his classroom so that he could get to know me and become comfortable with the idea of working with me individually. When I arrived in his classroom to take him to the playroom, he went into a rage, throwing a chair at the chalkboard. His teacher and I held him down, and the boy spit in my face. Immediately, I spit right back. "There! You see what that feels like? You don't like it, and neither do I!" I said. Wide-eyed and visibly calmer, he gave me his hand, and we began what was to be a successful 2-year treatment.

I didn't know what to expect when I went to clinical supervision, and my voice wobbled as I described this incident to the experienced child therapist sitting before me. She looked at me steadily for too long. "Well, I wouldn't ever advise a supervisee to spit at their clients, but I will tell you this," she said. "I don't know where it came from, but you had the courage to really interact with this very angry, frightened little boy, and to take matters into your own hands." I recount this incident because it captures my dilemma as a young clinician in training. It seemed clear that whatever capacity I had for clinical work was related to my ability to *relate to* very ill people displaying irrational or agitated behavior. What else could I conclude, except that I had developed this capacity in my relationships to my family members? And what did that say about me? Was I exploiting my sisters, then, using the experiences that I had had with them to help me in my career?

It is now my third year in graduate school. I have survived the breakup of my second marriage, a relationship loss that I had not anticipated and that threw me into a very deep depression. I am able to ask my parents for help, however, and they provide financial support so that I can continue graduate school and see a psychoanalyst. I wonder, of course, how it could be that I have been divorced twice and I'm barely 30.

And then—I still remember vividly the phone call, from which I learned that Teresa, the youngest of my older sisters, had attempted to take her own life. I remember being in my graduate student apartment, talking with the man who would become my third husband and with whom I would have a family. The minute I heard that it was my sister's husband on the phone, I knew. We had so little contact; I had only met him twice in the 12 years Teresa had been married to him. "I'm sorry to tell you this, Laura. Teresa's in the hospital." I hadn't even known she was depressed. She was not at all a communicative person, and all

I heard about her for years was how her research was going, and how successful she was as a woman scientist.

Teresa's suicide attempt was a shock. It was a complete miracle that she had survived, so violent was her effort. And she herself had not seen it coming. She had been offered a prestigious academic position. She had always suffered from a kind of agitated perfectionism, but to me it had seemed that it was the price she was willing to pay for spectacular achievement. This job offer was what she had been working toward her whole life, but when it came, she collapsed. Teresa asked me not to tell our parents or our sisters about what had happened, although over the years, she was eventually able to share with the family that she suffers from severe, recurrent major depression.

WHERE ARE WE NOW?

My husband tells me, whenever he and I talk about my family of origin, how surprised he was when he met Addie. He had been told so much about her diagnosis and about her psychotic breaks that he was not prepared for what a charming and warm person she is. Addie cares about people; she is curious about the likes and dislikes of others. She has always had a marvelous knack for choosing gifts, which certainly requires an awareness of another person's age and taste and interests.

Anne is quite different in this regard. I have no memory of her being interested in me, of responding to her little sister with adoration or curiosity. I can't recall a single time I was left with her as my babysitter, yet I have many memories of Addie or Teresa taking me places or being "stuck" with me. The lack of relationships in Anne's life is a staggering manifestation of the form that her mental illness takes. I am not the only one who has no contact with Anne; the same is true for Teresa and our parents. I know that Anne does not work, that she never answers her telephone, nor does she call any of us. Addie stops by and says hello to her a couple of times a month, and if it weren't for that, my parents, Teresa, and I would have no information about her. She does not work, and her health is bad. Anne is, quite literally, out of contact with the world, living in complete isolation. She cashes the checks my parents send and lives in a small condominium they purchased for her. I assume she lives on some kind of social security or disability.

And what of Teresa? Instead of taking the more high-powered position, the thought of which had driven her to attempt suicide, she became a professor at a fine university, trying to become realistic about her expectations for herself. She has been on medication and in psychotherapy for 20 years now and has been hospitalized three more times over the years, when her mood has plummeted.

There is a kind of cynical folklore about psychotherapists to the effect that people who want to work as clinicians are the "nuttiest" bunch of all. In other words, people choose this profession as a way to solve their own problems. I have been vulnerable to these ideas. Even when my younger daughter was 11, she said to me, "I think I know why you became a psychologist, Mom. I think it's because when you were growing up you were very, very curious about what was going on with Addie, and no one would tell you. And so when you went to college, that's what you wanted to figure out." In this vein, there is a statement attributed to the eminent clinician Harold Searles that a person is motivated to become a clinical psychologist after failing to heal a member of his or her own family.

For years, I have identified with this statement, although at the same time, it has made me uneasy. Did I try to heal Addie? Or Teresa? How much is my choice of profession ruled by survivor guilt or some other effort to solve my own problems or the problems of my sisters?

Slowly, I have come to realize that it is *not* simply the presence of an emotionally or mentally ill family member that set me moving on the clinical path I have taken. ALL families have some kind of trouble, and the more we learn about the epidemiology of psychopathology, trauma, and the effects of poverty and social injustice, the more I am convinced of the astounding prevalence of serious, diagnosable psychological suffering.

No, it is not that having troubled sisters left me feeling I needed to heal others. I think that my relational and emotional qualities set me on the course of wanting to care for Addie in the first place. I have had these instincts since my childhood and early adolescence.

Another way of thinking about this is to ask whether I would have become a clinician without my sisters. There's no empirical answer to such a question, of course, but one way to think about it is that neither Anne nor Teresa responded to Addie's breakdowns by becoming more concerned or more involved with Addie. I do not mean this as a value judgment at all, but rather to accentuate that it was something about me that brought me closer to Addie and to Teresa in response to their illnesses. This "something in me" was my interest in and capacity for interacting with people, including people in distressed emotional states.

I did come to graduate school with a lot of experience, then, in relating to all kinds of people, including clinical populations, and this experience deeply informed my approach to people and to clinical work. I know what it's like to be achingly close to irrational outbursts and paranoid states of mind. I also know what it's like to stay involved with people in these states rather than to withdraw.

It continues to be a great source of grief and sorrow for me that I could not "cure" Addie, or Anne, or Teresa. I "know" that the mental illnesses that afflict my two oldest sisters are incurable, just as I "know" that a diabetic must always take insulin. But mental illnesses express themselves as—and they are almost equivalent with—who the person is. I cannot escape the view that my sisters' conditions are who they are; these disorders have taken them over in some fundamental way. Such illnesses operate in the very realms that make us human: the ways we express, share, and experience emotion; our capacities for relationship and concern; our very thoughts and ways of making meaning out of life.

Today, as I write this narrative, I feel so bad for all of us. I know now that Addie and Anne (and to a lesser extent, Teresa) suffer from real illnesses, illnesses that express themselves in and through their very sense of self, permeating their behavior and their relationships.

If serious mental illnesses are "incurable," then what do I hope to offer people in my clinical work? How can I offer any hope or help? When I was first in private practice more than 20 years ago, a young woman who had already been diagnosed by her psychiatrist as having paranoid schizophrenia was referred to me. She'd had personality tests that confirmed at the very least a paranoid personality disorder. I remember my work with "Sally" so well. I recall especially that I thought, "Whatever the tests say, she seems like she's a real person, not just an illness, she has a real life and real relationships." She had a respectable job as an office manager, she took courses at the local junior college…and, at the same time, had complicated, absolutely paranoid delusions.

But she could talk with me about her delusions, and together we built a narrative that allowed us to get some perspective and control over them. After a while, she and I could talk about her diagnosis, about the medications she would need to take forever, and about the types of stresses that would exacerbate her symptoms. Eighteen years ago, I was a guest at her wedding. I am still her anchor, although we meet only once or twice a month now. She is a loving and stable mother to her 12-year-old daughter. Sally and her husband are open with their daughter, their extended family, and their immediate social circle about her thought disorder. This is the kind of outcome I hope for and work toward.

CONCLUSION

There isn't a "happily ever after" ending to my story. There was no great breakthrough or powerful honest moment when I began or reinitiated a grand, intimate relationship with any of my sisters or with my parents. When Addie began to fall apart, WE ALL FELL APART. There was no one to talk to, and no place where it felt SAFE to talk. There was no way to hide Addie's breakdowns; they were unraveling for all of us. It wasn't that there was an explicit message not to talk about it; rather, there was no way to talk about it that helped us survive as a family. The theories from the field of psychology held us accountable, whether the "cause" was bad parenting or bad family dynamics. Even genetic theories left me feeling damned; what horrible legacy would any children of mine inherit?

I have struggled, and denied, and tried just as much as I can stand to come to terms with my family's limitations and my own. I was finally able to reveal to my parents that I had not actually finished college, and I did eventually earn a PhD. Through the guidance of a clinical supervisor, I went into treatment with an attachment-theory-oriented psychoanalyst more than 20 years ago. We worked together intensively for 8 years, and I still see this woman twice a week. Within the safe space this analyst created with me, I was able to put together so many of the bits and pieces and selves and experiences that had been operating in separate compartments since I was a little girl. I took the risk of loving and marrying for the third time and of having children. I have found incredible meaning and purpose in my work as a clinician and clinical professor.

I know that my experiences with all of my sisters shaped me profoundly. But especially crucial were those cold Chicago afternoons when I was just 12 or 13, when I sat with Addie in silence as she cried or told me bizarre stories. Those afternoons are a touchstone for me. And just as I felt guilty as a sixth grader when I told my teachers that I was having trouble at school because of my sister's illness, I feel guilty sometimes even now that my capacity in my work is due in part to my experiences with my sisters' conditions.

Yet I also feel grateful, as I sit with my clients or my graduate students, that I know the human face of psychological suffering so well. With all the important scientific developments in psychopharmacology, empirically supported treatments, and transdiagnostic processes, it is central to me to also hold in mind the person inside the symptoms and the suffering. Who is that person? Who held her or tried to comfort her? Did anyone?

Perhaps I can try. And so can the students I train. Without that effort, where are we?

NOTE

1. Beardslee, W. R. (2002). *Out of the darkened room: When a parent is depressed: Protecting the children and strengthening the family.* Boston: Little, Brown.

2   Finding My Mind

Ruth C. White

PROLOGUE

SUNDAY, AUGUST 18, 1990, 3:30 A.M.

I now know that when everyone was telling me I was crazy I really was very unbalanced. I knew it then—at least I felt it then and I was terrified. The reality of mental "illness (?)" was too much for me.

At the time I wrote this I was 26 years old and struggling with the knowledge that I was "different." And although some of this difference related, I felt, to my giftedness, I knew that the way I moved in the world was problematic. I was not in control of my emotions, and I worked hard to control what people saw in me—and also what they did not see in me. In the 15 years that followed, I suffered a variety of depressions and manic episodes, all documented in my various journals. I tried to make sense of my behavior, but I would not seek help, even as I worked in a variety of mental health settings. Often, I would use the *DSM-IV* to self-diagnose, but I treated it more like a game than my life. I became diagnosed with adult ADHD, accompanied by depressions. As hard as this was for me to accept, I ultimately learned that manic depression was the more accurate diagnosis. In my mind, for much of my life the *DSM-IV* did not apply to me. It was for the mentally ill, and I was NOT mentally ill, despite matching all the symptoms for bipolar disorder.

The only consistent pieces of evidence for my mental health problems were my performance reviews at work. Spanning group homes, research institutes, and academia, I was always described as inconsistent, with bursts of creativity and excellence and then flakiness and lack of productivity—reflecting both mania and depression. I searched for order and consistency and tried to escape from feeling "haunted" and restless much of the time. I treated my mania with hours upon hours of dancing, night after night. It took the edge off. Unlike many people with manic depression, I did not use drugs or alcohol to self-medicate because, more than anything else, I hated feeling out of control. I already felt that way, and I was going to hold on to any bit of control that I had. It took many years before I lost all control.

The author, in London, her birthplace (2006)

NOVEMBER 1O, 2OO5

So I am here at Fairfax Hospital. What the @#$* happened to my life?!!
I'm taking my 1200 mg of lithium at night with my 20 mg of Prozac in
the morning and still have to be babysat to be safe. Two nights ago I put
a knife to my wrist as my daughter slept. It's like my brain is trying to
destroy my body. I think of suicide all the time.

INTRODUCTION

The following is the story of 3 years of my life. These 3 years could probably
be clinically constructed as one long episode of manic depression with various
degrees of severity. These years are marked by two crises, but throughout this
time period, I struggled almost constantly with regulating my moods, with taking
medication, and with achieving my new identity as someone who is mentally ill.
I also ended a long-term relationship, began life as a single parent, got a promotion, and then later lost it. This 3-year period has recently ended with an unprecedented "run" of stability and a newfound resolve to let others know about my
life and my illness.

Prior to the period I describe here, my worst episode had been a year-long
experience with the hell of postpartum depression that lasted from mid-1997
to late 1998. I functioned in a dark cloud, but I never sought help. I had a reputation for coping with anything and everything, and although it was clear to
anyone who knew me that I was not coping very well, I soldiered on in denial.

But that denial probably led to the severe episodes I describe in this chapter, because the longer manic depression goes untreated, the more severe and more frequent the episodes are likely to become. This was definitely my pattern.

I have been keeping a journal since age 14, and almost 30 years later, I still record my feelings, thoughts, and the random daily goings on of my life. This chapter is interspersed with excerpts from my journal (written in italics) that illustrate my experiences much more viscerally than hindsight ever could.

DIAGNOSIS, CRASH, AND REDIAGNOSIS

APRIL 25, 2003

A week ago I received a tentative diagnosis of ADHD. It's been a challenge to accept it....I went to see a therapist because I really wasn't feeling good emotionally. I'd been having a lot of anxiety with marked periods of depression. I felt like I was on fast forward in my brain. I couldn't focus, I was not sleeping and I felt emotionally out of control.

At that point in my life my official diagnosis was attention-deficit/hyperactivity disorder (ADHD) with significant depression. For a year I had not been able to get rid of the depression, and I had refused to take medication for either condition. Instead, I visited my therapist weekly, exercised almost daily, tried stress-reduction techniques, and even attempted yoga. I did not want to be medicated, because for me it meant that my life was out of my control—and it meant admitting that I was mentally ill. I also did not like the idea of having a somewhat "trendy" diagnosis of adult ADHD. At the same time, my high energy, distractibility, talkativeness, and so forth all made ADHD a strong possibility, especially given my struggle with these symptoms from early childhood.

Although the ADHD diagnosis did make sense to me, I thought it was a bit embarrassing to be part of the fastest growing diagnosis in the United States. I was prescribed Ritalin, and although I did not want to take it, I was desperate, so I took it as prescribed. Yet my second dose made my heart race and my hands tremble, and I thought I was going to die. No more Ritalin. Lots of therapy kept me from going over the edge.

THURSDAY, MAY 9, 2003

So the last week has been hard. I always feel like I'm on the verge of tears but I have nothing to cry about. I really feel like I'm going crazy....I don't want meds for all the typical reasons but I would really like to have my brain do what I want it to and to be able to not bounce off the walls so much (or to feel as if I'm going to explode if I don't). What's hard is to feel like I've been holding it together for all these years and now I can't. About 13 years ago I wrote in my journal that I felt as if I was held together by tiny strings and I guess they all just broke…but there has got to be a way to deal other than taking medication I keep thinking.

FRIDAY, MAY 16, 2003 (LATE THURSDAY NIGHT)

Sleep is not going to come easy tonight. I am tortured by my thoughts. Stuck on the theme of death. My death. I want to be dead. I think about all the ways I could die without [my daughter] feeling abandoned and lost. I think about my parents blaming themselves. And [my partner] too. And the shame. And the drama. I won't do it but it's all I can think about. I've had three crying spells this evening. Triggered by nothing but overwhelming sadness. And thoughts that are dark and shameful.…I feel like checking myself into a hospital. I really do. But then everyone will know my dirty secret: the overachiever with the "great" life who cannot handle daily living.

MONDAY, MAY 19, 2003 12:40 A.M.

Well what a weekend. My mood was all over the place. Great therapy session on Friday. Saturday I was an emotional mess. Deep depression. Thoughts of suicide. Lots of crying. No energy. Stayed in bed much of the day. Thought that if I spent another day like that I'd have myself admitted to hospital. I wanted to die. It was horrible.

WEDNESDAY, MAY 21, 2003

Went to an ADD support group tonight. It was the most amazing feeling. First, I was very uncomfortable with being in a group full of "sick" people. Even though I don't consider ADHD a "sickness." But I felt strange being in a support group. But at 8:30 P.M. when the meeting was over it was fabulous. To meet all those people who were like me. It was very "normalizing."

I was identifying with the ADHD diagnosis at this time. In fact, at almost any point in my life, I would have been easily classified as a classic case of ADHD. My childhood teachers often had no idea what to do with me. I was a brilliant student—somewhat of a child prodigy, who had reached sixth grade when I was 8 years old. I also disrupted the class, could not keep still, talked constantly, and was easily bored. People jokingly diagnosed me with ADHD all the time. As I grew into my adolescence in Canada, my mother would say that if I had spent my childhood in Canada (instead of Jamaica), I would have been prescribed Ritalin. Perhaps I do have ADHD, given that many people with manic depression also have comorbid ADHD.

From spring 2003 through the following winter, I spent the year in frequent contact with my therapist, trying hard to avoid taking the medications my psychiatrist strongly recommended. I tried yoga and ran up to 6 miles per day. I was still functionally depressed, however, thoughts of death ever near, with an external affect of someone hopped up on cocaine—clear evidence of the mixed-state form of manic depression in which one is both manic and depressed at the same time. But that was not yet the diagnosis.

FEBRUARY 4, 2004

Three days ago I got diagnosed with bipolar disorder I. It's an interesting story. I'd been on a manic run since December: 4 research proposals, 2 abstracts, 2 papers and 1 book review; all on different topics. I wasn't sleeping or running and I was feeling like I was going to "crash." So I called my psychotherapist and asked to see him as soon as possible. I fell apart in his office because I told him I was scared of being depressed since [my partner] left. Anyway, I decided on "no drugs" but weekly sessions.

I had been worried that I had no one to pick up the slack if I got depressed, and so I tried very hard to keep it all together for my daughter's sake. Then came THE CRASH.

How could this be happening? I sat on the floor of my home office, crying hysterically, one of my closest friends talking me down from near psychosis. I had called her to say that I had locked myself in the office because I had a very strong urge to smother my 6-year-old with a pillow and then kill myself. My only child (whose father lived in another city) had been sleeping in my bed, and I actually had the pillow in my hand when a moment of clarity made me run out of the room.

Afraid of being one of those "monsters" who does the unspeakable, I overcame the shame of owning those thoughts—and saved my life and that of my daughter by making that call. I suddenly understood how it happens that seemingly normal mothers kill their children, because I had almost become one of them.

I was still dealing with the ADHD diagnosis, but this episode was beyond what people with ADHD were likely to experience, and I knew enough to realize this. I was terrified. I no longer knew who I was.

My girlfriend, to whom I had made the call, suggested that I call 911. Yet we both knew that this would mean that my daughter would be removed from my care, given that I would be in a hospital and that I was the primary caregiver, with her father hundreds of miles away. I could not take that chance, so my friend promised to stay on the phone all night with me if she had to and that she would call 911 if we disconnected. Eventually, I gave her a break and called my daughter's aunt, who put herself on call to get on the next flight if needed. After I got my emotions under control, I fell asleep exhausted in the guest room, still afraid to go near my child in case my urges took control of me instead of the other way around.

The next morning, barely holding myself together with the strength of motherhood, I took my daughter to school. Afterward I drove directly to my therapist's office, where I fell apart: shaking, suicidal, and bawling my eyes out.

I was diagnosed with manic depression (my preferred term for bipolar disorder). The misdiagnosis could be explained by the fact that although my depression was acknowledged, my mania had been misinterpreted as hyperactivity and attention deficit. The cyclical nature of my emotions and the suicidal/homicidal urges were clues that ADHD was not the culprit for my behavior. Instead, I was a classic case of bipolar disorder, type I. I felt like a failure as a mother and as a person, especially when I was told that for the next few days, I would be hospitalized unless I had someone to stay with me or unless I had somewhere to go where someone could be responsible for taking care of my child's daily life. I was scared, ashamed, disappointed, confused, and lonely. Intellectually I knew that this was not my fault, that I had nothing to be ashamed of, but intellectual and emotional knowledge can be two different things.

Although I had been called "crazy" all of my life, the actual diagnosis of madness was more than I could accept. It was difficult, too, for many of those same friends who used to call me crazy to accept this new diagnosis. They questioned whether I was not simply stressed out from the many changes that had been going on in my life: a new job, a new city, my partner's move, and my new single-motherhood status. Ironically, some of my friends thought that I was just being overmedicalized and overmedicated. That angered me because I was the type of person who did not even keep aspirin in her home; I had received herbs and had minimal medical intervention even during my labor and delivery. For my friends to think that I was basically being emotionally lazy hurt me deeply. I knew that if I had called to say that I had cancer, the response would have been significantly different. I would have received empathy instead of being challenged on the validity of my diagnosis.

I also understood that the change in diagnosis from ADHD to manic depression made them question the accuracy of my diagnosis, causing them to wonder whether I was just a victim of "big pharma." I explained the difficulty in making accurate diagnoses of a disorder that goes in cycles. Difficult as it was, I also admitted to them how long I had been dealing with the symptoms of mental illness and the relief I felt at finally having a name for whatever it was that I was dealing with. I was not simply "crazy" anymore, I was mentally ill. It was validating, and yet it challenged the very core of my identity.

Things had been building for some time, clearly. With only me as my child's parent, there was no one to pick up the slack when things were falling apart.

And they were. My performance at work was sliding. I was going to bed at 2 A.M., my brain going in many different directions at once. I had difficulty focusing, I was talking all the time (and fast), I was forgetting to pick up my daughter or her playmate from one event or another, and I was going off on tangents during lectures, not being able to find my way back.

As a professor in social work, I knew there was something wrong, but I was in denial. I did not want to be mentally ill. Being hypomanic in this culture gets one lots of praise for productivity and creativity. I wrote articles on different topics and did the same with presentations. Instead of being the narrowly focused academic, I had ideas about everything, ideas that came hard and fast. I felt as though I was on a bicycle with the pedals going faster than my legs could go, as my body could never seem to catch up to my brain.

Finally, at that point I was ready and willing to take whatever medication was going to be needed to get me out of my misery. The clonazepam I got from the psych nurse made me so wobbly I had to tell my students I was on medications so they would not think I was drunk.

I had coped with being hypomanic (with intermittent depressions) for 25 years, but the longer my manic depression went undiagnosed and the more cycles I went through, the more frequent the cycling became, and the more severe the symptoms were. I was at that age at which undiagnosed manic depression begins to take its toll on the brain. My diagnosis was officially bipolar disorder I, mixed states, severe. Severe. That stuck with me. What did it mean for my life that I was severely mentally ill?

COPING

I did not know what to do about taking care of my daughter. I lived thousands of miles away from my family and close friends. I had only been in the Pacific Northwest for a short time and barely knew anyone. My daughter's father had moved us here for a fantastic career opportunity from which he later got laid off. Hating the Pacific Northwest, he returned to Northern California. I did not want to call him. How could I tell him what I had been thinking of doing? Would he take our daughter to live with him? Would he think me an unfit mother?

So I called the one person I knew beyond passing conversation: Kristen, the mother of my daughter's best friend in class. I told her that I needed somewhere to stay and had nowhere else to go. With open arms she took my daughter and me in, for as long as needed, which turned out to be only for a few days. It could not have been easy for her to have us there: a scared and confused child with a mother near the brink of madness undergoing the unpredictable journey that is "finding the right chemical cocktail" to bring her back to normal. My daughter's aunt soon arrived from Northern California to take over caring for my household as I got used to my new prescription regimen and slowly recovered from being put through the emotional wringer.

During all this, I never missed a day of work. It gave me something to look forward to, some sense of normality. Normality was my experience of it, but that was not true for my students, several of whom went to my superiors with complaints that my teaching had taken a dive: I was disorganized, behind in grading, and going off on tangents during my lectures.

I explained my shaking hands and wobbly gait (side effects of lithium and Klonopin) to my students by simply saying I was taking some medication. I wanted to say more but did not know how. I was comfortable that my students would know the truth, but I was scared that I would be seen as more than the absent-minded professor I already had the reputation of being. I also did not know how it would play with my colleagues. So I stayed hidden. In the closet. Like my sexuality. Being with a man meant I was perceived as straight, and yet I identified as queer because of my relationships with women. I felt like a fraud.

And yet the thought of ruining the image of "doing it all" kept me from telling anyone. As I noted before, when I did tell my friends, they did not want to accept the diagnosis because in their minds a highly accomplished woman did not suddenly get a diagnosis of mental illness. They questioned the diagnosis and my willingness to accept it. A graduate of McGill and Berkeley did not fit their image of mentally ill, even though many of them had thought me "crazy" for many years.

My colleagues and my peers did not know of my mental health advantage: mania. I would simply smile when asked how I did all that I did while parenting a child alone. What was I to answer—that it's my mania? I shared a floor in my university building with many psychologists. One day one of them commented that if he did not know better, he would think I was manic. I admitted that I was. That led to a good conversation, and then to many more, in which we explored current treatments and how I was doing. I was playing with my medications, as I knew that my love of the rush of energy and creativity that was mania had brought me to this point in my professional career. I had mixed feelings about using medications to give up mania in order to overcome depression.

Even a year later, the debate was raging in my mind:

> Madness
> Lurks around the edges of my mind
> Watching. Waiting.
> For me to let my guard down.
> So it can invade.
> Or perhaps…

Madness will creep in
Under the cover of my denial.
I close my eyes and try to wish it all away.
But I'm no genie.
My genies are pink and green and white.
And they must escape their bottles often.
Or madness moves in and stays. (May 19, 2005)

ACCEPTANCE

FRIDAY, FEBRUARY 6, 2004

Ruth White is mentally ill. Ain't that a bitch?!

FRIDAY, FEBRUARY 13, 2004, 11 P.M.

I'm at Kristen's house. I'm not doing well tonight and yet today was so good but around 5:30 P.M. I started to get mixed moods again. I wanted to cry and was on edge and just a wreck. I ended up eventually crying in the bathroom.....I saw [my therapist] today and told him how good I felt and here I am again feeling crappy. I swear if it wasn't for [my daughter] and my parents I'd just kill myself. It is miserable feeling like this. Tonight I thought about what it would be like to hang myself or jump off a building. I've thought about crashing the car but I'd just end up being bipolar and in a wheelchair. I feel like I'm going mad. I can't turn off my brain except with pills and they're not working. I called the advice nurse and she said I needed to give the double dose at least 72 hours to kick in. I'm just so frustrated. I need to write a paper for Trinidad and Tobago (conference) and I have 2 weeks and I haven't written one word. I wish I could just be manic for a little while. It would be done in days. So here I am at Kristen's for Valentine's weekend. Sad, messed up, and barely holding on.

TUESDAY, FEBRUARY 17, 2004

Well mania is upon me. There I was at 3:30 A.M. sweeping the baseboards....It's so frustrating. I haven't even yawned. I've swept, done laundry and now it's 4:30 A.M. and I'm doing pushups and situps.

SATURDAY, FEBRUARY 21, 2004, VANCOUVER

Anyway today was a bad day re: BPD [bipolar disorder]....Wild mood swings that are hard to deal with. One depressive mood hit so hard I had to grab [my cousin's] hand at dinner. Waves of sadness from out of

nowhere then shifts of mood I couldn't even keep back. I was very irritable. Couldn't deal well with [my daughter]. I apologized a lot. . . . I think I may have forgotten a lithium pill today so I bought a pill reminder to keep in my purse.

MARCH 16, 2004

To give up control of my brain to medication is surrendering my power. I want the mania back. I' m really considering stopping my meds. I don't have anymore "great ideas" and I miss that. I do like the calm. I don't miss the confusion. The feeling of always being in a hurry. I don't miss that.

MARCH 17, 2004

I want to stop taking my meds just to see. I'm wondering if they are keeping me messed up with their various side effects. I don't want to take them anymore. I just want to be me again. I've got one more Prozac a day to reduce my depression? Who am I now? I'm medicated to "normal." . . . I am a much better mother and for the first time since she's been born I don't think that having [my daughter] was a mistake. Who knew drugs could change that?

APRIL 1, 2004 12:30 A.M.

Well I tried an experiment. I skipped the lithium and Prozac today. I took the clonazepam because of its potential for me to have withdrawal symptoms [if I skipped it]. I felt great. I wasn't sleepy during the day. . . . I felt creative and energized. Low-level mania but I liked it. I worry about how that will affect my relationship with [my daughter] but I'll just try it and if I start messing up I'll get back on. I still resent walking around with a bunch of pills.

APRIL 3, 2004

Today is my third day without lithium or Prozac and I feel fine. I'm a little nervous about this drug vacation but it gives me the confidence to know that I don't have to be on them all the time.

APRIL 8, 2004

I'm feeling manic again. Not the simply good manic but also the edgy, wired, talk-a-mile-a-minute manic. I'm scared but I'm coping. I revised a paper I was supposed to have done two weeks ago. Worked on another. Worked on my second year review file. Ran errands. Got daughter to bed late with no bath. Got her to school late and forgot her show-and-tell.

Picked her up after 6 P.M. but another mom signed her out for me. I think I'm reacting to my very low teaching evaluations from last quarter where first I was manic and then depressed. It was such a psychological blow to see my average scores drop by a whole point. Especially after receiving "greatly exceeds expectations" on the teaching part of my APR [annual performance review] for the previous calendar year. Now I have to "explain" it in my second year review file, which means I have to say something about being ill. I am not "ashamed" of my illness but I don't want people to look at me trying to see if I'm okay.

APRIL 20, 2004

Mixed states. It sucks. Depression clear. With edge.

APRIL 28, 2004

It's late. I'm up. I can't even say what my mood was for the past few days. I just don't feel good. Feel on the verge of crying a lot but nothing takes me over the edge so I can let it out.….At times I want to simply crawl out of my skin I feel so emotionally "uncomfortable."

I did not like the side effects of lithium in the beginning, and as my journal shows, over the next months I took control of the science experiment that is life with a mental illness and ordered up mania—that is, I stopped taking my medications. What I hated most about taking medications was that they made me "normal." I got tired in the afternoon and called my psychiatrist to complain that getting tired in the afternoon was a side effect I could not tolerate. Her response was that was how most people felt at the end of the day, so the drugs were working. Great! I had to get used to being tired before midnight. It may sound trite or silly, but I had no idea what life would be like if I had to go to bed before 2 A.M. My favorite work hours were 11 P.M. until 2 A.M.

My therapist helped me to get used to less creativity and less productivity but more peace. I missed the highs, but I did not miss the lows. But like most people with manic depression, I played fast and loose with my medications. Accepting that I was mentally ill—despite all I felt about rejecting the social stigma of that reality—was not easy to do.

I really had not accepted the consequences of being mentally ill, even though by this time I had accepted that I had manic depression. When I read that sentence it seems oxymoronic. The answer is that I could deal in some abstract way with being "sick": I understood intellectually that sometimes the body did not function as it should and things go awry. As a child I had the mumps and the measles, and in my 20s I had a bad case of the chicken pox; but overall I was a very healthy person. So I accepted being "sick" as a reality of being human.

However, being mentally ill—with its possibilities for hospitalizations, periods of incompetence, and the requisite feelings of being out of control—was totally unacceptable to me. When one is on the high of hypomania, there seems to be no need for medication. In fact, the creative bursts were what I had used to build my career. It was hypomania (and at times full-blown mania) that allowed me to complete all coursework for my PhD and MPH at UC Berkeley in 2 years, while getting an exemption so I could work 30 hours a week. I also knew that it was depression (postpartum) that made me spend more than 1 year wishing my child would die in an accident to relieve me of the emotional burden of parenting.

Being a mental health professional, I knew the consequences of what I was doing. I understood that I was being a classic patient with manic depression by being noncompliant with my medication regimen, and I understood what that meant for my short- and long-term recovery. But all that was still not enough to make me take my medications regularly for more than 2 or 3 weeks at a time.

One year later I was still struggling with taking my meds as prescribed. On February 6, 2005, I wrote, "*I am having some difficulty committing to my medication.*" And it continued that way for almost another year as my moods went up and down, and I stuck with my therapist, sometimes weekly and other times less frequently. But it was getting tiring. I had basically been in one long episode of more than 2 years, and it would take another year to work it through.

OVER THE EDGE

The summer of 2005—more than a year after my diagnosis with manic depression and over 2 years after the beginning of my 3-year, almost continuous episode—I spent a summer traveling all over the world. Before I left, my friend Geoff, who is a child psychologist, sat me down and told me he was concerned about my obvious symptoms of mania. I heard him. But I was not willing to let being mentally ill get in the way of my career and my fun. In June, July, and August, I made separate trips to the Caribbean, the East Coast, Europe, Australia, and Africa, often with little more than a day or two between trips.

This put my circadian rhythms out of alignment. It is now beginning to be accepted that people with manic depression need to regulate their circadian rhythms to maintain emotional and psychological stability. In particular, abnormalities in circadian rhythms are prominent features of bipolar I disorder (although the impact of medication, mood state, and chronicity are not yet fully understood). Furthermore, unhealthy circadian rhythms, such as inconsistencies in bedtime and wake times, may compromise the benefits of pharmacotherapy.[1]

Within a few weeks of returning from my last trip, I was in trouble again. I was agitated and wired, helped along by a new caffeine habit that I picked up in response to the "sleepy" side effects of lithium. I was snapping at my daughter, lying in bed for hours, and feeling scared. Slowly, I began coming apart at the seams. A friend sent me an e-mail saying that our instant messaging was very unpleasant for her because I was verbally aggressive and unpleasant to communicate with. I stared at the e-mail and knew instantly what it meant: a slide into mania, but not the good kind. This kind of mania makes me edgy, irritable, wired. Yes, I could tell you lots of ideas, but they were incoherent and incomplete, and I couldn't keep track of them long enough to even write them down.

That weekend I brought my daughter to San Francisco to see her dad, and I hung out with friends. After a few hours, my dinner partner asked if I were taking my medications, because she feared I was manic. That is where shame really kicks in: when friends are telling you you're out of control. It is like being told you've gotten fat—of course, it was more scary than that, but I felt no fear at the time, only shame and anger. The next morning I woke up with my mood in the toilet. I was back on the wild roller coaster, and this one was flying (and sinking) fast. I was trying to not let Melinda (the friend who was hosting me for the weekend) know what was going on. I really tried to get out of bed, but I did not get out fast enough. She came to my room, saw my condition, and asked what was wrong.

Upon hearing the word *suicide* she suggested that I call my doctor. I did. There was the usual discussion of hospitalization, medication tweaks, and so forth. I decided that, to save face, I could not end up in the hospital, and I would do whatever I needed to do not to go. That included a walk through an Oakland cemetery, which was sobering. I watched a group of family and friends of someone buried there visit a slab of marble and cry. I did not want my daughter or my parents to be those people. I just couldn't ride the roller coaster anymore. I was tired, even exhausted.

After I came back from that weekend, not much changed. I would pick up my knives and use them to play violin on my arms without cutting the skin. Other times I would wake in the middle of the night and put them to my chest. I told my therapist reluctantly, because I did want someone to know, even though I knew what the result might be. But I really wanted to get better, and so I knew I had to tell the truth if that was my goal. As a result of my disclosures, talk of hospitalization came up in therapy sessions. Yet I would not, could not accept being in a hospital as a possibility. I thought of the times I had to get a client hospitalized, and I did not see myself being like "them." I was still on the "us" side of the treatment fence, no matter how ill I got.

NOVEMBER 3, 2005

What a day! Up, down, all around—my emotions were everywhere.
Geoff, my psychologist friend, went with me to get my lithium levels
checked and to pick up my prescription of clonazepam. Me and my drugs.

By now, I was back on medications, but missing some doses of my 3×300 mg a day lithium prescription. I was not deliberately avoiding my medications, but because I did not want to reveal that I was on medication, I would not bring them with me to meetings that might have coincided with the time I needed to take a pill. I do not really know what I was afraid of, because I doubt anyone would have asked me anything about it, but this was how I felt. Even so, I was fairly consistent with medications. In fact, I am willing to believe that the Prozac may have precipitated my severe mania, because, months later, I have no mania, and I have no Prozac. Then again, the imprecise nature of pharmacological treatment of manic depression makes it hard to pinpoint the cause of my symptoms at any particular point. Instead, it appears that a confluence of factors that may have included my sporadic noncompliance, my out-of-whack circadian rhythms, the stress of settling postrelationship issues, and my biochemistry led me to this point.

That weekend I sent out an S.O.S. to three friends by e-mail. I could no longer take care of my daughter, and I needed a night off. I asked if just one of them could give me a break. These women, mothers of the children with whom my daughter frequently played, came to my rescue by arranging to take my daughter for three straight nights. They picked her up from school that day with no bag packed. She wore their daughters' clothes, and they packed her lunches and arranged for pickup and drop-off from school.

One week later my jig was up. It was hospital time. I was completely falling apart, and it was clear that there was no way to get me in check while I was outside a hospital. I had a choice of going in voluntarily or waiting out an involuntary admission, which was most likely to be the next step (if I had not done myself in by then). I was an emotional wreck even at work, going to the bathroom on many occasions to have a crying jag and then returning to teach my class. My students were concerned. They were social work seniors. I had told them casually about my manic depression. This decision had negative outcomes for my performance evaluation for that year, because of a work culture that did not support that kind of disclosure.

My treatment team had sent me to get a preadmission checkup. After the doctor did her examination and I was left to get dressed, I searched through the drawers of the examining room. I had no idea what I was searching for until I found it: surgical blades. I took two and put them in my purse. Therapists often ask about a plan and a weapon. I had a weapon. No plan, not even a thought: I was on automatic pilot. But I had been thinking about killing myself for days. In my rational moments I knew I was on the edge, but I was at the point where I was almost living outside of my body. It was as if my mind were trying to kill my body.

As I drove from my clinic to the psychiatrist's office, my psychologist friend Geoff called. He had spent the previous night at my house "babysitting" me—taking away the sharp objects, making sure that I took my Klonopin, and reading me to sleep when the clonazepam just could not do the trick. He had wanted to come with me to the physical exam but could not break his own practice commitments on such short notice. He was worried because in many ways he was much more cognizant of my mental state than I was. That morning I had questioned him about what could possibly go wrong between a clinic and a psychiatrist's office.

In his professional wisdom, he was worried enough to call. He asked how the exam went and then asked the one question that gave my secret away: "Are you safe?" I paused for a second, which was long enough for his skills as a clinician to tell him there was something wrong. (I was always a lousy liar.) I admitted that I had stolen the surgical blades. And with the threat of a call to the police now over my head, I went immediately to my psychiatrist's office and handed them in. Geoff had called ahead and let my psychiatrist and psychotherapist know that I had the blades, so they were waiting with arms outstretched when I arrived. My doctor reaffirmed to me that going to the hospital at this point was not really a choice anymore.

When my therapist left his office to do some paperwork, I took a pen and tried hard to draw blood from my wrists. I only made marks that took days to wear off. Within an hour I felt shame at the stupidity of that move. (Within a day I was laughing at the memory.) My therapist entered the office and made a comment about now having to remove pens from the office. He had to leave the office again but left the door open this time. I then threw a chair and ended up sitting on the floor in a corner, crying. When my therapist reentered the office, he gave me a blanket and calmly dealt with the business at hand. My offer to drive myself to the hospital was met with a smile. I was told that was not a possibility and waited for my friend Kristen to come to drive me. At the door to the hospital, I decided to walk away, but Kristen appealed to my desire to mother my child, and I walked in. Within an hour of my arrival I was voluntarily submitting my earrings to the staff, as I had tried to put them into my wrists. I never did get those earrings back—just one more loss to add to the list.

THURSDAY, NOVEMBER 10, 2005

I really didn't want to be here but if I'm not here I will end up hurting myself. It's hard to own that. What has happened to my brain? Why is it trying to do this to me? I wish I could control my body but it seems as if I can't. What made me poke my earrings into my wrist? I don't want scars that belie my disease for the rest of my life.

I slept for the first day and a half, exhausted from having been manic for so long. I had packed for 2 days because of my own denial about my mental state.

I had to ask Geoff to bring me a blanket, sweater, and socks. The few moments I spent awake over those first 2 days I drank a cup of tea to pop my pills and went back to bed. My brain was in a fog. Getting me emotionally stable and trying to find a combination of medications that worked without bad side effects eventually took a week.

FRIDAY, NOVEMBER 11, 2005

Pharmasoup: Risperdal, Zyprexa, Seroquel, Lightbox, Lamictal, lithium, Prozac, blah blah blah blah. How can anyone keep the options straight? Make the right decisions? I just want to stop thinking about killing myself. The rest I can deal with. I have for years. I'm accomplished, fairly sane most of the time, a great mom, colleague, and friend. My brain is doing a chemical dance that is keeping the doctors on their toes. Bipolar Disorder I mixed severe with rapid cycling. Yeah. Yeah.

It sure is strange to be a patient on the other side of the treatment wall....

How hard is it for a mother to admit she has thoughts of killing her child? Yet in the thought of it, it is to save the child from life with a mother who committed suicide. No one needs that kind of psychic pain. I love my baby so much. And I love my life a lot too. I don't want to have scars on my wrists or my thighs that will remind me and everyone else what my past was.

I am motivated to get through this and not have to ever go through this again. I'll commit myself to the chemistry experiment that will start today and who knows how it will all end.

FRIDAY, NOVEMBER 11, 2005, MIDNIGHT

After a long day it's time to sleep. I spent much of the day sleeping. I feel like shit and keep trying to find ways to hurt myself.

By the next day I had the first med change. The major change was no Prozac, with the doctors agreeing that it may have contributed to my manic episode. I had become engaged in one of the great psychiatric debates of our time: Should people with bipolar disorder be treated with SSRI antidepressants to deal with depressed phases of their illness? I did not care one way or the other: I just wanted to be better, and I wanted out of the hospital, so I took whatever they told me. The ingredients of my new chemical soup were as follows: 1200 mg of Lithobid at bedtime, 2.5 mg Zyprexa at bedtime, 25 mg Lamictal (slowly increasing to 200 mg), and 0.5 mg of Klonopin (with a switch to Seroquel after weaning from Klonopin). Before I left the hospital I had also tried trazodone (made my heart race and made me feel extremely dopey) and eventually left the hospital on Depakote, Lamictal, Lithobid, and Klonopin. (The Lamictal eventually gave me a rash, which could have led to more dangerous complications, so that was later stopped.)

NOVEMBER 11, 2005, CONTINUED FROM MIDNIGHT

All so I can be "normal" in my moods. The docs are confident that I will be fine and that makes me hopeful. I don't feel "possessed" as I was feeling before. No exorcism is needed. The urge to kill myself is decreasing even though I still have thoughts of self-harm.

I began to ask a lot of questions of my doctors, and, because I was a mental health professional, they engaged me in long discussions about many clinical issues and controversies related to manic depression. I also started to gain much more understanding of the medication compliance issues that frustrate so many clinicians working with the mentally ill, especially those with manic depression. I had understood these issues from my own perspective, but my gradual politicization had made this a broader issue for me. Now, the issue was not simply one of intellectualization of my own noncompliance, nor was it simply about the high of mania. It was about being mentally ill and distancing myself from that identity. I knew that I was going to need to bring this experience into my teaching.

One of my doctors urged me to consider writing an academic paper in which I would include my experiences. It was a challenge that he thought would make me an expert on my own illness. He also thought that the subjective experience of a mental health professional would make a contribution to the work being done in this area.[2]

STIGMA AND ACCEPTANCE

NOVEMBER 13, 2005, 3 P.M.

Talked to a [social worker] friend today. She's not coming to visit. I resent that. I feel hurt and abandoned....She told me that she was afraid to tell me the truth about not wanting to visit. That was related to a family member's mental illness in her childhood. She also did not want to "see me like this." That this is shifting the way she thinks about me. That was hard to hear but it is what it is.

So there it was. A friend did not want to visit me because of what mental illness meant to her. Granted, her own family history of mental illness was connected to this, but she was also a mental health professional who did not want to see a friend in a mental health facility. I could not help but wonder whether she would have felt the same if I had had some other physical illness. (I say this because manic depression *is* a physical illness; it is not simply in my mind. It is about biochemistry.) I cried. I felt lonely at the hospital. Visiting hours were split between lunch and dinnertime, but lunch visits were out of the question for most people. And I had few friends and no family in the area.

My daughter visited me with my friend Kristen one day at the hospital on the only evening on which visiting hours were held. It was good that she was only 8 years old and had no idea of the stigma and shame of mental illness. She just wanted to see me, as I wanted to see her. And I wanted to be better—for her, more than for me. Other friends visited me, and it meant more than they would ever understand, because a mental health facility can be a very isolating place.

It was also very hard for me because I like being outside, and I walk 3 miles around a lake at least three times a week. Being indoors all day was stifling. Going to groups felt like school; I felt infantilized. I once asked for a pair of scissors to do an art project in my room, and I was very angry and frustrated when told no. I was no longer having ideations of self-harm, but it did not matter. I understood why, and it was exactly that understanding which angered me. It was just another reminder that I could not be trusted—because I was crazy!

I could have left because I was there voluntarily, but I really did want to get better, so I struggled with the conflicts in my mind about being ill. Here I was, a mental health provider who could run the groups I was having to attend and yet knowing I needed to go to them.

The shame I had already felt was intensified by my hospitalization. At the time I gave birth, I had not even spent a night in a hospital in my whole life, and I had not been in a hospital since the half day I spent during labor, delivery, and recovery. It was also difficult to be on the other side of the treatment fence after spending years working in mental health facilities. But I was trying to be just another patient working through an individualized treatment regimen. I felt that I already knew "the game," but I opened myself to learning more and growing.

I had been forewarned that nursing students from my university did their psychiatric rotations at the facility, and I had been asked if I preferred to go elsewhere, but I didn't. Anyway, the other option was more than 40 miles away, and that would have meant no visitors at all.

POLITICIZATION AND DISCLOSURE

Hospitalization politicized me. Everyone I talked to inside that hospital was carrying the shame of being mentally ill. And because of that shame, we were all struggling with medication compliance.

I was considering the work I had done on AIDS stigma and antigay sentiment in Jamaica. I saw how the power of stigma could make a person choose
death over life because he or she did not want the mark of being a person living
with HIV/AIDS, preferring to go undiagnosed or untreated. That work had also
given me the privilege of meeting people who chose to step out of the shadows to educate an ignorant, prejudiced, isolating, and often violent community
about life with HIV/AIDS. I also had to deal with the death of one study participant a day before I presented findings to which he had contributed. He was
killed because he was out as a gay man, and he knew that was the risk he took,
but he had wanted to open the closet doors. I thought about these people and
made a choice not to be ashamed of something I had no control over—an illness
that was due to a biochemical imbalance, an illness that had upturned my life at
home and at work. But, of course, not everyone felt as I did.

In recent months, revealing to my students that I have manic depression
inspired several of them to talk with me about their own mental health issues.
This included one student who was struggling with her own identity concerning
mental illness and had stopped taking the antidepressants she had been taking
for 10 years. She was having trouble coping with the resulting depression, but
she felt "weak" for needing medications to function healthily. As she stated in
an e-mail:

> I just wanted to thank you again for talking with me and following up. It
> was hard for me to actually sit down and talk to you about it because this
> is something that I have tried to hide and be "strong" about for so long,
> but you were so incredibly wonderful. Telling myself that I don't need my
> medication or trying to prove to myself that I am stronger has only dragged
> me down. I know this is a constant battle that I will have to deal with for
> the rest of my life, thank you for not tiptoeing around it like everyone else
> has seemed to.

This student later told me that my willingness to put myself out there inspired her to rethink her own stigmatized position. I was later able to convince her
to go to the counseling center, which later led to her restarting her medications.

Since then, other students have appreciated my disclosure, which has
prompted their own admissions of mental health challenges. They have admitted
to feeling relieved that someone understands, because of the difficulty, shame,
and embarrassment they feel when explaining their experiences to family and
friends. Another student to whom I had disclosed my issues worried, after her
own hospitalization, about completing her assignments. She was embarrassed
about what she saw as her inability to cope. In an e-mail message, she said:

> It is really nice to have someone who understands the situation…nobody
> else (friends, family) seems to, and that makes me ashamed and embarrassed

to talk about it. It is really refreshing to finally hear someone say, "I understand."

Yet another student who was struggling over a long hospitalization that had occurred in her youth and who was experiencing major resistance to taking her medications stated it this way:

> So I don't know how I am supposed to get over this since I can't talk about it. I really respect you and your ability to be so matter of fact about yourself in the hospital because it is so hard for me to accept and understand my own experience. I don't have any negative judgments about you or see you as any less of a person for going to the hospital, yet I am very, very critical of myself and see myself as bad and crazy.

I believe that modeling openness about mental illness and incorporating it into my teaching was and is a good thing. As teachers and trainers of mental health professionals, we have, I contend, an explicit responsibility not to reinforce the stigma that is attached to many of our clients. Yet disclosure of my mental illness to students became problematic in my work environment. One colleague felt it was a burden I need not share with my students, as they would feel the need to take care of me. But no student seemed to have that need—at least no one ever expressed it to me. From the official stance, however, the reality of my mental illness was something that was to be minimized into nonexistence.

It had been hard to see my course evaluations drop and hear about complaints from students to my superiors about my performance and behavior while I was symptomatic. Not being able to address the situation directly or explain it was very frustrating. There is no mention of my illness or hospitalization in my annual performance review. So as a free-standing document, my lower-than-expected teaching performance is not contextualized. Still, thanks to my manic productivity, I had enough publications to get an "above expectation" evaluation for the research aspect of my review.

I teach Race and Ethnicity, and my identity as a Canadian of Afro-Caribbean descent is something I use in my class to illustrate various points. Why should I not do the same with manic depression? Was it any scarier than being black in America? Or was it that I could not hide my blackness but I could hide my mental illness? If I could hide my blackness, would I be expected to do so as well?

Disclosure of one's own mental illness to a client is deemed to be "unprofessional." Would it be unprofessional for a doctor to reveal her own diabetes to a patient with the same illness? I don't think so. In the treatment of or teaching about addiction, it is considered useful, and even advantageous, to have survived one's own battle with addiction, and counselors in treatment programs are open about their own journey to being, and staying, sober.[3] So why is it not the same when treating or teaching about mental illness? Although we are not yet at the point at which people will walk onto a talk show and announce their mental stability after years of madness and get the cheers that one receives from noting 30 days (or 30 years) of sobriety, the story I tell in this volume is written in the hope that there will be such a day.

FINDING MY MIND AND FACING THE FUTURE

THURSDAY, DECEMBER 8, 2005

Today I met with my boss and she basically told me to go on medical leave for one quarter while I focus on getting better. Seems that things in my classes were worse than I thought. I shed a few tears then signed paperwork. What else to do? I am surrendering to all of it. I don't feel like the fight. I'm blah emotionally today but I was productive.

This was just one of many meetings and communications related to my performance under the influence of manic depression. None of them were pleasant, and I began to feel that the nature of my illness was at the heart of the matter. What was perceived by my university as a "performance" issue was for me a "manic depression" issue, although administratively they may appear to be one and the same. But being held professionally responsible for behavior I could not control is more than a little frustrating. Because of my disastrous fall quarter and medical leave in winter quarter, I lost 1 year in my quest for tenure. I also lost directorship of the program because of my inability to keep all the balls in the air. My study-abroad activities were cancelled—related, it seems, to a lack of trust in my ability to safely manage a group of students when my own behavior was suspect. My doctor in the meantime had given me a clean bill of health. I was hurt, angry, frustrated, and sad. It was all part of my life with manic depression, and it reinforced the need for more of us to come out of the darkness. It also made clear why we stay hidden: the costs of exposure just may be too high, especially in the professional context.

The more disclosure becomes the norm in academia, the more our academic institutions can develop policies that respond to the unique experiences that each employee with a mental illness may present. Our institutions, and faculty who are mentally ill, should also become knowledgeable about their rights under the Americans with Disabilities Act and their institution's human resource policies with regard to medical leaves. Also, health insurance that provides equal coverage for mental health treatment is one way of ensuring that people with mental illness not only have access to treatment but also are not singled out for "different" coverage.

As I argued earlier, disclosure to students makes it easier for them to understand that the mentally ill are all around us, that we are not to be feared, that treatment can work, and that career and life success is indeed possible. Disclosure "normalizes" mental illness. When I disclosed in class, I did so because I was in a moment of using an "us/them" dichotomy, which was a struggle for me to play out one more time. I was "them" and I was "us" at the same time. I suppose I could have found a mentally ill person to drop in for the one minute of that class in which I disclosed—that is, I could have had another "model"—but there I was, a live example. And it was but a 30-second part of a longer statement. But it was enough to make a difference in my life as a professor: I felt so free and real, and my students got to see me as human—and to learn what the mentally ill look like outside of the institutions in which they are often treated.

I remember the first student with whom I shared my secret. She was in my office and crying. She revealed that she did not think she could make it through school, as she had been diagnosed as having ADHD as a child and had been put on Ritalin. Although no longer on Ritalin, she was feeling the limitations of her diagnosis and prognosis. When I revealed that I too had a mental illness, she was shocked because she did not think that it was possible to be mentally ill and successful. Eventually, she would end up overloading on credits and walking away with grades of A.

In the spring of 2006, after my first months of stability in 3 years, I was ready to be done with all the medication tweaks. Eventually I was weaned off Depakote, taking only lithium and clonazepam. It felt liberating. But my battle with my symptoms was not over, and I was getting worn down with the ordeal. I was questioning whether I should be the primary custodial parent of my child, whether I could really hold a job, and whether I needed to be institutionalized.

MARCH 9, 2006

Being even is a strange thing. I'm still engaging and I still have emotions but my ups and downs are predictable and not wild and it's weird to not be manically writing papers and doing 10 things at once. This almost feels strange.

MONDAY, MARCH 20, 2006

I am in a shithole of a depression. I am frustrated, angry, and feeling no hope that I'm ever going to spend more than a few months at a time being stable. This depression creeped up on me from some pre-menstrual blues, morphing into suicidal ideation and trying to play violin on my arm with a knife. I thought I could slog through it cognitively and physically. When I couldn't, I surrendered and called [my psychiatrist] who got me into her office today. I have a regular appointment with my [psychotherapist] on

Wednesday and back to see the doc on Monday. Of course I had blood test today as well and an increase in my lithium dose.

APRIL 2, 2006

I'm getting over the frustration of the past week when I found out that my thyroid may not be functioning—either due to age or the lithium [or both]....I suppose it could be cancer but it doesn't mean I'm not annoyed by the tweaking of meds, etc.

Having my work taken away from me through the medical leave process was emotionally, psychologically, personally, and professionally devastating. I felt ready to give up, move on, and start over, and yet I knew that I had to stick it out. How would I explain my year to a new employer? I had no choice but to stay and work my way back to being the high achiever that I had always been throughout my life—whether in track and field events, in the pool, or in the classroom. This time I had to do it without manic energy, as I did not want manic disorganization and loss of control. It was time to find out what was me and what was my illness. Although it scared me to find out, I knew that being ill was not an option, so whoever I was going to be on medication was the person I was going to have to learn to live with for a very long time. I had spent 40 years ramped up, roaring down the highway faster than my driving skills could manage. Every now and again I would wipe out against the wall or surrender to the darkness and exhaustion and sleep along the side of the road.

MAKING MY PEACE AND KEEPING MY MIND

I am writing this chapter in late May of 2006. After tweaking my meds at least a dozen times in 3 years, and after dozens of blood tests and therapy sessions, I am now officially "in remission." After weaning me off Depakote, my doctor is now considering reducing my dose of lithium to the minimum needed to keep me even. I no longer take an antidepressant. I am back in the classroom and happy to feel in control of my brain for the first time in years. Perhaps because of a combination of lithium, age, and family predisposition, my thyroid no longer functions well, and I have to take thyroid replacement meds. I am trying to lose the 20 pounds that I put on during the first month that I took Zyprexa. (This medication is used to rapidly reduce manic symptoms, but the risks are rapid weight gain and diabetes. What a choice! I had to decide whether my sanity was worth my pancreas or a new wardrobe.) Those 20 pounds may not seem like much, and my concern may reflect a certain degree of vanity, but I had been within 5 pounds of my high school weight for 20 years. The weight gain was one more shift in my perception of who I was. I was now one of the legions of women who had a "second size" of clothes. I can hardly fit in my pants or skirts, so off to the thrift stores I went, assuming that in a few months life would go back to normal.

I religiously take my thyroid medication, in addition to my lithium and clonazepam. The latter still gives me pause because of its addictive properties, but I will not sacrifice sleep for fear of two little pills per night. To reduce noncompliance I now take all my lithium at once at night. That method of dispensing the drug maximizes my ability to sleep and minimizes the sleepiness that would occur when I took daytime dosages. My coffee drinking is down from three to six cups a day to one cup in the morning. (Drinking a cup after noon may also reduce my ability to fall asleep, so I mostly stick to that rule.)

NOVEMBER 13, 2005

> *My chronic illness is not a character flaw*
> *It does not define "me"*
> *It's not a lack of will*
> *Nor does it bestow me*
> *With the weight and burden of fragility.*
> *My spirit is not broken nor is it flawed*
> *If my brain chemistry is dysfunctional*
> *For me to exist in this world*
> *I choose to find a way to help me survive it.*
> *Thrive in it*
> *I don't want to die*
> *Neither do I want to hurt myself.*
> *After suffering years of misery*
> *I have chosen to surrender.*
> *I have fought long and hard*
> *To not be med dependent.*
> *Right now, this works.*
> *And I'm not quite ready to*
> *Risk my sanity to explore some other way.*

I do not know how long this period of sanity will last. I know that I am not the only one who has these concerns, as I have heard the phrase "in case something happens" used when it comes to my teaching schedule. Even as professionals we tiptoe around and avoid naming mental illness—as if saying the words will be an incantation that conjures up its scary head. Owning my manic depression now comes easy to me, as I have told colleagues that my position as one of "them" brings useful perspectives.

I know of the benefits of manic depression, so well explored by Kay Jamison in her various books. Had I not had manic depression, would I have been at the head of my sixth-grade class at 8 years old? Would I have scored near the top of the nation (Jamaica) in the high school entrance exam nearly 2 years later? Would I have been able to party several nights a week and work several jobs while getting grades of A and A+ in a demanding graduate school program? I am not sure, and I will never know. To be honest, I am glad I had the opportunity to experience the benefits of mania: living on little sleep, having bursts of creative and productive energy, and being the life of the party. In a go-go world, hypomania provides the ultimate advantage.

Now it was time to say good-bye not only to those productive hypomanic highs but also to the dark, gray, sad, self-destructive, and dragging days of depression and the high-wire balancing act, agitation, and mental confusion (successfully passed as clarity much of the time) of full-blown mania and of mixed states. Because I have a doctor who is a minimalist in her medication regimens, I am still engaging, funny, and creative. Because I want to keep my circadian rhythms going smoothly, I go to bed by midnight (11 P.M. is still my goal, but old habits are hard to break). Because I want the high of endorphins to stave off depression and burn off the edge of stress through a good sweat, I exercise regularly. (Although my athletic past has already given me a taste for the pleasure of exercise, I am much more consistent, ever vigilant for any breakthrough symptoms.) New research suggests (though there are conflicting findings) that vitamin B and omega-3 fatty acids improve the performance of mood stabilizers, so I have added them to my diet.[4] I consider that these nutrients are good for me anyway, so why not? Anything to keep depression and mania away.

I like who I am on medication: I enjoy my life more than I did before. I am still impulsive enough to run naked into the Pacific on a cold winter day or jump off a cliff into the Caribbean. The quality of the experience is more pleasurable, though less intense. I now enjoy each moment instead of flying through them. For now, at least, I am beyond the battle of the meds. There is no more fight. My daughter deserves the best mother she can have, and, with some talk therapy, a handful of pills, and a healthy maintenance plan, that is who I plan to give her. I will continue to speak and write about stigma and discrimination experienced by the mentally ill so that my daughter will not have to feel the stigma carried by her mother.

NOTES

1. See Mansour, H. A. et al. (2005). Circadian phase variation in bipolar I disorder. *Chronobiology International, 22,* 571–584; and Newman, C. F. (2006). Bipolar disorder. In F. Andrasik (Ed.), *Comprehensive handbook of personality and psychopathology:* Vol. 2. *Adult psychopathology* (pp. 244–261). Hoboken, NJ: Wiley.

2. This was 6 months before I had the opportunity of writing this chapter.

3. Culbreth, J. R. (2000). Substance abuse counselors with and without a personal history of chemical dependency: A review of the literature. *Alcoholism Treatment Quarterly, 18*(2), 67–82.

4. For discussion, see Coppen, A., & Bolander-Gouaille, C. (2005). Treatment of depression: Time to consider folic acid and vitamin B12. *Journal of Psychopharmacology, 19*(1), 59–65; Gao, K., & Calabrese, J. R. (2005). New treatment studies for bipolar depression. *Bipolar Disorders, 7*(Suppl. 5), 13–23; Hakkarainen, R. et al. (2004). Is low dietary intake of omega-3 fatty acids associated with depression? *American Journal of Psychiatry, 161*(3), 567–569; and Young, C., and Martin, A. (2003). Omega-3 fatty acids in mood disorders: An overview. *Revista Brasileira de Psiquiatria, 25*(3), 184–187.

3   A Field Agent in Our Midst

Tara S. Peris

Today, as on many, many days before, I open my laptop and sit before a blank screen. I sit, waiting for the rapid-fire movement of my fingers on the keyboard to begin, for my perfectly worded story to fill the pages. I am waiting for that articulate, well-executed story about my mother's mental illness to emerge and for the content of my story to take shape, even though its substance was determined long ago and remains, as always, well beyond my control. I am waiting for a voice for this story to make itself known, fully aware that the only voice that can tell it is my own.

Hours roll by, a new crowd fills the coffeehouse, and my screen remains blank. I read the paper, skim a month-old, discarded copy of the New Yorker, *and make a detailed to-do list that includes things like buying milk, living abroad, and owning a beach house in Malibu. I get up, do a few languid laps around the room, stretching my legs and talking to other struggling writers. I start to feel as if my task is infinitely more challenging than theirs, as if I could write a successful Hollywood screenplay in a heartbeat before saying anything meaningful about mental illness. (This is more than a little concerning, given the field I've chosen.) I consider asking the disheveled boy in the corner if he will write about schizophrenia in exchange for my writing his dissertation on Kantian ethics. Periodically, I look up to find the screen still blank. Sometimes I give in under its expectant glare, complacently typing a word or two. On a good day, I crank out a few sentences, knowing they are terrible and won't see tomorrow. I will carry on in this vein for a few hours before closing up shop for the day. "Work on book chapter" will be checked off an existing to-do list, and I will be absolved of the guilt that comes with procrastination and avoidance for yet another week. It has become a well-worn routine, irritating in its familiarity.*

I agreed to write about my mother's struggle with mental illness some time ago, with the idea that I would be doing something good for myself. To draw on my favorite psychological training jargon, I thought it would be good for me to spell out an experience about which I've never really spoken and be forced to just *sit with it*. As a first-year graduate student, I was amused by the ease with which this phrase was dispensed as time-honored advice. Therapy supervision for a client in distress: have her just sit with it. Counseling a friend through the sadness of a bad breakup: just sit with it. Bad grade on the statistics exam: sit with that, too.

What does it mean, anyway, to "sit with it"? Don't our challenging experiences stay with us simply by virtue of having occurred? Aren't we *always* sitting with them? Leave it to the field of psychology to state the obvious and then hand it back as "therapy." More than a few times, I have questioned the wisdom of accepting this writing task. I have challenged the necessity of doing something akin to eating emotional vegetables, with health benefits that will pay off only at an unspecified future time. There are important stories to be told, but I wonder whether mine must be one of them. I wonder whether it is even that important. I wonder whether it is worth it.

As I've attempted to write about my mother, I've come to realize that sometimes, rather than sitting *with* our difficult experiences, we are sitting *on* them, in an effort to keep them pinned beneath the surface, to keep them confined to the nice manageable places where they don't mess up life too much. For those who revel in their own resilience, it is deceptively simple to push down these experiences without a second thought, ignoring, minimizing, and concealing in turn. We focus on other things because life is full and crazy enough as it is without dredging up ancient history for a new round of analysis.

At other times we sit *under* our difficult experiences, trapped beneath the weight of them and burdened by all they bring with them. I'm not sure where you'll find me at the moment. I suspect I'm perched precariously at the junction where all three places meet. It's why the story gets so mangled, you see, because I'm never sure of the vantage point from which I'm telling it. And there are so many ways to tell it. Somewhere between a child's account of firsthand experiences and an adult's attempt to make sense of them, the narrative thread gets lost, and I forget who is telling the story. I lose sight of whose account is right and whose voice to use.

Once upon a time, however, it was simple. In fact, for the better part of my life, the story about my mother was quite straightforward: she moved to Japan when I was 12, and, with the exception of one visit there when I was 13, I have never seen her again. Her correspondence with me gradually faded to the point at which she stopped responding to letters or phone calls entirely. Over the years, I found this to be a good story, short and sweet and to the point. Admittedly, its merit rests more in its brevity than its sweetness, but I found that it sufficed quite well. When the subject of my mother's absence arose, I would matter-of-factly discuss it as "perplexing" and "puzzling," but one for which I had no answers. It was an account that inevitably sparked more questions than it answered. After all, "losing touch" is a phrase reserved for casual acquaintances and early childhood friends, not *parents*. The questions that typically followed were predictable, and I grew quite masterful at deflecting them. By the time I was 18, I had virtually memorized my response to all of the relevant questions.

I felt like an automated telephone system. If you'd like to know what happened to my mother, press "1" and I will casually tell you about how she left to take a teaching offer overseas. If you'd like to know why she stopped writing or calling, press "2" and I will tell you nonchalantly that we gradually drifted apart, as if this is the most natural thing in the world for mothers and daughters to do. Is she okay? Press "3," then watch me muster all the self-confidence I have in me to say yes, I'm sure she is, wherever she is. Like those automated responses, the information I learned to give was always of some use but never exactly what the person was looking for. Indeed, I became a polished presenter of a sad but somewhat sterilized story about a girl whose mother disappeared.

Accounts of family tragedy are difficult for both the storyteller and the listener, eliciting a degree of discomfort all around. To ease my way out of conversational tight spots, I learned to counterbalance my story with descriptions of my father, who raised me on his own from the time I was 6 and with whom I have always been exceptionally close. "Oh, but my dad is the best. He's been there every step of the way," I would say, eager to point out that I have had a good life, that I have been loved and cared for, and that there is no need to dwell on my mother's absence. My efforts to anticipate and dampen the discomfort in handling family questions usually sufficed. After all, we are taught to avoid so many subjects that are taboo, to back off when people put up their conversational barriers.

Yet, for a handful of people, most of them my good friends, I couldn't dispose of the subject quite so easily. Have you tried to contact her? Is something wrong with her? What do you think happened? These follow-up questions—posed by people who knew me well enough to gauge when I wasn't telling the truth—were infinitely more painful. It was evident that my story didn't add up, and despite the practice, I was a terrible liar. Nonetheless, I soldiered on. I stuck to the story, persisted with the "I don't knows," and waited until, eventually, they too backed away.

I'm not sure why I took this approach. Perhaps it is because I wanted to relay only what I knew with certainty—just the facts. She was gone, and although I could speculate about the reasons for her absence, I knew nothing for sure. Part of me wanted to pretend that I *didn't* know what accounted for her absence. All members of my family walked around feigning the same initial confusion, no one stating the obvious. With time, we learned to stop talking about her absence altogether.

But, of course, I did know what was wrong with my mother. I had shared a home with her and seen her in her most unguarded and vulnerable states. Long before I was introduced to the *Diagnostic and Statistical Manual* or the

International Classification of Diseases—the manuals that describe psychiatric diagnoses—or to formal clinical descriptions, I knew all too well and in a way, I suspect, that no one else really did. I knew about the CIA and the KGB and about wiretaps that made us unsafe. I knew about neighbors who were not to be trusted and about fearful stories that didn't make sense. I knew about conspiracy. I knew about softly muttered dialogue spoken when no one was in the room. I knew that doctors would say she was sick and, later, that the term for her illness was *schizophrenia.*

There is little glamour in schizophrenia. The accounts of artistic genius associated with bipolar disorder or major depression typically do not apply here. There is no Handel, no Emily Dickinson, no Abraham Lincoln, no flagship celebrity to sweeten the identification. It seems strange, even bold perhaps, for me to assign a label to my mother's condition, to give her the diagnosis that no one else did. Although the reality of her symptom profile remains the same no matter what one calls it, schizophrenia is such a devastating disease that years later I find that I would still prefer to describe the symptoms in some very general way rather than put forward a specific diagnosis. I have a persistent need to avoid that label, a terrible sense that I am handing down a death sentence. Clinical experience has taught me that all forms of mental illness bring distress and heartbreak, but resistance to this diagnosis lingers—and denial remains the ever-enticing easy out. Despite my best efforts at acceptance, I have a persistent desire to hope or believe that my mother's condition could be something else. I find myself yearning to make it something other than it is, something better understood by scientists and clinicians. Something associated with better outcomes, something that might actually have a solution.

BRILLIANT

I am trying to piece together my mother's early history, to learn about her life before I was born. I want to provide some context for her story that extends beyond a child's piecemeal recollections. They're so old by now, so altered by time and my wishes of what could have been, that I cannot trust them. I get frustrated easily as I write about my parents. Despite my age, I am forever the child in this story, feebly attempting to provide the clarity and objectivity of an adult as I render my account. It doesn't really work. The story is ceaselessly incomplete, missing links and loose ends continually confusing my understanding of the past.

So much of what I know of my mother comes from other people's accounts. She has been gone for well over half of my life, and my memories seem equal parts family folklore and reality. As I write, I've taken to asking people about my mother in an effort to unravel her story. My brief foray into investigative journalism has been largely unsatisfying. Everyone is forthcoming when I ask, but by now it's ancient history, and memories are blurred with nostalgia, doubt, confusion, and regret. I get the sense that no one really knows what to say. I am looking for descriptions that foreshadow what was to come, for telling labels about my mother—offbeat, odd, and withdrawn.

Instead, I am told only that she was brilliant. Brilliant. If there is a single word that sums up how most people describe my mother, it is brilliant. Not crazy, not delusional, not paranoid or unstable, but simply brilliant. For as long as I can recall, friends and family have been quick to dole out praise for her intellect. Perhaps it is because we are a family of academics, and there is a premium placed on this type of virtuosity. Perhaps it is because my mother's academic achievements are among the more objective things one can say about her. Perhaps it is because discussion of her brilliance seems to offset the larger reality of her suffering and illness.

I ask my aunt about what my mother was like as a child growing up in Wisconsin, and she tells me that she was independent and bright. Not popular, not unpopular, just brainy and competitive. Strange? No. Aloof? Not really. Just smart and occasionally haughty in that older-sister kind of way. I ask my godfather, who knew my parents when they were students in Cambridge, Massachusetts, and he tells me that she was sharp and brilliant. He adds that I was an adorable baby. We then digress quickly to a story about the time he and my godmother were left to care for me as an infant, when, despite being a generally good baby, I cried incessantly the entire time my parents were gone and scared my godparents out of having children for many years to come. These are the stories I hear, and although I believe them and bask in the affection with which they are told, they leave me stuck for a way to convey my mother in complete terms.

It is such descriptions as these that have made it all too easy to leave myself guessing about what was wrong with my mother, to sidestep a reality that was bleak no matter how you labeled it. To be sure, the descriptions themselves are rooted in objective fact: it is clear that my mother was a highly successful woman for many years. She received a PhD in English from Berkeley, taught at Stanford, and was completing a fellowship at Harvard when she met my father. He describes her as "your typical early-70s Berkeley type." I think this translates roughly into "she smoked a lot of pot." He also describes her as shrewd and ambitious, well regarded professionally. She was on track for a top-notch academic career and had an active social life built around her friends and colleagues from the Cambridge community.

Did she seem crazy? I have often asked, trying to break through memories as sanitized as my own. Even through the lens of 20/20 hindsight, my father struggles to answer. He suggests that her friends were kind of "out there," that much of the liberal ideology of the times pervaded their discussions. She may have been more carried away by themes of political espionage than most. Still, in the age of Nixon, it was hard to fault someone for being swept away by notions of governmental dishonesty. Everyone was dubious about politicians; everyone played the part of the conspiracy theorist at one time or another. Taken in context, there was nothing crazy about her, he tells me, and I can tell that he is as plagued by the same tendency to second-guess things as the rest of us are.

What my father can tell me with more certainty is that my mother had me at the age of 33 and that up until that point she seemed to remain more or less on track—somewhat quirky, perhaps, but a woman who seemed capable of functioning successfully. After my birth, however, she developed severe postpartum depression and began to experience bizarre neurological symptoms, such as tingling in her fingertips, semiparalysis of her legs, fainting spells, and high fever. She was eventually hospitalized for several months at Massachusetts General Hospital as doctors struggled to determine the source of her illness. She never received a formal diagnosis but was released when her physical symptoms remitted. Through countless evaluations and months of hospital care, no one questioned her sanity in the slightest.

Yet my earliest memories are of someone who had clearly crossed over into mental confusion. Shortly after I turned 4, my parents, then living in Los Angeles, filed for a divorce. They had started to argue incessantly, and, in what was perhaps an early sign of what was to come, my mother had become increasingly fearful that I would be lost or kidnapped. Her concern spawned countless arguments that never seemed to resolve, and, eventually, divorce papers were filed, and I went to live with my mother. It was within the shelter of a modest apartment in East Pasadena that I watched as she let down her guard. Slowly, our apartment became a collection of assorted thrift-store and garage sale finds. Large pieces of used furniture were acquired and positioned at odd angles that seemed to form an obstacle course in our living room. Mismatched curtains were clipped to the windows in a bizarre mosaic of colors and fabrics. For a while, my mother placed her bed in the living room. Stacks of paper proliferated, and newspapers, manuscripts, and old magazines spilled out of every corner. She was unbelievably messy, and the kitchen frequently overflowed with dishes and bizarre herbal products she picked up at the local natural foods store. When cleaning lapsed, there were roaches in the kitchen. The apartment was kept inexplicably dark for long stretches of time.

I don't remember having many toys or interacting with my mother all that much. I was able to occupy and care for myself without, it seemed, that much effort. I would use our shadowy apartment to play hide-and-seek with my dolls, and I would wait obsessively for *Little House on the Prairie* to come on each day. I recall watching a lot of TV. When that failed to entertain, I would walk down the street unsupervised and talk to the people in the Laundromat. I loved the smell of the place and the orderly rhythm of people coming and going. I loved the hum of the machines and the hypnotic rotation of sudsy water and clothes. I was not particularly shy, and, not knowing any better, I was rarely afraid.

It is hard to trust memories that are more than 20 years old, and I cringe as I reread portions of this; it's a bit more Dickensian-orphanage or Lifetime Movie of the Week than I'd prefer. It's at odds with my more salient memories of myself as a happy child, and, although I know each of these things to be true, I end up feeling as though the story is not quite right, not entirely fair.

I think, in part, that this discontent stems from knowing that my mother also managed to do many things well. She was good with routines, so that school, church, and time with my father all proceeded with great regularity. She was also meticulous with my grooming, and, like many mothers, she battled with me on a regular basis to brush my hair, refusing to concede my point that pink and red hair barrettes matched. We spent a fair amount of time picking out school clothes and arguing when I wanted to wear my favorite butterfly T-shirt every day of the week. In short, we did a lot of the things you would expect a mother and daughter to do. It just took place in an environment that looked nothing like your typical family home.

SIFTING THROUGH MEMORIES: CONFUSION AND DISCONTENT

Somehow, I am never satisfied with how descriptions of my mother hit the page. Perhaps I don't like to think about the reality I convey. Surely, I know that some degree of resistance sits at the heart of this. Decades later, it is difficult to sit with many of these experiences, the emotions they stir up still raw and overwhelming. Yet the account never feels accurate. I flit between feeling irritated that I have minimized my mother's impairment and feeling frustrated by accounts that seem too extreme. Some days I produce descriptions of my mother so stripped of feeling or personal detail that they seem more fit for a journal submission than a personal narrative. Other days, my flair for the dramatic seems to know no end. I find that, in the struggle to get this on the page, my recollections of childhood are coming out trite, clichéd, and forced. When I give a draft to a friend to look over, she notes in the margin that my writing is "exasperatingly devoid of emotion." She indicates that, even now, the account is sterile and distant. Bring her to life, she says. Give us a sense of who she really was. But that's the whole point, I tell her. There's no single answer. There are so many ways to portray my mother, no one in isolation adequate. So I put them down, terse and disorganized, hoping they will speak for themselves.

Ask me for a story about my mother, and here's one you might hear. It's about the time I shoplifted from a Boston department store at the age of 3. It was Christmas time, and I was bundled up in full winter gear, padding along beside my mother as we did last-minute shopping. The store was a mob scene, and I remember clinging anxiously to my mother, overwhelmed by the frenzied movement of the crowds. I had the distinct impression that, amidst the chaos, I was bound to get lost or stepped on. Keeping my hand firmly in her own, my mother kept telling me I was doing a good job and reminding me that I would get a reward for my good behavior when we got home. It was all I needed to hear. I was nothing if not reward-driven, and I began eyeing store merchandise for potential prizes like the proverbial kid in a candy store. It wasn't long before I was seduced by an attractive store display and found myself pleading persistently for a pair of Holly Hobbie house slippers. I wasn't sure what kind of treat my mom had in mind, but these seemed as fitting a reward as any. Holly Hobbie was my favorite cartoon, and my mother was well versed in managing my growing obsession. Gently, she said no, not today, suggesting that I put them on my Christmas list. Maybe Santa would bring them.

I suspect most children would have found this response acceptable, or perhaps voiced their discontent aloud. I, on the other hand, waited until she wasn't looking, stowed the stash in my snowsuit, and zipped my jacket closed with the ease of a veteran shoplifter. It wasn't until we returned home some time later that my mother unzipped me and watched the slippers fall out of my snowsuit, tags still attached. I watched her hands slow to a stop, her face beginning to reveal confusion. I knew I was in trouble. It took a moment for it all to register and for my mother's image of her charming, well-behaved little girl to be reconciled with one of her daughter's budding criminality. She tried to be stern, and I still recall her saying, *Tara Sophia, what have you done?* But the humor of the situation was not lost on her, and her amusement kept breaking through by way of poorly suppressed smiles and giggles. As punishment, I had to draw a picture saying I was sorry, and I was not allowed to listen to my favorite record that evening. I remember this, too, because the removal of my "Rainbow Connection" record was just about the stiffest punishment she could have administered at the time.

I still have those tiny house slippers, and they never fail to bring forth warm, happy memories. Early-onset conduct problems (remitted) and shoe fetish (chronic) aside, I smile as much at my mother's humor and sensitivity as I do at my own misbehavior. It's the same warmth present in the birthday parties she planned so carefully, the back-to-school shopping trips she coordinated, and the comfort she dispensed when I was upset or sad. It's the same gentle spirit that prompted her to provide regular help to the elderly people in our neighborhood, carrying their groceries and driving them on errands when their regular rides fell through. She was compassionate and kind, and at times she could do things remarkably well.

Although I marvel that my mother didn't attract more attention, that she never received a concerned inquiry, or even, it seems, a second look in those early years of my life, memories such as these remind me of why it may have been easy for people to assume she was okay. She held a job, paid her rent on time, and had a healthy, happy child. Our apartment was where the true chaos lay, and few people, including my father, ever saw the inside of it. Even this seems strange until I remember that the pickups and drop-offs between the two of them occurred at school or at church. My father rarely came by the apartment and almost never went past the entryway when he did. I don't think he had a clue as to the physical disorganization of the place or what it suggested about the inner workings of my mother's mind.

Ask me for another story, and I might tell you about the time I hid under a church pew while my mother argued with a priest during the middle of his sermon. Consistent with our usual routine, we had arrived on time for the 8 A.M. service dressed in our Sunday best. For me, a flowery summer sundress, subject to strict maternal screening for neatness, cleanliness, and color coordination; for her, an outfit characterized by total neglect of these features. My mother was never grossly inappropriate in her dress, but her style reeked of hippie chic gone awry. On this particular day, she was wearing a long pastel sundress, white open-toe sandals, black pantyhose, and a heavy winter blazer. I remember the blazer not because it was out of place in the middle of a Los Angeles summer but because I took it with me when I ducked for cover under the pew. There, from the coolness of the tiled church floor, I remember looking intently down the row, observing pairs of feet that were rocking nervously as my mother stood to shout. Staring at her mismatched shoes and hose, I remember thinking that you could tell she was different from her feet alone.

I don't remember what the priest said or what about it was upsetting to my mother. The incident began as soft mumbling under her breath, accompanied by a slow, decisive shaking of her head. It was clear that she disagreed with a point in his sermon. Eventually, her discontent grew unmanageable, and she spoke at full volume, her rant now fully directed at the priest. I think he tried to carry on for a minute or two, ignoring her and hoping (or praying) she might go away. I didn't wait around. I slid under the pew and sat cross-legged while my mother went back and forth with the priest, vigorously insisting that he was wrong.

I was 6 at the time, and this incident set in motion a week of events that provided the first clear evidence that something was very, very wrong with my mother. When we got home that day, she refused to let us leave the apartment.

She then boarded up all the windows and wouldn't answer the phone for the next several days. Eventually, people from the church came by with groceries, offering help and expressing concern. My mother refused to see or talk to anyone. She perceived imminent danger for both of us, and she was terrified. When my father showed up a few days later to pick me up for a scheduled visit, he found a darkened apartment with few signs of activity. The soft sound of muffled footsteps was the only clue that we were home, and he began to battle with my mother to open the door. She relented only when he threatened to call the police, and she did not speak when she opened the door. She had tape on her mouth and communicated only with a chalkboard, indicating that she was being watched and it wasn't safe to talk. My father took me home, both of us wide-eyed and frightened, and he proceeded to call the police.

My mother was 39 and it was the first concrete, undeniable indication that she was mentally unstable. Yet no one had a clue what to do about it. The call to the police set in motion an endless string of inquiries, and my father began to negotiate an impossibly complex maze of health and social services resources. My mother's sister, a Veterans Administration nurse in San Francisco, was called; together with my father, she made an attempt to have my mother committed. Despite their best efforts, however, the team from the community services board was unable to make progress, stating that despite her troubling behavior, my mother had no previous diagnosis and she did not present as committable. By the letter of the law, she was not a danger to herself or to others.

Both as her child and as a mental health professional, this monumental failure of the mental health system continues to overwhelm me. Couldn't it be argued that my mother was a threat to *me?* Wouldn't that have been compelling evidence to put before a judge? What exactly did she need to do—how crazy did she need to be—in order to earn herself a diagnosis? Somewhat harder to think about: Did my family really want a diagnosis, or did they just want my mother and all of her bizarre problems to go away?

Although I remember the incident in the church and the week that followed—perhaps more vividly than I'd like—my understanding of what followed from there is based entirely on family accounts. It is, at best, a very poor understanding, and I find that family narratives raise more questions than they answer. Most of the time, these questions simply represent an effort to understand how it was that things transpired, a feeble attempt to fit adult accounts of what happened into my own fragmented recollections. I would be lying if I said that they haven't lapsed into feelings of anger and resentment from time to time. At the end of the day, I never really understand why my mother didn't get help after this incident. I fail to grasp how people stood back and let her slide further into the ruins of her condition. And in the midst of this confusion, I start assigning blame. I blame my father for not pushing harder to get her help. I blame my mother's sisters for not getting on a plane and coming to help manage her problems in person. I blame the rest of her family for ignoring signs of a problem that must have been brewing for quite some time. It is an utterly useless path, I know, but it's the sorry detritus of years of grief and confusion that leaves families looking for someone, anyone, to blame. When you can't blame the sick person, it's all too easy to blame one another.

LOOK THE OTHER WAY

I suspect that my mother was allowed to remain in her home, resting precariously on the fringes of normality, because of the shame attached to mental illness. Certainly, my father speaks of an upbringing in India that taught him to view mental illness as a form of moral depravity. My mother's goals, accomplishments, and fundamental personality were so incongruent with his perception of mental illness that for many years he simply did not believe that she could be ill. Even when the evidence before him seemed undeniable, my father was reluctant to pursue the matter too vigorously because of the stigma he thought a formal diagnosis would attach to her. He did make efforts to get her to see a therapist or a priest from our local parish. Yet with little understanding of the nature of her problems and even less awareness of what could be done, he backed away from the issue when he saw how angry it made her.

The suggestion that she needed help of any kind did, in fact, make her furious. Her life was none of his business, she said. What right did he have to pass judgment on her beliefs? He was part of a conspiracy to harm her, she claimed. Although her perspective was seeped in distrust and paranoia, she could argue with a lucid, cogent force that silenced even my father. She dragged him into philosophical debates about free will and personal agency that left him wondering whether, in fact, he had misjudged the situation—whether, in fact, he had misjudged *her.* In the end, there was nothing he could do. His only recourse was to sue for custody, a process that was quite challenging for fathers in 1982, let alone Indian fathers without citizenship status. It was a bitter and protracted custody battle, but one my father ultimately won.

My memories of life with him are much clearer. I moved into his house, where I already had my own room and toys, and suddenly my life changed dramatically. My father's solution to single parenting was just the opposite of my mother's, and I remember wondering from an early age how two people could be so different. On some intuitive level, I found myself constantly processing and assimilating the differences between my old and new environments. Whereas my mother was lax with rules, my father was firm. Whereas I watched almost endless amounts of TV in her home, under my father's care I was allowed no TV during the week. Instead, I was enrolled in every extracurricular activity possible, from violin to tap lessons. My father's love of books and music was contagious, and I soon began to use my free time for reading or writing my own short stories. Some of my fondest memories are of sitting in an overstuffed armchair, hearing him read a story before bed each night, giggling with delight as he assumed the voices of the different characters through his Indian accent. There were daily rituals in place for the first time in my life, and they provided a degree of structure that allowed me to flourish. Single parenting by necessity relies on some degree of organization, and if my father's parenting philosophy could be summed up in one word, it would most certainly be *routine*.

The new routine did not include a specific prescription for visitation with my mother, and my interaction with her remained chaotic and inconsistent. I saw her every weekend at first, and then, over time, every other weekend. Mostly we went to the movies or went shopping. I loved these visits because we did things I would never do with my dad. Had it been left to my father, I suspect I would have been reciting Rudyard Kipling and drafting *New Yorker* contributions as creative ways to fill my time (we joke that these are childhood activities for which he'd still advocate strongly). However, my mother seemed committed to keeping me rooted in real childhood. Superman, *Star Wars*, and trips to McDonalds were all within her domain. These excursions were the fun parts of her visits.

Much less pleasant were the times spent in her apartment. Over the years, she moved a few times, but each apartment soon became the same disorganized mess as the last. I don't remember much about these dwellings except that there were papers and junk everywhere and that during my preteen years our rooms probably looked about the same. At first, I tried to help her clean, envisioning how much she could accomplish if she could actually see the floor. I had this sense that if I could impose physical order, everything else might just fall into place. There was a fleeting, desperate hope that I could fix things. This hope gradually faded as I realized there was no way to get her out from under the mess for very long. Try as I did to believe otherwise, those apartments were always one of my most concrete reminders that something was not right. Even at the age of 9 or 10, I knew that adults were not meant to live amidst that kind of disorder.

My mother's employment also started to slip during this time, and she went from being a full-time professor to gradually "temping" at community colleges. No one ever commented on this clear and steady slide downhill. Perhaps it was politeness; perhaps it was because, somehow, she always managed to stay above water, paying her rent and her bills and finding a new job to replace the last. Yet there was a picture of a woman who didn't quite have her act together. Her rapidly rotating collection of jobs made her resemble a migrant worker more than a woman with a doctoral education. However, in the absence of events such as the one in the church—an episode never repeated, which came to seem increasingly anomalous with my mother's coherent day-to-day appearance—we all seemed inclined to just look the other way.

By the time I was 12, the idea of regular visitation had been long since abandoned, and visits with my mother were quite sporadic. Sometimes, if we hadn't heard from her in a while, my dad would give a nudge and suggest I call to set up a visit. I remember feeling more or less okay with this, as life with my dad grew busier and visits with my mom remained an unpredictable blend of fun and anxiety. I was old enough to know very clearly when she was saying things that didn't make sense, and my efforts to reason with her were exasperatingly fruitless. There were no incoherent speeches, no rants or diatribes, just the occasional vague reference to a plot or a scheme that I quickly learned to ignore. On the whole, her offbeat comments were rare and somewhat related to the topic at hand. With generous interpretation, I could believe that they were relevant or appropriate. I knew that they weren't, of course, but it was so much easier on both of us for me to look the other way.

By this time, however, I knew not to take chances with what other people might think. I never brought my friends around my mother, and I knew to hurry her away when she showed up at school events. Because I would sometimes do this with my dad as well (for an entirely different set of reasons), I don't think this struck anyone as odd. Early adolescence had taken hold, and I was so full of disdain and embarrassment for all things my parents said and did that I would have locked them both in a closet if left to my own devices. My mother existed on the outskirts of my life, a confusing blend of warm, maternal traits and frustrating, embarrassing, and odd ones. If friends and family knew the real reason for my avoidance, they never let on.

DEPARTURE, LOSS, AND RELIEF: A MEMORY OF GOOD-BYE

I am dubious about so many memories I have of my mother, always wishing for some kind of litmus test to probe their accuracy, checking and double-checking with others to make sure I have the story right, hoping that my mind isn't playing tricks on me. They're all still there, in remarkably good shape, given that they've been boxed up and shelved for a good portion of my life. Some stories, however, need no fact checking. My mother's departure is one of them.

I am sitting at the dining table studying for a sixth-grade geography test. I fidget with the torn hem of my school uniform, trying to remember whether Guatemala is in Central or South America, wondering how many countries I can misplace on the map while still keeping an A in social studies. My father is in the den reading a student's thesis, emitting heavy sighs and periodic bouts of displeased muttering. Someone will be faced with a lot of revisions. Dinner is cooking, and I am distracted by smells of pasta coming from the kitchen. My dad loves cooking and can be quite creative with our meals. Nonetheless, his food always smells vaguely of chicken curry, and I'm wondering what form it will take this evening. I've moved on to Costa Rica (always tricky—Central America or Caribbean?) when Dad calls out and asks me to turn up the stereo. It is tuned to USC's classical music station, and he asks if I can identify the piece that is playing. I cannot. I earn my own defeated sigh from my father. "But you play this on the violin, Tara. You play this yourself." Oh. I am trying to decide whether my father actually cares about my stunted music appreciation skills when the phone rings.

"Hello, Tara, it's Diane," the caller announces, adding belatedly "your mother" as if I need the title to identify her. She has been doing this intermittently of late, going by her first name rather than by "mom." I have no idea what the change is about, nor do I ask. I am accustomed to all manner of odd things from my mother by now, this one neither especially noteworthy nor distinct.

"Hi, Mom. How are you?" I ask, the irony of that simple question not lost on me at this age. I am standing in the hallway, phone in one hand, still fiddling with my torn uniform. I'm feeling guilty because I cancelled our last visit so I could play with my friend Amy instead.

"I'm doing well. I've got some exciting news for you," she says, her tone of voice somewhat flat and incongruent with her words. I am trying to decide what constitutes excitement that my mother would want to share with me. Free movie tickets? Perhaps a trip to the Magic Mountain theme park? I am at a loss.

"I'm moving to Japan." She continues. "You have a geography test this week. Do you know where that is?" Unfortunately, I know exactly where that is, and it is nowhere near Pasadena, California. My knees buckle and I sit on the hallway floor. She must be confused.

"Japan?"

"Yes. It's part of the Asian continent, you know, near Korea." I do know. But I don't believe. I am about to seek clarification, but she goes on. "I've been offered a 5-year contract for a faculty teaching position in Kyoto. I'll be teaching advanced English, and they'll provide housing and a full package of benefits."

I am stuck on the word benefits. At age 12, I take this literally and am lost when I can identify no tangible benefit to my mother living in a foreign country. She continues, "I've been looking into it, and Japan has a number of excellent boarding schools for you to attend. There's also an American school in Kyoto." I am now in an alternate universe. Her voice fades to the background as I start to imagine being shipped overseas and forced to learn Japanese. A few moments later, she is winding down her account and says she'll call in a few days when she knows all the details. Having said almost nothing thus far, I respond with the only thing I know to say. "Okay." I hang up the phone and sit on the hallway floor, silent and stunned, tears streaming down my face, until my dad comes to see who was on the phone.

Two weeks later, my mother moved to Japan. Although my dad was quick to comfort me after that phone call, reassuring me that my mother would not go to Japan and that I would not go to boarding school, he was only partly right. No doubt in part because of her impressive academic training, my mother had, in fact, managed to secure a long-term job in Japan. She left quickly and quietly, and although I remember being sad, I also remember feeling relieved that she was going to have stable employment and housing for the foreseeable future. I clung to a small, persistent hope that she would fit in better over there and that her eccentricities wouldn't stand out so much. There was still this sense that maybe things weren't as bad as they seemed. She could be so convincingly normal at times that I remained hopeful for her future.

During a brief visit to Japan 1 year later, I realized that whatever the nature of her problems, she was taking them with her wherever she went. Initially, I was relieved to see her. As always, she knew how to make a great first impression. She looked fantastic: tall, slim, and fit as ever. She sounded great, talking of work and her travels through Japan. She sounded *normal*. Although 1 year later she still spoke not a word of Japanese (my father could not get over this fact), she seemed comfortable and at ease in her environment. As we strolled the streets of Kyoto during our first few hours alone, I told her eagerly about my first trip to India, my progress at school, and my desperate battle with my father to be allowed to audition for cheerleading. She was full of warmth and laughter, teasing me playfully about my refusal to eat half of the things on the Japanese menu. As we finished our dinner and made our way home, I actually thought the place had cured her.

The sight of her apartment was a harsh reality check. The clutter was all too familiar, her living arrangements providing an instant blow to my cozy denial. With my father lecturing in Tokyo, I was back on my own in the familiar but terrifying world of my mother's disheveled apartment. Papers and books were piled over all sorts of everyday goods, from food items to boxes of tampons. In keeping with Japanese urban planning, all of it was crammed into a studio about one-fourth the size of her other apartments. I could not believe that she actually lived there, that someone so seemingly together in other respects could have this kind of chaos lurking underneath the surface. During the course of my stay, other features of her disorganization emerged as she began to speak of my neighbors at home who were not to be trusted and of my father's plots to turn me against her. Her statements remained vague and confusing, and I had little tolerance for them. I was tired of playing make-believe with her sanity, tired of being the only one who had to deal with it firsthand.

I didn't shout. I would have done that with my father, but somehow I knew it was unacceptable with her. Instead, I threw every bit of early adolescent condescension and sarcasm her way, as I argued with her incoherent logic. I dissected my mother's arguments as if I were auditioning for the debate team, knowing my reasoning was as lost on her as hers was on me. I left Japan dejected, knowing full well that she remained completely the same.

My mother continued to write or call occasionally over the next few years. However, by the time I was 16, our correspondence had waned, and she eventually stopped responding to letters and phone calls. Although my father and others also made efforts to contact her, they were as fruitless as my own. I have not seen her since.

DIAGNOSIS

The girl sitting across from me has loosened up. She's finally starting to talk, and I'm thinking I may just get my intake done. She was admitted to the hospital late in the day and, like most kids, is reluctant to talk about the events that brought her here. Instead, we've covered the usual teenage fare, spending ample time on her fascination with the television show American Idol and her various boy-band crushes. It's been nearly 45 minutes, and I'd like to go home. I remind myself that she'd probably like that, too. I watch her nervously twirl a strand of matted blond hair, my eyes drifting to marks on her wrists. Slowly, she begins to talk of more substantive matters, of a death in the family and her 6-month descent into withdrawal, isolation, and academic failure. She tells me of fitful sleep (check). She mentions that she's not hungry anymore (check), that she's made a terrible mess and knows she can't fix it (check, check). I'm on my way, trying to ward off my fatigue and complete her intake form thoroughly.

"What do you do to feel better?" I ask. " I listen to the radio," she tells me. (Coping skills, check). "Does it help?" " Sometimes." "Do you ever talk to friends?" "Not so much. They don't understand." "So mainly the radio?" "Mmm hmm." "What kind of music do you like?" I ask, prompting myself to slow down, to maintain the rapport I'm slowly establishing. She names a few bands. I continue to write. "But it's not the music. It's the message," she says matter-of-factly. "Pardon?" "I listen to the message."

Within the context of what we're saying, it sort of makes sense, but I get a
bad, familiar feeling. I want to do what I've done in the past, stop asking
questions and just move on. She seems so lucid compared with the other
new patient down the hall. Last time I saw him, he was shouting over his
shoulder to an invisible demon. "You listen to the message of the lyrics?"
I ask, my hopefulness adding an exaggerated lilt to the end of the ques-
tion. "No, to what they're saying." I can hear irritation rising in her voice.
"What who's saying?" I press. "Oh, I don't know." She exhales a deep
sigh and I can see I've been derailed. I try again. "You said you listen to
the radio?" "I listen for the messages. They come through the radio to the
transmitter in my head."
*   I put the chart aside, realizing that I will need to formulate a whole*
new set of diagnostic hypotheses.

Having come this far in my account, it occurs to me that the "I don't knows"
that I have given to people over the years are ultimately the most honest answers
I could have given. I do not know where my mother is, and I do not know if she
is okay. Equally tough for me, however, is that I don't actually know what was
wrong with her. Schizophrenia is nothing more than my own makeshift effort
to match murky, disjointed memories to diagnostic criteria that are themselves
far from perfect. Aside from observations of the disorganization of her physical surroundings and her occupational impairment, the only thing I know with
certainty is that she was delusional. I suspect that she was responding to some
sort of internal stimuli—some inner messages—during spells when I would see
her gazing off inexplicably, but I cannot be sure. Her medical problems following my birth and her early experimenting with drugs only muddy her clinical
picture further. Among the host of disorders in the schizophrenia spectrum and
the delusions and paranoia that can be associated with other conditions, it is
hard to make heads or tails of my memories and what they mean. My mother's
actual diagnosis remains a mystery.

As my clinical psychology training progresses through the end of my degree, this gets harder and harder to grasp. I've wanted on more than one occasion to round up the world's leading clinical researchers, stick them in a room,
and subject them to a case conference on my mother, hoping for just a bit of
diagnostic clarity. I've wanted PowerPoint slides and schematic diagrams that
distill my muddled memories down to a single, solitary name, a label that helps
me to make sense of my experiences (and hers). Yet I'm equally aware that in
some respects, the label may not matter. Her illness is what it is. The symptoms
and impairment are the same no matter what you call them. Even if my mother
were to have received the most airtight of diagnoses and the most comprehensive treatment, we would still never relate as most mothers and daughters
do. There would always be that subtle, instinctive role reversal that kept me

wondering and worrying about her welfare. My childhood would still have been what it was.

At the same time, the possibility of understanding the nature of her disorder is alluring. Whether I view it from the standpoint of a psychologist who anticipates its course or simply that of a child afraid of being contaminated by it, there remains a pressing need to know, to understand. Perhaps I am looking for concrete answers that the field is not yet prepared to provide. I know from firsthand experience how complicated and inexact differential diagnosis can be. Moreover, I know that diagnostic labels do not bring with them all the answers we'd like, especially in terms of treatment. And despite my professional training, it is not for me to diagnose my mother. Even if she were still a part of my life, my role will always be, inexorably, that of daughter.

Even when I put aside my own inclination to diagnose her, I remain mired in disbelief that no one else did. I am often left wondering how it is possible that could she make it as far as she did with no diagnosis from anyone, without any intervention at all. I think back to my mother's months in the hospital after I was born and reflect on the fact that no one seemed to think she needed a psychiatric consultation. If she had one, it certainly didn't reveal that she was on the brink of psychosis. Maybe the onset of her disorder was too insidious for that. It is hard to believe that she made it through the 12 years between that hospitalization and the time when she moved to Japan with no intervention. There were countless incidents, both small and large, that never seemed to garner enough attention to get her into the mental health system. I know that at least some of this stems from my mother's staunch refusal to seek assistance, but there is little comfort in that. For me, the saddest part of her story—the hardest part to accept—will always be that she didn't get any help. And whether I attribute it to a failure of modern mental health care systems or a failure within my family to acknowledge and address her problems, I know that my mother is the one who paid the most profound price.

Making sense of this has been a challenge. Second-guessing yourself comes with the territory once you've entered that no-man's land of do-it-yourself diagnosis. To some extent, it's only natural when trying to understand the fact that someone who is sick did not receive care. In desperation, I let my logic twist and turn. I deduce for a fleeting moment that if my mother didn't find her way into the mental health system, it's because she wasn't really that sick. Or perhaps my assessment was wrong—perhaps it wasn't all that bad. Perhaps the memories are distorted. I've tried to step off the merry-go-round of self-doubt, but it's too easy to hop back on for another spin.

Deep down I know better. But I get the sense that within my family, we have all wanted to believe that perhaps it could be something else. It's my only explanation for our well-regimented denial of the reality she placed before us. At no point as I was growing up did anyone speak to me about mental illness specifically or even about the more general idea that my mother had difficult and very real problems. I think it was easier to look at the things she managed to do well, such as remembering birthdays and planning parties, and to use these strengths to delude ourselves about the gravity of her condition. Just the simple fact that she was able to live and care for herself independently undermined the idea of psychotic mental illness. It's so much easier to keep quiet about something when you don't know what you're dealing with.

It is what it is, I tell myself. Label or no label, this is the hand she was dealt. Suppose I had pursued a diagnosis. I know all too well that diagnosis is only the tip of the iceberg. Although certainly critical to understanding matters of onset, course, and genetic risk, a diagnostic label does not tackle the larger matter of what to do next. Finding effective treatment is itself a formidable challenge; the juggling of alternate approaches and treatments seems by design to bring equal parts hopefulness and heartache. In my mother's case, the scenario is much bleaker. The refusal to get help, the skirting of the mental health system, and the burden of escalating, untreated illness remain as devastating as they would without any label at all. In the end, a diagnosis would be useful, but it wouldn't provide the panacea I seek.

SILENCE

I am visiting with family friends, and we are lingering around the table after dinner. Wine glasses are refilled, and we each sink a bit lower in our seats, reluctant to bring the night to an end. I smile with contentment as I hear chatter and laughter on all sides. These are my favorite people, and the sight of them alone is enough to warm my heart. I've been giving the grad school update, complete with all the requisite gripes, and they are chiming in with their own horror stories. Multiple conversations proceed in tandem, and laughter rises as they compete to put Kingsley Amis's Lucky Jim character to shame. The jokes turn to my father, and I'm told that his graduate office could have passed for fully functional living quarters, complete with a futon, a stereo, and a mini-fridge. I'm rolling out of my seat, envisioning my father as a slacker grad student sleeping through office hours. A photo album comes out to provide tangible evidence. The laughter rises yet again, and the conversation turns quickly to topics of bad haircuts, hideous hippie outfits, and early '70s home décor. I am holding the album and howling with laughter at the youthful images staring back at me. We are making a ruckus that will surely peeve the neighbors, but I don't care. I'm enjoying the trip back in time.

I turn the page, eager for more, and it is then that I see my mother, peeking out from behind the sticky, yellowed plastic. I feel the laughter

*die down. I've never seen these pictures before, and I slow down to take
in new details. It occurs to me for the first time that I have some of my
mother's features. To someone else, this might be obvious, but I've spent a
lifetime hearing that I am my father's daughter, and it takes a moment to
register the new information. "I look like her," I say, noticing that my voice
suddenly seems loud without all the laughter. "Mmm. You do," someone
says. "I guess it's just my nose," I say, looking up to find people fidgeting
with wine glasses and cloth napkins. "Mmm hmm," someone says, leaning
over and squeezing my shoulder affectionately. We sit there a moment longer, awkward and uncomfortable, before someone punctuates the deafening silence. "Dessert, anyone?"*

It's hard to comment on the silence in my family without feeling as though
I am criticizing or passing judgment. As I get older and learn to speak about this
more, I realize that we have all done the best we could, that this is a sad story
with no winners. Yet the tragedy has been exacerbated by the fact that we have
all suffered in silence. Whatever struggles have been endured, whatever grieving
has occurred, or whatever attempts to make meaning have transpired, I sense
that we have all navigated the challenge on our own. There has been a collective
decision for all of us to make sense of the situation and move on.

Until recently, the silence was both so welcoming and so ingrained that
I didn't even notice it. My dad and I have always been close, and we have spoken openly about most subjects. In childhood, he was my refuge of first choice
when something went wrong at school or with a friend, and I have always had
this general sense that I could talk to him about anything. When it came to my
mother, things were no different. My father seemed more than happy to answer
any question I might have, and if the subject of her disturbed him, he never let
on. He would talk in the same levelheaded manner in which he spoke about
everything else. But it was always up to me to broach the subject. Somehow,
I rarely did. Occasionally, inevitably, I grew upset about something she had said
or done and went to him for comfort. There were always hugs and reassurance
and soothing reminders that things would be okay, but the nature of her problems was never discussed. He acknowledged the sadness I was feeling and the
challenges I faced in the most comforting of manners, but the heart of the situation, her illness itself, was never once mentioned.

Instead, the focus of our discussions was on seeing the positive wherever
it could be found. There was acknowledgment that things were tougher for me
than for other kids in some respects but that everyone faced challenges in life.
The key was to be grateful for what you had, to play the hand you were dealt.
Among our circle of extended family, wonderful friends, and the educational
and extracurricular opportunities I had growing up, it was not hard to shift my
focus elsewhere. Over time, I internalized this approach. I have come to view

my experiences with my mother as truly sad, but as just one piece of the puzzle constituting my life this far.

It wasn't until college that I ever suggested to my father that my mother might be ill. It wasn't until many years afterward that I described the apartment and what it was like there. As he listened to my story, my father was marked by a different kind of silence. This time I could tell that he was struggling to put the pieces together in his own mind, to make his own sense of things. It was less a denial and more a reckoning of accounts.

RESILIENCE

I am driving across Route 66, slowly making my way into Alexandria and cursing the D.C. traffic that has delayed my arrival. I am meeting my cousin for the first time in 20 years, and I have spent most of the drive up from Charlottesville, my graduate school home, trying to recall what I know about her. The answer, apparently, is not much. The first and only time Jess and I met was when she was 7 and I was 8. My mother and her two sisters had arranged a reunion in Northern California, and Jess and I enjoyed a brief stint of family togetherness before beginning to fight relentlessly over a Barbie doll. That is about all I remember of her, that she had the good toys and that I was given a time-out. The 20 years that have passed have brought her sister's birth, her father's death, and countless other things I've heard about only in bits and pieces. It is her new job in D.C. that brings us together again, and, as I make the 2-hour drive, I wonder what our interaction will be like this time.

I find the restaurant, nearly hitting a jaywalker as I crane to evaluate the décor. I am wondering whether I am appropriately dressed. What does one wear to these types of events? Are they formal affairs, or is the goal to dress casually? There's not much choice on my end: from the grad-student couture that has slowly invaded my closet, I am in my standard uniform of jeans, sneakers, and a faded Cal sweatshirt that dates from my first year of college. I am wondering what Jess will be wearing, and, as I inch forward along the crowded city street, I entertain images of 20-something hipsters, D.C. politicos, and young sophisticates in turn. It is in the middle of this fashion parade that it occurs to me that I have absolutely no idea what she looks like. I strain to call her face to mind and get nothing. Not a clue. Did we discuss how to identify each other? I vaguely remember telling her that I am small and brown, a description of myself borrowed from an old boyfriend. It leaves me momentarily fearing that she will be inclined to look for a hamster rather than a long-lost cousin. Did she say anything about herself?

In the end, the details are irrelevant. I enter the restaurant and realize that there is no way I could have missed her. The resemblance is striking. The hair is darker, the build of the woman who stands to greet me a bit less tall and lanky, but the fundamental features are unmistakable. I am caught off guard by luminous fair skin, clear blue-green eyes, and a smile I have known only in pictures for as long as I can remember. She looks so much like my mother that my breath catches and I struggle momentarily for air.

Lunch is a haze. We both speak about college and graduate school and career plans. I ask about growing up in the Midwest; she asks about childhood in Los Angeles. It's a worthwhile introduction to a wonderful individual, who I subsequently learn is climbing the ranks within the CIA and who is fond of dogs, themed parties, and exploring the family tree. But it's lost on me. I can't stop staring. I am completely distracted, taking note of every feature and every idiosyncratic movement or turn of phrase that brings someone else to mind. Back from the dead, my mother's image is haunting me, and it doesn't really matter how much real resemblance exists; the shock is visceral, and I struggle to keep my composure.

We say our good-byes, promise to do a better job of keeping in touch, and part ways, knowing that it will be a long time before we see each other again. It's been an interesting experiment in reassembling the family, but the two of us are starting from scratch, and it will be a while before these visits feel natural enough to schedule on a regular basis. I get in the car and head for the highway still in a trance. I have no clue where I am going, heading for the suburbs of McLean when I should be going the other way. It is only when a friend calls and asks how it went that I snap out of it. I open my mouth to answer and out come the tears I've held in for an hour. And, indeed, for so much longer.

People who know my story always comment on how smoothly I navigated my childhood experiences, how well I've done given the circumstances. Indeed, much of my adult identity has been crafted around a strong sense of resilience. I lived with a mother with schizophrenia for the first 6 years of life, but I came through it, and I came through it pretty well. I know what the scientific literature says about kids like me, and it is not often so favorable. For me, however, the concept of resilience has been a double-edged sword. The idea that life can be tough but that all you can do is try your best and move on clearly has been adaptive. Yet I've noticed that the pride I take in my resilience at times allows me to minimize or dismiss the gravity of what I experienced. It is exactly what maintains my silence about my mother's condition. Underneath it all, there has been this sense that if I am doing fine, if I am truly okay with all that has transpired, there should be no need to talk about it. And, of course, implicit in silence is a negative evaluation of the mental illness itself, a shame and embarrassment that linger.

I have also dreaded the pity that would come with disclosure. I remember the first time I expressed this fear to one of my close friends. She laughed affectionately and said, "Oh, but I *do* feel sorry for you. It's a really sad story you tell, and I'm sorry you had to live through it." My initial reaction was one of terror, complete panic setting in and making me want to impale myself on the spot. At the same time, the ease and warmth with which she said this shed new light on my view of things, and it began to dawn on me that it's okay to get sympathy. It spurred a nascent awareness that I'm not alone in my family struggles.

These kinds of revelations have been furthered by my experiences in therapy (both giving and receiving). Clinical interaction has reminded me that acknowledging and accepting other people's sympathy is painful because it forces you to confront the gravity of the situation before you. It forces you to confront your own sadness and loss in a way you might otherwise avoid. It is only as people around me help me to normalize my difficult experiences with my mother's mental illness, to place them on the continuum of other family tragedies, that I start to grow more comfortable with the idea that talking about family problems does not undermine my way of life, my coping, my resilience. And it is slow progress, indeed. I've reached a point at which my closest friends now know about my mother and will periodically bring her up in conversation. Their concerned inquiries remind me of how loved and blessed I am; but they still catch me off guard, making me instantly uncomfortable. My body tenses and my heartbeat accelerates, the physiological signs of anxiety hard to suppress. Talking about her is still a foreign exercise, and I stumble through as if speaking an entirely new language. Practice will make it easier, I know, but it is tough to remember this when you've lived your whole life comfortably in silence.

A FUTURE UNFOLDING

The irony of my career path is not lost on me: a clinician who prefers silence, a researcher marked by firsthand experience. However, I am hesitant to attribute my interest in psychology to such a convenient, single source as my mother. Her influence is no doubt real, but it's always struck me as a bit of an easy out, an explanation that undermines my own intellectual inclination toward the field. In fact, my clinical and research interests have never revolved around adult psychopathology but have centered on children and how families shape the course and treatment of childhood disorders. My work provides a vehicle for understanding my own childhood experiences, but its focus and direction (still evolving) are not dictated by these experiences.

I see the impact of my family less in the content of what I have chosen to study and more in the approach I have taken with it. Whereas many students have an intellectual preference for using a scientific framework to study psychology, I often feel I have a visceral need for it. I need clear answers about mental illness, and, in the absence of them, I need a structured approach to finding them. One of the things I like most about clinical science is the opportunity to take a subject such as mental illness—something that is inherently emotional—and approach it with objectivity. I look to science to impose a modicum of clarity on complex and often irrational emotions. And, of course, I look to it to order my own experiences while keeping them at a comfortable distance. Like many people in my shoes, I've grappled with this strategy, aware that my academic approach allows me to intellectualize (and perhaps diminish) what I have experienced. At the same time, I see clear benefits in being able to assess and process from a safe vantage point. It's a delicate balancing act, and one I am still learning to manage.

There have, of course, been times when scientific objectivity is impossible, times when the emotional weight of my experiences resurfaces and psychology becomes a much more personal endeavor. During my first year of graduate school, we were required to read Irv Gottesman's classic book, *Schizophrenia Genesis*, as part of our experimental psychopathology course. Until that point, I read and sometimes reread each article, taking notes like the best of eager-to-impress new graduate students. Here I did no such thing. I did read the beautiful, poignant first-person narratives from people with schizophrenia but left untouched anything related to twin studies or genetic risk. I would like to say that it was that time in the semester when we students had grown a bit lax in our habits, but I know better. Something hit too close to home, and I didn't want to read any more material related to the genetic risk of first-degree relatives of people with schizophrenia or about the complexities of diagnosis and course. I didn't want the wholly unsatisfying answers it would give me. I didn't want to reflect on the fact that since the book was written, our treatment of schizophrenia has not improved terribly much.

I've come to realize that in the realm of schizophrenia, hopelessness and despair are my sovereign emotions, holding court over the cautious optimism I try my best to practice. It's a sour view born of firsthand experience and fueled by a constant displeasure with what science has to offer. It's a sharp counterpoint to my own work on child anxiety, a topic about which I feel passionate, idealistic, and eager to make a difference.

Not long ago, I was working in an inpatient psychiatric ward with a supervisor whose compassion and clinical skill I greatly admired. He had worked in the hospital for more than 20 years and was known as one of the best in his field. On the day of orientation, I huddled into his office with my fellow trainees and listened to his introduction to the unit. We were going to see the full spectrum of serious mental illness, he said, and it was going to be illuminating. The stories were bleak, the treatment outcomes more often than not imperfect, he told us. As part of his overview, he took a moment to brief us on two of psychiatry's more perplexing illnesses. Bipolar disorder, he contended, was a difficult condition, but one that, with the right medications, could be well managed. Schizophrenia, he continued, well, that was a different matter altogether. It's bad stuff, he said repeatedly, *really* bad stuff. Putting aside his sketch, he then began to address the genetics of schizophrenia and to speak of recent developments in the field of gametic imprinting. He explained that the first-degree relatives of people with schizophrenia carry genes for the disease that may be accentuated or suppressed depending on their partner's genes. It could be that neither person in a couple has schizophrenia, but the nuanced interaction of their genetic material could produce it in their offspring. Even if one person's family history was perfectly clear of schizophrenia, he said, the other person's genetic loading remained a significant liability. You don't want that, he kept saying. You really don't want that.

That schizophrenia is a devastating, disastrous illness, I already knew. That no one would elect to have it in his or her own family, I also knew. That it made me a liability, a form of damaged goods, was a new and painful twist on an already brutal lesson. Perhaps it was because this man was an expert in the field that I felt the sting all the more keenly. The familiar swell of embarrassment and shame engulfed me as he spoke, and I sank further in my seat. I felt immutably flawed. I felt helpless against my damaged DNA. It was not only my mother I had to worry about, it was myself. His words touched a deep and as yet unresolved fear about what lies ahead for me. I began to wonder whether, down the road, a would-be partner would take that chance on me, whether *I* would take that chance on me. I began to wonder whether I should ever have children.

I would have expected to be angered by this supervisor's words and the unsettling emotions they evoked. Instead, I felt only quiet resignation. I had no ill will toward this man. He had devoted his life to treating youths with severe mental illness, and he knew exactly how heartbreaking it could be. He knew, as I did, that it was really bad stuff.

Experiences such as these have reminded me that I am not an objective participant in the field and that I cannot be. Try as I may to strive for perfect clinical distance (whatever that is), I am bound by my history. I have intimate experience with mental illness, and it has shaped my life dramatically. It has taken my mother, and it has taken my peace of mind. The effects of these experiences are profound. But they need not constitute a professional liability; rather, they may be valuable tools for sharpening my skills in both clinical and empirical domains. Certainly, I prefer to see them as a vehicle for insight, compassion, and persistence.

I know that others might not share this view, believing that my personal lens may be viewed as a handicap or hindrance. With this in mind, I have kept my experiences to myself, aware of the reactions they may earn from my colleagues. I have been a double agent in the field, with a secret identity kept well under wraps. I suspect it is why I did not get angry at that supervisor; I knew he did not appreciate the level on which his words would resonate. Although I maintain that he could have been more sensitive to the influence he wielded over trainees, I believe that in some misguided way, his goal was to evoke empathy for the plight of individuals with mental illness and their families. He could not know he had a field agent in his midst.

LESSONS IN THE FIELD

I learned to break my silence about my mother the hard way. I would have been more than happy to keep quiet about her indefinitely, relegating memories of her to the deepest recesses of my mind, steering clear of her in casual conversation, acting as if she never really existed. Like the rest of my family, I had put her in the past. Her story, when it arose, was told in final terms, the conclusion already in place. In one of life's more painful lessons, I came to realize that this is not how it works.

> It is the morning after my 27th birthday. I am traipsing around my apartment in my pajamas, still groggy after the previous night's birthday celebration. I'm in no rush to get ready. It's my designated writing day, which means that I don't have to leave the house. I turn on the coffeepot, boot up my computer, and go outside to grab the paper. In mid-April it is still freezing, and I dart back in. I return to my computer, wrapping my robe a little tighter. I bring up my e-mail, and I see a message from my aunt. We don't correspond via e-mail, but somehow I conclude that she is sending me birthday greetings. A look at the date stamp confirms what I have already assumed: her message was sent at 8 P.M. the previous night. My eyes scroll over to the subject header, and I see the following: "News about your mom." It does not compute. I am still expecting birthday wishes when I read these words:
>
> Tara, I just spoke with someone from the US consul in Japan. Diane has been detained in a cell for the last 6 weeks because she was found in an abandoned house in Japan and found to have an outdated visa by many years. Spoke with an official who said she was not making any sense, etc. and did not release any information until yesterday when she mentioned she had 2 **half**-sisters. She will be deported to the US. . . .

For a brief moment, the words don't register. It's too foreign, too far off the map from what I am expecting. The notion of my mother reentering my life after a 14-year absence resides firmly in the realm of the impossible. I can only stand there in the early morning hush, staring blankly at the screen, trying to make sense of the message staring back at me. When it registers, I am instantly sick, my body hijacked by anxiety and my brain completely overwhelmed. I run to the bathroom and throw up. As I drop to the floor and lean against the toilet, I start to feel as if my brain has been sucked out of my head. Detained. Cell. Deported. Words and phrases from the e-mail are floating in front of me, but my brain has short-circuited and it feels like everything is scrambled.

Slumped on the floor and lost in a suffocating haze, I start willing it not to be true. This is not happening, I say to myself. There are no tears, not yet. Just a simple mantra repeated again and again: This cannot be true. A few moments later, I stand up and move back to my computer, leaning against the wall as I walk, not entirely sure of how my feet are still moving beneath me. I continue muttering to myself the whole way down the hall. This cannot be true.

I reread the e-mail, and that is when complete panic sets in. In my shock, my mental faculties quickly begin to abandon me, my thoughts racing a mile a minute and my body moving as if in a dream. I realize that I need help. It is 4 A.M. on the West Coast, too early to call my father or my aunt. As my heartbeat accelerates and my breathing quickens, the need for help grows more urgent. I have amazing friends in graduate school, but none of them knows anything about my mother. They live right down the street, but I've rendered them all useless. How can I start to explain at a time like this? Where do you begin? Who will help me now? The answer, apparently, is no one. In an instant, a lifetime of silence back-fires on me. Transformed, my quietude now holds me captive. I sit alone in silence for another hour until I reach my father.

Several years later, it is still difficult for me to sort out the flurry of emotions that accompanied my mother's unexpected return. They came fast and raw, piercing me with their force. They came all at once—anger, disbelief, despair, sadness, anxiety—and they were sucked into a vortex that rendered them a single entity. There was no way to sort or order them and, for the first time in my life, there was no way to minimize them. The result was an emotional landslide that left me utterly incapacitated. Even now as I write, I find my fingers halt at the keyboard, paralyzed in a strange and frustrating parallel to my frozen state that day. It's what I remember most: being instantly immobilized and completely alone.

The first lesson from that day, a bitter pill to swallow, came in the form of powerful rage. Unfettered, all-consuming rage was something I had not yet had the occasion to feel; my life, despite its ups and downs, had been too good for that. My family hardships had produced only a sense of heartbreak for my mother and for all that she had lost. It was an outlook that did not leave me room to feel sad for myself. I had not devoted time or energy to my own loss, and I had not thought about what I had been forced to endure as a child. I had been too busy being resilient. It therefore came as quite a surprise to feel rage, that ugly stepsister of sadness, rise to the surface within minutes. Sitting alone in silence, all that I had lived through became real, and my sadness and disbelief were matched by a deep sense of anger at my lot in life. It was in the midst of this naked fury that my first clear thoughts emerged: *This is not fair. I have already dealt with this. I have put this behind me. This cannot be true.*

My line of thinking reflected a gap in logic that the brain mercifully allows in an effort to preserve the heart. In hindsight I recognize that the error in my reasoning was bound to be unveiled eventually. You do not "deal with" mental illness. You do not put it behind you. It stays with you, always. It does not afford the courtesy of a neat conclusion.

But I could not know that then. It was another lesson to be learned. I realize now that in my mother's absence, I had made sense the only way I knew how: I had come to think of her as dead. Much like a small child, I had skipped the ugly details of her death—the pain and suffering, the how, when, and why—and sent her off to some innocuous, other-worldly place. Her return blindsided me, catching me completely off guard. There was no longer any refuge to be found in cloudy childhood memories or pat denial. My mother was back, and she brought with her clear, irrefutable evidence of her illness. And it was terrible evidence, indeed. The circumstances of her reappearance forced me to think about the gravity of her condition in new light. They forced me to consider exactly how she had spent the last 14 years. At what point did she lose her job? Her home? How had she been getting by? It was a brutal schooling in the realities of severe mental illness. It was, and still is, excruciating for me to think about.

In those first weeks, I would find myself transfixed by the sight of melting snow banks, haunted by images of my mother, age 60, living in an abandoned building in Japan in the dead of winter. I wondered if she had been scared and lonely. I wondered if she had been cold. I wondered what inhumanities she had endured. Raised in privilege, I had no mental framework for organizing these kinds of musings. The people I knew did not end up homeless; they did not have to worry about how to stay warm in winter. Their hardships, although difficult in their own right, were familiar and commonplace. They were your garden-variety accidents and illnesses, those unpleasant, unwanted, and unavoidable events endemic to any life journey. When it came to my mother, it was more than I could get my head around. I tried desperately to rein in my

imagination, to tell myself it wasn't that bad, that I had no way of really knowing what her life had been like. The image of her squatting in an abandoned
building was so far beyond what I could envision that the effort proved futile.
Her downfall was complete, her descent from successful scholar to drifting va-
grant, a reality far worse than my most fantastic invention.

My worry about what she had lived through was matched only by fear of
what was to come. By the time I was 27, my mother had been gone more than
half my life. She was a foreign figure built from cracked, aging photos, murky
memories, and a handful of selectively told tales. I had no idea what to expect
from her. I was terrified by thoughts of what she would look like and what state
she would be in. I envisioned her with posttraumatic stress disorder exacerbating her psychotic symptoms. I envisioned her aged, decrepit, and deranged.
I envisioned having to care for her for the rest of my life. The nightmares began
the night I received that e-mail, and they stuck with me for weeks to come.

In the midst of so many unknowns, there was nothing to anchor me. Bowled
over by shock and trampled by panic, the only thing I knew with certainty was
that my mother needed help. There were no guideposts other than that. Help
her. The form of help, its method of delivery—these details were all mysteries
to me. Should I get on a plane and go to wait for her in San Francisco? Should
I let her settle in with my aunt first? Harder still, what was I to say to her when
I saw her? Would she even know who I was?

I felt helpless and alone, the burden of her care resting squarely on my
shoulders. Objectively, this was not true. From the moment news of my mother
surfaced, my father and my aunts were instantly involved in coordinating her
return, and they consulted with psychiatrists, attorneys, and advocates as they
prepared for her homecoming. They too recognized her need for help, and they
were doing all they could to secure it. Yet I found myself mistrusting of their
efforts, skeptical of their competence, and dubious about how much they were
really willing to do to help her. In the end, I harbored a lingering resentment
over how it was that they had let her fall this far. I felt it was up to me to do
what they had failed to do in the past.

I became obsessed with getting my mother a psychiatric evaluation. I had
a little over a week before her return, and I swore to myself that this time it
would be different—this time she would get help. I understood mental illness,
at least better than others in my family did. I had resources, and I was convinced
that with the right strategy, I could find help for her. I spent endless hours on
the Internet reading about the laws for commitment. I knew that my mother
would not enter a psychiatric facility voluntarily, that she wouldn't step off a
plane and simply head, at my behest, to the hospital. Nonetheless, I was determined to get her there. I had faith that if I worked hard enough, if I researched
matters sufficiently well, I would be able to find a way to get her the help she
desperately needed.

Without any medical or psychiatric records, it proved more difficult than I could have imagined. To be admitted involuntarily, a person must pose imminent danger to herself or to someone else or must be so disabled as to fail to provide care for herself. I had nothing to demonstrate my mother's impairment—no diagnosis and no previous treatment history. She hadn't even been in the country for the past decade and a half. It was as though she hadn't really existed. I had no time and nothing to work with, and I could see history gearing up to repeat itself. Somehow my mother seemed destined to slip through the cracks, too sick to care for herself but not sick enough to pose the kind of threat that society is inclined to address.

In my desperation, I fell back on a familiar crutch: I tried to educate myself. Beyond the cool letter of commitment law and beyond public policy, I learned about what others in my shoes had done. My family was not alone in facing this struggle. We were not the only ones to wrestle with how to get help for a loved one who was ardently convinced that there was no need for help. Frantic for whatever anecdotal advice I could find, I visited countless chat rooms and websites for families of people with schizophrenia. It was a demoralizing journey filled with the same worn tales of people unable to persuade their loved ones to seek help. They came in all shapes and sizes, bleak no matter their form. There were mothers who lied to the police and claimed that their children had assaulted them in an effort to get the children committed to the hospital. There were those who prayed that their family member would get caught stealing and enter the mental health system via the criminal courts. The tactics varied, but they were always those of pure and utter desperation.

It was the kind of desperation that I understood all too well. I was terrified of what would become of my mother without sound mental health services. Even with treatment, I worried about how things would unfold for her and for me: Where would she live, and how would she support herself? I ruminated about what would become of her as she grew old. I agonized over who would assume responsibility for her care. I could envision the scenario many different ways, but one element remained fixed: as her only child, it was up to me to care for her, whatever the cost.

"Don't let this derail you. You could be a star in the field," a professor said to me shortly after I told him what was happening. Those were among his first words on the subject of my mother, and they sharpened the budding sense I had that caring for her would somehow shortchange the rest of my life. It was a horrible thought, but the alternative was worse: my mother would disappear again, lost to the void. And this time, there would be no hiding behind my denial, no safe haven where I could mentally store her. I would know the precise situation to which she was ineluctably bound. I would know the depths of her illness, and I would know what it had in store for her. It was pure fear that propelled me as I searched in vain for help.

In the end, she came and went quickly. It happened so fast I never saw her. From what I am told, she stepped off a plane in San Francisco looking great. It was as if no time had passed, my uncle later said. She was wearing a suit, looking well groomed and professional. She provided her usual smooth first impression, and it was hard for my aunt and uncle to reconcile this with the fact that she had been found homeless and unable to identify herself just a few weeks earlier. They took her to Stanford to meet my cousin for lunch, hoping that while they were there, they could get her to agree to see a doctor for a physical examination. After all, she had been through so much over the last month; a checkup couldn't hurt. She would have none of it. She staunchly refused help and immediately grew suspicious of their motives. My mother stated that her plan was to go to Holland and that she intended to stick around only long enough to obtain a visa.

Within a matter of hours, the veneer cracked, and she claimed she was royalty from Holland. My mother stayed with my aunt briefly and then asked to be taken to Palo Alto, to the area where she had once lived as a young professor. My aunt tried to reason with her, tried to encourage her one last time to seek help, but it was to no avail. My mother promised to call. She hasn't been heard from since.

It has now been 3 years since my mother's fleeting reappearance, and I find it is still immensely difficult territory to tread. I can't help but feel that it was all a cruel joke, a vicious prank on an unsuspecting victim. I lost my mother early in life, and I learned to do without. The shock of her return, the promise of a reunion, and the recapitulation of her loss remain more than my heart can bear. Life has gone on, as it must, but the mark of that experience remains. I know she is out there—how near or far I have no idea—and I know that she suffers.

I suffer with her, useless and unable to help, despite all my professional training. I suspect it is one of the bigger lessons I've learned. We are all helpless in the face of mental illness, all brought to our knees by the heartbreak it brings. Everyone suffers, and respite, if it is to be found, is brief. I wanted so desperately to help my mother. I pursued every avenue I knew to explore. In hindsight, however, it always seems that there was more that could have been done. It's a view that I know will linger. I will always be unsatisfied until she gets help. Nothing short of that will ever have been enough.

It's been a journey in forgiveness as well, forgiveness of myself, of her, and of others. I now know what it is to try your best and fail. I know what it is like to wrestle with the ambivalence that comes with caring for someone with mental illness. I understand that the need to preserve some personal distance is human, necessary. These were things for which I once assigned blame, but in living them myself, I have come to see them differently.

I also understand what it is to make mistakes. Looking back, I see that as I prepared for my mother's return, I dove headfirst into the practical matters of her homecoming. I worried about flight plans, accommodations, and finding mental health services for her. Our actual relationship was more than I could manage. I did not know how to negotiate that or even, truthfully, where to begin. I was afraid to see her and afraid of enduring another round of trauma. I was afraid to stir sleeping memories of shabby living quarters and painful, confusing interactions. I regret that I was sidelined by fear. I regret that I wasn't there to greet my mother on her return, that I missed what may have been my only chance to see her again. Those pieces came together too slowly for me. I waited, thinking I would get my chance, and I learned too late that I had passed it up. It was a lesson learned the hard way.

Coping with this final episode has been an ongoing process. There is no tidy ending here, and I now know not to look for it. My greatest fear has been realized. My mother, more likely than not, is homeless; she is one of the masses lost to mental illness. It's more than the human heart can bear, and anticipating it years ago, I thought I would surely collapse under its weight. Sometimes I still do. Passing homeless people on the street was once a minor inconvenience for me, a mildly uncomfortable reminder that life's blessings are not equally distributed. It is now acutely painful. I can't help but look at each one, somehow seeing my mother in each muddied face. I will often find an ordinary day interrupted by thoughts of how this stranger got there, what accomplishments have fallen along the wayside, where loved ones are waiting. There's no looking the other way for me, no avoiding reality. I have tried that strategy and it doesn't work.

My mother's brief return uprooted all sense of order in my world. I realized that life is unpredictable and unfair, and that its toughest lessons are to be learned again and again. Yet I also realized that I do not have to endure these struggles alone. I started talking about them the hard way, first in stumbling, halting sentences and now in fluid narrative. I gain strength with the practice, and I realize that, with support, I am always stronger than I think.

4

Laura's Story: Making Sense of and Deriving Meaning From Her Life With Mental Illness

Elizabeth B. Owens

HER STORY

My 4-year-old daughter tells me that her Piggy (a deeply loved stuffed animal who is usually her best friend, sometimes her baby, and sometimes her punching bag) has a baby sister who died. She asks me about her aunt Laura, my younger sister, who died. "Why did she die?" she asks, even though her concept of death is underdeveloped, at best. Interestingly, my daughter asks "why" and not "how." Can I explain *why* my sister's life ended as it did? For now, I say to my daughter that Laura was very sick and died, and I talk about how I miss my sister. Now that my daughter has a 2-year-old (and therefore sometimes annoying) little brother, I talk about what it was like for me to have a little sister and how sometimes she made me angry, too.

Why did Laura die of a lethal drug overdose? Well, I can't explain it in the sense of tracing the series of causes leading up to the event. Of course, as a behavioral scientist, I wish I could. Everyone in my family and many of Laura's friends have struggled with the questions Why did this happen? and How did this happen? My answer involves references to genetic vulnerability—for instance, my maternal grandmother died at 56 of medical problems related to alcoholism—negative peer influences, and the effects of early substance abuse on a developing brain. These things are probably causally relevant but basically unsatisfactory as a real explanation. I mean, why Laura? Why her and not others with similar vulnerabilities and experiences? Why Laura and not me?

I can't explain, but I can at least describe. I'm going to give two different accounts, each different but both entirely accurate.

One Account of a Horrible Death

The first portrayal is of how, in the very early morning hours on Thursday, May 10, 2001, my 34-year-old sister was left brain dead after a massive cocaine-induced stroke in a dingy and dirty Days Inn motel in Seattle, Washington, far from family and real friends. Paramedics had been called to the scene by a guy with whom Laura was using, and somehow they technically kept her alive by injecting a medication into her chest to restart her heart (well, this is what I gathered from the guy who called the paramedics), but she clearly was no longer alive in any real sense of the word. Her undernourished and fragile body and soul had simply been abused beyond repair. She died the next day when her life support system was unplugged.

Her death occurred after 22 years of alcohol and drug abuse, beginning with marijuana and alcohol in junior high and then high school. She continued to drink and smoke pot but also graduated to abuse of prescription pain medication and all forms of cocaine and heroin in college and beyond. Prior to her death she had not been employed for approximately 3 years, lied constantly, wrote bad checks to buy booze, and moved frequently from place to place. She had been homeless, living and sleeping God only knows where. I'm sure she was attacked and victimized by others on the street, and even 5 years after her death this is a wrenching thought. She repeatedly sought respite (and prescription pain killers) in emergency rooms and brief inpatient stays in psychiatric and medical hospitals. Her medical record read like that of an 80-year-old: repeated bacterial infections, gallbladder surgery, chronic pancreatitis, osteoporosis, and liver disease. Honestly, I can hardly bear to think about the conditions in which she was living, or "essentially dying," during the last few years of her life.

If you live in an urban area, you probably frequently see people in your neighborhood or hanging out on sidewalks living as my sister ultimately did. What do you think and how do you feel when you see them? Do you ever think, "Why don't you get a job? Why don't you stop drinking? Start taking care of yourself!" Do you turn away from them? Do they irritate you? At times I thought these things about my own sister. Forget irritation, sometimes I was downright furious with her. When we were both living in the Bay Area and then Los Angeles, she would sometimes stay with me and then get drunk or use drugs in my apartment. Couldn't she refrain for just one day so we could be like normal sisters for a few hours? Couldn't she stop calling me at 6 A.M. (which was early before I had children) or at 11 P.M. crying, asking for money, telling me how her boyfriend set fire to the bed when she was sleeping in it, or otherwise worrying me? These phone calls would often leave me overtaken with anger, helplessness, and sadness.

Despite my sometimes being overwhelmingly sad and angry when trying to help or simply live with my sister, I didn't really begin to cry about her death until I was home in California on the night of Sunday, May 13, 2 days after she died. The phone rang close to 10 P.M., and my body reacted as it always did to late and early phone calls, with a flush of dread because calls at that hour were almost always from my sister and almost always difficult. However, less than a moment after my initial automatic bodily response, I realized that of course it wasn't Laura, and I burst into tears. Throughout the rest of my life I would never again receive a phone call from her. Despite the negative impact those phone calls could have on me, the thought that (God willing) I may live for many more decades and will never, ever again hear her voice is still hard to believe.

The Life and Death of a Wonderful, Troubled Girl

Now let me begin the second account of my sister's death, followed by a much more detailed account of her life. After more than 20 long years of struggling with anxiety, depression, eating disorders, and substance abuse, my sister slipped away from us in a hospital in Seattle, Washington. On the morning of Thursday, May 10, 2001, I received a call that she had been hospitalized after being found near-dead in a motel. How did the hospital social worker find my phone number? I still don't know. That afternoon, 5 months pregnant with my first child (who is named after my sister), I traveled from California to Seattle, accompanied by my husband. He worked on arranging accommodations while I visited with my sister. Laura was pasty and limp, dressed only in her flimsy hospital gown. Her eyes were completely vacant. She was intubated and poked full of intravenous needles. I chatted with her, or rather at her, for a long time, stroking her beautiful, soft blond hair and her warm but lanky, scarred, lifeless arms. Her blood pressure, which of course was being constantly monitored on a machine next to her bed, seemed to rise slightly when I did this. We watched TV sitcoms—one of her favorite activities—together. I called my parents to forewarn them. I had difficulty describing how bad the situation was. I didn't say she was dead, but I tried to imply it so that they didn't have to experience the shock I had when I first walked into her hospital room.

By Friday morning my parents and younger brother had come from the East Coast to be at her bedside. By noon we had consulted with the doctor about Laura's condition. Her brain had been irreparably damaged by a stroke, and she would not continue to live if life support machines were unplugged. The doctor did not and would not suggest what we do, but it was obvious that this was the end for Laura. We stood around her bed holding each other and her, and we each said good-bye. How did my parents do this and not literally collapse with grief? I feel weak just recollecting our good-byes. We watched her go after the machines were unplugged, and we left her room, silent and stunned.

The next few days felt flat and lifeless. Food had no taste; we couldn't sleep. We didn't talk much among ourselves. But we were very busy. Among her countless symptoms, Laura was a hoarder. She had trouble letting go of anything that might be useful at some point. We had to collect her things from an apartment where she had been staying and from the guy who had been with her when she collapsed. Then, in our motel rooms, we had to rifle through it all, deciding with haste what to keep and what to give away. Almost all of the smoke- and perfume-laden clothes were given to Goodwill. There were dozens and dozens of large bottles of prescription medication, literally pounds of pills, obtained from multiple unknowing (but should have been knowing) doctors and pharmacies unable to detect her hoarding patterns and substance abuse history. I kept a few things that I had given her (and 5 years later they still smell vaguely of cigarette smoke and perfume—her signature scent), and we kept her many photographs and all of her notes and curriculum plans from her days as a preschool teacher. I saved the extensive collection of puppets she used when teaching, and my own children play with them frequently now. We also kept her stuffed animals. Despite my absolute abhorrence of cigarette smoke, I find its lingering scent on these cute and fuzzy stuffed creatures to be rather charming because the juxtaposition reminds me of my endearing but brash and sometimes caustic little sister.

From our motel rooms in an unfamiliar city, we had to obtain a death certificate and plan for Laura's cremation and the transport of her remains. We began planning a memorial service to be held in our hometown in Westchester County, New York, a few weeks hence. Throughout, my mother never cried, which is odd because a beautiful sunset or a bouquet of flowers can make her cry. She cried during each and every *Little House on the Prairie* episode we watched together in the 1970s. But I know that she had done much of her grieving for Laura's lost life long before her final death, as had I. My father, however—whom I had never seen cry—cried on and off for 2 days. He couldn't help us by going through or even looking at Laura's things. He mostly kept to himself, and sometimes buried his face in a pillow as he wept. Because I have my own children now, I can just begin to understand how he felt. But I can't dwell on it for more than a moment because knowing that my father and mother have faced the excruciating pain of the death of a child is almost unbearable for me. I think that everyone who is lost to serious substance abuse has someone grieving for her or him, as we did for my sister. I always remember this when I come across substance abusers on the streets in Berkeley, which is a frequent event. Where is his family? Who is wondering and worrying about her?

My sister Laura was born in 1967 and was almost 2 years younger than I. My mother reports that I had an exceptionally difficult time when she was born and perceived her entry into the world as a rude dethronement from the position of the only, cherished child. My mother also reports that Laura was an extremely irritable and inconsolable young baby. It was perhaps 3 months before doctors realized that Laura had an obstruction in her gastrointestinal tract that had been causing her much pain. Once it was surgically corrected, her irritability and crying were considerably reduced. My parents and I have wondered whether Laura's first few months of continuous, unrelieved pain contributed

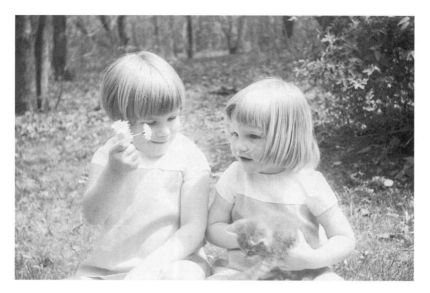

Laura, right, age 3; Liz, left, age 5

to her eventual reliance on alcohol and drugs to relieve any hint of physical or emotional discomfort. Even before she began using alcohol and street drugs, she abused over-the-counter nasal decongestant sprays and was clearly addicted to them. Throughout much of her life, even minor nasal congestion was so intolerable for her that she always had a bottle of Afrin with her and used it multiple times each day. It is a medication that is not supposed to be used for more than 3 days in a row. She might have used it every day for more than two decades.

Laura was very attractive and very sociable. From the beginning, she was outgoing and popular, with many close, enduring friendships, because she was an attentive, considerate, loyal friend. Later she had many boyfriends, as well. Laura was fun-loving, warm, and generous. People simply flocked to her. She was a "life of the party" girl, even before she started using. She had a quick wit and a fabulous, sharp sense of humor that could stop people in their tracks. For example, I loved her phrase, "Well, excuse me for talking while you were interrupting," which she often used humorously when she felt pushed out of a conversation.

When we were children, and certainly when we were adolescents, I was jealous of her popularity, but I maintained my superior attitude (she called me a snob) because of my good grades and good-girl image. Laura was also very bright and did well in school, although I'm sure she would have done better if she hadn't been the second, middle child. I had already filled the academic-achiever niche in our family, so, as she once explained to me, at age 9 she decided to choose other pursuits. When she was physically healthy, in her teenage years before eating disorders robbed her of strength, she loved camping and living outdoors. And she loved animals and always had a variety of pets, including her beloved Sidney, an adorable lop-eared rabbit named after Sid Vicious, the deceased bassist of the Sex Pistols (he died of a heroin overdose). Her sweet, shy, and pillowy (i.e., soft and fat) cat named Nona still lives with my parents.

For some reason, a reason I wish desperately I could pinpoint even though I know there was no single cause or turning point, she began drinking and smoking pot when she was 12. At the time, between 1978 and 1980, we were living in Brussels, Belgium (my father was an executive at an international food company and was transferred from New York to the company's European headquarters). In Belgium, no one thought twice about teenagers drinking in bars. There was no concept, legal or otherwise, of underage drinking. I do think that easy access to booze helped to get her started, but she probably would have started anyway under other circumstances. I'm sure her friends were hanging out in bars and drinking, as were mine, even though they were all nice kids from upper-middle-class families and not what one thinks of as "deviant peers."

From my perspective at the time, Laura's emotional and behavioral problems began to surface in high school, after we had returned to New York from Belgium. However, in retrospect, problems had certainly been brewing during our 2 1/2 years in Belgium, when Laura was 10 to 12 years old. One month she chalked up a $400 phone bill (in 1978 dollars) calling her friends in the United States. She was beginning to be secretive about how she spent time with her friends in Belgium. My parents began to offer her money in exchange for better grades, which really upset me. I had never been offered a reward or even much recognition for good grades; why did she deserve one while I was essentially overlooked?

Then, 1 year after we had returned to New York, Laura went off to a private boarding school, which my parents hoped would provide containment and correction of her increasingly out-of-control behavior. Even though she performed well academically there (she won the Latin prize that year), her behavior was very problematic. After 1 year she returned home and to our public high school. At the time I didn't understand why she had left or why she had returned home, but I did see that in the interim she began cutting her forearms and wrists and upper thighs, apparently with razor blades, leaving dramatic scars. For the rest of her life she never wore short-sleeved shirts, something I realized only after knitting her a short-sleeved sweater one Christmas that she obviously couldn't bring herself to wear.

As Laura's troubles were escalating, I began college at Stanford in 1983 and was fairly out of touch with her for a few years. We saw each other perhaps twice a year and talked on the phone occasionally. But our relationship for much of the previous decade had been quite contentious (that is an understatement; we hated each other), and I was not sad about being out of touch. I honestly didn't think much about her as I started my new life in California.

Laura graduated from our local high school and went to a state college in New Paltz, New York. But, again mysteriously to me, after 2 years she transferred to another state college in Purchase, New York. Knowing what I know now, I suspect she was trying to get away from her drug-using friends in New Paltz. She performed very well at Purchase, obtaining a grade-point average of 3.8. Nevertheless, by the time she graduated in 1989 she was a serious substance abuser, something we realized only years later. I was married in 1988, and she, my maid of honor, age 21, was doing cocaine in the bathroom at my reception. Before you repress the urge to shake your finger at her, know that there were at least three other wedding guests using with her. Remember, too, that it was the 1980s and that many of the guests were right out of college. She was also quietly complaining about looking fat, at 115 pounds, in the dress I had chosen for her. In fact, she was struggling with bulimia by then, too.

But no one in my family seemed to realize what was going on. At least I didn't. I just knew that Laura was often difficult and rebellious and infuriating. But she was my sister, and despite our history of deep-seated conflict—which had been greatly relieved by our physical distance from each other—I cared about and loved her, which is why I asked her to be my maid of honor. I don't think my parents knew what was going on, either. But sometimes I think: How could they not have known? Did they not see it, or did they see it and ignore it? My parents were quite permissive with all of us. They completely avoided confrontation and limit setting, and I believe that this strategy had dramatically different effects on Laura, on me, and on our younger brother. Without limits, Laura pushed and pushed to see what she could get away with, which was almost anything. I, on the other hand, self-imposed my own set of overly stringent and punishing limits, which were intended to ensure that I perform well and stay in control. I was anorexic in high school and bulimic in college (something that almost seemed fashionable among girls at Stanford at the time; and, yes, 19-year-olds are girls, not women) and have suffered from repeated, but thankfully infrequent, episodes of mild to moderate depression since my freshman year in college. My younger brother, remarkably, was totally unscathed by this hands-off and permissive parenting style and is, and always has been, completely well adjusted and happy.

I used to get angry about my parent's permissive style and their refusal or inability to rein Laura in, but I don't any longer. I do the best I can with my children every day, and I often fall short. It is very clear to me now that my parents did the very best they could with all of us. Despite this, the fact is that, before any of us knew it, Laura's life had spun totally out of control. I wish I had more to say about how her life had gotten that way. What really happened? But I am at a loss.

When I got married in 1988 I was living in California. A few months after the wedding, Laura moved from New York to California. At my wedding she had met and started dating the best man, who was my husband's best friend and a very good friend of mine during college. They moved in together in 1989 and were living in Oakland, while my husband and I lived in San Francisco. It was that year, when Laura was 22, that she declared her need for help. She did so, after drinking too much, at a Christmas celebration with my family at my aunt's house in Atherton, California. And this is where her story really begins. What 22-year-old has the presence of mind and courage to announce to her family that she is an alcoholic (and more) and needs help? That was an incredibly brave thing to do. I can't imagine asking for help as she did, if I had needed it. Over the next 12 years Laura surmounted obstacles that I don't think I would have even attempted to face. She always, always wanted to clean up her act and get her life back on track. In fact, one of the reasons she moved to California was to get away from her drug-using and drug-pushing friends. She continuously reached out for help, sought treatment, and worked hard in school and in her jobs. At least up until the very end, she never gave up. Despite outward appearances, I think she was a much stronger person than I am in many ways.

After her request for help at our family Christmas gathering in 1989, nothing happened right away. I remember being somewhat surprised or maybe confused by her announcement. I remember thinking, "She is an alcoholic? Huh....Well, that explains a lot of things. I thought she was just a pain in the ass sometimes." For the previous 10 years I hadn't been able to distinguish sober Laura from high Laura, and I had been confusing her personality with her state of intoxication. So it took a while for her announcement to sink in.

I'm not sure what my parents thought or how they reacted. It seemed to me that we all sort of ignored Laura's declaration, as no one jumped to action. Maybe my parents acted privately, but it was not something we discussed. Then in the spring of 1990, a few months after her plea for help, Laura returned home to New York. She checked herself into Northern Westchester hospital, the local medical facility, for a 3-day detoxification program. But apparently she brought a suitcase of vodka with her and was walking around the hospital drunk. This is not the only time she was drunk during inpatient treatment. If trained medical professionals had no idea what was going on, how could my parents?

During that brief stay a psychiatrist convinced her to check herself into an inpatient psychiatric facility called Four Winds. Apparently she was not cooperative with treatment there, but she heard about an expert in the treatment of eating disorders who worked at another local inpatient psychiatric facility called Silver Hill. Laura checked herself out of Four Winds, got in an ambulance, and asked to be taken to Silver Hill, where she stayed for 6 months. At discharge a psychiatrist at the hospital said they had done all they could. My mother recollects that this discharging doctor was not very optimistic about Laura's future, despite her youth and the 6 months of inpatient treatment she had received.

After these intensive treatment experiences in New York, Laura returned to Oakland, California, in 1991. That summer, while the rest of our family was on vacation in Maine (a trip we had wanted her to take with us), she made what might have been the first in a series of suicide attempts. Because we were 3,000 miles away, everything my parents know about the event came via telephone. And because everything I now know about the event was filtered through my mother, the details of the suicide attempt were lost to me. However, needless to say, even 15 years later the memories of that vacation make me sad and anxious.

Frankly, over the next 10 years Laura went in and out of hospitals rather frequently, so it is hard for me to exactly reconstruct the time line of her inpatient stays. Many of these followed suicide attempts. She was painfully aware of her need for help and often desperately wanted it. At those times she would check herself in somewhere but would then often bolt from these facilities, checking out abruptly, against medical advice, almost in a panic. At one point in 1991, I helped to check her into the eating-disorder inpatient unit at Stanford. I arrived at her apartment, and she was totally wasted, on vodka I assumed, barely able to stand up. I literally dragged her to my car, and when I pulled up to the hospital, staff helped me to pour her into a wheelchair. She couldn't sit up straight, and her head and left arm drooped over the side of the chair. I was embarrassed wheeling her into the hospital like that, but now I think of how my feelings paled in comparison with hers. I think the only way that she could face treatment, which she perceived as necessary agony, was to obliterate her consciousness so that she didn't have to experience the fear, disgust, and panic that accompanied checking into a hospital. During that stay she lied to hospital staff about having dentist appointments. Even though she was a hospital inpatient, they let her go to these "appointments," which were really walks to Safeway to buy vodka, on her own. This, to me, is unbelievable, but true.

Later in 1991 my husband and I left San Francisco so that I could begin a doctoral program in clinical psychology at the University of Pittsburgh. Again, I fell somewhat out of touch with Laura. It was during this time that she stopped drinking and using for a period of years. A stay at a residential treatment facility in Sonoma County, called Mountain Vista Farm, precipitated her long period of sobriety. I don't know exactly what it was about Mountain Vista Farm that helped her. It was a very spiritual place, and she made good friends there. We were all thrilled and amazed that she was clean and sober. After a time we thought it was for good.

But at the same time Laura's already low weight plummeted, and during much of her mid-20s she weighed between 75 and 80 pounds. It was during this time, when Laura was not using, that the depth and complexity of her emotional problems became apparent to me. Saying that Laura was a polysubstance abuser (i.e., she abused alcohol and a variety of drugs), which perhaps was her most prominent and impairing behavioral problem, does not begin to capture the extent of her mental illness. The drinking and drug use were gut-wrenching and terrifying to us, but her wasted body, her significant and highly impairing anxiety, and her deep depression were heartbreaking. How could so much mental illness be packed into such a tiny and beautiful person? At various times between her teenage years and her death, and often simultaneously, she met diagnostic criteria for many disorders, as defined in *DSM-IV*, the manual of psychiatric classifications. These included major depressive disorder, dysthymia, generalized anxiety disorder, obsessive-compulsive disorder, agoraphobia, bulimia and anorexia nervosa, borderline personality disorder, and many types of substance abuse and dependence disorders. This description of Laura's illness is nonparsimonious at best, which I think reflects on the field's current inability to fundamentally understand and classify mental illness. Although the classification system that exists is necessary for study, few ill people with many co-occurring symptoms are well served by it.

This is how I make sense of the extent and variety of Laura's emotional and behavior problems: I believe that anxiety and fear were at the core of Laura's illness and that the substance abuse and eating disorders were attempts to relieve or at least control these overwhelming feelings. The depression, on the other hand, was secondary to the substance abuse and eating disorders. In other words, she was depressed about how drugs and starving and purging had wrecked her life. This is not to deemphasize the extent of her very serious depression, which fueled her repeated suicide attempts. However, it seems to me that whereas she binged and purged and self-medicated with drugs and alcohol in order to deal with her symptoms of anxiety and depression, for Laura depression was not a precipitating or initial condition.

It was clear to some of her treatment providers, but not to me, that she had borderline personality disorder. How did this condition interact with the other symptoms and disorders? I'm still not sure. To me she appeared to have symptoms of borderline personality disorder only when she was high, which means that it wasn't a fundamental component of her illness. Maybe I just don't want to admit that she had a personality disorder. My own view is that the personality disorder classifications in *DSM-IV* are toxic because they are indictments of a person's whole self. There has to be a more humane way to describe people whose behavior and symptoms currently fall under these classifications.

The truly amazing part of Laura's story is that during this same period she received a master's degree in education and an early-childhood teaching credential from Mills College. She graduated in May 1994. She cherished the memory of that day, and we continue to do so. Our entire family, some extended family, and a few of her close friends were there. In the many pictures we took that day, Laura looks genuinely happy and proud. She was a fabulous, amazing preschool teacher and became the head teacher at a well-regarded university preschool. I visited her classroom a number of times, but I wish so much that I had spent more time watching her teach. She related to young children in such a loving, understanding, playful way. One of my favorite pictures of her was taken when, dressed as a witch for Halloween, she presided over her class of 3- and 4-year-olds in costumes. Laura had also clearly been well educated at Mills, knew a lot about what preschoolers needed, and had mastered many best-teaching practices. She loved teaching, and I'm sure her little students loved her. It was her saving grace.

Then in 1997 a new director took over at Laura's school, and she lost her job. At first I assumed it was because her physical appearance—she was literally skin and bones—was beginning to be of great concern. She was obviously very sick. (Incidentally, at one point my mother and sister tried to check into a hotel together and were denied. My mother assumes that the reason was that the desk clerk thought Laura had AIDS.) Although I never understood the full story, I do believe that the new director, who did not last long at the school, was very difficult and perhaps mentally ill herself. Laura's job loss was probably just a very unfortunate mistake. It precipitated a period of almost autistic concern with self-preservation. Because Laura was continuously in so much distress, she had always been preoccupied with her own emotional needs. It took me years to understand that behaviors I interpreted as selfish really reflected her continual concern with getting those needs met. I think this self-absorption is true of many people who are mentally ill, and it can certainly trigger angry responses from others who view it as selfishness.

It was at my beloved grandfather's funeral in March of 1997 that the extent of Laura's preoccupation became so apparent and made me extremely angry. Instead of letting my mother participate in the reception after her own father's funeral, my sister literally cornered my mother and flooded her with anxieties and concerns about her lost job and uncertain future. Laura also hounded my mother to make long-distance phone calls related to her job search. My mother arrived 2 hours late to the reception because she had been dealing with my sister's anxieties instead.

Somewhat ironically, because of my grandfather's death and the money my family inherited, my parents were able to pay for an expensive 6-month stay at Montecatini, a residential treatment facility just north of San Diego for girls and women with eating disorders. I had moved to Santa Monica, California, in 1996 in order to become a clinical psychology intern at the Neuropsychiatric Institute at UCLA. So I was fairly close by and able to help Laura check in to Montecatini during the summer of 1997. My mother was there as well. As usual, Laura had mixed feelings about being subjected, yet again, to the confinement and scrutiny of round-the-clock treatment. She was sassy and confrontational with the director of the program, and the director's cool but challenging and authoritative response to Laura was a joy to witness. It put Laura at ease, as well. In that moment I think we both believed that finally Laura would be understood and really helped. The house was sun-filled, lovely, and welcoming, too; it overlooked the grounds of a world-famous resort. I knew Montecatini was going to be a good place for her. She agreed to stay for 6 months in exchange for financial support from my parents when she was discharged. The deal was that if she left before the 6 months were up, she would be on her own.

The program worked wonders. I visited Laura a number of times during her stay there, and over time I saw a person emerging I had never seen before, or at least hadn't seen since we were children. I will never forget attending one of their group sessions in November, about 4 months into Laura's stay. In front of all of the other residents and with the help of the psychologists running the group, Laura and I actually had a truly reciprocal interaction. It only lasted a few moments, but that interaction brought to consciousness my experience as Laura's older sister. I talked about how my relationship with Laura had been hard for me because it was always about what she needed and wanted. It was always about me taking care of her or doing for her. What I wanted was a sister, an equal, a friend, rather than a dependent. It was during that interaction that I realized that for much of the past 20 years Laura's illness had robbed me of a sister, or at least a satisfying relationship with a sister.

Miraculously, Laura heard what I said. She was not defensive or angry. She was accepting, which was something I had never seen before and rarely saw again. In fact, during the next few months and for at least a short time after she left Montecatini and moved to Los Angeles, I had a real sister, and it was lovely. We went out to dinner, went shopping, and went to the movies. We went to church together. I cherish the memory of Thanksgiving 1997, a holiday that, given Laura's eating disorder, had typically been a nightmare. She was still at Montecatini but was allowed to come to Santa Monica overnight for the holiday. Laura was happy and calm. She ate a normal amount of food and didn't throw it up. I spent almost no time worrying about her. I was simply enjoying her company. It is the lack of tension—in her, in me, and between us—that I remember most about that Thanksgiving. The next day we went to the San Diego Zoo and had a great dinner (also worry- and conflict-free) at one of my favorite Mexican restaurants before I dropped her off at Montecatini.

Laura left the facility in January of 1998 and found an apartment in Los Angeles, in Westwood near UCLA. From the beginning something seemed amiss. Why did she want to share an apartment with two guys in college? They did seem nice enough, and it was good for Laura not to be alone, but it was weird, too. For a while things seemed as though they were going to work out. Laura's education and teaching experiences made her highly prized, especially among private schools in Los Angeles, although she had to explain where she had been the previous 6 months. She landed a good job teaching fourth grade at a Catholic school, and she was very excited about the opportunity. However, Laura seemed to have left Montecatini without any referrals to or connections with mental health service providers. My one complaint about her treatment there was the lack of discharge planning. She went from a very sheltered environment to a life without any kind of safety net except her family. I think this was true of the many inpatient and residential treatments that ultimately failed her. Laura needed to learn how to live in the real world and to tolerate the anxieties and challenges most people face daily without resorting to drugs or other self-destructive behavior. Her inpatient stays removed her from and protected her from the world but didn't adequately teach her the life skills she needed to deal with her anxiety and manage her symptoms in a constructive way on a day-to-day basis.

The more significant problem, though, was that shortly after she moved to Los Angeles, she met a man at an Alcoholics Anonymous meeting who either caused or was an accomplice to the chaos that ensued. He got her using again. He verbally and physically abused her, as he had previous girlfriends. His abuse of one of them had resulted in his incarceration. The thought of the ranting, angry messages he left on my answering machine for her still turns my stomach. He stole or helped Laura to spend the $13,000 she had saved (remember, she was a hoarder) on heroin in a matter of a few months. What was completely heartbreaking to me was that she really didn't think she deserved any better. My sister was so pretty and funny and kind and intelligent—how in the world did she develop the idea that she deserved a no-good criminal for a boyfriend? It was absolutely stunning to see how quickly Laura's life went from near normal to utter chaos. Needless to say, she was fired from her job after she stopped showing up.

It was as though she dived head first into an abyss that was even deeper than any into which she had sunk before. Part of her, it seems to me, needed the chaos. Her daily life had been constructed around dealing with emotional pain and mental illness. When that foundation was gone, she was driven to re-create it because it was the only life she knew how to live. Getting through each day the way we all do, by basically spending our time accomplishing some kind of work and caring for ourselves and for others, was just too difficult or too scary for her. I can't say she preferred the chaos, but it was familiar to her. I can't say she actively chose it, either, but she was driven toward it.

Just a note about Laura's boyfriend, whom I hold partly responsible for her death because I think it is quite possible that she would still be alive if she had never met him. He was seriously mentally ill himself. At a minimum he was an antisocial, paranoid, drug- and alcohol-abusing asshole (although "asshole" is not a mental illness). I wondered whether he was frankly psychotic and suspect he had schizoaffective disorder. Yet despite my clinical training and my own experiences with a mentally ill sister, I completely blamed him for the terror he introduced into Laura's life and mine. But then I think: He is one of five children. One of his brothers is a priest. I am sure his family grieves for him as we did for Laura. Although intellectually I can put his behavior into perspective, I still hate him. I often wished I had possessed the nerve to murder him, and I imagined shooting him the chest with a shotgun. I've never held a gun, though; perhaps I could have run him over with my car? Maybe poisoned him? Despite some effort to be understanding (although, I admit, not my best effort), I have little empathy for him. This upsets me because a major impetus for this chapter was the generation of empathy or at least sympathy for substance abusers and others with serious mental illness. If I can't feel sympathy for him, I wonder whether you'll feel any for Laura. The difference in their stories is that Laura was not knowingly and actively antisocial, aggressive, and destructive, as he was. Of course that makes her more deserving of sympathy than he. However, if his aggression and antisocial behavior were due to a mental illness, is he to blame for it? Professionally, I would like to say that he wasn't, but that is not how I feel.

So 1998 was a bad year, except for the fact that I defended my dissertation and finished graduate school. For various reasons, I didn't take a job right away, and I was very glad to have the time to try in vain to help my sister. Life with Laura that year was emergency after emergency. One of the saddest moments of my life was when I showed up at her apartment after she called me in a panic stating that she needed to be taken to a hospital. I don't know the word(s) to describe "far beyond simply intoxicated but not yet passed out," but that was the state she was in. Laura was tangled in sheets on her futon on the floor with her hair a mess and mascara smeared. Her sweatpants, which hung off her bony body, were on backward, and she was not wearing underwear. She was awake, but had a great deal of troubling making volitional movements. It was like she wasn't fully alive, but she was. It absolutely broke my heart. The remains of the biggest bottle of vodka I had ever seen were next to her futon. Apparently it had been delivered to her door, and she had paid for it with a bad check. I am still so, so angry at whoever made his living delivering lethal amounts of alcohol to peoples' homes, no questions asked. How on earth can that be legal? And if it is legal, it is completely unethical. Why doesn't that person just show up and murder his customers? That is essentially what he was doing.

On that day and others I took her to emergency rooms when she pleaded for help. I tried to keep her from her boyfriend, especially after he lit her futon on fire while she was sleeping in it. At this I was entirely unsuccessful. In fact, they ended up getting married during a drug-saturated trip to Las Vegas. Within a few days she had filed for divorce, but to my surprise there is no such thing as a quickie divorce in Los Angeles County (the process takes a minimum of 6 months). I spent time just sitting on the floor of my apartment crying, which I am not at all prone to do. I was utterly sick with worry. With help from friends I cleaned out her apartment and her storage areas after she had run off to Seattle with another drug addict. At least that one wasn't a paranoid criminal.

After she left for Seattle, I moved to Berkeley, California, where I live now. I came here to do a postdoc and now work as a research psychologist at UC Berkeley's Institute of Human Development. I never saw Laura in Seattle, but we phoned each other a lot and talked about my visiting, which was always contingent on her sobriety. Needless to say, I never visited. So except for those few hours before her life support machines were unplugged, I never saw her alive again after she left Los Angeles. A few days before she died she called me, and we had the best phone call I had experienced in months or even years. Laura was almost never at peace, but during this call she was palpably calm. I can't remember what we discussed, but I remember vividly how the phone call felt; Laura was not at all frantic or on edge. Although of course it didn't occur to me at the time, she may have known what was coming and was willing to leave her tortured, tormented life behind. The last thing I said to her was "I love you," and I truly felt it and meant it. I thank God for that phone call and for the opportunity to feel that way and to say those words.

LAURA'S IMPACT ON MY CAREER

The relation between experiences with a mentally ill family member and one's career choices is a theme that runs throughout the chapters of this book. Thus I would like to comment briefly on this issue. It would seem that the differences between Laura's development and mine would have inspired my current work, much of which involves the notion of resilience, which signifies positive adaptation or "doing well" among children at risk for developing psychopathology. As I have noted throughout this chapter, I often wonder about why Laura became ill and I did not. But her illness and our juxtaposed lives did not prompt this interest of mine.

First, resilience requires risk, and I don't believe that I have had major risks in my life (either inherited predispositions to substance abuse or family environmental ones). Furthermore, my interests in resilience, and in clinical psychology more generally, predate any real knowledge of Laura's illness. I chose to become a clinical psychologist during my junior year in college, inspired primarily by volunteer work with autistic and severely emotionally disturbed young children. At that point I still believed Laura was a troublesome little sister who partied too much. I had no idea she was a drug and alcohol abuser and did not think of her as mentally ill. However, it is probably not entirely coincidental that throughout my career I've been interested in explaining why one child becomes mentally ill and not another. That is certainly an obvious question that has been asked in regard to my sister and me, although as I've noted, my own personal history is not devoid of mental illness, either.

Relatedly, although Laura's illness did not consciously inspire my career choice or research pursuits, I do think the different developmental outcomes among my siblings are related to my interest in a well-accepted but poorly documented phenomenon in developmental psychology called "goodness-of-fit."[1] The idea essentially is that certain types of parenting work well for some children, whereas other approaches work better for other children. What matters, in this view, is the fit between parental behavior or style and the child's attributes, behavior, and temperament. It is remarkable to me how this idea, as sensible as it is, is so often overlooked in studies of parenting and child development. Typically, variations in parenting account for rather small (or at most moderate) effects on children's developmental outcomes. But these modest effects hide the true impact of parenting. The implication for me is that a particular parenting behavior or style has certain effects on some children and different effects on others, which may not be revealed when child differences are not considered. Consequently, through my 15 years of psychological research, I have been interested in and have tried to directly investigate this issue, typically through analysis of how parent and child factors (e.g., maternal responsiveness and child negative emotionality) work together to explain differences in developmental outcomes.

Finally, when I was working as a therapist (which I haven't done in almost 8 years), there certainly were times when my personal experiences with mental illness enhanced my empathy for my clients and their families. In graduate school I was taught to avoid disclosing personal information in a therapeutic relationship, but at least one time I broke this rule and was very glad I did. I was working with adolescent girls on the eating-disorders inpatient unit at UCLA. One girl, whose primary diagnosis was bulimia, worked very hard for months to appear that she was complying with treatment guidelines regarding eating and exercise, but even in the hospital, she was not (e.g., she was exercising quietly in her room in the middle of the night). Her stepmother was growing increasingly angry at her stepdaughter's covert resistance to treatment. The stepmother saw me as the girl's ally and also was clearly frustrated with me, too. She asked me point blank if I'd ever had to deal personally with someone like her stepdaughter, and I responded with an authoritative "yes." I told her briefly about my sister and my firsthand knowledge of frustration and anger toward a family member with an eating disorder. The stepmother then seemed to abandon her "us" (the girl's father and her) versus "them" (the daughter and me) mentality. I think this minor disclosure on my part was a key move because it saved my relationship with the stepmother and helped to keep her invested in her stepdaughter's treatment. This was so important because successful therapy with children and adolescents almost always involves working closely with their parents. This is just one example of how my personal experiences with mental illness probably increased my effectiveness as a therapist.

WHAT LAURA'S LIFE HAS TAUGHT ME ABOUT ILLNESS, CHOICE, AND SHAME

Laura's life was about so much more than substance abuse. But a cocaine binge ultimately killed her. So I begin this section with my thoughts on the status of substance abuse and dependence as forms of mental illness. I think it is hard for many people, even some well-educated and well-trained mental health professionals, to accept them as such. Instead, many consider substance abuse or dependence to be a character flaw, a lack of strength, or a moral corruption. There was absolutely nothing defective about my sister's character or will. Laura was a completely moral and caring person. She was a beloved preschool teacher. She *always* tried to do the right thing. She studied and worked hard. She often looked to God to help her. She wanted desperately to be faithful and religious, although I don't think that fire was ever really lighted in her heart.

So why did Laura continue drinking and doing drugs? Why couldn't or didn't she stop? It was because she was *ill*. Her brain, a physical organ, did not function healthfully. In this way, mental illnesses are just like the physical illnesses. When someone has cancer and is tired, irritable, in pain, worried, and afraid, does anyone ask him or her to stop having cancer because it is causing problems for people around them? Obviously they don't, in part because it would be incredibly unsympathetic but more so because it is impossible to will oneself well. But this is how people with serious substance abuse problems are treated every day. They are asked, often angrily, to stop being ill. Over and over again I desperately, impatiently asked my sister to "just stop," or at least I wished she would stop using even if I didn't make this silly demand of her directly. "Just say no" (yeah, right, Nancy) seems so simple. Couldn't users cure themselves simply by refusing to put substances in their bodies, substances that made them crazy and ruined their lives? Many of us do recognize how difficult this would be for any addict, but we still believe that the solution is simple. Yet for Laura, despite the fact that drugs and alcohol certainly perpetuated her problems, sobriety and getting clean—although certainly helpful—would not have been a cure. Even when she wasn't using she was quite ill, although remarkably well functioning at times, too.

Laura's mental illness was deeply rooted in her emotional and biological makeup. In particular, I believe that Laura inherited a disposition to metabolize alcohol (and drugs) in a way that most people, including me, did not. She felt very good when she drank and rarely felt especially bad the next day. Or perhaps she did get hung over, but in some way it didn't bother her. I love to drink. But the buzz I get from a couple of drinks is pleasant at best, and when I drink more than that I pay for it with a hangover the next day. I *hate* being hung over, and I thank God for this. I strongly believe that Laura inherited a biological disposition to be an alcoholic (not a surprise given the history of alcoholism or heavy drinking on both sides of my family), and my good fortune was that I did not.[2] If I had been made the way Laura was, I certainly might have traveled the same path she did. Furthermore, given that I was a boring goody two-shoes in middle and high school, my brain had 5 or 6 more years than Laura's did to develop normally, protected from the seriously damaging influence of early drug and alcohol exposure. Even without a biological disposition apparently as strong as hers was, I might have become a substance abuser myself if I had started early enough.

Clearly, Laura's illness was partly rooted in her biological makeup. So did she really have the choice to stop using, however difficult that would have been given her mental illness and its biological basis? I knew that Laura's recovery was up to her. I wanted desperately for her to *choose* to be well, but ultimately I came to the decision that the choice was not one she had the power to make. Symptomatic behaviors of those with mental illness are not volitional. If she could have chosen to be clean and sober, she would have been. How would anyone in her right mind choose to live as she did? Refraining from using drugs and alcohol was either not a choice for her or she was not of "right mind," which also implies that she did not have the capability to choose. I remember learning in graduate school about a study in which rats were taught to operate devices through which they could stimulate the dopamine pathway in the brain now believed to be responsible for the positive, pleasurable effects of drug use. They were given opportunities to eat and procreate but did not. Some rats continued to self-stimulate the rewarding neural pathway instead of eating until they died of starvation.[3] Obviously, animal behavior does not precisely parallel human behavior, but I found this finding quite compelling. Because the stimulation of this reward system in the brain is overwhelmingly reinforcing, drug addicts may essentially be robbed of their choice to stop stimulating it.

I also think about the bad habits and "addictions" many of us have. Isn't there something, a food or a person or an activity perhaps, that it is very hard for you to resist? Something you feel biologically wired or driven to want? I certainly have cravings of this sort that make me rather miserable, because they are always for things I shouldn't have. From my limited knowledge of behavioral psychopharmacology, I know that people addicted to drugs, especially crack or heroin or alcohol (three of my sister's favorites), have to deal with these cravings on an unimaginable scale because of the neurophysiological changes induced by substance use. I, literally, can barely resist premium ice cream and good quality chocolate. Remembering how my addictions, silly in comparison, can nevertheless be impairing helps me to be empathic with those who are struggling with alcohol and/or drug addictions, which generate cravings and have reinforcing powers on a scale far beyond anything most of us have ever felt or experienced.

Addicts are constantly blamed for choosing destructive behavior, but I argue that they shouldn't be because they suffer from a pathology or illness of the brain. However, I do struggle when attempting to embrace this idea, because I believe in personal responsibility, and I often make internal, if not also stable and global, attributions for many of my own undesirable behaviors. In other words, I often not only blame myself for specific things I've done wrong, but I also interpret my negative behaviors as reflecting general, enduring personal faults. But I try not to make these types of attributions for others' behaviors, especially those who are mentally ill. People who are mentally ill should not be blamed for their problematic behavior. I don't mean that continued substance abuse should be excused or condoned. Some abusers do stop and become permanently clean and sober, which leads me to believe that this is a reasonable goal for many.

But accepting responsibility for one's behavior and working to improve it are different from accepting and internalizing blame for such behavior. My 4-year-old daughter is working on this subtle distinction. When she accidentally does something wrong (e.g., kicks me under the dinner table, knocks over her brother's block tower), she believes that the "I didn't do it on purpose" excuse absolves her. I try to explain that yes, she did not mean to kick me or knock over the blocks and that she should not be blamed for a bad intention, but she is still responsible for her actions. Obviously, I have not yet figured out how to explain this distinction to a 4-year-old, but I trust that over time she will get the idea.

What I perceive to be a fine line between blame and responsibility is the death knell for many suffering from addiction. Addicts need to take responsibility for their recovery, but they should not be blamed for their illness, if for no other reason than that blame is pointless and destructive. Blame generates shame, and my sister was incredibly ashamed of her behavior. At times she literally seemed crushed by the weight of her shame. At one point when we were both living in Los Angeles, I picked Laura up at the airport (I can't remember where she had been). She had obviously been drinking and said that the man sitting next to her had bought her a drink, which is entirely plausible given how pretty and friendly Laura was. But as she explained this to me, she began quietly crying. As we sat on the filthy sidewalk outside of LAX's Terminal 1, she looked up at me with a quivering lip and, like a terrified small child, whimpered, "I need help." Her shame, and her fear and desperation, were so strong they almost seemed to physically exist in the space between us. I think this was another of the other saddest moments of my life. From the airport we called my mother in North Carolina and began arrangements for another stay at Mountain Vista Farm in Sonoma County.

I was first asked to write this chapter just 2 years after Laura died. I hesitated to accept the offer and did not commit to and begin writing for 3 more years, in part because Laura would have objected, angrily, to having her life displayed for all to see. Ultimately, however, I came to believe that if this chapter and the others in this book increase empathy for people with serious mental illness, especially substance abusers, the posthumous shame it would have caused her will be outweighed by the good work accomplished by the sharing of her story. Despite the difficulty she would have had with this chapter, I know that Laura would have come to the same conclusion because she was a genuinely caring, generous person and was always willing to help anyone. I began to write only when I came to this realization and knew that Laura would have agreed to share her story in the hope that it might positively influence how people afflicted with mental illness are viewed and treated.

There were many moments when a look on Laura's face or a tear in her eye gave me a window into how she felt about herself. Knowing that someone I loved so much hated herself so passionately was terribly distressing to me. I wanted so much for Laura to see herself as her family and friends did. I wanted her to see herself as the caring, funny, beautiful person she was. I wanted her to believe that she was worthy of help and deserving of a better life. But instead she internalized the hatred and intolerance we as a society feel toward substance abusers. To a large degree that shame served to perpetuate her substance abuse. The disgust and self-hatred that came from her repeated failures to stop using and make herself well were almost unbearable for her. More drugs and alcohol (and more binging and purging) relieved some of that pain, but continuing to use and to binge and purge made her all the more ashamed. It was a terrible, vicious cycle. If we as a society could stop ostracizing, stigmatizing, and angrily blaming substance abusers for being ill—something I don't know if I ever truly accomplished with my own sister—perhaps this particular causal link between shame and perpetuated substance abuse could be broken.

ACKNOWLEDGMENTS

I want to thank Mike Larkin, Monica Garcia, and Steve Hinshaw for providing me with very thoughtful and helpful feedback on this chapter, the writing of which was a journey in and of itself.

NOTES

1. Thomas, A., Chess, S., & Birch, H. G. (1968). *Temperament and behavior disorders in children.* New York: New York University Press.

2. Eng, M. Y., Schuckit, M. A., & Smith, T. L. (2005). The level of response to alcohol in daughters of alcoholics and controls. *Drug and Alcohol Dependence, 79,* 83–93.

3. Routtenberg, A. (1964). Self-starvation caused by "feeding-center" stimulation. *American Psychologist, 19,* 502–507.

5 In My Voice: Speaking Out About Mental Health and Stigma

Jeffrey Liew

FINDING A VOICE

I entered this world knowing how it felt to be alone and misunderstood. Born with a cleft palate, I had corrective surgery shortly after my first birthday. I do not remember many details from this traumatic event; perhaps I was too young—and perhaps our minds protect us from what we are not ready to handle. After the operation, I remained at the hospital for several days. My parents visited, but when evening came and visiting hours were over, they had to leave me. I imagine that I must have felt alone in darkness. After the corrective surgery, as I gained expressive language, I spoke with a minor impediment. Many people found that it took extra effort to understand me. To avoid unusual reactions or ridicule, I often kept silent as a young child. With treatment and intervention, my speech improved, but I had already known the pain and shame associated with making my voice heard. So I remained silent. It took years before I realized the distinct value of speaking in my voice rather than echoing the voices of everyone else.

With my voice, I now speak of my mother's experiences with mood disorder. I am honored that she has granted me permission to speak for her in hopes that we will live in a society in which individuals touched by mental illness could share their experiences without shame and be heard with compassion and understanding.

BRAVING A WHOLE NEW WORLD

I was 6 years old when my mother gave birth to my sister. My baby sister ushered in a world of change within our home. But the world outside the walls of our home soon began changing, as well. One year later, our family moved from Hong Kong to the United States. In addition to caring for my baby sister, my parents busily prepared for our major migration. We were uprooting and starting over. Imagining myself boarding an airplane and jetting across the world for the very first time, I was bursting with excitement. My father's mother (my grandmother) lived in Brooklyn, and she periodically sent packages with audio-tapes and photographs. On the tapes my grandmother described how we would go pick big red apples from tall trees in gigantic green orchards near Long Island. Luckily, she sent photographs, because such images were beyond the imagination of a child who knew only the hustle and bustle of an industrial city such as Hong Kong.

My grandmother also cautioned us about the extreme winters in New York. Accustomed to living in the subtropical climate of Hong Kong, my mother preferred to avoid the cold of New York by settling in San Francisco. Famous for the magnificent Golden Gate Bridge, San Francisco was equally well known for earthquakes, fog, and rain. However, I could never have foreseen that my family would be shaken to the core and weather the darkest of storms.

Without familial or social connections in the Bay Area, my father luckily found work as a waiter in Chinatown. As he toiled tirelessly until midnight, my mother juggled child-rearing and household duties. I remember her as able to handle everything. With my baby sister swaddled on her back and towing heavy bags full of groceries in both hands, my mother would lead my younger brother and me home from school. After trekking home, she always had after-school snacks prepared for us and would tutor us on homework for about 2 hours.

She always kept a Chinese-English dictionary nearby because her English was proficient but not fluent. After homework, my brother and I were allowed to watch our favorite television shows while a flurry of sounds filled our home. Chopping, the clanging of pots and pans, and hot oil exploding and crackling in the wok alerted us that we would soon need to turn off the television for dinner. My father's work schedule rarely allowed us to have dinner as an entire family. When my father was home, he was in desperate need of rest.

THE SCREAM: FIRST EPISODE OF MAJOR DEPRESSION

Managing two rambunctious sons and a baby daughter in a foreign land must have been lonely and frustrating. On the surface, my mother was exhausted by the stress of family life and the transition to a new environment. Although that was part of the problem, explanations of life's complexities are rarely as simple as they appear on the surface. Only 8 years old, I was blind to the internal turmoil broiling within her. But even at that age, I noticed that she was no longer herself. Instead of her usual strong and independent self, she displayed a lethargic, helpless, and hopeless side that I had never seen. One morning, I walked into the kitchen and noticed my father quietly hiding the knives and cleaver. How can Mom cook without her knives and cleaver, I wondered. Although my father was hesitant to alarm me, I sensed something was seriously wrong.

Later that afternoon, my 2-year-old sister napped while my brother and I watched our favorite television shows, just like any other day. After the show ended, I realized that nearly half an hour had passed since I had seen or heard from my mother. The usual sounds of chopping, pots clanging, and oil popping were missing. Instead, silence filled the home. Feeling panicked, I feverishly searched the rooms of the house. With no sign of my mother, I told my brother to stay with my sister while I frantically hurried down to the basement.

When I found my mother, I felt relieved. I saw her atop a chair, as she tied a rope around one of the wooden beams that ran across the ceiling of the basement. Suddenly, my relief at finding her turned into panic. In a matter-of-fact tone, my mother asked, "What would you do if I hung myself?" Immediately, I shouted for my brother to hurry downstairs. My mother began to position the noose near her chin and neck. Without a second to waste, I ordered my brother to help me grab our mother's legs and to lift so we could support her weight. Knowing that we could not shoulder her weight for long, we started screaming for help.

Afraid that our noise would wake and frighten my sister, our mother asked us to stop. She cared about and thought of her children even in her darkest moments.

Instantaneously, I knew what I had to do. I screamed louder and louder until my mother shifted her weight onto the chair and then got her feet on solid ground.

After this incident, my grandmother moved from New York to live with us. Ironically, my grandmother's arrival signaled my mother's departure. My father told me that he was taking a short leave from work to go back to Hong Kong with our mother. I was sheltered from much of the chaos and details, leaving me with much uncertainty. I only knew that my parents were gone. Without our mother to pick us up after school, my brother and I now walked alone. Walking to and from school during days with heavy rain, I felt as if a mighty force was casting stones from the sky on me.

My siblings and I were careful to be well behaved for our grandmother so that my father would not need to worry about us. I knew that he had enough concerns with my mother. My grandmother had immigrated to the United States when I turned 1 year old, and I knew her only through photos, phone calls, and audiotapes. During her stay, she taught me to do household chores, such as cooking, cleaning, laundry, and sewing, so that I could take care of myself. To this day, I use those life skills; I will always be grateful.

Although my grandmother was there to help, I also knew that I was partially responsible for my younger siblings. Not even 9 years old, I felt as if I were a miniature adult. After seeing my mother standing atop a chair with a noose in her hand, I felt incredibly numb and confused. I blocked most of these images and emotions; letting them in would be too threatening, especially when I was left with little or no information on what was now happening with my mother.

Shutting out traumatic events was not overly difficult. I learned it well when I was very young, after my corrective surgery for my cleft palate. But the price was never fully processing the fact that my mother was gone. My parents' disappearance left me feeling rejected. Evenings were the worst. As I lay in bed, questions echoed within me. Why did they not take us back to Hong Kong? How could they leave us here with grandma? I felt alone in darkness.

STICKS AND STONES: SHAMING LIES AND GOSSIP

After spending about 6 months in Hong Kong, my father returned without my mother. I was happy that he returned, but life was not the same. For the next 2 years, my brother and I continued walking to school alone. Because my father worked late into the evenings, our grandmother became our surrogate mother. She attended teacher-parent meetings and open houses at school. I felt ashamed because I was different from most of my peers. Fortunately, I had an understanding teacher and a small group of good friends who helped me adjust at school.

Among my friends were three brothers who lived in a neighboring home. After school or on weekends, we often played football or rode our bikes. One day during our games, one of the boys asked us where our mother was. Before we could respond, the youngest of the brothers said, "Your mother was talking crazy, and the police took her away." Embarrassed and hurt, I instantly suppressed the urge to punch him.

As a child, I did not know that my friend was not intentionally being insensitive. Reflecting on this experience, I wonder how he got the idea that my mother was "crazy," taken away by the police. Were people gossiping and spreading lies and half-truths about her? Is the image of a person suffering from mental illness that of someone in a straightjacket, taken away by the police while kicking and screaming? As a 9-year-old, I felt the bruising slap as I came face-to-face with how society perceives and stigmatizes individuals suffering from mental illness.

OUT OF SIGHT BUT NOT OUT OF MIND: SEPARATION, SECRECY, AND SUSPICION

Two years had passed since our mother vanished from our lives. My father and grandmother veiled most of the details about our mother's condition, fueling uncertainty and anxiety. Where was she? How was she doing? Is she coming back?

During late evenings when my father was working, my grandmother sometimes spoke with relatives on the phone after my siblings and I had gone to bed. Despite her attempts to keep her voice low, her whispers often escaped into the bedrooms like balloons on strings, floating away from the weakening grasps of children. Sounds traveled especially well from one room to another through the heater vents. As I quietly tiptoed out of bed to kneel next to the vent, I heard the words "electricity" and "shock." In the darkness of my bedroom, I felt chills as I envisioned my mother enduring electroconvulsive therapy (ECT).

With my mother gone for 3 years by this time, I felt disappointed that my father had not brought her home. As a child, I was not ready to understand how my father must have felt. In retrospect, I can only imagine the pain, longing, and hardships that he endured as he forged ahead with three young children without the support of his wife. But at the bleakest moment, my aunt called from Hong Kong to give us news. Like sunlight breaking through the usual haze and fog of an early morning in San Francisco, we heard that my mother was well enough to return home.

THE REUNION: WOULD I REMEMBER HER FACE?

On the day that I would see my mother again, I hoped her return would offer answers to the questions that had haunted me for the past few years. She was scheduled to arrive back in the United States in the morning, when I would still be at school. That day, my attention drifted from my lessons to scenes of reuniting with her. The ringing of the school bell knocked me back to reality. Walking home with my brother, each step intensified the anxiety within me. It had taken me nearly 3 years to forget that I was living without her; how long would it take to remember how to live with her? Would I recognize her face? Equally important, would she remember and know me? No matter how slowly I walked to buy myself time to prepare, I eventually arrived home. Climbing the stairs of the house, I noticed the doorknob turning and the door cracking ajar. Our thumping footsteps must have alerted her. The door swung open to reveal my mother standing in the doorway. I immediately noticed her hair. Three years ago, she had had long, straight hair. Her hair was short and curly now. "Don't you remember your own mother?" she joked. I nodded silently. "I haven't seen you for so long, and you two are so tall now," she continued with a smile.

To ease the tension, our mother told us that she had brought us some gifts. Hearing this news, my brother jumped up and down. As the oldest child, I chose to curb my enthusiasm, but I felt excited nonetheless. Our mother went to an adjacent room and returned with new backpacks, pencil cases, and handheld electronic games for us. We were most thrilled with the games. We immediately popped the batteries into them and began playing. Meanwhile, our mother

Liew family (1990); Jeff at far left

brought out some candies and snacks for us. Having snacks after school with my mother reminded me of how things had been.

When my mother had returned to Hong Kong, my sister was a babbling toddler. Now, my sister was 5 years old and finishing preschool. While my brother and I played with our video games, I heard my mother talking and playing with my sister. Her lively and cheerful demeanor reminded me of how nurturing and warm she had been before her depression. Amidst our reunion, I noticed my father watching us with a faint smile. Toiling for years at the restaurant, my father had finally struggled his way to being a manager, giving us more time as a family. For 3 years, I had longed for such moments when we could truly be together. I deeply treasured common, everyday events such as family dinners that many people take for granted.

CULTURE AND THE MEANING OF HELP-SEEKING

Although my mother appeared much better, she was still not fully recovered from her depression. Despite her reluctance to expose her illness to those outside the family, my father convinced her to seek professional help. Cultural beliefs were a major reason that my mother (Chinese and an immigrant) resisted seeking professional help. Most important, my mother and father did not have a clear understanding of depression. Certainly, they did not acknowledge severe depression as a serious mental illness. Their misinformation was also indicated by their belief (perpetuated by many in the Chinese community) that eating healthy foods and taking herbal remedies could cure depression. As a child, I, too, sensed that depression was temporary and that a person could overcome depression with a strong will and conviction.

Fortunately, such home remedies and folk assumptions were balanced with help from professionals. My father sought help for my mother at a low-cost community health clinic with a Chinese-speaking psychotherapist. An entirely Western concept, therapy was foreign and even antithetical to my mother's beliefs. Most traditional Chinese people are uncomfortable sharing private or familial information with people outside the family. Because individuals afflicted with mental illness are stigmatized, seeking professional help would reflect poorly, bringing shame to self and family.

I met her psychotherapist once after their sessions. In somewhat broken Chinese, she struggled in translating to my father that my mother was doing well. I instantly recognized that language was one of the barriers that kept my mother from truly connecting with her; she probably saw her therapist as an "outsider." The guilt and shame of leaking deeply personal or private information to such an outsider made it easy for my mother to abruptly terminate treatment after only a few sessions.

Although my mother had cut short her treatment, her condition appeared to improve. At the very least, seeking treatment meant that she had confronted the fact that she suffered from mood disorder. In addition, the responsibilities of motherhood gently nudged her toward independence and confidence. After my sister entered kindergarten, my mother decided that it was time to reenter the work force. Despite our family's limited budget, my mother worked hard to arrange for after-school activities and supervision. A babysitter cared for my sister, while my brother and I participated in educational, sports, or musical activities. Doing so freed our mother to pursue her goals.

Applying for jobs was a major step forward in my mother's recovery process. At the same time, it exposed her to risks of disappointment, rejection, and stress. Was she ready to handle it? After several interviews, she found part-time work operating a photocopying shop independently. She enjoyed the autonomy, and her naturally gregarious personality helped her to easily make friends with the neighborhood customers.

After settling into her job, she decided to enroll in an English course, designed for immigrants, at the local community college. In addition to improving her English skills, the course gave her a chance to connect with other immigrants. In the evenings, my mother enjoyed talking with her classmates for hours on the telephone. At the end of the semester, she brought my siblings and me to a holiday party to meet her classmates. At that age, I thought of school as a place for children or teenagers. My mother changed my misconception by showing me that education is a lifelong process. Admittedly, I felt embarrassed as she introduced me to her classmates and teacher, but I was thrilled to see that she had a supportive group of friends. Afterward, she attended additional English classes and some computer courses. She had such enthusiasm and connectedness that I wondered whether her teachers and classmates could have guessed that she had recently battled severe depression.

With no obvious signs of relapse after many months, my mother appeared fully recovered from depression. She worked particularly hard at providing us with enriched educational and recreational experiences. Perhaps she was compensating for not being available during her illness; perhaps she was just showing us what her depression had previously veiled. All I knew was that she was an incredibly dedicated and caring mother. If we ever experienced problems at school, she advocated for us by meeting with our teachers to propose and find alternatives and solutions.

For several years, I was in a bilingual classroom. However, there was a lag in my transition, and I was falling behind in my course work. My mother grew concerned and hired a private tutor. Despite working tirelessly for low wages, my parents never hesitated to invest in their children's education. Seeing how committed my parents were helped reduce my anxieties and insecurities that lingered from times that they had been gone.

THE UGLY FACES OF INSECURITY AND INADEQUACY: GOOD ENOUGH IS NOT GOOD ENOUGH

After my mother's condition stabilized, some sense of normalcy returned for my family. I felt relieved at not having to try so hard to block out the vivid images of my mother's attempted suicide. Perhaps, more accurately, their powers to intrude on my consciousness were waning. Nonetheless, those early experiences of witnessing my mother's depressive episodes changed me forever. As the oldest child, I felt deeply obligated to make things perfect for my family at a time when everything appeared so imperfect. Living with a depressed parent, I learned empathy and sympathy for others who were suffering or were in need. When my parents were gone, I felt deeply responsible for my siblings. Over time, I began caring for everyone else except myself.

Entering early adolescence, I finally felt as if my family could pass as "normal." But the rumors and gossip about my mother's depression and institutionalization still echoed within me. "Saving face" is an extremely important concept and social custom in traditional Chinese culture, related to social perceptions of a person's status or prestige in the community. To save face, people should not embarrass themselves or their families. Consistent with such values, I hid the fact that my mother suffered from depression.

By the time I reached high school, I became accustomed to working incredibly hard to excel in a variety of activities. If I earned good grades and won awards for art, music, or athletic activities, perhaps I could disguise how imperfect my family once was. I wanted to show others and myself that we were, if not perfect, at the very least "normal."

During my late adolescence, my mother appeared fully recovered from depression, and I shifted my attention from the brokenness of her life to mine. My adolescent years felt chaotic. When it came time to consider college applications, I felt lost, because my parents knew little about the American educational system. When my high school career counselor advised that my grades were good but that additional extracurricular activities would enhance my applications, I felt as thought I were not quite good enough.

The loneliness and shame that I experienced from my mother's mental illness continued shadowing me. Anticipating college applications, I engineered a schedule that I thought would prove I was in fact "good enough." A typical school day felt incredibly packed as I rushed to choral practice 1 hour before classes even officially started. How else could I fit everything into a single day? During lunchtime, I took only 15 minutes to eat so that I could squeeze in music rehearsals or meetings of social clubs and organizations.

After school, I trained for and competed on the high school cross-country or the track and field teams. Studies and homework were frantically completed before dinner, followed by an hour of rest so I could digest the food before rushing off to private gymnastics training. During workouts, I cycled through about 1 1/2 to 2 hours of bending, stretching, contorting, and somersaulting to sculpt my already exhausted body. Workouts ended around 9 o'clock, when I waited for the bus to return home. Before crashing into bed, I completed studies or homework that I hadn't finished earlier.

Waking up in the mornings, I would lay motionless in bed with sensations of soreness and pain saturating my battered body. The slightest shifts or movements triggered sharp aches. But I had become good at enduring pain. And, with only piano lessons on Saturdays and church activities on Sundays, I had the weekends reserved for recuperating and resting.

CROSSING THE BRIDGE: TRANSITION TO COLLEGE AND ADULTHOOD

Both despite and because of my outrageously imbalanced lifestyle, I won several academic scholarships and awards during my final year of high school. I was relieved that I was accepted into my first-choice college, the University of California, Berkeley. My parents didn't know much about American universities, but they knew two things about Berkeley. First, they knew that it was only across the Oakland Bay Bridge from San Francisco and were thrilled that I would be near them. Second, they knew that Berkeley is renowned as one of the best public universities nationally and internationally. To this date, I cannot recall feeling as ecstatic about any news I had ever received as I was the moment I discovered that I would be going to Berkeley.

Heading to one of my first courses at the university, I fought through a sea of students as I found my way to the lecture hall. Getting a little lost along the way, I entered the building about 5 or 10 minutes late and found an auditorium filled with nearly 500 students. With all seats filled, I found a spot on the floor and sat in the aisle of the auditorium, along with a swarm of other students. The room was so enormous that the professor spoke with a microphone. The professor asked us to look to our left and right, warning us that more seats would be available after a few weeks when many of us would drop out. The auditorium was silenced. Seconds later, silence swelled into rumblings as students began feeling tense and wary.

Amidst the furious pace of assignments and exams, I was unprepared for university life but had little time to learn to adjust. My mind was flooded with so much information that I barely knew why or what I was studying. I was uninterested in my premedical courses, but my parents had made it clear that they wanted me to become a doctor, and I did not want to disappoint them. Miraculously, I survived my first semester of college despite very average academic performances amidst an anything-but-average student body.

THE NIGHT A BULLET WAS FIRED INTO MY FACE

Performing progressively worse with each semester, I wondered if I belonged at the university. During my fourth semester, my most dreaded course was organic chemistry. I was on the verge of failing the course, and everything appeared meaningless as I struggled to memorize rather than to understand. As the final exam approached, I was sleep deprived and overdosing on coffee, which left me feeling constantly jittery and anxious. On the last night before the final exam, I desperately crammed and memorized information that appeared disconnected and incoherent. I no longer cared whether I was learning; I only wanted to pass the course.

Exhausted, I realized that I had 4 hours before my final exam. I felt that it was useless cramming any longer, so I napped briefly to be refreshed before the exam. I woke screaming, with the image of a gun pointed at me, a bullet fired into my face. I rarely had nightmares, so this really disturbed me. Heading into the exam, I hoped to pass the course after spending so many hours memorizing facts. After the exam, I was relieved. It was over.

The end of the semester marked the beginning of winter vacation. I was glad to escape the university environment but ashamed to face my parents. After being silent and moody for days, I eventually disclosed to my parents that I had probably failed one course. My parents were understanding but encouraged me to continue pursuing premedical courses. "Just try your best and work harder," my mother consoled me. "Keep trying and work harder," my father advised.

There is something about the phenomenon of actually seeing something that forever leaves a mark on you. The day that I witnessed my failing grade printed on my transcript was the day that I felt officially branded as a failure. When spring semester started, I returned to the academic world feeling stupid and worthless. I felt that I didn't belong, but I mustered enough effort to repeat and pass my organic chemistry course. Despite running on the last traces of faith within me, I refused to give up on myself.

Such a last-ditch effort left me emotionally bankrupt. It took a long time, but I finally realized that I could no longer continue traveling down a path only to end up at a place where I never wanted or was meant to be. In my bedroom in my apartment, I sat alone on the floor in darkness. All I wanted was to sit silently with the lights off, hoping I could somehow fade and disappear into the darkness. As a child, I was known as a relatively fast runner. As an adult, I knew I could never escape myself, no matter how fast or far I ran. I wept quietly but aloud, breaking the deafening silence within me. Crying was not something I did easily. For years, I was afraid I had become so numb that I had forgotten how to cry. Growing up without my parents for a period of time during my mother's depressive episode, I was often stoic. Throughout my childhood and youth, I wished that I could become a mechanical robot, because humans have emotions and could feel pain.

I felt the stinging, yet healing sensations in my past wounds. I resisted wiping my eyes so I could feel the tears stream down my face to my lips. I wanted to taste the salty waters that would wash away the years of silence and pain. Loosening the grasp of my childhood patterns that had helped me survive thus far, I was afraid but finally ready to look at myself, scars exposed. I knew that I had to take control of my life, and part of that meant taking control of my education. I decided to pursue a career in psychology, a field of my own choosing. Although my parents saw psychology as impractical, the mission and philosophy behind psychology resonated with my life experiences and goals.

BLINDSIDED BY PERFECTIONISM AND PANIC

Earlier in my life, I had learned to cope with the chaos and brokenness of my life by trying to make myself and my environment appear in control or "normal." I blamed myself for messing up the first 2 years of college. Now that I was pursuing a major of my choosing, I felt that I had to redeem myself by proving to myself and to my parents that I made a good decision. I relied on my old habits, orchestrating an array of academic and extracurricular activities that bound me to a rigid schedule. I exercised religiously as an outlet for the anxious energies that were pent up. I also volunteered with several campus and community organizations. By such immersion, I thought I was grounding myself. I wanted predictability or control in my life, even if it was only an illusion.

As I pressed forward with my rigid routine of activities, I crashed into a roadblock. On a seemingly typical morning, as I fought my way across campus through a swarm of students, out of nowhere I was blindsided. It took me some time before I realized that I was struck by panic. Strangers' eyes immediately felt like daggers targeting and darting at me. My heart pounded as beads of sweat formed and felt like boulders rolling down my forehead. Heat spread like wildfire through my face. I worried how flushed my face must have looked to bystanders. I felt as though I was being choked and suffocated but dared not gasp for air. To minimize any movements that might attract attention, I tensed my muscles so tightly that I was in excruciating pain.

Soon, similar panic attacks struck me in the middle of lectures in class, while reading at a coffee shop, or when I was in public places such as a store or restaurant. I was constantly vigilant as I anticipated the next panic attack. The anxiety and wariness of anticipating the next panic attack were worse than enduring the attack itself.

My fear of being labeled as "crazy" kept me silent and only exacerbated my anxiety. The more I bottled up my anxieties, the more they rebelled to be set free. On my way to class one day, I noticed a neon-colored flier on a bulletin board in the hallway of the psychology department advertising counseling services for students at the health clinic. I quickly ripped the flier off the board and stuffed in it my backpack before anyone saw me. When I got home after classes, I took the crumpled flier and tossed it into the trash bin, annoyed that I had wasted my time taking it. The next morning, I saw the neon-colored flier peeking out of the trash container. Opening it up, I saw big bold letters spelling the "Stressed?" at the top of the flier. My answer was an emphatic "yes."

But why would I seek counseling services from the student health clinic? Coming from an immigrant Chinese family, I felt particularly conflicted about sharing or entrusting personal and familial information with strangers. Most important, I resisted seeking help because I did not want to reveal or admit what I perceived as my vulnerabilities and imperfections to myself, much less anyone else.

Somehow I had mislearned that only crazy, strange, or weak people sought counseling or mental health services. But no matter how hard I tried, I could not "will" myself out of my panic attacks. My emotions continued to disrupt even the simplest daily events. Seeing no end to suffering alone, I eventually made an initial appointment at the student health clinic. Walking to the clinic for my intake visit, I felt nervous because I had no idea of what to expect.

After this visit, I met with a psychotherapist, who helped me learn ways to alleviate my distress, panic, and anxieties over five brief sessions. For example, I learned muscle relaxation, breathing, and visualization techniques. I also learned to identify specific environmental triggers that generally preceded my anxieties. By doing so, I learned how to interrupt the sequential pathway that led to my attacks. I felt empowered, knowing that I could consciously disassociate my feelings from those triggers. I also learned cognitive-behavioral techniques that helped minimize the intensity and duration of my distress. With practice, the attacks subsided. After my emotions were in balance, I was in a position to explore the issues underlying my anxieties. Working through such issues, I was informed by, rather than enslaved to, my past experiences and the emotions associated with them.

PURSUING A CAREER IN PSYCHOLOGY

I was now able to invest my attention and energies toward academic and research activities. With my academic record already blemished, I struggled to complete my bachelor's degree with respectable grades to have any chance at continuing on with graduate studies. At the same time, I knew that my parents were unenthusiastic about the social sciences. If I listened carefully, I could still hear their voices echoing that fields such as medicine, law, or business were legitimate, practical, and successful careers to pursue. I felt like a "bad son" when I chose to pursue a career in psychology. The lonely and abandoned part of me hungered for my parents' approval, but the hurt and angry part of me wanted to rebel and prove that I could succeed in a field not of their choosing.

With ideas of becoming a clinical psychologist, I became friends with a cohort of classmates who also planned to pursue graduate studies in psychology. I finally felt a sense of community that I had yearned for throughout college. Clinical psychology has often been perceived as the most desirable area in psychology, and it is clearly the most competitive in terms of admission to graduate programs. I saw this as a chance for me to redeem myself from my dismal undergraduate career. Furthermore, my positive experiences with counseling and therapy convinced me that this was a field worth pursuing. As a senior, I applied to a list of extremely competitive programs, all of which were in California. My parents had not hidden the fact that they wanted me to remain as close to them as possible. In truth, I was not completely prepared to separate from my family and friends. Aware that my tarnished academic record and unimpressive entrance exam scores seriously handicapped my chances, I was disappointed but not surprised when I was rejected by all the programs.

Feeling unwanted, I resorted to handling my feelings of rejection as I did when I was an 8-year-old child without my mother and father: I blocked out my feelings so that I could press ahead. I was determined to reapply to clinical programs the following year. After consulting with others who advised me to focus on aspects of my application that I could improve, I spent my time studying for the graduate entrance exams and upgrading my research and applied skills. I blamed myself for inadequate preparation and soon developed frequent stomach pains or migraines. By the time that applications were due for my second attempt, I once again applied to competitive programs that were mostly in California. Although I was a stronger applicant than a year before, I still did not get in.

Like a scratched record or a skipping CD, phrases such as "it's over" and "you really messed it up" repeated in my mind as I faced another round of rejection. I wanted to barricade myself from the world in my bed with blankets, burying my head in my pillows to muffle the critical words echoing in my head. I hated myself. I was acting as my mother did when she was depressed. To counteract this, I committed myself to a string of work, research, and volunteer activities. But even the simplest of tasks appeared unusually challenging, as every day ended with me on the verge of emotional breakdown. At the time, I had no idea that I was pushing myself deeper into depression by being overly demanding of myself.

Similar to my mother, I avoided seeking counseling or mental health services. Was I too proud, embarrassed, or ashamed—or simply not ready to share my feelings and thoughts with others? I avoided professional help for all of these reasons. Instead, I found emotional release through music. As an avid music collector, I spent many hours sifting through my collection of songs for the lyrics that spoke the words that I did not know how to express—or words that I was too afraid to speak myself.

Eventually, I grew dissatisfied with merely listening. Having been tormented as a child about my speech impediment, I hated hearing my voice, as it was associated with shame and pain. But I reached a stage at which I was finally ready to go beyond listening. With one note, I shattered a lifetime of silence. Singing at the piano, I discovered my voice. I realized that I could not understand myself, let alone be understood by anyone else, if I muted myself. So began a process of playing music, songwriting, writing poetry, and creating artistic sketches. It was not easy to listen and look at myself honestly, especially when it came to parts of me that I felt were dark or ugly.

I seriously evaluated what drove me to clinical psychology. What was I trying to prove by gaining admission into the most competitive area of psychology? Ever since performing poorly in the first few years of college and ultimately failing a course, I had been constantly trying to show everyone, including myself, that I was not stupid or too lazy to perform. It was exhausting to spend so much time and energy trying to convince everyone else about my self-worth. But perhaps I was the one who needed convincing.

Having experienced 2 consecutive years of rejection, I thought carefully before applying for a third time. This time, I approached the application process in an entirely different way. In selecting programs to target for my applications, I focused on research match. Because I was interested in studying emotions and self-regulation, I identified potential mentors who were conducting research on those topics. Awaiting the results of the application process, I felt relatively calm because I did the best that I could. Upon learning that I was accepted to developmental psychology programs in California and Arizona, I decided that Arizona State University's program was the best fit. I was at ease even if I was traveling farther away from home.

EMPTY NEST: TRANSITION FOR EVERYONE

Although pleased with my decision, I felt torn about leaving behind family and friends. San Francisco had been my home ever since leaving Hong Kong as a child. Questions roared within me: "With all the sacrifices that your parents made for you, how can you abandon them now? How can you be so selfish?" Guilt-ridden, I saw my move to Arizona as a decision to put my own needs above those of my family.

Both of my siblings were encountering major developmental milestones of their own. My brother had just graduated from college and started a desirable but demanding job in San Francisco. My "baby" sister had just left home to start college at Davis, 75 miles east of San Francisco. At a time when my sister and I were leaving home to pursue higher education, my parents, now in their 50s, were experiencing rocky times at work.

Since arriving in the United States, my father had given his entire working life to the restaurant business. He did not expect to be laid off abruptly when the restaurant's business declined and eventually went bankrupt. I felt secure growing up, not because he worked in a prestigious or lucrative profession—in fact, he toiled for meager wages in a restaurant in Chinatown—but because he showed his care, dedication, and determination by providing for us without complaint, even when my mother was institutionalized in Hong Kong. Even though I was now an adult who could earn a living and help support my family, my father's unemployment still signaled impending instability for the family. Finding employment was challenging for him, especially as he did not have educational credentials from the United States. After scrambling for months, he finally found work in the hotel industry doing housekeeping.

At the same time, my mother felt intensely pressured to maintain some kind of income at the bank where she worked. This coincided with major changes in the entire banking industry that included "phasing out" of the traditional bank teller through the introduction of self-service and computerized banking. Consistent with such trends, my mother's workplace began major reorganization and downsizing. Her bank began testing the employees on the new banking procedures on a weekly basis. I saw her memorizing thick training manuals late into the evenings. Nearly three decades older than many of her coworkers, she also began experiencing hot flashes, heart palpitations, dizziness, and lapses in memory indicative of menopause.

On the night before I drove to Arizona, I slept uncomfortably and woke early the next morning to the sounds of my mother preparing breakfast. As I ate, she advised, "Don't eat too much fast and fried foods. Eat more fresh vegetables and fruits." My father hurriedly interjected with his reminders, "Remember to change the oil in your car regularly, and check your air filter and antifreeze." Although our farewells apparently revolved around trivial matters, I understood that they were expressing their caring and concern for me. Pulling out of the driveway, I saw the images of my family diminish, fade, and eventually vanish in the rearview mirror as I trekked from the Pacific Ocean of California to the Sonoran desert of Arizona. I was awed by the statuesque Saguaro cacti, some nearing 30 feet tall, lining the freeway. Approaching Phoenix, I was captivated by the beautiful hues of red, green, and copper in the mountains that fortressed the city.

Shortly after settling into my apartment in Tempe, a suburb of Phoenix, I received a call on my mobile telephone from my brother, alerting me that our mother had collapsed at work. I asked to speak with her on the telephone, and she faintly whispered that she was "dizzy and overheated." The next morning, my father telephoned her workplace to request a sick leave for her. Concerned, he prepared soups and forcibly fed her to sustain her, even though she had little appetite and refused to eat. Over the next few days, she disappeared behind the bedsheets and blankets, reappearing only to use the restroom.

RELAPSE INTO DARKNESS—AND MANIA

Continuing to shield herself underneath her blankets, my mother isolated herself in the darkness of her bedroom. My father and brother could do little to convince her to leave her room; soon, they could not ignore the stench that permeated the air from the bedsheets and blanket. Although the bank manager insisted that she return to work only when she was in good health and ready, my mother began panicking that she might lose her job if she stayed home too long. She decided that she would have to upgrade her computer skills if she was ever to return to work at the bank.

As if bursting out of the dark bedroom in which she had imprisoned herself, she stayed awake for 2 or 3 days to memorize her computer manuals. Exuding a frighteningly intense and frenzied force, she made her way to the local community college and enrolled in computer and English courses. She also found energy for aerobics classes at a local gymnasium. We were initially relieved to see her outside of the home. But soon, I sensed that her frenetic energy would ignite and launch her into a relapse of severe depression. In fact, this turned out to be the case: she was experiencing hypomania, and a repeated series of manic episodes and depressions followed.

The longer my family and I denied that my mother was afflicted with mental illness requiring medical or psychological treatment, the longer we delayed reexperiencing the pain that we felt from her first major episode. In a strange way, we earnestly believed that we could properly care for and heal her. Although we wanted to hide her illness from others, we could not keep her hidden.

Relatives and friends who knew about my mother frequently advised my father on how to painstakingly prepare ancient Chinese remedies of soups or herbal teas that could allegedly cure her illness. My brother and sister did their parts: tediously sifting through scientific and medical articles on depression in the libraries or on the Internet, my brother researched the latest information on diagnosis and treatment, and my sister gave up time bonding with her peers during her first year in college to stay with our mother every weekend. As the only child living far away from my parents, I felt powerless to help.

From Arizona, I felt as if I were a despicable and ungrateful son who had chosen to live away from his family. Given that familial connectedness is heavily emphasized in traditional Chinese culture, how could I be so disloyal and selfish? How could I choose to pursue a doctorate in psychology at a time like this? I began feeling that graduate studies were utterly unnecessary and self-indulgent.

One evening, my aunt (my mother's younger sister) telephoned me from Australia. She asked how I was doing in school and how I liked living in Arizona. I kept my update brief and shifted our conversation to my mother. A registered nurse, my aunt had cared for my mother in Hong Kong during the first major depressive episode, so she was familiar with some of my mother's symptoms. My aunt questioned me, "You're studying psychology, so why don't you help her? Is it possible to take a leave of absence from school?" I told her that I would think about it. Her words haunted me long after our conversation. I began seriously questioning whether I was secretly using graduate school as an excuse to escape the responsibilities and burden of caring for my mother.

My father and siblings were supportive of my decision to continue with graduate studies, but my mother sent conflicting messages. During her depressed state, she often told me over the telephone to "quit school and come home. People your age should be working and making money already." On the other hand, during her manic phases, she told me in a matter-of-fact tone to "never come home because there is no room here for you." With such opposing messages, I didn't know what to expect from her anymore.

As a child, I had witnessed firsthand some of my mother's early symptoms during her first depressive episode. As an adult, I was now experiencing her problems primarily from afar. Only after contrasting and then integrating my experiences as an insider and outsider was I able to appreciate how my mother's depression incapacitated not only her, but our entire family, physically and emotionally. When my brother informed me that she had locked herself in the bedroom, I knew that her silence and stillness forecasted an impending shakeup. We were familiar with waiting through the days or weeks of lethargy, which eventually swelled into a seismic force.

When my mother finally unleashed the manic energy that had lain dormant, her behaviors were excessive but initially benign. She frequently telephoned every person listed in her telephone directory. Even late into the evenings, she disturbed many of her long-time friends to complain or engage in self-blame. Sooner or later, her friends came to ignore or reject her telephone calls. With few outlets for her rabid energy, she began leaving the house to shop. Eventually, her excessive shopping morphed into persistent and aimless roaming and wandering in the streets. The contrast was striking: whereas she could hardly be forced out of the home during her depressed states, my father could barely prevent her from leaving the house during her manic phases.

Because she needed constant supervision, my father and brother soon became captives of her mental illness. Working the graveyard shift, my father remained home with my mother during the day. After work, he rarely got the sleep that he needed. Although in-home professional care was an option, it was extremely expensive and would expose her condition to more people outside of the family. When the situation became unbearable for my father, my brother rearranged his schedule to work from home as often as possible. It became clear that they could not properly supervise my mother without additional help.

During her manic episodes, my mother often forced her way or snuck out of the home. One evening, our neighbors complained to my father, "Your wife was bothering us. She said that she was homeless and wanted us to take her into our home. What is going on?" My father questioned my mother about what happened and was left stunned to discover that she had routinely been asking strangers for shelter. On the telephone with me, she lamented, "Your father is better off without me. He should remarry and just put me out on the streets so I could be homeless. Your lives would be better without me." She also told me that she occasionally asked strangers to give her rides if she roamed too far from home. Hearing such news sent chills through me, as stereotypes of a homeless mentally ill person, roaming and babbling in the streets, flashed across my mind.

Our fears that her manic behaviors would get her into serious trouble were confirmed late one evening when my brother telephoned me to inform me that "the police took mom away." Momentarily, I felt as if I were 9 years old, with the voice of my childhood friend, taunting me about the police taking my mother away, echoing in my mind. The neighbors were upset that my mother rang their doorbells and claimed that she was homeless and needed shelter. "The police took her in for trespassing," my brother explained in a calm yet uncertain voice.

With police intervention, my father escorted and admitted my mother into a publicly funded psychiatric hospital. After three evenings, she was released, with medication to suppress her anxiety and psychotic symptoms. On returning home, she cocooned in bed nearly every day. Sedated by the medication, she remained relatively disoriented. She frequently complained of dry mouth, loss of appetite, and constipation from her medication. By that point, we were happier with the choice of her being sedated at home rather than roaming the streets.

ROADBLOCKS TO RECOVERY: DENIAL, RESISTANCE, AND NONCOMPLIANCE

Although medication alleviated some of my mother's depressive and manic symptoms, it could not help her accept that she was suffering from mental illness. Insisting that she was not depressed, she challenged any notion of needing professional help or medication. Initially, she flushed her pills down the toilet. When my father and brother began closer monitoring, she developed increasingly clever methods to outmaneuver them, for example, hiding the pills under her tongue or in her cheek. When confronted, she adamantly roared back that she was "not really sick, but only acting sick." She insisted, "I acted sick because I don't want to work. I am lazy. I just want to stay at home."

My mother's explanations angered my father. Awed by her stubbornness and damned by her illness, my father combusted, "Just get better! Why are you torturing yourself and your family?" Perhaps he was unable or unwilling to truly understand her illness. Perhaps, like my mother, he was resisting the realization that she truly suffered from a serious mental illness. Maybe he did not realize that her psychotic and depressive or manic symptoms were often beyond her voluntary or volitional control. His outrage eventually subsided to desperate pleas: "I beg you. Please, stop doing this to yourself and your family." On hearing such updates by telephone, I felt deep sorrow for my father. In his early 60s and working the graveyard shift to sustain some kind of medical insurance for himself and my mother, he did not deserve such punishing circumstances.

REUNION REVISITED

Thanksgiving gave me the first opportunity to have somewhat of an extended visit with my family. The days prior to my visit were smeared with chaotic swirls of longing to see my family blended with anxiety, guilt, and apprehension. My father confided what he expected from me: "With all your years of schooling, you must speak with your mother. What good is all your education if you can't use it?" Despite the fact that I was specializing in developmental rather than clinical psychology, my family desperately hoped that I could do something to help. They did not comprehend that I was not a trained therapist or counselor. In truth, I also wished I knew how to help my mother.

On my flight to San Francisco, I felt pushed and pulled in multiple, conflicting directions as I rehearsed scenes of the upcoming reunion. Oddly, I felt trapped in a film, one that was looping in an old film projector. I was still embodying the life of a lonely and frightened child who marched up the stairs in anticipation of reuniting with his mother who had disappeared for nearly 3 years. As the wheels of the airplane touched ground, I was snapped back into the moment by the jolt of the landing. I felt harried as I darted through the crowded airport to the meeting area where my father waited. On seeing him, my eyes strayed from his warm smile to the lines and wrinkles that carved his gaunt face. In just 6 months, he had markedly aged and weathered.

On our way home, he warned me, "Your mother is not doing well. She is always in the bedroom. You have to talk to her." As I stepped inside our home, I noticed down the hallway that the door to my parents' bedroom was slightly ajar. Although I wanted a little time to gather myself before seeing my mother, I forced myself down the hallway and knocked gently at the door. Not sure if she was awake or asleep, I waited, in silence. I was somehow relieved, thinking that she might be asleep. But weak murmurs broke through the dead air trapped within her room. Peeking inside, I saw that she was under the covers with her back to me. To get her attention without startling her, I tiptoed toward her and quietly whispered, "Mom, I'm home."

Spiritless, my mother summoned enough strength to toss the covers off as if struggling to free her from a cocoon. As she slowly turned her body and head toward me, she appeared both familiar and unfamiliar. Her grayed and tangled hair framed her flushed and bloated face. Squinting, she appeared as if fighting to keep her eyes from shutting. She mumbled in a hushed but assertive voice, "Why are you here? You should not have come to see me. You can't stay here. Go back to Arizona. I am dying here." Unsure how to react, I told her that I was visiting for a few days and asked about her rest and appetite. "I just lie in bed all day, but my mind and my heart stay awake. My mouth is dry. I am not sick, but the medicine makes me sick." I listened, but I had no solutions. I prompted, "We should do something while I am home. Where do you want to go?" She responded in an insulted manner, "How can I go anywhere? I don't know how to walk anymore. My legs don't work." Puzzled, I told her that we could do something after I unpacked my luggage.

Shortly after I went to unpack my suitcase, my mother stumbled out to the kitchen and hurriedly shoved foods such as grapes and breads into her mouth. As she ate, I noticed spurts of physical tremors in her hands and occasionally through her face and mouth. In addition, I noticed that her feet tapped when she stood still. Ironically, she was moving but going nowhere. Her "pitter-patter" footsteps reminded me of the aftershocks that I felt as a 16-year-old during the 1989 Loma Prieta earthquake. Might she be showing signs of neuromuscular or psychosomatic problems? Because she was under the supervision of a psychiatrist, I tried to reassure myself that her physical and mental health was being monitored and that her behavioral symptoms might reflect the side effects from her medication.

MOTHER, WHERE ARE YOU?

My return home made me realize how the distance during graduate studies had blinded me to, and protected me from, how severely her mental illness had affected her entire being. Yet such distance gave me an "outsider" perspective, allowing me to see my mother's condition through different lenses. I did not see a woman who was acting or pretending in ways to cause chaos for her family. Rather, I saw a woman who was acting in ways not under her volitional control—a person with a mental illness. Similar to people with many types of illnesses, such as diabetes, she could function and live a happy, productive, and healthy life with proper diagnosis and treatment. However, the critical hurdle was breaking down the resistance that kept her from accepting that she was mentally ill so that she would seek and benefit from treatment.

As the Thanksgiving weekend came to an end, I knew that my time with my mother was precious. Too often, I rushed through life, with people, things, and events blurring and fading into the background. I slowed things down by momentarily staring at her face. I could finally see my mother as the person who had made the suicide attempt I witnessed as a child and one also in the midst of severe depression. Her face was flushed red and bloated, and her eyes were glassy. She was not the woman I once knew. I wondered to myself, "What can I do to reach you? How do I connect with you? Mother, where are you?" I was staring at a woman who was strong and independent, but also broken and vulnerable.

With the chronic stress of caring for my depressed mother, my father and brother were developing health problems. My father suffered from chronic coughing, and my brother experienced recurring bouts of stomach and chest pains. Although my mother routinely berated my father and brother, she was more harsh with and critical of herself. She lamented, "I am not a good mother. I did not raise you properly. And I don't know English. You kids don't know English either. We all have very bad education." I was baffled, wondering if she felt that she had sacrificed her own educational or career opportunities so that her children could achieve at least a college education. With these questions burning within me as I departed, I struggled to keep pace with my graduate studies.

LISTEN WITHOUT JUDGMENT: MAKING SENSE OF NONSENSE

I made subsequent visits every 2 to 3 months over the next 2 years, spending much of my time listening to my mother ramble endlessly. She routinely declared, "Our family is cursed. We are dying!" But the more I listened, the more I learned to see my mother. Dispersed within her nonsensical ramblings, she revealed, "I lost my mother when I was only a teenager. She died from breast cancer. The doctors discovered the cancer very late, and they could do nothing. Even my uncle who was a doctor tried everything to save her, but it was too late. Because I lost my mother when I was so young, I don't know how to be a good mother to you." Hearing about her loss at an early age, I imagined the loneliness and fear she must have experienced as a youth and into adulthood. Even though I sympathized with her, I realized that I don't truly understand the depth of her loss. Although my mother had returned to us after seeking treatment in Hong Kong, her own mother had never come back.

My mother rarely talked about her mother and her youth, and I finally understood why. As the oldest daughter of seven children, she naturally assumed the role of caregiver with the passing of her mother, shouldering the housekeeping responsibilities for her family and parenting her younger siblings. Pressured into forsaking her educational aspirations to help with her father's business, she pursued a degree in accounting. She recalled having to do accounting and bookkeeping for her father's business that left her little time to pursue her goals.

Over the following 2 years, my mother vacillated between periods of depression and mania. While the psychiatrists experimented with the types and dosages of medication for her symptoms, she continued avoiding taking the prescriptions. With such noncompliance, she cycled through extreme depressive and manic states that lasted from a few days to a few weeks each. As if needing some rest before lurching from one extreme to another, she would enter the "calm before the storm." During such periods, she appeared relatively serene and logical.

Because my father continued holding out hope that my mother would recover from her depression by "snapping out of it," these calm periods reinforced and prolonged his denial. Inevitably, he would be gravely disappointed when his wife slipped back into depression. I grew increasingly concerned for my father's health. Despite frequent visits to the doctor, my father's cough persisted. After months of taking cough syrup that the doctor prescribed, the cough worsened. When he began coughing blood, the doctor prescribed him an asthma inhaler.

IN THE CLUTCHES OF ABANDONMENT

Three years into my graduate studies, I struggled to find motivation and focus in order to complete my master's thesis. Writing late one evening, I was surprised by a telephone call from my brother. It was nearly 2 A.M., and I immediately wondered whether our mother had been arrested after having wandered off. In a calm voice, he explained, "I'm at the emergency room now with Dad. He couldn't breathe in the middle of the night. He was rushed here and they performed an emergency tracheotomy. Can you call home to check on Mom? She's alone." I asked him to call me when he had more information. I then called my mother, who sounded disoriented. I comforted her as I silently worried how my siblings and I would manage with both parents afflicted with serious illnesses.

Early the next morning, my brother called to inform me about my father's condition. Had my father not been rushed to the emergency room, the doctor indicated that he would have suffocated and died in his sleep. To save him from suffocation, the doctors had to immediately puncture a hole in his neck to create a breathing passage. Somehow, it took me several minutes to realize that such a procedure meant the destruction of my father's larynx, or voice box. It hit me that I would never hear my father's natural voice again. I barely had time to process my thoughts and emotions before my brother braced me for additional news. After the tracheotomy, the doctors discovered a lump. Was the tumor malignant? Statistically, my father was at relatively low risk for cancer. He did not have a family history, he did not smoke, and he was an identical twin whose brother did not manifest similar problems. No matter how much I rationalized, I knew the tumor could possibly be cancerous. Awaiting the test results, we all felt powerless.

Several days later, my brother called to say that the test results indicated that my father was already in a very late stage (stage 4) of laryngeal cancer. I momentarily felt numb, but then I felt a swelling seed of anger burgeon within me. For over a year, my father had visited the doctors complaining of coughing and throat problems. How could they have ignored him, and then prescribed him an asthma inhaler? Would an inhaler prevent him from nearly suffocating to death in his sleep from a cancerous tumor blocking his airway? How did such a flagrant misdiagnosis happen? I silenced the inner screaming so I could focus on the immediate situation of keeping my father alive. With no time to waste, my father was scheduled for immediate removal of the tumor and all the tissues surrounding his larynx. At such final stages of cancer, the doctors recommended "gutting" the inside of his neck to remove lymph nodes to which the cancer might have spread. After informing my academic advisors about my father's condition, I immediately booked a flight back to San Francisco.

On my flight over the Sonoran Desert toward the Pacific Ocean, I constantly glanced at my watch and wondered how my father's operation was going. After I landed, my brother rushed me home so we could pick up our mother and sister before heading to the hospital. At home, I found my mother still wearing her pajamas, pacing frantically from room to room. I hurriedly asked her to change her clothes so we could go see my father. She wailed, "I am not going. What if your daddy dies? What will I do then?"

Although I knew that she was mentally ill and not herself, I became frustrated and angry. How could she be so focused on herself at a time like this? Likewise, my brother became upset and demanded, "You're coming with us. Dad needs to see us." After much arguing, we arrived at the hospital. Before entering the patient room, I hesitated. Was his neck mutilated? Would he be awake? I entered cautiously and saw him asleep. His neck was heavily bandaged, soaked and stained in crimson. As my siblings and I approached him, his eyelids convulsed like little earthquakes as he fought to barely crack open his eyes. As soon as he recognized us, he struggled to raise the corners of his mouth to signal a barely noticeable smile. My mother stayed away from my father, and I heard her "pitter-patter" footsteps from a distant corner of the room. Eventually, she shuffled toward us, looked at my father, and mourned, "He is mute. How could our family go on? He is crippled!" My siblings and I were horrified, and my heart ached as I saw tears streaming from my father's eyes down his face.

When my father returned home, we tried our best to accommodate his needs. We gave him a bell to signal for help in case of emergencies. We also made sure he had pens and paper readily available to communicate with us. One of his first written requests was for us to initiate legal paperwork for wills and trusts for the family. Seeing such a request on paper made me realize that losing my father was a very real possibility. His prognosis was not good. The doctors recommended aggressive radiation therapy soon after his wounds healed. Despite the potentially debilitating effects, my father agreed without hesitation to any treatment that might give him a chance at survival.

Whereas my father was a model patient who complied with doctors' orders, my mother continued to resist treatment and medication for her mood disorder. I increasingly resented the way that she intensified stress for my father as he fought to stay alive. In retrospect, I recognize that the possibility of losing her husband to cancer must have left my mother feeling extremely threatened, as it had with her own mother so many years ago. Given her severe depression, perhaps lashing out against my father was her way of showing how much pain she felt.

PERCEPTION BECOMES REALITY: THE MENTALLY ILL AS NUISANCE AND OUTCAST

My mother's yo-yoing from the extreme lows of depression to the extreme highs of mania for more than 4 years was wearing out the tattered string that held our family together. With the added stressor of my father's battle with cancer, that string was at risk of snapping. With my sister and me in school, my brother was the only family member working full time. Living with my parents, he had become their primary caregiver and an easy target for my parents' displaced frustrations. Juggling professional and familial obligations, he soon became visibly worn and unnaturally gaunt. With chronic stress, he developed a persistent cough in addition to the stomach and chest pains he had been previously experiencing. Despite multiple visits to the doctor, his cough persisted.

Sounds of my brother's cough triggered anger from my father. If the coughing continued, my father often picked up his voice machine and berated my brother as if he were doing it intentionally. My brother recounted that my father would frequently stomp out of the room while slamming the door behind him. I imagine that every time that my father heard my brother coughing was probably a painful reminder of his too-late diagnosis and subsequent loss of his larynx to cancer.

My mother reacted to my brother's declining health very differently, becoming more convinced than ever that she was responsible for the physical illnesses of my father and brother. Seeing herself as a nuisance to her family, she pleaded for a divorce.

Sadly, we had also begun seeing my mother as an annoyance. There were times when I felt so upset that I partially blamed her for the hardships that our family had to endure. I had lost sight of the fact that she deserved sympathy and understanding as a person who was suffering from mental illness. After years of watching her failure to comply with medication, my brother and I contemplated whether electroconvulsive therapy (ECT) was the only viable and effective treatment.

Initially, we had kept our mother's depression relatively hidden. But after my father was diagnosed with cancer, we reached out to relatives and friends for help and support. In particular, the minister and church members offered significant help. My family had been Christians for at least three generations, and my mother was a relatively religious woman. But it was not until after my father's bout with cancer that her manic episodes took on religious themes. She became obsessed with studying the Bible, convinced that her depression was a sign of weakness in her faith and a punishment from God. To ward off Satan, she rabidly recited Biblical scriptures throughout day and night. Her religious fervor often lasted for several days before transitioning to periods of obsessive house-cleaning or excessive shopping. She then progressed to socially inappropriate or risky behaviors, such as roaming and disturbing bystanders and neighbors.

NO PLACE LIKE HOME: BACK ON
TRACK TO RECOVERY

After vacillating about whether to keep our mother home or admit her into the psychiatric hospital, we finally conceded to professional consultation and intervention in a hospital. The psychiatrist recommended a variety of treatment options, including ECT. Given my mother's experiences with ECT in Hong Kong, I felt extremely uncomfortable with this treatment. But I also learned that it was a relatively safe procedure involving mild risks of memory loss. Still, my mother refused to consent to the procedure. We agreed on medication even though she had a history of noncompliance with such treatment. After a week in the psychiatry ward to stabilize her condition, my mother was released and returned home.

My brother and I felt desperate to try something that could possibly help her. We collaborated on a plan to create an environment that would support her taking medication on a daily basis. I relied on my experiences working with aggressive and defiant children in devising a behavior modification program. My brother would be responsible for implementing the program, consisting of concrete activities, rules, reinforcers, and consequences. We also focused on en-gaging our mother in physical and social activities within and outside the home. The basic rules were simple: we expected her to comply with her medication and to leave her bed and/or the home at least once a day. Yet enforcing these rules was not easy at all.

Initially, our mother did not take my brother seriously. When she did not comply, my brother enforced mild but effective consequences. For example, he poured small amounts of cold water on her when she refused to get out of bed for most of the day. After testing the limits several times, she quickly learned that there were consequences.

With continuous medication and at least some social engagement outside the home, over a 6- to 8-month period my mother's manic and depressive epi-sodes became relatively brief and less intense. One day, she said that she was making an appointment for a haircut and permanent. The day after her hair appointment, she took the bus to go shopping for new clothes and skin care products. I was ecstatic about these simple, everyday events that had been miss-ing from her life for so many years. She continued visits with psychiatrists every few months, finally receiving a diagnosis of bipolar disorder rather than major depressive disorder. Given that she had bounced between depressive and manic episodes for over 5 years, I was surprised that this diagnosis had not been made earlier. But an accurate diagnosis was difficult when the psychiatrists did not know whether her symptoms stemmed from a wrong prescription or from non-compliance with medication.

My mother began to direct her time and energies toward meaningful and productive goals. For example, she volunteered at nursing homes. At church, she volunteered as a caretaker for infants and toddlers whose parents were attending services. In addition, she actively participated in Bible study, prayer groups, and the choir. After gaining greater self-confidence with volunteer work, she felt restless and found part-time work as a housekeeper and babysitter. I was proud that she was finally integrating the activities that she enjoyed into her transition to a new stage of life.

Why had she resisted treatment for so many years? Why did we, her family members, enable her denial and noncompliance for so long—effectively serving as accomplices? Deceptive yet protective, denial is powerful and sometimes functional. Denial was what helped my mother as a teenager survive the loss and pain associated with the death of her mother. Denial was what helped her as an adult to survive the sudden changes in her world when she immigrated to the United States. But denial of her serious mood disorder proved to be devastating.

Although medication suppressed her manic and depressive symptoms, it offered no insight into what gave rise to her depression. I felt that she could benefit from psychotherapeutic treatment. Was she ready to reexperience all the losses in her life? How does one truly become ready to embrace the loss of a parent to cancer? I felt that I would be a hypocrite for pushing my mother to seek therapy when I had been so resistant to doing so myself. I can only imagine that after a lifetime of suppressing her own pain, she preferred to keep her feelings in hibernation.

BREAKING THROUGH STIGMA

After a year of recovery, my mother has resurfaced by living a satisfying, meaningful, and productive life. Until recently, I was incapable of fully grasping or accepting that my mother would likely need professional assistance throughout her life. Perhaps the 15 years between her first and second major depressive episodes had fooled me into believing that her depression had been "cured." Although the time was ripe for her to benefit from psychotherapy or counseling, I struggled with whether it was my role to nudge her toward psychotherapeutic treatment.

Given that it had taken nearly a decade for her to accept medication, I realized that she would need time to become receptive to psychotherapy. Not surprisingly, she declined when I asked her to consider seeing a therapist or counselor. Her primary reason was that she needed a Chinese-speaking therapist. After searching for a while, my mother decided that she had no need for therapy because she had nothing to say to the therapist. Whereas medication is a relatively private form of treatment, psychotherapy requires sharing or exposing personal information with another person.

Given the stigma about mental illness, such exposure could be extremely threatening and shameful. False messages that psychiatry is a pseudo-science and that individuals who need antidepressants are weak continue to infest public consciousness. Internalized stigma is not just a theoretical construct to be discussed within academic circles; it lives within and among us, infecting each of us often without our knowing. Even when my mother's depressive symptoms were relatively under control, she lived in fear. These fears were not completely unfounded: what if parents of the toddlers and children she babysat for learned about her past struggles with mental illness? Would they avoid her? Would they treat her differently? My mother's concerns alerted me to the harm caused by misinformation and stigma.

Early in life, I learned lessons about stigma from my childhood friend who taunted me that the police had taken my mother away because she was "talking crazy." As a child, I could not understand why my friend made such accusations against my mother. I now know that these comments reflected the way popular media and culture have traditionally portrayed the mentally ill: as social outcasts who should be taken and locked away. Unfortunately, misperceptions often warp our reality, and we act according to such generalizations and stereotypes that disrespect, discriminate against, and mistreat individuals with mental illness.

As a child, all I could do was swallow the gossip and lies I heard. In the process, I unknowingly accepted and legitimized the negative messages and stereotypes about my mother and everyone who suffers from mental illness. In writing about my mother's experiences with bipolar disorder, I initially hesitated discussing my own struggles with anxiety and mild depression. But only through writing this chapter did I discover that I must stop swallowing the lies. I have learned that, as with any person afflicted with physical illness or unfortunate circumstances beyond their volitional control, individuals with mental illness deserve respect, sympathy, support, treatment, and healing.

Rather than being ashamed, I am proud of my mother for what she has achieved while living with mental illness. The fact that she has granted me permission to write about her experiences battling depression represents a significant step forward in breaking through her internalized stigma about mental illness. Only after escaping a great wind from the wilderness that threatened to tear my family apart did I understand the frailty and the strength within my mother—in fact, within everyone who lives with and tries to overcome mental illness by moving toward mental health.

As for my father, I am equally proud of him for his dedication to our family. More than 6 years in remission, he leads a productive life with stable health. In the process, he has demonstrated supernatural strength and courage in coping with and surviving cancer in the midst of my mother's depressive episodes. He will never have the use of his natural voice, but he has discovered other means of expression.

SURRENDERING TO AND CONQUERING MY OWN WORST ENEMY

Now in their mid-60s, my parents have found ways to remain active and productive with part-time work or volunteer activities. As I near the end of this chapter about my mother's battles with mental illness, I ironically arrive at the end of a significant chapter in my life. During the 7 years that I lived in Arizona, I was undergoing personal and professional growth amidst my parents' illnesses and my graduate studies. As I neared the end of my graduate career at Arizona State University, I never expected that my next steps would lead me back to counseling and psychotherapy.

On the evening of my 31st birthday, I was blindsided with relatively sudden news from my partner of 4 years that he wanted a separation. I was nearing completion of my dissertation, and this left me distracted and feeling completely abandoned. I felt that seeking professional counseling would be wise during such a traumatic time to keep myself physically and mentally healthy especially as I needed to prepare to go on the job market. But I hesitated and felt embarrassed. As someone in the field of psychology who (logically) believed in the healing powers and benefits of psychotherapy and counseling, I continued harboring the negative messages about mental illness and the mental health services that I've swallowed since childhood.

A lifetime of holding in all the negative messages and images of the mentally ill had left me bloated and mired in misinformation. I now tasted what my mother experienced as I fought against seeking professional help. I did not want to succumb to what I perceived as weakness for seeking support to heal my emotional and psychological pain and injuries. Such stigmatizing messages, when applied to physical pain and injuries, sound absolutely absurd and foolish. For example, I would not hesitate to seek professional help to treat and heal my leg if I injured or broke it. Would we recommend that people who were experiencing chest pains to ignore it or deal with it on their own? Why should society look down on those who seek treatment for emotional or psychological injuries and pain? Having internalized so many lies and half-truths about mental illness, I became my own worst enemy by denying myself acceptance, respect, and the right and access to a meaningful and productive life. Through the process of writing this chapter, I have come to realize that I must surrender my past in order to command my future.

To do so, I let go of the shame that I felt about my mother's mental illness and my emotional breakdown during college. Until I took responsibility to liberate myself from a lifetime of devaluing and discriminatory messages, I remained a slave to oppressive lies. For example, I recognized that self-reliance and individual strength were characteristics that were strongly valued in North American culture (especially in males). One myth or stereotype that I had to confront, challenge, and shatter was the notion that independent, strong, and brave individuals (especially men) should endure, ignore, or suppress their emotional, psychological, or physical pain. By recognizing and confronting my internalized stigma, I was finally able to benefit from treatment, healing, and growth. With the help of skilled therapists at Arizona State University's Counseling and Consultation Services and the support of my family, graduate mentors, and friends, I was able to complete the journey that I began as an inspired undergraduate studying psychology at Berkeley. I am now an assistant professor in educational psychology at Texas A&M University.

A major step in overcoming stigma is confronting and conquering it within ourselves. Reliving the memories of my mother's experiences with bipolar disorder and my experiences with counseling and psychotherapy has been a painful process. But writing this chapter has freed me to overcome a lifetime of negative and discriminatory messages living within me. Only after surrendering to my sorrows, fears, and pain was I able to conquer and slay my own worst enemy, my internalized stigma. Such a rebirth has allowed me to grow into a new stage in my life. Feeling alive and liberated, I can finally live rather than relive.

Having entered this world knowing how it felt to be alone and misunderstood, I now realize that I am connected to a community of others who, personally or through familial experiences, live productive lives in spite of mental illness. I no longer feel alone in darkness as I did when I was a 1-year-old child staying in the hospital ward after surgery. Individuals with mental illness live with extraordinary challenges that most people could never imagine or know. To overcome such challenges requires extraordinary strength, courage, and resilience. In fact, many individuals afflicted with mental illness are able to move toward or maintain mental health through preventive care or through accurate diagnosis and proper treatment. Reflecting on my mother's experiences since her youth, I now see her as a whole person who lives with great strength counterbalanced by great vulnerability. I am grateful for the lessons of compassion and understanding toward people who encounter extreme emotional or psychological distress, and that includes me. Through speaking of my mother's life circumstances, I have discovered my voice in a chorus of voices from individuals touched by mental illness.

6   Columbus Day, 1994: A New World

Kay S. Browne

This chapter is about my now-31-year-old son's mental illness. A major theme is my feeling of betrayal by my psychiatry residency and by my earlier training, which fueled my anxious expectations and my devastation once mental illness invaded our family. It is also about what happens to a family when serious mental illness arises. A lot of the chapter is about what would have been and what could have been very helpful had proper help been available and what mental health professionals can do to help a young adult and his or her family when mental illness arises. And, most important, it is about the possibility of the achievement of recovery. As I state herein, my firm belief is that professionals treating schizophrenia and bipolar spectrum disorders should always be aiming at full recovery.

I am recently 61 years old, trained as an MD at Harvard Medical School at a time when our class contained only 10% women (12 out of 120). I had wanted to be a doctor since before high school. My mother was a nurse, and as a child I read her nursing textbooks, memorizing the bones of the skull to the applause of the adults in my family. I have much-older half-sisters on my father's side, but I was raised as an only child of older parents (54 and 42 when I was born) who wanted (and could afford) to give me an excellent education.

ORIGINS, FAMILY, AND MEDICAL TRAINING

Because my parents were home and together most of the time, I learned to "read" adults and probably did more than my share of intervening when there was any friction. Although this ability has stood me well in my chosen profession, attaining it as a child was stressful, and it may have made me particularly sensitive when I began a family myself. My family of origin was very close, and my current family is, too, with emphasis on a great deal of communication and love. My older son Nathan's return home floridly psychotic, at the beginning of his sophomore year in college, was a shot out of the blue, totally out of any thought or context we had as individuals or as a family.

I decided early in my college career that I wanted to go to medical school. I loved my psychology courses but could not take any more advanced courses in this field because I was a chemistry major and also had to fill my liberal arts requirement. I looked diligently for summer work, and my mother intervened as well. She had been a nursing classmate of one of the head nurses at Boston Children's Hospital who had good connections. Much as I didn't want family intervention at that age, her assistance paid off, and I worked in Boston, first as a nurse's aide at Boston Children's Hospital and then as an assistant in biochemical research at Harvard Medical School. While there, I chose every opportunity to see and participate in as many types of patient treatment as possible. An early meeting with Dr. Charles Janeway, pediatric medical chairman at Children's Hospital, led to my getting a letter from him that introduced me to the heads of all of the various departments at the hospital.

After forceful personal negotiations, I was also able to watch open-heart surgery from a viewing gallery and visited various clinics, just like a medical student. I talked with women doctors about their lives. Many of them discouraged me from becoming an MD because of the difficulty of balancing responsibilities of home and medicine. We were on the cusp of the women's liberation movement at that time, and any form of equality in home responsibilities was just beginning. Older male physicians were not used to women in the profession, and it was significantly harder and often embarrassing for women in medical school.

From my earliest years, I had always wanted a baby and had played for long hours with my dolls. When I was 14 years old, my sister gave birth to her fourth child, and with my mother's supervision I was able to take total care of the new baby for a few days while her family was moving. As a consequence, I wanted even more to have my own children.

Much earlier, when I was very young, prior to knowing where babies came from, I asked my mother when I would be old enough to have a baby. Caught by surprise, she answered "21." From that time on, I always believed that I would have my first child when I was 21. Perhaps it wasn't just chance that I was married for the first time in June 1966, on the day of my 21st birthday. Yet my sons, Nathan and Tim, were not born until I was 29 and 31 years old.

After medical school I did a pediatric internship in Boston and then moved to the University of California, San Francisco, for a pediatric residency. I had been divorced in the middle of medical school and thought moving to San Francisco might help with my after-divorce blues. The training regimens at that time were grueling: during my internship in Boston, I had worked a 2-week cycle, going to the hospital at 8 A.M. on Saturday morning and living there until Monday at around 5 P.M. I left the hospital until Tuesday morning at 8 A.M., leaving Wednesday evening but returning again on Thursday morning, this time not to leave until Saturday morning, when the weekend people, in the parallel cycle, reported for the long weekend duty. During that time I was sleeping fitfully in on-call rooms next to the heating plant. There were no fans or air conditioning, even in the Boston summer. Whatever sleep there was became interrupted by calls to perform hospital ward emergency admissions, emergency room visits, or immediate care needed by the critically ill children, with diagnoses such as diabetes, meningitis, or acute leukemia. I occasionally tried to sleep in an empty room on the ward so that I could be immediately available to an extremely ill child.

There was also the teenage patient suffering postpolio respiratory paralysis who still used an iron lung, had pneumonia, and periodically needed me to take blood from his artery to test his degree of blood oxygenation. In the late 1960s house officers (interns and residents) performed most of the lab tests currently done by automation. This was particularly true in the middle of the night when only X-ray, operating room, and blood bank technicians were available.

I had always been interested in psychology. I still remember the Skinner box and positive and negative reinforcement contingencies from my college psychology course. I've used those principles more than any I learned in my chemistry major. I briefly considered a psychiatry residency, but psychiatry seemed less scientific, and those in my class who went into it, though often brilliant, did not seem interested in the laboratory methods for diagnosis employed in the other specialties. I note that my graduation year was the first that did not require psychiatry residents to do a general medical or pediatric internship before going into psychiatry. Eventually, those selecting psychiatry were no longer required to do neurology training as part of their psychiatric residencies. I often wonder about this reduced rigor in the psychiatry field.

My fascination with psychiatry was fueled by my medical school psychiatric rotation 36 years ago at Massachusetts General Hospital, which remains particularly vivid in my memory. Our first day of orientation was held in the offices of Dr. Seymore Kety, who had just published work revealing the substantial heritability of schizophrenia. He had done twin research in Scandinavia showing that identical twins had a much higher concordance for this disorder than fraternal twins.[1]

As to patients, there was the 19-year-old college student with schizophrenia. His father, a dentist, kept signing him out of psychiatric hospitals against medical advice, believing that his son was not particularly ill. I heard later that this young man had committed suicide shortly after a psychiatric hospital release.

There was also the 50-year-old divorced woman who had nursed her adult daughter through a terminal illness. When the daughter died, the mother's life seemed to languish into severe depression. The medications then available didn't work for her; I remember her extreme, tangible sadness and the inability to treat her effectively.

My interest in psychiatry led to my doing a psychiatry residency in Indianapolis between the births of my two sons. Included were rotations in adult female psychiatry and adolescent psychiatry, as well as 6 months of psychiatric research. At that time I was trained as a pediatrician, and the psychiatric training included giving uncontrolled shock treatment to a group of women, mostly diagnosed with schizophrenia. They shuffled into the room, lay down, and had brief sedation followed by an electrically induced generalized seizure. At one point I went to court to testify in support of shock treatment for a woman in her 70s with severe depression. I had been following her for some time as an outpatient: medications had not worked, as there were few available antidepressants in the early 1970s. She deteriorated and was forced into hospitalization. The idea of legally forcing a woman the age of my mother to undergo shock treatment appalled me, but there did not seem an alternative at the time.

I reacted to the psychiatry residency with overwhelming anxiety. There was a definite psychological separation between staff and patients, an "us versus them" attitude that was palpable.[2] This stance was particularly brought home to me when the wife of a good friend of my husband's was admitted with recurrent severe depression. There was open discussion in staff meetings of the details of her home life, including her husband's excessive drinking. She had no privacy, and I could not help but feel that the experience might exacerbate rather than help her depression. Interviewed in front of the staff of about 20 people, she cried openly. I became even more anxious and depressed.

In addition, a young woman, the daughter of two neuropsychiatrists, was admitted with a psychotic episode. There were long discussions about her diagnosis, schizophrenia versus bipolar disorder. I don't remember any resolution of the question, nor do I remember any discussion with the family—or much sympathy for their situation.

Still another woman in her 30s was admitted. She was beautiful and highly educated, with a long history of paranoia and recurrent, very subtle psychosis (she was very quiet and isolated with her delusions). Her ex-husband was a senior resident in psychiatry in Boston, at one of the elite psychiatric teaching hospitals. I remember my feelings of inadequacy when I interviewed him on the phone. I felt far less educated in psychiatry than he and wished I had more experience to treat his former wife adequately. In this case, the medications available had very uncomfortable side effects; she "cheeked" them and refused to be treated.

My anxiety and depression during my psychiatric residency led the staff to recommend that I receive therapy. A recent graduate of the program, a woman, was recommended. The sessions were a disaster, primarily because she did not seem to understand the stress that the residency was putting on me. She was part of the system that I found so disturbing and was judging me from that perspective. She repeatedly offered me sleeping pills as each session ended, despite the fact that insomnia was not a part of my symptoms. Also, I had an infant at home that I was still breast-feeding, consequently having to be awake sometimes in the middle of the night.

I obtained another referral from a psychologist friend, a man who listened with empathy to the difficulties I was having. He actually agreed with my concerns and supported my criticism of the psychiatry program. I learned that he was considered a bit of a maverick in the psychiatric community; some of the psychiatric staff were clearly not supportive of my using him as a therapist. He suggested medication for my anxiety and depression, but I reasoned that my situation was a response to my environment. I also believed that being medicated for psychiatric symptoms was succumbing to a weakness.

At one point during that year, another of the staff psychiatrists recommended that I see a movie that had just come out. It was called *One Flew Over the Cuckoo's Nest*. She understood, on some level, what I was going through. I learned later from a fellow Harvard Medical School graduate, who had gone immediately into psychiatry, that psychiatric training programs in other places routinely offered supportive group sessions to help psychiatry residents deal with just these issues. My residency did not offer them and instead pathologized the symptoms, adding to my stress.

The growing sense I had was that practice was not up to par, that concern for patients' families was not often in evidence, and that questionable practices were in place. Little did I know that I would confront these issues head on, years down the road.

I did a 6-month rotation on an adolescent inpatient unit. I had wanted to do outpatient adolescent psychiatry, but my psychological difficulties led the administration to decide that I would be better supervised by the staff on the inpatient unit. This unit was in crisis, as the psychiatrist in charge was in the midst of a bitter divorce and custody battle. In fact, the infant of the head nurse (also married) was said to look very much like him. Midway through my 6 months there, they both decamped with their children to Canada, apparently to avoid their respective spouses' obtaining custody of the involved children. The unit was then temporarily assigned to a psychiatrist who had just completed her residency and had little experience in psychiatry, let alone adolescent psychiatry.

Among the patients whom I particularly remember, one was a young, naive teenage girl from the local farm country who had attempted suicide. I established a very trusting relationship with her. Over weeks, in the course of my therapy with her, she revealed that she had been molested as a child. She also disclosed that she was sexually attracted to women instead of men. When I revealed this at our twice-weekly staff meetings, the rest of the staff decided that she was not appropriate on the inpatient unit and, above my objections, discharged her. She had no loving people or family to return to. I do not know what happened to her.

CALIFORNIA AND FAMILY

I was divorced from my second husband more than 20 years ago and raised my two sons, Tim and Nathan, much as a single parent. We moved from Indiana to a small town in the Sierra Nevada mountains (Truckee, California). I was the first and only pediatrician in more than a 40-mile radius, including the North Shore of Lake Tahoe and surrounding communities. I was "on call" all of the time. Much of the work was acute pediatric newborn and emergency room care, something that I hadn't done at all for at least 8 years. It required my being called from home at unpredictable hours, and I had to hire multiple live-in child-care personnel. I was making little money and consequently could pay only limited amounts for long, unpredictable hours of child-care backup. One night a woman came to interview in response to my ad for live-in child care. She had hired a cab to Truckee from Reno, Nevada, 30 miles east. She was very clearly psychotic. I got a friend to take her back to Reno, down the mountain, and paid for her cab.

Nathan and Tim did well in school in Truckee. They skied for the Squaw Valley ski team; Nathan was highly nationally ranked in his age group in ski racing. We spent most weekends at races. Even after we moved to the San Francisco Bay Area a few years later, we continued to travel to the mountains every weekend so the boys could ski race.

The support for this move was the death of my parents. Both had lived to old ages, and their passing generated financial support. We moved to Marin County, just north of San Francisco. I started work as a part of a multidisciplinary team (speech and language, educational specialists, psychologists, behavioral pediatricians) assessing very complex child cases for the California Department of Special Education. The children have, for the most part, severe neurodevelopmental and behavioral disorders; they have often been multiply labeled and often treated with multiple medications. Although some are clearly in need of pharmacologic treatment, the side effects of the medications are sometimes worse than the initial behavior being treated.

I can remember my boys at the time of the move. The older, Nathan, age 10, was a Tahoe-type guy: big and athletic, a ranked ski racer. The younger, Tim, age 8, was a milder personality—he acquired words and reading extremely early and learned quickly.

The three of us spent a great deal of time together as a family. In Tahoe we hiked and camped out in the summers and skied in the winters. We took several week-long vacations with the Sierra Club, camping and hiking with a family group on Kauai and the big island of Hawaii. The boys played sports year round: swimming, ski racing, and soccer. Later they both played varsity water polo for their winning high school team. Nathan was captain during his senior year. Nathan also spent some of his high school years in the mountains, enrolling in the high school up there or being home schooled by me, so that he could continue to train and ski race competitively. I always included Nathan's and Tim's friends in our activities, as I had regretted so much being an only child and liked introducing their friends to camping and hiking. To give a flavor of the types of adventures we had, I recall that one night I took four boys and our two dogs for overnight camping in the High Sierras. It started raining in the middle of the night, and the boys slept soundly. By the time that I put up the tent, the rain had stopped.

1994

The summer of 1994 was different from my previous 10 years. For the first time since my sons were born, I was living in my home by myself. Nathan had, by then, successfully completed a first year of college, ski racing and making reasonable grades. Ominously, his freshman year had been preceded by his rolling his four-wheel-drive car down a mountain in Oregon on his way to his small college in Washington. Miraculously, he climbed out of the car window unhurt. He therefore started his college career year without a car and without the bike and several sets of skis that had been crushed in the accident. This loss made his freshman year in college even more stressful than it would have been ordinarily.

The summer after his freshman year, in 1994, Nathan was touring the country with a college friend in a rainbow-colored Volkswagen van (stereotypes and all, that's what they traveled in), while Tim was in Paraguay for 2 months with a volunteer group called Amigos, digging latrines and teaching about health. Other volunteers in the group obtained iodized salt for people and gave rabies shots to the canine population. He lived with a local "healer" and became very immersed in the culture. I wrote him thoughtful long letters that he found important. It's funny how a separation can lead to writing things down that one doesn't say in person.

At the age of nearly 50 years, I was leading a good life. I was dating a man whom I liked and recreating a life for myself without my boys in the nest. My multiple cats and two golden retrievers kept me company and required regular care and exercise.

When Nathan returned from his cross-country trip in late August 1994, he seemed depressed. In fact, he was withdrawn, and he had become very thin (he was by this time a total vegetarian). He was reading a form of religious writings not traditionally biblical. During a brief trip, his friends later said that he was "lighter" than the rest of them, in a better mood. But back at home, he wandered on our hillside and then took the ferry to Angel Island, a beautiful but isolated island in the San Francisco Bay, spending the night hunkered down. The first ferry brought him home in the morning, as he was told that it was illegal to stay on the island after sunset.

Soon after, he shaved off all of his rather long, dirty-blond, Jesus-type hair. One night, he cried in my arms. I was concerned that something stressful had happened during his traveling and questioned him about depression, which he denied, along with any indication of stressful encounters. He did claim to feel a lot of fear and confusion. After several days at home, he left in the very early morning hours with a college friend to return for his sophomore year. He had not packed anything and had to be pulled out of bed to get on the road.

After several weeks of silence, there came a series of out-of-context phone calls. Nathan was fearful, not sure he could continue in college. He eventually took the bus home. On the way he lost most of his college textbooks, the coin collection from his banker grandfather, and his internal-frame backpack. We later had a college classmate pack up his remaining belongings and ship most of these items home.

In the days prior to Nathan's return home, I had asked the dean at the college to talk with Nathan. The report from the interview was that Nathan was fine but depressed and needed some time at home. Once Nathan came home, I talked with his college friends, and I found out that he had been wandering the campus, sometimes sitting in the dark in a lotus position with a book in his lap. He had been spending nights in the infirmary. One of the nurses there called me when she found out Nathan had left college; she felt that he was coming to the infirmary because of difficulty sleeping prior to midsemester examinations. I feel that it might have been a connection to the fact that I am a doctor and that he felt safe in the medical facility.

When Nathan arrived at home at age 19, on Columbus Day weekend in 1994, he was very thin and extremely withdrawn. He pulled away from the kitten that I had brought with me in the car to greet him and was, it became clear in the next 24 hours, experiencing both auditory and visual hallucinations. These were not particularly threatening but certainly distracting.[3]

PSYCHOSIS

Just at the time that Nathan arrived back home, his dad and his dad's new wife were visiting from Indiana, and Tim was in the first semester of his senior year in high school. None of us got much sleep the first 24 hours. Nathan was not sleeping at all and would wander out of the house at all hours, leaving doors open, allowing indoor-only cats to escape. He would not engage interpersonally through eye contact or conversation. He was clearly distracted, but not by anything that we saw or heard. Tim and I sat up with him that first night, and I asked him about voices. He described a black wall or veil that was keeping him from perceiving the world. He admitted to hearing voices, though with no particular content. The following morning, while out on our porch dressed only in undershorts, he seemed to be twirling and communing with the sunbeams and described the "little people" that he was talking with.

During that first day Nathan's father and I talked. His wife is an army nurse turned attorney and judge; all of us, except Tim, were knowledgeable about psychosis and the need for medication treatment. I had been taught that schizo-phrenia, though treatable, remains a chronic disease from which the individual never really recovers. My belief was that individuals with this condition were probably somehow neurocognitively uneven to begin with. Though at times quirky, Nathan had been psychologically sound throughout childhood and ado-lescence, with a great sense of humor and full enjoyment of all things athletic. A strong boy with very strong nonverbal cognitive skills, he could from a young age figure things out and fix them quite easily. He also was artistic, particularly with carving and wood arts.

That first night home, late in the evening he went up to the undeveloped area behind our house and took off his shoes and left them up there. (After much searching we found them the next morning.) During the night I started calling people that I knew. I had been doing histories and physical examina-tions for our local child and adolescent psychiatric inpatient facility, and I knew which psychiatrists I wanted to evaluate Nathan. Because of the limitations of our insurance and because Nathan knew that I worked on the local psychiatric unit (meaning that I was friends with many of the local mental health person-nel), I called a psychiatrist friend in San Francisco, chief of child and adolescent psychiatry at a major medical center. The following morning, he arranged for a semivoluntary admission to a locked adult ward. Given our friendship, as well as professional relationship, he oversaw Nathan's care at a distance.

Tim was up with me most of the night prior to Nathan's hospitalization. He failed to report to water polo practice early the next morning, and the coach took him to task. Tim was angry and blaming of the coach for reprimanding him, so I called the coach and told him what was going on. Nathan had been captain 2 years previously, and the coach expressed deep sympathy and support for Tim, as well as the rest of us.

Similarly, Tim's senior-year English and physics teachers had also taught Nathan during his senior year and remembered him. During that initial week, Tim wrote an essay about Nathan's return home, and the English teacher was extraordinarily supportive. Similarly, I called the physics teacher, as he had liked Nathan a great deal. I believe that he also offered Tim a measure of support.

After an initial evaluation, including an EEG, Nathan began treatment with the antipsychotic medication Navane. This was started at a relatively low dose to avoid side effects that might keep him from being willing to take it. Even so, he immediately developed significant neurological side effects and hated the medication. But the medication also led to a reduction in his auditory and visual hallucinations. It was apparent to me when he had taken his medication and when he hadn't; he was distracted and unavailable when he had not taken medications in the preceding 12 or so hours.

He was miserable in the hospital. There were few, if any, other people his age, and he did not feel that he had any problems. He called his father and me repeatedly, asking to be let out so that he could come home. His treating physician finally told me that they would be unable to keep him long because he was not sick enough to impress a judge that he needed to be hospitalized against his will. Nathan was also wearing us all down with his phone calls and expressed misery. His younger brother almost put his hand through a wall on the ward when we visited his brother. Tim was strongly opposed to the hospitalization and overwhelmed by the changes in his brother. He called the nurses "Nurse Ratched," invoking the name of the autocratic head nurse from *One Flew Over the Cuckoo's Nest*.

After he had been in the locked ward for 4 days, Nathan went before a judge. We had been told that if I was willing to give him a place to stay, the judge would be unlikely to decide to hold him against his will. Nathan was consequently released "against medical advice," which caused our insurance company to threaten not to pay his bills in the future. That was a stress I hardly needed just then. Because Nathan's hospitalization was partially involuntary, he still feels a deep resentment against me and his father for putting him there.

When he returned home, Nathan was clearly very disabled. I took him to the grocery store, and he could not make any decisions about what he wanted to purchase, picking up one loaf of bread only to return it and pick up another. His inability to make decisions, along with the strange affect he showed (with the accompanying attention it caused), made such trips intolerable for me. I dreaded meeting our friends on outings. It wasn't something that could be explained in a few sentences, and Nathan would get angry if I insinuated that there was anything wrong. Whereas Nathan had previously been a source of pride when I was out with him locally, his presentation was now alien and uncomfortable.

Nathan was also "cheeking" his medications and then spitting them out. Tim found out and told his father, who had come back to California after Nathan left the hospital. They decided to try to get Nathan to take his medications without telling me. I found out and was able to convince Nathan to take them by clearly stating how important it was to me that the medications were taken. He related to me with strong ambivalence. His initial reaction was always to go against anything that I suggested, but if I pushed hard he would do it. We had been close, with similar personalities in many respects, and had clashed a lot through his adolescence.

At that time I was not functioning very well. I could not go to work because I could not leave Nathan alone in the house safely, and my anxiety levels were well beyond what is healthy or tolerable. Coincidentally with Nathan's psychosis, I was starting involvement in a major study conducted jointly by the Berkeley Psychology Department and the University of California, San Francisco, Child Psychiatry division. Contact with this group of professionals was a support during the following years. Even so, nobody was particularly trained in treatment of acute-onset psychosis in a young adult. I had difficulty from the start finding the right kind of psychiatric help, despite all of my connections. One of my hopes is that that this chapter, and this book, will help other parents to be able to seek and find the right kind of help for their mentally ill son or daughter.

The main source of my anxiety was that I believed, based on information I learned during my psychiatry residency, that schizophrenia was a deteriorating and incurable disease. Logical thinking was one of the most important givens in life for me and most everyone I know, and Nathan's inability to think logically was devastating to him, his brother Tim, their dad, and me. In retrospect, my prior training was a deterrent rather than an asset, as my anxiety and fear diffused through our whole household. Being calm and matter-of-fact helps a lot when dealing with a mentally ill relative, and it helps immeasurably to believe that psychosis is a curable entity.

Another hurdle was that Nathan was 19. Although living in my household and financially dependent, his rights of privacy as an adult kept involved professionals from being able to talk with me. I tried to find him vocational services and authorized neuropsychiatric testing. Done at a time at which his thinking was very abnormal, the testing showed an average IQ (101), with attentional difficulties noted. I assumed that if his psychotic symptoms had been in check, the scores would have been higher.

Nathan saw a psychiatrist weekly after his hospitalization. I paid privately because I needed to find a clinician who was not a friend. His medication was not changed despite ongoing neurological difficulties, stiffness, and restless extremities. He would take the medication only under coercion. Indeed, he was very disorganized. At one point the psychiatrist suggested that he take public transportation, not realizing that he was so disorganized mentally that he couldn't even begin to negotiate the system by himself, even if carefully scripted.

I drove him to his appointments on my days off (I have worked part time for many years), and we often had breakfast together afterward. Sometimes I would participate in the sessions. They were often very painful, and there was no real progress. There was no discussion of diagnosis and no suggestion of change in medication. There was always the undercurrent that I was part of his difficulties. The symptoms were by now subtle, hard for others to appreciate.

Nathan's symptoms continued to keep him from participating successfully in life. He did not take showers or participate in household activities. He would frequently engage me in conversations about "dreams" that he had difficulty separating from reality—and about his father in the Midwest and the telepathy that they had together. I encouraged Nathan to do activities, but he would only do so when I was working by his side. We swam laps and moved a half cord of wood to the back of our house together.

Nathan gave up quickly and only tolerated brief periods of time in public places, such as art museums or restaurants. He would often worry about a situation and not be able to participate, though he couldn't tell me why. He tried to jump out of the car on our way to Tahoe for a family visit with a group of old friends. He decided while on the way to the airport that he could not go on a trip to the Caribbean with us, hiring a cab and going home rather than getting on the plane. Fortunately, a good friend was tending our pets and could keep an eye out and reassure me by e-mail. It was extremely difficult, though, for me to make the decision to continue the trip without Nathan.

Much of that first year is vague to me; I was deeply lost in anxiety and depression. I do remember telling my younger son a year later, on Christmas day, that I didn't want to go on. He yelled at me that I should never tell him that and that it was unacceptable. He was right.

At one point, in the middle of another heated discussion with Nathan about what was real and what was not, I remember curling up in tears on the floor of the kitchen in frustration and probably as an attempt to let him know how very distressed I was. He did get the message. It is strange that when I really escalated my actions—although I feel that I did so in an unacceptable way in this instance—he did hear me through the haze of his psychosis.

Nathan managed to find a number of jobs over the next 2 years. Indeed, he got his first job within a few months of his hospitalization. He presented himself well and had references from high school summer jobs in the community. Among other jobs, he worked in a hardware store, as a pizza delivery person, as a summer water polo coach for preadolescent children, as a substitute preschool teacher, as a busboy, and as a driver at a moving company. His first job, in the hardware store, ended after a few weeks. He came home laughing about having dropped a whole pile of lumber from a hoist. He also started missing days because he would stay up all night, unable to get up in the morning.

At his substitute teaching job, the preschoolers loved him and would crawl into his lap and talk about the fact that he hadn't brushed his hair (he hadn't) that morning. He was well liked there.

He applied for a job at a local sporting goods store. They had all applicants fill out a form that was supposed to assess their reliability. Nathan answered a few questions truthfully, such as saying "yes" to the fact that he had knowingly purchased stolen merchandise. On the basis of this response, he did not get the job. A friend of his, with similar experiences, later found a job at the same store. When I asked the manager about the test, he said that he felt people should have the judgment to lie on certain parts of it. Nathan did not have that awareness.

In all, from late 1994 through January of 1996, Nathan held at least six different jobs. I had called our local vocational services and met with them and Nathan about potential work. Unfortunately, they were more oriented to helping individuals who were physically or cognitively handicapped. They had little understanding of mental illness, and Nathan disliked the idea of getting any kind of "agency" help. He lasted only 1 day at a "job corps" position. Part of the problem was that the hot temperatures and Nathan's medication did not get along. Another was that most of the other people working had mental retardation. The group leader was Nathan's age, and Nathan felt he belonged more in that position than as a "worker."

Nathan continued to be unreliable and would take off in the middle of the night to cruise Napa or, once, to drive to Oregon to visit college friends. These friends called me because they knew of his difficulties. After a few days, they were able to persuade him to drive back home. Fortunately, he had retained his good driving reflexes. Yet in 1 year he got three speeding tickets for driving at speeds over 80 miles per hour. He lost his license, which was a big relief for me. But he got claustrophobic on buses, partially because of his size and partially because of his discomfort at being in a closed space with strangers.

MY REACTIONS

I have already indicated that I was extremely anxious during this first year of Nathan's psychosis. I had trouble finding practical information on what I should be doing. I called our local alliance for mental illness and went to a few meetings, but the leaders were very pessimistic about any kind of recovery. The young adults with mental illness represented here had significantly more difficulties than Nathan (e.g., having been in prison, on the streets, out of touch for years), and I was more educated about mental illness than was the group. I felt unsupported, and the meetings exacerbated my anxieties and depression rather than reducing them. That was when I first resolved to try to fill the obvious need for better resources and support for families in such crisis.

I went online and tried to get as much information as I could. Though it would be potentially very taxing of my finances, I would have paid for a residential school or treatment center if one had been appropriate and helpful and acceptable to Nathan. I had a pretty good idea of what the program might consist of, but I couldn't find anything that seemed even remotely promising. His symptoms were at once so subtle and so disabling that he fell between the cracks. Even many of my closest friends, who had known him much of his life, had trouble seeing his symptoms.

On the recommendation of a family counselor whom I was seeing for supportive therapy, I hired a nurse who was supposedly gifted in coming into homes and helping to mediate for disturbed patients and their parents. There was, unfortunately, an immediate disconnection, as she was a nurse of the old school and I was a physician. That is, she was not comfortable in coming into my home and advising me. As well, my mother had been a nurse, and we had clashed repeatedly through and after my adolescence.

Her immediate take was that Nathan was simply depressed. She felt that if I were more structured and demanding of him, it would relieve much of his symptomatology. Her training and experience were related to individuals with retardation; again, Nathan's psychotic features remained subtle to those who did not know him well, including her.

In an attempt to follow her mandate, I became more matter-of-fact and less flexible. Nathan grew worse over the next few weeks, even threatening to shoot and kill me and then kill himself. His brother, home for college for winter break, heard him on the phone ordering a gun clip from a local sporting store. Things escalated, and, after Tim had talked with me, I guessed that Nathan may have obtained a gun. I looked in his car while he was asleep one January morning in 1996—he was still having problems sleeping and often slept in all morning. I found a gun under some blankets in the back of his car.

I called the local sheriff's office and gave them the gun. They later told me that it was a "hot" gun, stolen from Oregon. Nathan told us that he obtained it by trade for his brother's electric guitar in our local downtown community. The sheriffs responding to my call talked with Nathan, still in his bedroom. He was not willing to say that he wanted to kill himself or anybody else, so involuntary hospitalization was not in order. Later that day I wrote out an agreement between Nathan and me stating that he would not kill himself. He signed it with some formality.

I also called his dad in the Midwest and his three half-siblings (more than 10 years older than he), along with their spouses and children. In the next few days all of them called him to express their concern and love for Nathan. Some weeks later he admitted to me that during this time he had taken a shotgun and held it to his head (he has long arms) but couldn't pull the trigger.

All of these events occurred during or just after the winter holidays, December 1995 and January 1996. It seemed that Nathan's symptoms had escalated in the late fall. Nathan's psychiatrist was away for a month of vacation, and the backup psychiatrists covering for him would not help me without seeing Nathan. Yet Nathan refused to go with me to see anybody, so we were stuck.

I finally found a psychiatrist who was willing to talk with me on the phone. He was relatively local, but I had not known of him. He said that he was not taking patients who required acute hospitalization but that he would be glad to see me if I felt that it might help. We later found out that his sons and mine (of similar ages) had known each other through soccer and water polo. I started to see him regularly and still see him, though now only several times a year. He convinced me to try antidepressant and antianxiety medications. I continue on these medications, and I am eternally thankful for this intervention. He was and continues to be a huge support for me.

This same psychiatrist helped me when I felt that Nathan's care was suboptimal. He actually participated in a meeting, just after Nathan's gun incident, with me and Nathan's psychiatrist to discuss the diagnosis and treatment plan. Nathan's regular psychiatrist was a bit evasive but said that he thought the diagnosis was schizoaffective disorder. When asked about Nathan's suicidality (I had just taken the gun away the month before), he thought that maybe antidepressants were in order. In Nathan's few visits since the gun incident, his regular psychiatrist had minimized the significance of the episode and consequently did not believe that any pertinent treatment was needed.

Despite the talk of antidepressant medications, I do not remember that any were prescribed. Nathan continued on the Navane. In retrospect, he should have been systematically tried on the new antipsychotic medications available, the so-called second-generation agents that have a different mechanism of action. Some of these were available at the time and could have been an excellent choice, I now realize.

In retrospect, all I can say is that I did not know. I still harbor resentment against Nathan's psychiatrist for being unresponsive.

At my urging, Nathan was finally switched to Risperdal, a second-generation antipsychotic. The Navane was tapered as the Risperdal was started. In the middle of this process, he had a temporary period during which his thinking became much clearer. I later talked with a researcher on psychotropic treatment of schizophrenia, who said that others had noticed this phenomenon. As I think about this now, I wish that I had thought to suggest that Nathan remain on both medications at low doses.

On Risperdal, Nathan immediately started to gain weight and to eat constantly. At 6 feet 5 inches, very athletic and slim, he ballooned from around 200 pounds to close to 300 in about 4 months, developing signs of endocrine imbalance now known to be related to the newer antipsychotic medications.[4] Over the next year or so, he was tried on additional second-generation antipsychotic medications.

A few months later, Nathan's dad in the Midwest suggested that Nathan come for a visit. Both Nathan and I were ecstatic to accept this offer.

INDIANA WITH DAD AND BACK HOME

Nathan went to Indiana but had a very long unexpected layover in Denver (10 hours or so) that worried us all a great deal. He arrived and ended up unexpectedly spending close to a year, at his father's urging and to my great relief. Living with a mentally ill relative is intense and draining. It certainly occupied a significant proportion of my thoughts on a daily basis.

A vignette from Nathan's stay in Indiana is as follows: One day he was helping his older half-brother plant some trees outside the half-brother's new house. The bulldozers were creating the yard, and Nathan was supposed to be planting a tree. When the family looked out to find Nathan, however, he was asleep on the ground near the tree. Things still weren't quite right.

Encouragingly, Nathan's half-sister, an attorney, trusted him to take good care of her two young sons. In fact, all three of Nathan's much older half-siblings were a tremendous help, through his suicidal and threatening phase during the 1995–1996 holiday season and then during his months in Indiana.

When Nathan returned home to California, he was significantly overweight but continued to eat all day and night, gaining even more weight. In the morning I would find multiple pizza boxes and fast-food containers in the kitchen sink. For a while he dressed like his 60-year-old, Midwestern-attorney dad. Gone were the Grateful Dead scarves, tie-dyed shirts, and baggy pants more typical of California. He had also adopted some of his dad's speech patterns and mannerisms, reacting to situations in a manner more typical of a moderate Midwesterner than a liberal Californian. I have realized that his psychotic period and its aftermath must have made him very uncertain about his persona. He therefore did what younger individuals do, which is to copy the mannerisms and personal characteristics of the same-sex adult they spend the most time with.

Needless to say, having a son back in the household with the clothing style and personal characteristics (not to mention politics) of my ex-husband was not an easy situation for me. It has taken years for Nathan to evolve back, with confidence, into his own persona, to do his own thinking about his views. I feel that a lot of this has had to do with poor self-confidence. That is, he lost a significant part of the experiences that help form a young adult identity, and I believe that he is still in the process of making up the gap. He now will take chances, stating his own opinion and then substantiating it in discussion with me or others.

There is a lesson here. After he had returned from Indiana, I often had a great deal of trouble listening to his rambling explanations about things. I was embarrassed when he talked this way to strangers; I would dismiss him quickly and not give him the time to fully explain himself. His brother and his school friends, in contrast, were more patient and provided sounding boards for these early attempts at solid individual reasoning. I believe that it is difficult for parents to distance themselves enough to let expression develop, especially after a period of serious disturbance. I hope that I have learned to back off and let him find his voice.

Nathan now works as an activities director at a local exclusive nursing home. The staff, as well as the elderly individuals at the home, have consistently enjoyed his companionship and provided an objective and nurturing sounding board for his continuing adult maturation.

CONTINUING TREATMENT AND REFOUND IDENTITY

When Nathan returned home from Indiana, I was able to find a local psychiatrist who would take on his care. This man was very nurturing; his liking for sports and physical fitness and his therapy training background were similar to mine.

Nonetheless, it was a difficult set of interactions. Nathan was very uncooperative when it came to medications and maintaining a therapeutic relationship. He was still very inattentive, his thinking was tangential, and he had very poor short-term memory. We soon learned that I needed to write grocery lists down if there was any hope of his purchasing more than one item.

A major additional problem was that I still was very anxious, and the relationship between Nathan and me was often adversarial. He felt that I was to blame for the fact that he had no money and was not able to successfully negotiate a successful adult life in school or in a job. In turn, I wished that somebody would do something, anything, to help him return to more solid thinking and more solid identity, faster.

I made many very long, anxious phone calls to his new psychiatrist in an attempt to communicate the difficulties that I was seeing at home. We finally developed a plan: I would write a letter to this new psychiatrist. Nathan would read it first and then take it in and discuss it. Sometimes the follow-up would be a direct phone call to me from the psychiatrist in Nathan's presence. The goal was to make communication clear, so that Nathan could air out his strong individual views about his home life and treatment and I could be involved, too.

At some point a year or more later, Nathan was treated briefly with a low dose of the SSRI antidepressant Zoloft. After 3 to 4 weeks he began exhibiting very pressured speech and stealing my checks and credit card numbers to make extravagant purchases. He bought a $300 pair of earrings for an old girlfriend whom he hadn't seen in a very long while. It didn't take too long to diagnose mania (actually, probably just hypomania), and the Zoloft was tapered and discontinued. At the same time, despite Nathan's spending and pressured speech, he seemed sad and irritable. I now know that there is such a thing as a mixed state in which individuals can be both manic and depressed at the same time. So the schizoaffective disorder diagnosis made some sense.

During this period there were delays in getting Nathan started with some of the newer second-generation antipsychotic medications. I think that part of the reason for this delay was that I thought that antipsychotic medicines were useful in treating only the truly psychotic features of the illness, the so-called positive symptoms such as hallucinations and delusions. I now know that these medications have the potential to also treat the disordered thinking, as well as the attentional and memory problems, which can exist after the blatantly psychotic features have abated. Indeed, Nathan has not been actively psychotic for a number of years. Only recently, however, has his full personality returned and has he gained the ability to self-reflect. He will now say, for example (with resignation), "make me a list" when I ask him to go to the store on the way home from work.

Recent research affirms the importance of the all-too-often-ignored "thinking problems" that accompany schizophrenia, as well as the fact that most of the current medications do not adequately treat the core problems with attention and short-term memory.[5] After many years, Nathan does not currently take any medications, and his thinking has gotten progressively better over time.

I have been keeping myself current in the psychiatric literature, and in the past year, numerous articles have been written about the neuropsychiatric cognitive deficits that can be residual after the acute psychosis is successfully treated. There is, fortunately, a move to treat these cognitive deficits with newer medications and with cognitive therapy. My biggest frustration with the process of Nathan's illness has been that people seldom recognize the debilitation caused by these cognitive weaknesses. The acute, florid symptoms of psychosis grab people's attention, but the subtler problems in planning, memory, and reasoning ability often escape detection. Only those close family members who have known Nathan all of his life seem to recognize these changes and the consequent extent of their influence on his motivation, successful college completion, and work attitudes and attendance.

It is only recently that I have been able to speak clearly about these issues and be understood. In fact, I doubt that this would be so clear to me if I had not had long-term work experience in assessing children and adolescents as part of a multidisciplinary team. Cognitive deficits *can* be reversed with treatment; more aggressive identification and treatment of the attentional, motivational, and memory deficits that can accompany severe mental illness are huge priorities.[6]

Nathan has always had significant symptoms of depression, as well. Indeed, some of the psychiatrists who know him believe that he probably initially suffered a psychotic depression. This view is further supported by my own long-term struggles with depression and my older half-sister's recent bout of severe depression in her early 80s. She recently told me that, in retrospect, she had experienced several other clear episodes of depression earlier in her life. Her generation is even less willing to talk about mental illness, though certainly depression has a more acceptable reputation than schizophrenia.

1998 TO THE PRESENT

The years from 1998 through 2004 were somewhat similar. Nathan tried many types of college courses and many different jobs. He was most successful working in theatrical productions. He was able to learn to work a lighting board and to work on stage production. For several summers he had odd jobs for an outdoor summer theater production company; he also had a small role in a Marin theater company production. The social milieu of the stage seemed to suit him and support the return of more normal thinking processes. The more time that Nathan could spend with peers out of the household, the better things became. Nonjudgmental social support is crucial for people recovering from mental illness. At the same time, given the stigma related to mental illness, such support is difficult to find.

In 2004 Nathan took a course in nursing home activities and rehabilitation. As before, however, he started losing motivation and stopped attending classes about midway through. Fortunately, his instructor and fellow students provided support and encouragement. He was able to catch up and complete the course and then do an "internship" at a local nursing home. In fact, there was a job opening there, and he was hired as an assistant activities director in the late fall of 2004.

He has consistently worked full-time at this job since then. His fellow workers and the elderly patients have provided considerable support and contributed to Nathan's increased self-esteem. There have been times when he has impulsively "quit," but the owner of the nursing home has continually encouraged him, and he consequently has persevered.

A continuing issue is that Nathan still is very overweight. As I noted earlier, this became an issue when he began taking second-generation antipsychotic medications. Even though he is no longer taking any medication, one of his key goals needs to be weight loss—but his motivation to do this is low.

Overall, much has changed over the dozen years since Nathan came home psychotic. Psychiatrists now recognize more clearly the subgroup of individuals who are in remission from the floridly psychotic symptoms of schizophrenia. There are a variety of new medications that address the range of symptoms, including the thinking problems, associated with schizophrenia. There is a spectrum of disease, and active work can help to deal with the huge stigma that accompanies mental illness.[7] Even so, I continue to read novels that portray an extremely inaccurate image of mental illness and the individuals who suffer from it. It is amazing that even though the incidence of mental illness is as high as it is, most novelists seem to have no idea of the reality of the issue.

CONCLUSIONS

I have been writing and rewriting this chapter for well over a year now. This year has brought tremendous growth in our household, and at least part of it is due to my writing this chapter and, as a consequence, presenting my perception of these dozen years to Nathan. We have now begun to talk about his hallucinations, with the discussion initiated by Nathan. When I presented a partially finished version of this chapter to him, Nathan unexpectedly made printouts and took them to the head nurse at his workplace and to an intelligent, bedridden resident. All of this openness is a huge breakthrough, given that Nathan had never "owned" any of his behavior patterns of the past decade-plus. I believe that his newfound willingness to be reflective is a good sign for his recovery.

One of the greatest difficulties that I have had through this journey is that Nathan's illness and course were very different from others that I had personally known or heard about. I soon came to feel that nobody could really say what would happen. I had been taught in medical school and later in my psychiatric residency that people were either psychotic or not—and that if they adhered to an antipsychotic medication regimen, then things would go well, and they could be relatively normal.

But this was not so for Nathan. Although the hallucinations and loss of contact with reality were clearly suppressed with the initial antipsychotic medications that he took, difficulties with judgment, short-term memory, and attention remained in place. Indeed, some of these symptoms—especially slowed thinking and tiredness—may have been side effects of his medication. His lack of motivation could well have been part of his primary disorder. It could also have been related to the understandable psychological impact of the huge changes in his life over a short period of months. Perhaps too little attention is paid to the fact that individuals who become psychotic have had a huge and frightening experience and would be expected to have a prolonged stress response.

Even though I read all the popular books and saw the movies as they came out—including *A Beautiful Mind* and Steve Hinshaw's book about his father, *The Years of Silence Are Past*[8]—these all made me feel very uncertain. Despite the similarities in the symptoms portrayed in these works to Nathan's, I could not personally relate to the specifics of their illnesses. Of course, these authors have a perspective that comes from the opposite pole—looking back on the past and knowing outcome. My perspective was always uncertain and doubtful of the future.

The attitude, even among well-meaning professionals, that there was not a possibility of a "normal" future in store for Nathan constantly dragged me down. I liken the uncertainty to riding a unicycle on a tightrope two stories up (and note that my balance has never been very good). I have long felt that there is a vast spectrum of schizophrenic and bipolar disorders, with the vast majority falling in between the two in terms of presenting symptoms and course. I simply didn't know of the possibility of long-term recoveries during Nathan's first years with his condition. When I raised the issue of recovery and of the need for aggressive, thoughtful treatment (not simply high doses of medication but also frequent reevaluations), I was told, even by mental health professionals that I knew and respected, that "this was the way it was."

Several of Nathan's friends seem to have had near misses and gone through withdrawal, paranoia, and sleep disturbances. Their families were deeply concerned. I know several of these individuals, now in their 30s and having graduated from college. They are doing well with their lives and are happy. Indeed, there are now ongoing studies of individuals with such prepsychotic symptoms, and the best information is that about 40% of these individuals go on to develop positive symptoms of psychosis.[9]

One close friend of Nathan's is still not doing well. He became psychotic after his freshman year in college, has continued to have difficulties with drug and alcohol abuse, and lives a marginal existence. My understanding is that he still is quite paranoid. He had several very close family members with diagnoses of paranoid schizophrenia.

Because I knew his psychiatrist, I asked his mother to mention to the psychiatrist that these two young men, who had been such good friends, had both had onset of psychotic illness within a year of each other. The psychiatrist apparently chalked it up to their being drawn to each other because of early symptoms. I felt put down when hearing this view. Why not reason that perhaps they were drawn to each other because they were both captains of the water polo team over several years?

In 2003 an HBO documentary was produced called *People Say I'm Crazy.* It follows a young artist, John Cadigan, and his battle with the onset and course of schizophrenia.[10] This was really the first production I've encountered that mirrors many of Nathan's and our family's struggles with mental illness over the past 12 years. Having watched it, we subsequently met John, his sister Katie, who produced the film, and his mother. At one particularly poignant moment, John asks his mother: "What was the hardest thing?" She said that there were many hard parts but that the hardest was seeing the pain and struggle produced in her son by his "brain disease."

During the summer of 2005 Nathan and I participated in the San Francisco NAMI (National Alliance on Mental Illness) fund-raising walk with John and his family. One year later, before the walk, I was told that John had "changed his look." He had lost the 130+ pounds that he had gained as a result of side effects from medication; he had also cut his hair and beard and wore stylish new glasses. When I saw John, I would not have recognized him. He looked not like the "old John" but like a young, handsome professional artist. I exchanged looks with John's mother and immediately sensed the importance of this transformation for John and his family. She sighed, "John is back."

The overwhelming experience of mental illness and the neurological and metabolic side effects of medication can create a person who "looks mentally ill." This "look" contributes to the social burden of the individual, as well as family members, contributing to a feeling of loss in the family—and judgment by society. Helping to achieve transformations to a different state of mind, and even a different appearance, is important for full recovery.

Recovery is a continuing process. John still cannot work full time and continues to experience medication side effects. Nathan, though off medications and working full time, still grapples with his weight, a lack of full self-confidence, and societal stigma. Families look deeply into their offspring's behaviors and physical appearance, hoping for signs of full recovery. The fight, for all those who experience severe mental illness, is a long one.

COLUMBUS DAY, 2006

I have learned a great deal over the past 12 years, and I am a better physician and parent for it. I now know that my initial reaction, to push for full recovery, was the right one. As more and more is known, and as better medications and interventions are created, many if not all of the symptoms of mental illness will be able to be treated. My first response, were I to do this over, would be to find a psychiatrist for Nathan who is very knowledgeable about the current treatment of first-episode psychosis and the medication options. I would want a person who also knows about the responses of family members, particularly those who have some mental health training, to the illness in their loved one. I would want that professional, with the permission of the patient, to actively include involved family members in decisions and planning. A team approach that includes knowledgeable members of the psychiatry, social services, and per- haps even legal and educational communities and that involves the individual, along with primary and extended family, is highly desirable. Although such an approach may not be cheap, the financial toll of inadequately treated mental illness on family, community, and, ultimately, tax resources is overwhelming. In fact, a well-thought-out team approach would ultimately produce significant financial and emotional savings to all of society. My ultimate hope is that the world that my hoped-for grandchildren grow up in will indeed be a new world in the way that mental illness is understood and treated.

NOTES

1. Kety, S. S., Rosenthal, D., Wender, P. H., & Schulsinger, F. (1971). Mental illness in the biological and adoptive families of adopted schizophrenics. *American Journal of Psychiatry, 128*, 302–306.
2. Hinshaw, S. P. (2007). *The mark of shame: Stigma of mental illness and an agenda for change.* New York: Oxford University Press.
3. What of the role of any drug use that might have precipitated Nathan's onset of mental illness? He had done some experimenting during adolescence with marijuana and nitrous oxide. Adolescent marijuana use may be associated with onset of psychotic disorders in genetically vulnerable individuals, as reported in Caspi, A., Moffitt, T. E., Cannon, M., Murray, J., Harrington, R., Taylor, H. et al. (2005). Moderation of the effect of adolescent-onset cannabis use on adult psychosis by a functional polymorphism in the catechol-o-methyltransferase gene: Longitudinal evidence of a gene x environment interaction. *Biological Psychiatry, 57*, 1117–1127. But note that most adolescents who use marijuana (including a number of Nathan's friends) never develop psychosis. Overall, there must be a multitude of genetic and environmental factors that lead to an early adult psychotic break. Although Nathan, I, and our family do not discount the possible role of drugs in exacerbating the situation, I do not believe that eliminating illegal drug use (or alcohol use for that matter) would significantly eliminate these occurrences.

4. Lieberman, J. A., Stroup, T. S., McEvoy, J. P., Swartz, M. S., Rosenheck, R. A., Perkins, D. O., et al. (2005). Clinical antipsychotic trials of intervention effectiveness (CATIE): Effectiveness of antipsychotic drugs in patients with chronic schizophrenia. *New England Journal of Medicine, 353,* 1209–1223.

5. Milev, P., Ho, B.-C., Arndt, S., & Andreason, N. C. (2005). Predictive values of neurocognition and negative symptoms on functional outcome in schizophrenia: A longitudinal first-episode study with 7-year follow-up. *American Journal of Psychiatry, 162,* 495–506.

6. Erhart, S. M., Marder, S. R., & Carpenter, W. T. (2006). Treatment of schizophrenia negative symptoms: Future prospects. *Schizophrenia Bulletin, 32,* 234–237; but see Wirshing, D. A., Pierre, J. M., Erhart, S. M., & Boyd, J. A. (2003). Understanding the new and evolving profile of adverse drug effects in schizophrenia. *Psychiatric Clinics of North America, 26,* 165–190.

7. Cannon, T. D., & Keller, M. C. (2006). Endophenotypes in the genetic analyses of mental disorders. *Annual Review of Clinical Psychology, 2,* 267–290; see also Hinshaw (2007).

8. Hinshaw, S. P. (2002). *The years of silence are past: My father's life with bipolar disorder.* New York: Cambridge University Press.

9. Avehart-Treichel, J. (2001, March 16). Early symptoms may hold key to preventing schizophrenia. *Psychiatric News.* Available at http://www.psych.org/pnews/01-03-16/key.html

10. Cadigan, J. (2005). *People Say I'm Crazy.* Available at http://www.peoplesayimcrazy.org/film.html

7 The Meaning of Mental Health (and Other Lessons Learned)

Marc S. Atkins

It was a clear, late summer night in upstate New York. I was walking very fast across the quad of the small liberal arts college I was attending. It was the fall of my sophomore year. The quad was empty of Frisbee-playing students, and all was quiet save for the voices racing through my mind. I was heading back to my dorm, but the speed with which I walked bore no relation to my need to be in my room.

I was driven by something else, though I had no idea what. I stopped abruptly as someone approached. Did I know him? He seemed to know me. He said hello and asked where I was going. I glanced his way, wondering how I knew him and how I would answer him. My hair, down past my shoulders in curled randomness, looked wind-blown, though there was no wind.

I turned abruptly as I heard my name called out from across the quad. "What?" I yelled, apparently to no one. I turned back, smiling, but my acquaintance looked scared, the way I thought people look at the mentally ill. "Did you hear that," I asked him, "from over there?"

I don't remember his response except to know that his look told me that I needed help in a way that no one else had been able to communicate.

There are moments still when I remember the days and nights of my late teens with stark clarity. Mostly, however, they are memories that feel long past, although never far from my thoughts. You don't truly forget things like this, especially not when you work in the mental health field: a curious choice of professions in one respect, but an inspired one in another. Bridging worlds and perspectives is my work, and my own experiences, if harnessed appropriately, can be the basis for an unusual understanding of mental health in context. I am at once therapist, patient, neither, and both. My roles become confused, my perspective divided. And yet, though at first I found this frightening, I now understand it as a strength and an opportunity. I am, I realized long ago, a teacher with an unusual perspective on my work. I was there where the patient sits.

I felt misunderstood, maligned, but ultimately rescued. How can I communicate this to my students and my patients?

A few years ago I was jogging through the campus of the National Institutes of Health in Bethesda with a colleague whom I had met just a few days before. He and I served on a panel reviewing grants for the National Institute of Mental Health. As we jogged past the Naval Hospital I asked him if he was a veteran and could get us inside to get some water. He and I were similar in age, of the Vietnam War generation. He said that no, he had never served in the military, but that he had his own battle scars from that time.

We stopped running and talked on a bench. He described his battles with alcohol and drugs in his early 20s and his fear at the time that he would never recover. Even today, he said, he sometimes worries. He and I agreed that at times, when reviewing grants or reading studies related to mental health, we think of ourselves as recipients of the services we are reviewing—or, alternatively, we take the perspective of research participants. It was something that neither he nor I had talked about with anyone else, feeling the same stigma that we knew others felt. Unlike our current clients or research participants, we had made it out and now stood on the other side.

As we talked, what he and I realized was that we felt both a privilege and an obligation. We each believed that our own experiences gave us an insight into the world of mental illness that many of our colleagues would not be able to grasp. Neither of us had articulated this to anyone prior to this conversation. We were not proposing a privileged status, we agreed, but rather were allowing our own experiences to inform our work. Perhaps now, some three decades later, we had reached some form of clarity and comfort.

CYCLING OUT OF CONTROL

I was born in New York City, the third child in a family of four siblings. I grew up on the lower East Side of Manhattan, in a housing project known as Knicker-bocker Village, or KV, as it was known to its inhabitants. KV had a reputation as a hotbed of left-wing political activity, in part because it had one of the strongest tenant organizations in New York, and, perhaps more persuasively, because it was the home of Julius and Ethel Rosenberg, the only Americans to have been convicted and electrocuted for treason during the anti-Communist McCarthy era of the early 1950s.

My parents, both lawyers, were active in the labor and civil rights movements of the 1940s to 1960s, and my father was one of the lead attorneys for the KV tenants' union. Among my parents' proudest contributions was their lead advocacy for integrating KV's tenants, including the first interracial couple, in the early 1950s. When we left KV in 1960, the husband in this couple, an artist, drew a cartoon of my father holding back the moving vans that depicted both my parents' and their friends' great ambivalence about our leaving. My siblings and I accompanied my parents on many demonstrations and marches, including the civil rights demonstration in Washington, D.C., in 1963 at which Dr. Martin Luther King, Jr., made his famous "I Have a Dream" speech.

KV was built in 1924 to replace the tuberculosis-infested tenements known as Lung City. In fact, it was in the forefront of the affordable housing movement as the first housing project that was built with federal funds.[1] KV was a multi-ethnic community, nestled between the Manhattan and Brooklyn bridges, a few blocks from the now-abandoned Fulton Fish Market. With Chinatown a few blocks west and the Bowery and Little Italy a few more blocks north, there was no shortage of diversity of food, culture, and personalities. My family lived in KV from the late 1930s to 1960, when we moved to Forest Hills, Queens, at the time that I was 9 years old.

Although my parents may have been ambivalent about leaving KV, my younger brother and I were less conflicted. The neighborhood surrounding KV had deteriorated, and it was becoming progressively more dangerous. There were many reports of roving gangs, and I had experienced frequent bullying from older peers. Forest Hills, Queens, looked positively idyllic to my young eyes, and I recall feeling quite safe, especially during my elementary school years. On the other hand, as I approached my teenage years, my political precociousness—a logical carryover from the KV culture in which I was raised—was less accepted in the more conservative, middle-class community of Forest Hills. My passion through my adolescence was equal parts basketball and left-wing politics, with the later surpassing the former as I progressed through high school.

I entered Hobart College in 1969, a small liberal arts college in the Finger Lakes region of New York, at the height of the anti-Vietnam War movement. Given my background and interests, I was—though a college freshman—among the vocal leaders on this small campus as the antiwar movement escalated nationally. It seems to me that 1969 was an unprecedented time of student influence and although this was exciting at times, it was clear to me even at the time that it was more than I could manage. I frequently spoke in public, and when I did I spoke quickly, impulsively, dramatically, and more than a few times stupidly. I sought the spotlight at times. More frequently, however, I felt thrust in the lead when I would have preferred the shade of anonymity. I felt that the events were controlling me and that I had little choice but to respond.

The stakes increased when an undercover FBI agent infiltrated our campus and, bumbling though he may have been to most of us, managed to convince a few of my classmates to bomb the ROTC building on campus. I don't know if these students were ever arrested, but I knew who they were, and I was very concerned with the turn of events toward violence. The FBI informant, who went by the name Tom Thomas (his real name was Thomas Tongyai, but he was known to us as Tommy the Traveler because of his self-proclaimed widespread travels through the pantheon of left-wing political circles), was an irritant to most of us and not taken seriously. But I knew from my classmates that he had taught them how to make the bomb that they used to blow up the ROTC building, and I knew that he was agitating others toward similar acts.

About a month after the ROTC building was destroyed, Tommy the Traveler was exposed when he attempted a drug bust in the largest dorm on campus. By now he had become a well-known fixture at the college, and apparently the sight of him arresting students for purchasing drugs was more than the students could tolerate. The campus erupted as word spread of his activities that night.

Or so I was told. I was not on campus at the time, having taken off on a road trip to California with a few friends. Off the hook on that one, I thought—that is, until I received a subpoena to appear before a grand jury to testify against the students who were on trial for conspiracy to riot.[2] My parents hired an attorney to advise me, but this action did little to suppress my building anxiety. I was not much concerned for my own welfare, as I had broken no laws and I was not myself under investigation. But I was very concerned that my knowledge of others' activities could land them in jail.

I suspect that through all of this most people saw me as a reasonably well-functioning if somewhat brooding and intense young adult, despite what I imagine was an obvious sense of uneasiness. After all, given the events, it was not surprising that I would be troubled, and no doubt I was not the only one experiencing sleepless nights. Subpoenas and the like were serious stuff. But as my experiences during freshman year accumulated, I began feeling increasingly more overwhelmed and frightened. In retrospect, it seems inevitable that it would all come crashing down.

LESSON #1: YOU NEVER KNOW

The episode of auditory hallucination noted in the opening to this chapter led to my withdrawal from school to return home and receive psychiatric treatment, which I had resisted for most of the previous year. My parents had noted my agitation and anxiety, but I had dismissed their concerns (and my own) as a by-product of my political activism. Why shouldn't I be agitated? After all, we had a war to end!

My parents were very sympathetic to my antiwar sentiments but concerned with my well-being. A few visits to the psychiatrist, which I made to appease them, had little impact on me at the time. I argued with him and challenged his view that I was in need of psychiatric treatment. He said that if I changed my mind he would be glad to see me. Privately, I was curious about whether he could help me; he seemed patient and sympathetic. I have thought of this often in my own clinical work and teaching. You never know whether someone will want to return to your office. You never burn a bridge—always keep a door open.

It is easy to see now that I was not schizophrenic, but at the time my psychiatrist had no other explanation. Although it now seems clear that the voice I heard across the quad that dark lonely night was the culmination of a tumultuous year of antiwar politics, adolescent anxiety, and adjustment to a setting that often seemed alien and frightening to me, my psychiatrist saw it as a stress-induced schizophrenic break that was due to happen at some time. He told me that schizophrenia was genetic and that I would probably never fully recover. In fact, I could experience another break at any time. He impressed on me the need to receive treatment and told me that I could avoid going into the hospital by taking an antipsychotic medication.

I was in no position to argue. I was scared, demoralized, and exhausted. I didn't fully realize what it meant to be schizophrenic, but I did know that I needed help. He prescribed Thorazine to stop the racing thoughts and saw me three times a week to monitor my progress. I was getting plenty of sleep now and had no racing thoughts. In fact, I don't think I had any thoughts at all. It was as if he had given me cognitive air brakes. Everything stopped.[3]

I am not sure how it happened, but after several months I began to question his diagnosis. When I asked if he had anything I could read on schizophrenia, he gave me access to his office after one of our sessions and left me with a stack of articles to read. I didn't understand a lot of it, but I could see that my symptoms were only a small part of this devastating disorder. I think he saw this, too, although I do not recall discussing it. When I told him that I wanted to return to school, he said that it was possible but unlikely. When he began tapering my medication, it left increasingly longer gaps between doses, and I used this time to read more and to write. At first, the thoughts would come rushing back, leading me to welcome the return of my chemically induced calm when I reinitiated taking the medicine. But soon I was writing letters and prose during these times of relative clarity, racing thoughts notwithstanding. I was learning to channel my thoughts into my writing. I was starting to feel better and a bit more confident. I was going to return to school; I just knew it.

LESSON #2: NOTHING REPLACES REALITY

I am not sure why my psychiatrist allowed me to return to school that spring, but I suspect it was in part to get rid of me. I was now reading everything I could on schizophrenia and began to pester him with questions about its similarity to existentialism. I was influenced by the writings of R. D. Laing, along with Thomas Szasz's probing challenges that mental illness was a myth to maintain societal conformity.[4] Psychodynamic in orientation, my psychiatrist often suggested that my antics were disguising sexual frustration. Finally, we found something on which we agreed! Clearly, it was time for me to return to school.

But though I very much wanted to return to school, I was also frightened. It was a return to normalcy that I sought, yet one could certainly question whether that campus was a place for me to find anything resembling normal functioning. The college administration was very sympathetic and worked with me in reducing my course load. I also agreed to take frequent trips home and check in with my psychiatrist. I was no longer the reluctant patient but a willing participant in my treatment. I did not want a repeat of what I had experienced.

Once back at school, I had the support of my friends and many of the faculty. Everyone seemed to know me, which was not hard on a campus of a few thousand students. I had more free time than I wanted and accepted an invitation from a friend to join him as a volunteer at a new school that some of the faculty had started for their children. It was what was called in those days a "free school," meaning that the kids were free to do what they wanted. Naturally, this left plenty of time for recreation. I found that I enjoyed being with the kids and staff. I knew how to play with kids, having been trained by my nieces and nephews from the age of 13. I sought out more experiences in a local Head Start center and as a Big Brother. But, perhaps characteristically, I was overdoing it, becoming overwhelmed and stressed.

On one of my trips home, my psychiatrist worked with me on my schedule and suggested ways to reduce my stress, which included frank and explicit conversations about sex and dating. I didn't know it at the time, but his professional partner, with whom he shared an office, was a world-renowned sex therapist. These were very different sessions from our earlier ones. The information was concrete and useful. How he made this transition from insight-oriented psychotherapy to practical advice and skill development I am not sure, but I often think of my psychiatrist as my first and best introduction to behavior therapy.

But perhaps most important to my growing confidence was the development of a new identity. I now had a new calling, although I wasn't quite sure what to do with it. Quite simply, I found that working with kids trumped antiwar demonstrating by a long shot. That summer I took a job at the 14th Street YMCA in lower Manhattan working as a counselor at their day camp. I also took a course in personality theory at the New School for Social Research down the street from the "Y" to try to make up for some of my lost school time. I was especially impressed with theories of child development that we learned, such as those of Piaget and Erikson, but perhaps less for their ideas than for their methods. Working with and studying children was something that I thought maybe I could do.

LESSON #3: LEARNING FROM EXPERIENCE

Returning to school with a new focus and direction was both liberating and frustrating. I was highly engaged during my time in Head Start classrooms but noticeably disengaged from my college courses. I began volunteering at a state mental health hospital and met people who personified the real tragedy of mental illness. This was a difficult experience for me, testing my confidence that I was fully recovered from my troubles of a year or so before. I vividly recalled my psychiatrist's admonition that another "break" could happen at any time. Was I really that different from "Mr. President"—the man who greeted us on our arrival at the hospital, wearing shirt and tie with baggy pants and slippers? What was I thinking by taking on this experience?

The juxtaposition of the severely mentally ill individuals at the hospital with the preschoolers at the Head Start center led me away from considering myself as a mental health worker and instead encouraged an affiliation as an educator. The normative tasks of childhood provided a compelling basis for understanding my own struggles, far more palatable than identification as an individual with mental illness. Clearly, I was not schizophrenic, but neither was I yet like my better-adapted classmates. As my therapy began to help me through the transition to adulthood, I felt less like a patient and more like a student. If being sick got me the help I needed, it was the experiences with kids that provided the way out. And if there was a war still going on overseas, I didn't seem to know it. My political activism translated into a commitment to working with kids and my own personal discovery.

Given my newfound identity I was, perhaps inevitably, again unprepared for college. Book learning meant little to me; direct experiences were my classroom. Perhaps it was all just going too fast; from Thorazine to Thoreau just wasn't working. One of my friends told me of her aunt, who ran a laboratory school at the University of California, Davis, to train students to work with children. Whether I was retreating from schoolwork or beginning a career I was not sure, but that summer I left college again for the sunny skies of California and a chance at a new identity.

LESSON #4: FINDING MENTAL HEALTH IN ALL THE RIGHT PLACES

Northern California in the early 1970s was a place of personal discovery and untold possibilities, and the perfect place for me to start again. The free-speech movement at Berkeley had morphed into the hippie movement of Haight-Ashbury, and by the time I arrived both had been replaced by a counterculture that was decidedly less edgy and more personal. Davis, California, with its welcoming sign noting a population of 40,000 residents and 50,000 bicycles, seemed as far from the turmoil of New York as I could imagine. It is still remarkable to me that I could simply up and leave the way I did, perhaps aided by the foolish self-assurance of a 21-year-old who didn't know what he didn't know. I had a plan, to be sure, and in retrospect it was the best thing I ever did, but few details were worked out.

I traveled to California in a 1971 Datsun that my parents had bought straight off the floor for $2,000 cash. My parents were not wealthy, but they didn't question my need for transportation, and I am sure they were highly relieved to see me energized and excited. I told them I would pay them back, but of course I never did—and they never asked. I imagine that my psychiatrist endorsed this plan, because I don't remember anyone trying to block me. But, in truth, there was no stopping me. I had a calling and a need for new surroundings. Three thousand miles away seemed just about right.

I traveled with several friends who were looking for a new adventure that summer. We arrived in Santa Cruz, with its beautiful beaches and fully entrenched counterculture milieu, at the home of a University of California, Santa Cruz, student who was a high school friend of one of my traveling companions. I stayed a few weeks and then informed my friends that I was leaving for Davis to pursue my goal to work with kids.

Here is another decision that I often wonder about. My new friends informed me in very clear terms that *no one* leaves the beaches of Santa Cruz for the flatlands of Davis, unless the goal is to study cows. Although it was appealing to stay, I was determined to go—I suspect in part because of my discomfort with the lack of structure in what we now might call the *new age* milieu for which Santa Cruz is so well known, as well as my strong need for direction and focus. A bit too much New Yorker in me, I suspect. I found myself firmly reliant on my new plans, perhaps not unlike the way I had formerly embraced the medicated calm of psychiatric treatment. What cliff might await me in Santa Cruz I cared not to discover. I drove the short trip northeast to Davis with a friend who came with me to help me get settled.[5]

I remember my early days in Davis very fondly, the way most people talk of their halcyon days in college. But rather than a time of experimentation and rebellion, my second college experience was one of affirmation and serenity. To be sure, I can recall some lonely nights and a fair share of doubt at times, especially in those first few months. But after I made my way to the UC Davis campus and found my friend's aunt, Jane Welker, who ran the laboratory school, my optimism returned. Not that Jane knew exactly what to do with me. She was friendly and encouraging, but she also let me know that there was little I could do with her unless I enrolled in college. However, returning to college was not what I had in mind, at least not yet. And anyway, that would require an application, and that would take some time. In the meantime, I needed to find some work.

I volunteered at a local day care center run by the Davis school district and after several weeks was hired as a classroom aide. I found a place to live as a counselor in a crisis center, which provided me a rent-free room. A year or so later a position as a lead teacher became available at the day care center; I applied and received the job. I delayed college for a few more years, and with a coworker (to whom I have now been married almost 30 years) I took some extension courses on early childhood education. I quickly developed the new persona that I had been seeking. Most remarkably to me, there were no racing thoughts and no depressive episodes or anxiety-laden interactions. This transformation represented perhaps the most enduring lesson of my own experiences related to my work in mental health. Without denying my personal history, genetic and otherwise, it was clearly a toxic environment that had prompted my psychiatric symptoms and a beneficial one that had solidified my recovery. But how to explain what was nothing but a remarkable change, without the aid of therapy or medication?

LESSON #5: FAMILY AND FRIENDS

My professional colleagues have often noted a tendency of mine to embrace environmental influences on children's behavior to the exclusion of biological or genetic influences.[6] I certainly am not alone in such views, but I do not doubt that I am more passionate than most, as my own experiences provide a powerful reminder of the ways that I was helped through supportive relationships and experiences. It could be argued that it was the combination of therapy and medication that provided me the opportunity to take advantage of my new opportunities, and, to be sure, I am forever grateful for the wisdom and flexibility of my psychiatrist in those critical early days of therapy. And certainly, I must note that no one else I knew experienced the intensity of psychiatric symptoms that I had, even those who shared many of the same stressors.[7] Some personal vulnerability was clearly operative: who I was, with my own insecurities and vulnerabilities, did matter a great deal. Yet these same vulnerabilities have accompanied me throughout my life, and certainly so in those first few years of my time in Davis, without even a hint of any return of serious psychopathology. How, then, can one explain my apparent recovery?

If there is a lesson here, it is that everyone deserves what I had received to help me realize my potential. It is how I understand the job of the mental health profession, and perhaps this is where my political advocacy and my professional worlds have combined. I have worked for much of my career with children living in urban poverty, which, among other things, constitutes an overwhelmingly negative set of environmental influences that dwarf the influence of most biological traits. For example, my recent work is focused on developing new models of mental health consultation to urban schools, in order to enhance schools' potential to support children's educational and emotional development, in contrast to most models of mental health practice in schools that provide individual counseling to children.[8] There is little evidence that counseling is necessary or sufficient to overcome the pernicious effects of poverty, and I find especially misguided the assumption that children in poverty, independent of their parents and teachers, can effect change on their environments. Although my published arguments are based on an empirical literature, my inspiration clearly is personal.

As I understand my own discovery, I consider the various contributions to my successful transition to health. First, my parents' and siblings' support throughout my childhood, and certainly during those dark days of psychiatric impairment, provided me with a strong foundation and confidence. There was always a place to return, and I speculate that this in part explains what seems to me now to be a brave (if not foolish) venturing off on my own to California. My family did whatever they could to help me get back on my feet, and I cannot imagine how much more difficult this would have been had they been any less supportive. I often think now, as I am parenting my son in his late teenage years, how impressive it was that my parents maintained their support for me throughout the turmoil of that time. How easy it would have been for them to lose their confidence in me. The support I received extends to my brothers and sister as well. I remember vividly that my older brother, who was at the time completing his medical training in Philadelphia, drove up to my parents' home in New York City late the same night I returned from college because he wanted to talk to me himself, to see if I was OK.

Second, I needed to have something meaningful to replace my political advocacy, which I had embraced throughout my adolescence. Working with children gave me a new sense of confidence in my abilities and a new direction for my work. I struggle at times with my withdrawal from politics. But although the intense glare of political advocacy remains a distant (and not very fond) memory,[9] children's classrooms and playgrounds have become my new political forum. Meaningful work, however defined, goes a long way to overcome personal doubts.

Third, the type of therapy I received during my first year back in school was critical in allowing me to make that important transition successfully. Reworking my schedule, receiving advice on dating and sex, and having my day-to-day experiences taken seriously all focused me on tangible goals. I may never understand why the events of my life happened to me, and after a while I stopped trying to understand. Getting back to school and getting back on my feet were my goals for therapy. These *behavioral* objectives empowered me in a way that the prior therapy had not. I don't mean to second-guess my psychiatrist's attempts at uncovering my unconscious motivations during the year prior to my withdrawal from school. I don't suppose any therapy would have been acceptable to

Marc Atkins and his son, Lee, in Carmel, California (August 2005)

me at the time. However, the validation I felt when my daily experiences were taken seriously is a strong reminder to me of what matters most in therapy. I had been given the gift of a supportive environment to remake my life and establish new friendships. As I heard a colleague from the National Alliance on Mental Illness once describe it, I had the basic elements of mental health: a safe home, a good job, and a date on Saturday night.

EPILOGUE

I wrap up a review of a manuscript and greet a student waiting to meet with me. I had been working on this chapter early in the morning before my workday began, and the thoughts of my past are fresh in my mind.

The student begins by updating me on a case that she is concerned about, involving a very troubled teenager and the very worried mother of this girl.

The mother and daughter live alone, and their interactions look odd to us, as outsiders. The daughter, a senior in high school, is overly concerned with her schoolwork, isolated from her peers, and focused like a laser on the need to have her time free on weekends. Her concerns are leading to an accelerating cycle of frustration, as her intrusive thoughts are interfering with her ability to get her work done during the week, thereby increasing the amount of work she will have on the weekend. She cries frequently and withdraws into her room. She expresses no interest in college, despite her excellent grades. Her mother is becoming increasingly more desperate and frustrated.

Yet, on weekends, she and her daughter share many activities, such as household chores and shopping at the mall, which are enjoyable to both of them. The trainee has talked with the mother about withholding these positive activities from her daughter unless the daughter is able to complete her schoolwork, so as not to inadvertently encourage her daughter's difficulties. The mother reported that she would try, but the student and I are skeptical. They seem enmeshed, the student observes, by which she means that the mother and daughter are overly involved in each other's affairs. Although the student was using the term "enmeshed" to help understand the relationship between the two, the term struck a nerve with me. It felt judgmental.

I have a rule for my supervision of clinical cases that I began during my first faculty position. I ask my students to talk about the families they are seeing as if they are talking about one of my relatives. At the time, some 20 years ago, I did this of necessity. I was taking the students' negative comments about families too personally, and I was becoming angry with the students for their seeming insensitivity to the client's perspective. I asked them to help me understand the perspective of the client before we passed judgment on motives and behavior.

I knew at the time where this was coming from: I was identifying with the client and not with the therapist. I could sense that this view made the students uneasy, and privately I was unsure about this stance of mine, as well. Like them, I had been taught in graduate school to maintain my objectivity, and I recognized that I was little help to others if it was my problems we were focused on instead of theirs. However, I found that something interesting happened when we avoided judging our clients: taking the perspective of the client changed the focus away from our views to their views. However misguided we may have believed our clients to be, we now understood their actions in a new way, temporarily suspending our own worldview in order to adopt *their* worldview, which made their actions seem more logical and coherent.[10] Our goal now focused on providing clients with other perspectives that would lead to new actions and behaviors.

Students also became changed during this process. Rather than judging clients, they were now defending them. Mom has no other choice, they might say. How can we help her see that there are other alternatives? Judgment was replaced by concern and answers by questions.

A number of years ago, the chief of the Children's Hospital of Philadelphia, where I was on the faculty, sent an article to faculty members for discussion at the ensuing faculty meeting. Written by a physician who was on the faculty at a university medical center, the article described the deteriorating condition of his wife while she was a patient at his own hospital and the lack of care that he observed by physicians who appeared too distracted by their research pursuits to adequately care for his wife.[11] If this is the way the wife of a staff physician was treated, he asked, what might be happening with our other patients? He was especially concerned with what seemed like callous interactions between staff members in front of his wife and a lack of coordinated care that appeared to jeopardize her health.

The faculty discussion of the article was appropriately polite and respectful, but I wondered if they really got it, my own identify as a patient activated again. Certainly no one wants to do harm, but were they really listening? For that matter, was I really listening, or had I too become too busy with my own work to fully attend to the clients under my care? I recalled a visit I made many years ago to my brother, himself an academic physician, during which I attended rounds with him. One patient stood out especially. She was a woman probably in her late 50s, hospitalized for a severe asthma attack. While taking her history, my brother inquired as to how long it took her to arrive at the hospital that day. She said that it took several hours, involving numerous bus transfers and a considerable amount of walking. I asked my brother later why he asked her that. He said he wanted the medical students, residents, and other attendees to understand how hard it was for her to get there and how important it was to help her manage her asthma at home. He had, it seemed to me, changed their image of her from a patient to a person.

I have since assigned this article by Southwick to my psychology students at the beginning of their training year to promote a discussion of our role in ensuring a high quality of care. Regardless of how complex our cases are or how minor we may perceive our role in an interdisciplinary treatment team to be, we all share a responsibility to see that our clients are cared for respectfully and competently. Think of them as one of your relatives, I tell them. For me, that may be the largest lesson of them all.

NOTES

1. In his travelogue of New York City waterfronts, Lopate provides an engaging description of Knickerbocker Village and its place in the history of New York political activism. See Lopate, P. (2004). *Waterfront: A walk around Manhattan*. New York: Anchor Books. Knickerbocker Village's tenant union was part of a larger tenants' rights movement in New York that began in the early part of the twentieth century. This movement was closely tied to the organized labor movement that was

also emerging at that time. See Lawson, R. (1986). *The tenant movement in New York City, 1904–1984*. New Brunswick, NJ: Rutgers University Press. My parents were very active in both movements and inspired the political activism that I later embraced during my late teen and early college years.

2. The events at Hobart College attracted considerable national attention as part of an expose of active FBI infiltration of college campuses to curtail political activism. See Churchill, W., & Vander Wall, J. (2002). *The COINTELPRO papers: Documents from the FBI's secret wars against dissent in the United States*. Boston: South End Press.

3. Antipsychotic medication such as chlorpromazine (Thorazine) was widely used to treat psychosis in Europe by 1955, but its widespread use in the United States was delayed, particularly in outpatient settings, until the early 1970s by the enduring influence of psychoanalysis. See Lopez-Munoz, F., Alamo, C., Cuenca, E., Shen, W., Clervoy, P., & Rubio, G. (2005). History of the discovery and clinical introduction of chlorpromazine. *Annuals of Clinical Psychiatry, 17*, 113–135. In fact, my psychiatrist often commented that just a few years prior he would have had little recourse but to hospitalize me. For coverage of the strong tendency for any sign of psychosis to be labeled as schizophrenia in the United States for much of the past century, see Hinshaw, S. P. (2002). *The years of silence are past: My father's life with bipolar disorder*. New York: Cambridge University Press.

4. See Laing, R. D. (1965). *The divided self: An existential study in sanity and madness*. Baltimore: Penguin Books; Szasz, T. S. (1961). *The myth of mental illness*. New York: Hoeber.

5. Last summer I visited Santa Cruz with my son, who was looking at colleges. A day or so touring the city impressed on him the need to look elsewhere. "Looks like your kind of place, Dad." No, I told him, not really my kind of place, either.

6. For an example of my enthusiastic refutation of the biological influence on behavior, see: Peters, E., Atkins, M. S., & McKay, M. M. (2002). Adopted children's behavior problems: A review of five explanatory models. *Clinical Psychology Review, 19*, 297–328.

7. I found a 2003 description of the political events at Hobart College in 1970 from the perspective of a student who was observing the events but not participating in them. Clearly they were eventful enough to remain memorable these many years later. In contrast to the effects on me, however, he got up the next morning and went to class (http://www.hws.edu/alumni/alumnews/showwebclip.asp?webclipid = 1532).

8. See Atkins, M. S., Frazier, S. L., Adil, J. A., & Talbott, E. (2002). School mental health in urban communities. In M. Weist, S. Evans, & N. Tashman (Eds.), *School mental health handbook* (pp. 165–178). New York: Kluwer Academic/Plenum Publishers; and Atkins, M. S., Frazier, S. L., Birman, D., Adil, J. A., Jackson, M., Graczyk, P., et al. (2006). School-based mental health services for children living in high poverty urban communities. *Administration and Policy in Mental Health and Mental Health Services Research, 33*, 146–159.

9. Some 35 years later, during the last presidential election, I joined a local political organization only to leave and never return after the first meeting because it was too reminiscent of my late teenage years. I chose instead to canvass neighborhoods door-to-door, largely because it allowed me to work alone.

10. In his seminal work on cross-cultural influences on behavior-change processes, Jerome Frank was the first to coin the term "worldview" and the first

to understand the power of people's perspectives in guiding behavior. See Frank, J. D. (1961). *Persuasion and healing: A comparative study of psychotherapy*. Baltimore: Johns Hopkins Press. In addition, Carl Rogers long advocated the power of empathy in effecting behavior change. While an undergraduate at UC Davis, I participated in a month-long workshop by Rogers and his group that greatly influenced my work. Ironically, the workshop took place on the campus of UC Santa Cruz. Rogers wrote and read a paper during this workshop that he described as his most complete accounting of the importance of empathy in psychotherapy. See Rogers, C. R. (1975). Empathic: An underappreciated way of being. *Counseling Psychologist, 5*, 2–9.

11. See Southwick, F. (1993). Who was caring for Mary? *Annals of Internal Medicine, 118*, 146–148.

8 Memories of Parental Decompensation

Theodore P. Beauchaine

As many of the chapters in this volume illustrate, disclosure of mental illness in one's family, whether immediate or extended, is not something that most mental health professionals take lightly. This is especially true among academic clinical psychologists, who receive both implicit and explicit messages throughout their training regarding the imprudence of divulging personal anecdotes of familial dysfunction. As a result, most graduate students in clinical psychology and related disciplines are unlikely to hear examples of the impact of personal experiences on the professional development of their professors or supervisors. On reflection, I cannot think of a single instance in which a professor or supervisor disclosed information to me about mental illness within his or her family during the 11 years I spent as a student and intern toward earning my doctoral degree in clinical psychology. Given that my training exposed me to no fewer than 11 research supervisors and 12 clinical supervisors, it was not likely that this absence of self-disclosure meant that their families were free from psychopathology. For me, this sent a very strong message. Prevalence rates of mental illness virtually guarantee that each of us has at least one family member who is afflicted with significant psychopathology. Thus it is not possible that a group of 23 people could have familial pedigrees devoid of mental illness. In fact, one of my clinical supervisors eventually died by suicide as a result of bipolar disorder.

Although the taciturnity of my research advisors and clinical supervisors communicated an implied message, more explicit mechanisms also imposed a professional code of silence. I experienced the first when I finished my undergraduate education and applied to graduate programs in clinical psychology. Almost all such programs require a personal statement in which applicants describe their motivations for pursuing a graduate degree. Any well-informed student requests that a faculty advisor review this document. Although mental illness within my family had a tremendous influence on my choice to pursue graduate study, which was reflected in the initial draft of my essay, the professor who critiqued it removed all references to related personal experiences. She did not provide any explanation, yet I trusted her judgment, which in retrospect was sound. Most faculty members seek to ensure that those admitted for graduate study are capable of professional detachment, fearing that direct and emotionally evocative experiences with psychopathology could obscure prospective students' objectivity, particularly if they have not "worked through" any associated trauma. Furthermore, faculty seek to avoid admitting students who suffer from personality characteristics that could make it difficult for them to get along well with others in a research group or maintain clinical rapport. Accordingly, professors tend to avoid applicants who disclose significant psychopathology within their families.

The second experience that dissuaded me from divulging personal information was much more protracted. Clinical training almost invariably includes direct instruction to use self-disclosure sparingly, if at all. In classical psychoanalytic theory, the predominant psychotherapeutic paradigm for much of the 20th century, analysts are trained to behave as "blank slates," maintaining a neutral, anonymous, and nondisclosing stance at almost all times. This stance is intended to engender projections of clients' neuroses onto the analyst, which become fodder for the therapeutic process. In this manner, unconscious motives are brought to consciousness, where they can be examined and altered. Avoidance of self-disclosure is therefore canonical in psychoanalysis. Although more contemporary forms of psychotherapy may provide for instances of self-disclosure, these situations are typically quite circumscribed, and therapists are taught to examine their motives carefully to ensure that they are not bolstering their egos or placing expectations regarding proper behavior on the client.

These therapeutic conventions of non-self-disclosure are not related directly to faculty-student or supervisor-student relationships. Yet exposure to silence over years of undergraduate and graduate study has a profound effect on most trainees' approach to interpersonal functioning across professional contexts, particularly when there is a power differential such as that between a faculty member and a student. Through this mechanism, a professional code of silence is passed across generations of academic clinical psychologists.

Finally, mental health professionals are not immune to the effects of cultural beliefs about and prescriptions for behavior. In many Western societies, including the United States, behaviors often associated with mental illness, including alcohol and drug dependencies, aggression, melancholia, homelessness, and lack of motivation, are considered to be volitional. As a result, those affected by psychopathology are marginalized and stigmatized to an extent that is rarely observed for physical illnesses, of which affected individuals are perceived as victims. When this potential for stigmatization is coupled with professional knowledge of genetic risk for psychopathology, denial and silence can serve psychologically protective functions. One of my greatest fears in early adulthood was that my mother's mental illness would be passed along to me and that I, too, would gradually decompensate. This fear emerged over time as I came to understand through education that my mother did not choose her fate and that her genetic legacy could be passed along to me without my choosing. For me, this made it especially important to hide my family history from other mental health professionals. If they knew about my mother, they might construe my eccentric behaviors—which everyone exhibits from time to time—as indicators of active psychopathology or imminent decompensation, interpretations that could have considerable implications for my career.

For all of these reasons, I wasn't about to breach the code of silence as a graduate student, clinical intern, or assistant professor. Yet there is a profound irony in mental health professionals' guardedness about their personal experiences with mental illness. Those of us who are most knowledgeable about psychopathology are in the best position to destigmatize psychiatric disorders by letting others know that such conditions are prevalent at all levels of education and socioeconomic status. By remaining silent about our experiences, we engage in a form of elitism by objectifying mental illness and implying that it is always the problem of others. In this manner we reinforce rather than confront stigmatization. It is for this reason that I agreed to write about my own experiences growing up in the household of a parent with schizophrenia. What follows is a story that I have never written about before and that I am not accustomed to telling. In fact, it is the most difficult exposition that I have ever authored, and one that I postponed for quite some time due to its enduring personal poignancy.

THE NATURE OF SCHIZOPHRENIA

The pages that follow chronicle some experiences, as I remember them, of growing up with a mother who was afflicted with schizophrenia, a frequently progressive form of mental illness caused by heritable compromises in both the structure and function of the brain. People with paranoid schizophrenia, the subtype that my mother had, suffer from delusions and hallucinations. Delusions are incorrect assumptions about perceptions or experiences that are not shared by others who observe the same events. For example, a woman with schizophrenia may interpret mere conversation between her spouse and another woman as definitive evidence of an ongoing affair. Delusions of jealousy such as these were quite common for my mother, as were delusions of religiosity and somatization, which I describe in the pages that follow. In contrast to delusions, hallucinations are sensory perceptions that are not induced by external events. The most common form of hallucinations is auditory, with afflicted people hearing voices when no one is speaking to them. Such hallucinations oftentimes take on persecutory themes in which voices chastise or taunt the affected person for misdeeds, transgressions, and shortcomings. Although my mother did experience hallucinations, to my knowledge she did not do so until I became an adult.

Delusions and hallucinations are the most salient symptoms of schizophrenia, yet two additional symptoms characterized my mother's illness, both of which are also quite common among people with the disorder. The first was interpersonal aversiveness. My mother was very uncomfortable in her relationships with other people, owing in part to her paranoia and consequent feelings of mistrust, but also because of crippling anxiety. When faced with the prospect of a social engagement, my mother would almost invariably become ill with physical symptoms, including migraines, abdominal discomfort, and joint pain. By the time I was in high school, she spent most days completely bedridden with these symptoms.

Second, my mother experienced profound anhedonia, or inability to experience pleasure. She sought no friendships, had no hobbies, attended none of her children's sporting events, smiled infrequently, and expressed little if any eagerness to engage with the world. As with her other symptoms, her anhedonia progressed unremittingly over the years that spanned the time of my first memories at about age 5 until I left my parents' house at age 20. This time period encompasses several major developmental milestones that children, adolescents, and young adults face. With the support of competent and sensitive parenting, these milestones are usually negotiated successfully. Each success provides appropriate scaffolding for tackling subsequent challenges and life events. Unfortunately, serious mental illnesses such as schizophrenia adversely affect a person's capacity to form meaningful, trusting relationships with others. Nowhere is this more costly than in a mother's relationship with her children.

In the following sections, I describe my mother's decompensation during several important stages of my own development. Each of these stages is defined by one or more developmental transitions or challenges. My intent here is to illustrate the potential impact of parental mental illness on children's normative development and on the interpersonal relationships of all people within the family. I begin with brief description of my mother's own life history, which provides some necessary context for the remainder of the material.

BACKGROUND

My mother was born during World War II in Albany, the capital of the state of New York. She was the second of two children, with a brother who was 9 years her senior. In this respect, she was effectively an only child during her middle school and high school years, the latter being the sole portion of her youth that she recalled with any fondness. During my mother's upbringing, her father delivered milk door to door, and her mother worked a switchboard for the local telephone company. Although home milk delivery was commonplace at the time, working mothers were still somewhat of a rarity. Yet having two incomes enabled my grandparents to send my mother to private Catholic institutions through high school. In all likelihood, this schooling influenced the expression of her illness, which often took on religious persecutory themes.

After high school my mother worked as an office assistant for a large health care company, a job that lasted only a brief period of time until she met my father, whom she married within 6 months. Less than a year after their marriage, my brother was born, and my mother never again worked outside the home, although she often expressed interest in doing so. Unfortunately, the progression of her illness over the next three decades rendered her less and less capable of engaging in social interactions and goal-directed activities, as she spent a larger and larger portion of each day in bedridden isolation.

The two preceding paragraphs outline almost all of the objective knowledge that I have about my mother's family history. Most of the additional details that I present in this chapter are derived entirely from secondhand accounts conveyed by her. Given that her ability to understand objective reality has often been compromised, and given that she has always tended to either vilify or venerate others (including her parents), the veracity of such information is uncertain at best. For this reason, it should be kept in mind that the remaining descriptions of my mother's family history have not been verified and may well have been interpreted differently by others who were present at the time. Nevertheless, such details remain crucial for conveying both the nature of her illness and my understanding of her subjective experience of living in what she experienced as a very frightening and threatening environment. As I have learned from many years of interacting with my mother and with patients with schizophrenia during my clinical training, quibbling over the "truth" regarding the experiences of an afflicted person is almost always counterproductive. Gaining even a remote appreciation of a person's feelings—a prerequisite for empathy—requires that we attempt to value and accept their experiences *as they understand them.* This can be especially difficult for family members of a person with schizophrenia, yet it is exceedingly important when paranoia renders the person acutely aware of disapproval and rejection. It was not until my late 20s that I became able to accept my mother's condition without feeling compelled to change her thinking.

With these caveats aside, conversations with my mother indicated that her relationship with her mother was strained at best, yet she adored her father. At some level this is ironic because her father drank quite heavily for much of her childhood before sobering up during her teenage years and later dying of lung cancer when she was 19. Throughout much of my mother's childhood, her father's drinking left my grandmother to parent by herself. According to my mother, my grandmother was resentful about this, leading to a mother-daughter relationship characterized by significant acrimony. Although I do not know specific details, their mutual frustration was palpable in the few times during my adulthood that I was with both of them at the same time. My grandmother, a straight-talking, Rosie-the-Riveter type, had little tolerance for my mother's derailment, superstition, tangential thinking, and fixation on the past and would openly criticize such behavior. As is typical among people with schizophrenia—and perhaps with anyone castigated by his or her own mother—my mother would become deeply wounded, given her hypersensitivity to criticism and rejection. Nevertheless, she indefatigably tried to convince my grandmother that her delusions were true.

I recall one instance in which my mother was absolutely certain that a boyfriend from high school who was later killed in Vietnam was actually still alive (a recurrent delusional theme for her) and that he was trying to contact her through various messages left in unusual places, such as the BIOS sequence of her computer during startup. Although such delusions of reference are commonly experienced by people with schizophrenia, I could never understand why my mother was so persistent in articulating them in the face of negative and even hostile feedback. Why would anyone argue any point so faithfully and with such conviction—even if it was true—when it elicited harsh criticism, especially from loved ones?

I cannot count the number of times during my childhood that my mother would sob for long periods following a phone conversation with her mother that had degenerated into such an argument. My mother wanted desperately to be loved, yet she was convinced that her mother hated her. Although it was not known at the time, the interaction patterns between my mother and grandmother—characterized by considerable rejection and hostility—are especially harmful for people with a genetic predisposition for schizophrenia. In the psychological literature, such interactions are said to be high in expressed emotion, which may trigger earlier onset of illness among people with high genetic risk and which predicts earlier relapse among people who are in remission. Unfortunately, the behavior of people with schizophrenia often elicits the very reactions from family members that amplify genetic risk. This was the case in my immediate family for many years.

Shortly after being married, my mother and father moved from Albany to a small town 30 miles south of Rochester, New York, where my father worked for an aircraft servicing company. One of the reasons he took a job in the Rochester area was to get my mother away from Albany and the emotional instability that he attributed to her frequent contact with an overbearingly critical mother. Although I do not know the specific details, my father confronted my grandmother at least once about her harsh treatment of my mother, and the two (my father and grandmother) disliked each other strongly. Because Rochester was about a 4-hour drive from Albany, in-person contact between my parents and my maternal grandmother was restricted to once or twice yearly following the move. The result was that we were insulated from our extended family, including aunts, uncles, cousins, and paternal grandparents, something I have always regretted. Worse yet, in explaining our lack of contact with relatives to us, my mother maintained that we were black sheep and that they didn't like us anyway. As a result, when we did visit Albany for special events and reunions, I recall quite clearly feeling like an outsider within my extended family. To this day I have very little contact with the survivors among this group.

THE EARLY YEARS IN NEW YORK

Shortly after the move to Rochester, my brother was born, followed exactly 1 year and 2 days later by my sister and me (we are dizygotic twins). Although I know little about the years preceding my first memories, it must have been very difficult for my mother and father, who were just 21 and 22 years old, respectively, to adjust to having three children within 1 year, especially given my mother's condition. My mother clearly had a difficult time with the task demands of parenting, particularly with respect to my sister, whose misbehaviors, although pedestrian given her age, were almost always attributed by my mother to intentional, direct hostility. In this way, my mother projected the quality of her relationship with her mother onto my sister, which she continues to this day.

In fact, my mother's disdain for her mother and her adulation of her father generalized to all females and males, whether inside or outside the family. For example, she often expounded on her love for her brother while demonizing his wife and blaming her for the infrequent contact our families shared across the years, despite the fact that we were the ones who moved away. I cannot recall my mother saying anything negative about her brother or anything positive about her sister-in-law. This black-and-white, all-or-nothing thinking regarding her feelings toward others is also very common among those with schizophrenia. Within the immediate family, my mother often sought to strengthen bonds with my brother and me, yet she cared little if at all about doing so with my sister, to whom she delivered exceedingly harsh and abusive punishment. In one instance that is always quite troubling to recall, my sister was forced to eat a dinner that she disliked. By itself, this would not be traumatizing. However, following dinner my sister threw up, and my mother forced her to eat her own vomit.

Presumably as a result of such abuse, my sister was removed from our home by the State of New York and placed with a foster family when she and I were 5 years old. Both of my parents have always avoided discussing this occurrence. In fact, I recall its being mentioned only once, when my mother asserted that the foster placement resulted from a meddlesome neighbor's false accusations of abuse. One of my first memories is of the only time we visited my sister with her foster family, including the couple's biological children, who were about our age.

I remember all of us playing with toys in one room while my parents and my sister's foster parents met in another part of the house. Too young to appreciate the magnitude of the untoward circumstances, I thought to myself how lucky my sister was to be living in a house with such friendly people and such cool toys. Later we took my sister out for ice cream. Images of the driving rain on the windshield and my sister's fascination with the multispeed wipers of my father's car are indelibly etched on my memory, although any feelings I had at the time have long been forgotten. To this day I do not know the true extent of the maltreatment my sister incurred that resulted in her foster placement. Yet she continued to bear a heavy burden from my mother's treatment of her for many years to come.

In preparing to write this chapter, I spoke with both my sister and my brother about our upbringing for the first time in many years. Although my sister's memories of being removed from our home are sketchy, she did recall that the length of her stay was 6 months almost to the day and that she was not contacted by either of our parents until the final week of her foster placement, during the visit just described. This was the last opportunity for visitation before my sister's placement would have been extended indefinitely. Because of the lack of contact until that visit, she recalls wondering whether my mother and father cared at all whether she came back home. Yet very soon after we visited her, my sister did return. Even though she had attended kindergarten during her foster placement, she was required to do so again the following year with me to avoid any probing questions being asked by family members or school personnel. My parents were so secretive about the placement that they avoided telling anyone in the extended family. This meant that we—including my parents, my sister, my brother, and me—did not visit either set of grandparents or any other family members for the entire 6 months.

The details of my sister's mistreatment and foster placement will probably never be resolved fully. My parents are no more willing to discuss the issues now than they ever were, and the official records collected by the State of New York cannot be accessed because the building that contained them burned down many years ago. For me, this is unfortunate, even regrettable, because I would like to understand what happened. For my sister, it is tragic, because it precludes complete closure on a psychologically devastating chapter in her early life.

We remember events from our early childhood based on the very concrete thinking that is normal given our ages at the time. For children who are mistreated by psychiatrically ill parents, this means internalizing the messages communicated by the abuse—that we are not endearing, that we somehow deserved it, that we might have prevented it. In fact, contemporary psychological science has demonstrated that abuse and neglect incurred during childhood can elicit long-term changes in patterns of functional brain activation and that children who have experienced abuse are exquisitely sensitive to the negative emotions of others, often inferring anger from socially ambiguous behaviors and neutral facial expressions.[1] Through this hypersensitivity to negative emotion, reproachful messages about oneself become internalized and are not readily dispatched. Because our brains are not fully developed until early adulthood, we simply do not have the wherewithal to achieve relativistic perspective about our early experiences, which are processed egocentrically. These experiences influence our thinking about ourselves and others powerfully and pervasively, yet so routinely that most of the time we are insidiously unaware. Thankfully, my sister is hardworking, insightful, and resilient and has overcome many of the negative sequelae so often associated with abuse. Yet no one emerges from such experiences without psychological scars.

I spent many years wondering about the nature and the extent of the maltreatment that my sister endured. As a young child, I largely believed my mother's contention that my sister was irascibly unpleasant and that she elicited and even deserved the harsh treatment she experienced. I even remember getting an acute sense of satisfaction when my mother complimented me for being so complaisant compared with my sister (and sometimes my brother). This was an unfortunate paradox in my family: In the rare instances when praise was forthcoming, it was almost always at someone else's expense—usually my sister's. This created quite a dilemma for me because I, like most children, actively sought my parent's praise and admiration. Yet the only way to get it was to "one-up" my siblings, thereby imparting disapproval on them. As a consequence, accomplishments took on a strong approach-avoidance quality for me, the vestiges of which I experience to this day.

As a good example, I continued to feel so uncomfortable about achievement as an adult that I did not attend the graduation ceremonies for either my baccalaureate or doctoral degrees, nor did I inform my parents about either event. In the summer of 2006 I did attend a ceremony at the annual convention of the American Psychological Association to accept an early career award that I had recently received. This award comes with a tremendous sense of pride and accomplishment, but I did experience familiar feelings of guilt in the months preceding the ceremony. This is a well-established pattern, yet I hope that participating in the ceremony served as a corrective experience.

Despite the vagueness of my early memories, it is clear on reflection that my mother's condition was deteriorating progressively during my early childhood. Although I can remember her participating in outdoor activities, such as camping and tobogganing, when we lived in Rochester, especially early on, by the time we left for Los Angeles when I was 8, such occurrences were uncommon. Similarly, I can remember instances of her laughing and joking with family members when I was quite young, yet her expressions of positive affect became increasingly rare over time. At first, my mother complained of migraine headaches, which kept her in bed for 1–2 day stretches that slowly increased in frequency. Throughout these episodes, which I remember most clearly during the summers when I was home from school, my siblings and I had to keep as quiet as possible to avoid disturbing her. Although we could enter her room if we needed her, she was far along her progressive course of disengaging from day-to-day activities of family life. This is also the time period during which she began staying up later and later at night and sleeping more and more during the day. As a result, the morning ritual was for my father to wake up his three children, make us breakfast, get us dressed, pack our lunches, and drive us to school on his way to work at the airport. Rarely did I see my mother until I came home from school in the afternoon. Indeed, she became ever less available to us as a mother, for reasons that were inexplicable to me at the time.

As my mother's condition progressed, the burden on my father grew. On the mounting number of occasions in which my mother remained in bed all day, my father was responsible for making dinner when he got home from work. Furthermore, although my mother took driving classes, paralyzing anxiety prevented her from passing the behind-the-wheel exam. She therefore never obtained a license to drive, which increased the burden on my father even more, as he wound up doing most of the shopping, errand running, and shuffling children to dental and medical appointments. Because we lived in a rural location with no services within walking distance, the burden was especially high.

Shouldering all family responsibilities took a heavy toll on my father, whose temper was quick to flare up in angry, sometimes raging outbursts when my siblings or I misbehaved. He was also fiercely protective of my mother, harshly punishing any expressions of negativity toward her. In one instance when my mother and I were arguing at the dinner table, my father lost his temper and slammed my face into a plate of food, breaking my front teeth. Although he was extremely remorseful about this, his temper outbursts continued until I left home to attend college. As I reflect on instances such as these, which were fairly common experiences for me and both of my siblings, I suspect that my father was extremely annoyed with my mother, as well as with us, and that his frustration was expressed through the path of least resistance. In other words, it was easier to be harsh with us than to confront my mother's eccentricities and capricious expressions of anger and contempt.

This is not to say that my mother and father did not experience significant acrimony between themselves as well. On the contrary, it was common for them to engage in prolonged arguments during which they yelled at one another for what seemed like perpetuity after banishing us to a far corner of the house. Unfortunately, we could always still hear them. These arguments often ended with my father leaving the house and driving away after slamming all doors behind him. At one point no fewer than three doors were either broken or recently repaired in one of the houses we lived in.

One of the reasons that early experiences are so formative is that we have no reference point for anchoring them. Most of us grow up in only one family, and we assume implicitly that the behavior of our parents is normal. It is only after we get old enough to observe other adults that we begin to question the customs and rituals that we have always taken for granted. While in my mid-20s, I remember a very intimate conversation with my wife, whom I was still dating at the time. She had just experienced a very disappointing event—and she told me that she wished she was a child again, because if she were, her mother's comforting would render all of her problems inconsequential. I was truly bewildered by this statement because I could recall almost no instances in which my mother had been consoling. Rather, when I felt disappointment or distress, I learned to seek solitude because I knew there was little comfort or understanding to be garnered from either of my parents.

In fact, I recall only one instance in which I felt truly comforted by my mother. It is one of my earliest memories of my childhood in upstate New York. I had gone outside on a frigid winter evening with no gloves on, and I returned to the house crying because my hands were so cold. My mother placed me on her lap and warmed my hands by rubbing them gently between hers. As I write this I am smiling, yet I am also saddened because I do not recall a single other instance of seeking or receiving comfort from my mother. It was simply beyond her capabilities, given her increasingly serious illness. As with many who have schizophrenia, she had an exceedingly difficult time empathizing with others, despite being acutely aware of her own psychological distress, which was considerable.

GOING TO CALIFORNIA

When I was 8 years old my father was transferred to Los Angeles, so we moved across the country. I remember being very sad about leaving our home in upstate New York and very fearful about knowing no one at my new school. Yet this apprehension in no way foreshadowed the difficulties that my siblings and I would face in the upcoming years. Our move to Los Angeles was only the beginning of what turned out to be a series of transfers that placed me in eight different schools by the time I was 14. Although the constant uprooting had long-lasting positive effects on my ability to cope with change and acclimate to new situations, it also had a profound influence on my fledgling sense of interpersonal self-efficacy, especially given my mother's very limited ability to provide appropriate emotional support and comfort.

We moved into a tough, working-class neighborhood of Los Angeles. One lesson that I learned quickly is that socially dominant and aggressive males always victimize the new kid to establish their preeminent status in the playground hierarchy. Although I was extremely well prepared intellectually because the private schools I attended in New York were at least a year ahead academically, I was ill prepared for the bullying I would face. At each new school I attended between second and eighth grade, the same pattern emerged: for weeks I would attempt to be unobtrusive and morph into the milieu, avoiding contact with socially dominant males. Yet each time I was targeted by at least one such classmate, of whom I developed great fear. In a couple of cases, the bullying became so unrelenting that I ended up fighting the antagonist. Because I matured early and was therefore large for my age, I fared well, and I was usually not bullied again until we moved to the next new school.

Almost a year to the month after moving to Los Angeles, my father was again transferred, this time to Portland. Although I don't recall how my sister felt about it, both my brother and I were happy to leave, given the bullying we were facing. One incident in particular comes to mind in which the two of us, while walking home after school, were attacked by a gang of five or six classmates. Somehow we escaped the situation without getting injured seriously, and I remember feeling very afraid, yet fortunate to have an older brother who risked his own safety in coming to my defense. Despite being terrified, neither of us informed my mother about the incident, because her typical reaction was to blame us for not being socially sophisticated enough to be liked by others. Even though we rarely had more than a few months to adjust to any one school, I remember my mother saying, "I don't know why you can't make any friends. I had all kinds of friends when I was growing up." Thankfully, my brother and I had each other. Over the years, the bond between us strengthened progressively, and he remains the only person who I assume has truly unconditional positive regard for me.

During middle childhood and adolescence, I spent a good deal of time being very angry at my mother—more so than the modal adolescent. Most of this anger stemmed from her extreme and apparently senseless resistance to her children's attempts at individuation. This was especially true for my sister, who was not allowed to date, wear makeup, or participate in after-school activities. Furthermore, as the only female child in the family, she was burdened with the responsibility of caring for our decompensating mother (and, as I noted earlier, she was clearly the target of my mother's rage). Although our mother did complete household tasks such as washing clothes and cleaning early in our childhoods, by the time we were in middle school she had stopped contributing to household management almost completely. At first, these tasks fell almost entirely on our father, yet the burden on my sister was also excessive and became increasingly so as she matured into adolescence. By the time we were in high school, our mother was usually still in bed when we arrived home after classes. My sister was responsible for attending to her and performing many basic household chores. This meant fixing snacks, fetching medications, cleaning, and cooking dinner. My sister was also often obligated to stay home to dispel our mother's loneliness, which usually meant watching television with her for hours, sometimes until bedtime. As my brother put it in a written response to reading an earlier draft of this chapter, "If being born into our household as a male child guaranteed a life of familial dysfunction, having been born a girl was more akin to a prison term."

Through all of this, my sister lost many opportunities to engage in normal rites of passage during her childhood and adolescence. As with many "parentified" children, she was placed in an onerous psychological bind. If she did not perform up to expectation she was derided as lazy, but if she did too well she was blamed for upstaging our mother. These accusations, which placed my sister on a perpetual psychological tightrope, were but one manifestation of our mother's paranoia, which was becoming ever more discernible.

These paranoid delusions clustered around two primary themes: religion and sexual perversion. My mother believed in biblical literalism and was constantly interpreting world events as evidence of the impending rapture. In this sense, her strict religious upbringing fueled her paranoia, and this upbringing may have served as an environmental trigger and potentiator of inherited liability for schizophrenia. When I was a child, her predictions of the Last Days and her reminders that we would go to hell if we did not behave were frightening, but by the time I reached high school they just annoyed me.

My mother's fear of sexual perversion was more difficult to cope with, as it extended to all aspects of her life. She was always suspicious that my father was having an affair, and she therefore monitored his every move. On one occasion during my early adulthood she even accused my girlfriend (now my wife) and my father of being sexually involved with each other. Yet, as with everything, the largest impact of her paranoia fell on my sister, who was accused of promiscuity, forced to wear agonizingly frumpy clothes, and prohibited from dating. Although I rarely expressed it, I felt very sympathetic toward my sister. At the same time, I was able to minimize the time I spent at home by working a part-time job that my father arranged for me and by playing sports year round. I despised being at home more than anything.

My mother and father also continued to argue and fight with alarming regularity, and sometimes these fights became physical. Over the years, my sister, brother, and I had many conversations during which we tried to figure out why our parents bothered to stay married given their derision for one another. We naively concluded that my father was a coward for not leaving. This anger toward him derived in part from his unwillingness to stand up to our mother on our behalf, particularly when she set seemingly unreasonable limits. For example, in addition to the harsh restrictions placed on our sister, my brother and I very much wanted to play baseball, but our mother would not allow it because she was worried about us getting injured emotionally if we were not good enough to play a competitive sport. Our father would probably have let us play, yet he was unwilling to assert his view. We were also prohibited from playing football, attending school dances, and the like. Perhaps more important, all of us harbored anger at our father for allowing my sister to be treated so harshly by our mother. As my brother put it, "No parent, no matter how ill his or her spouse, should allow the near destruction of one of their children as a result."

My father was frequently angry and usually unsupportive but rarely displayed any signs of vulnerability. Because of these characteristics and the anger they elicited from my siblings and me, it took many years to recognize that things would have been much, much worse for us had my father left. Despite the fact that he was at wits' end much of the time, he provided for us and was a rational, predictable influence, and he even served as my brother's and my scoutmaster when we were young, something I will always recall fondly. It is not a fantasy to suggest that had he left, we might have ended up homeless. Ironically, it was my mother who eventually left, several years after we had all moved out. And she did end up homeless for a time.

THE NEXT CHAPTER

In *Straight Man*, a humorous yet poignant novel about the existential conflicts facing a middle-aged history professor, author Richard Russo makes the keen observation that most of us spend our lives seeking to either emulate or disaffiliate from our parents. He then notes that either way, we almost surely fail. Much of my late teens and early 20s were devoted to detaching from my family, and, true to Russo's word, I failed. As might be expected given the family dynamics described thus far, my brother, my sister, and I all moved away just as soon as we could. My brother was the first in our family to attend college, which he worked his way through in a series of temporary jobs, eventually earning a degree in electrical engineering. My sister worked for a fast-food chain before becoming a veterinary technician. I worked a series of odd jobs while attending college sporadically and then joining the Teamsters Union. All of us avoided our parents, visiting only on holidays that none of us felt we could avoid.

While in my early to mid-20s, two events were especially formative in directing me back to college and toward psychology. First, my coworkers, almost all of whom were at least 20 years older than I, were all very unhappy with their jobs, yet most felt boxed in because they needed to support their children. For me, this was "writing on the wall," and I decided to pursue college studies in earnest. Up to that point, however, I didn't find either of the majors I'd tried (engineering and chemistry) compelling.

Second, an event transpired that changed they way I thought about my mother almost overnight. Among the reasons that mental illness affects family members so powerfully is that inexplicable behaviors exhibited by those with the disorder are assumed to be volitional and are therefore attributed to malicious intent. When this is the case, anger is evoked instead of compassion. For many years, we had no idea that my mother was mentally ill; we just thought she was bizarre and vindictive. Consequently, I blamed her for almost everything that did not go well in my life and for the way she treated all of us, especially my sister. One spring day, however, she called to inform me that my father was producing and selling heroin. Knowing my father, I found this to be exceedingly unlikely, but I went over to their house anyway when she asked me to do so.

What transpired was bizarre beyond description. My mother was certain that my father had been "cooking" heroin in the oven, that he was having an affair with the next-door neighbor, and that they were getting high and distributing drugs together. Her proof was a greasy oven grate and her certainty that she could hear him shooting up in the bathroom.

This was her first clear psychotic break. Up until then, it was still possible to attribute her thoughts and behaviors to personality factors that, although strange, were not clearly delusional. This was different. I called a friend with an associate's degree in social work, and we thumbed through his *Diagnostic and Statistical Manual of Mental Disorders* to figure out what disorder she had. Given that psychosis is symptomatic of a number of disorders, we couldn't pinpoint her condition, so I called a therapist I'd seen who had a master's degree in psychology. After describing the situation, she correctly identified my mother's condition as paranoid schizophrenia. Thankfully, we were able to get my mother to a psychiatrist, who prescribed an antipsychotic medication.

Although antipsychotic drugs available at the time were effective for treating psychosis, they often induced considerable side effects, including blurred vision and reduced motivation. The former occurs because the drugs block dopamine, the neurotransmitter of the eyes. My mother found this intolerable because she could not read—perhaps the only activity that she enjoyed considerably. While taking medication, she also became uncharacteristically reserved, expressing very little positive or negative affect and showing little interest in engaging in conversation, even with family members. Due to these symptoms, she stopped taking her prescribed medication dosage after a few weeks. As she took progressively lower doses, her symptoms of paranoia gradually returned. This pattern, with acute psychotic breaks followed by transient medication compliance, self-initiated tapering of the dose, and eventual decompensation, has occurred several times in the two decades since her first episode. Unfortunately, evidence suggests that each psychotic break makes schizophrenia more severe.[2] Yet medication noncompliance is very common with the paranoid subtype, as I learned while on internship at the University of California at San Diego School of Medicine. There, I led groups for Vietnam veterans with schizophrenia and similar psychotic disorders. We spent about half of our twice-weekly sessions solely on medication compliance, which was always an issue for most of the patients. Yet my mother had no regular therapy appointment, and her motivation to take medication suffered as a result.

Although I could tell when my mother had stopped taking her medications by her renewed energy and vitality, convincing her to resume her medication regimen has always been impossible for family members, including me. By the time I can detect that she's stopped, she has become paranoid enough that she believes the medications are controlling her thoughts (in some sense they are)—and that anyone who promotes them is trying to kill her. Thus, as is common with paranoid schizophrenia, anyone who confronts my mother becomes part of her delusional system. Over the years, I've decided not to confront her because I'm much more effective in helping her when she trusts me. This has been frustrating for some family members, who expect me to do more for her because I am a clinical psychologist. However, a cardinal rule of the profession is not to do therapy with friends and family. I stick to that rule with my mother.

Given my training and the unambiguous nature of my mother's mental illness, it is now very easy for me to have complete compassion for her, with no lingering anger. Although this transition took many years, I remember the day it was completed in September of 2001. By this time I had completed my graduate training at the State University of New York at Stony Brook and my clinical psychology internship at UC San Diego, and I was a relatively new assistant professor at the University of Washington. While in the kitchen fixing myself lunch, I received an out-of-state phone call from a nurse who told me that my mother had been admitted to the inpatient psychiatric ward the previous night. I did not need any details, as I knew it was another psychotic break. I made the 3-hour drive to the hospital, and when I saw my mother, I was both horrified and overcome with compassion. Although divorced from my father for several years and living with a roommate at the time, my mother had become convinced that my father was stalking her with intentions to kill her. In an effort to avoid him, she fled to the streets, something she had done on a few other occasions. This, too, is common with paranoid schizophrenia, which afflicts a considerable proportion of the homeless population.

Unfortunately, fleeing to the streets was not effective, and she began to hallucinate, believing that she saw my father. She dove deep into a blackberry bush, where she hid for some time until a police officer coaxed her out. Blackberry bushes are formidably thorny, and every square inch of her body was lacerated and bleeding. I have never seen a sadder sight. Yet she was the happiest woman in the world at the sight of her son. I have never been angry with her since.

Currently, she is expressing delusions that an old deceased friend has been reincarnated in my father. She is also quite talkative. This suggests that she is not taking her medications regularly if at all. Although I gently remind her on occasion, I do not do so with force because I want to maintain her trust. My hope is that her condition will improve as she moves into late adulthood, which sometimes happens with schizophrenia. She is still quite angry toward my sister, which will probably never change. Even though this stance is difficult for everyone, particularly my sister, she (my sister) has gained considerable understanding, and she handles our mother's anger with aplomb. In contrast, my father, who now lives alone, is usually very angry with my mother because he still interprets her behaviors, including medication noncompliance, as volitional. Yet he is considerably happier overall because he sees her only on holidays, when the entire family gets together.

I do not have any children, but perhaps one day I will. If so, they will surely experience their grandmother as eccentric, and it will be satisfying to explain that she is sick and that she does not intend to hurt them. Because my mother was undiagnosed for so many years, I did not benefit from such an understanding. Many children of psychiatrically impaired people become quite protective when they have children of their own, often limiting their children's contact with the ill family member. I doubt that I would do so, as it would stigmatize her, and my children would lose an opportunity to learn about mental illness, which is so common but so often hidden from view. Perhaps one day mental disorders will be accepted the way that most so-called physical illnesses are now. The brain is a functioning organ. Yet because it is so complex, there is far more opportunity for functional impairment than there is with the kidneys, liver, or bladder. It is ironic that we fail to recognize this crucial point; I'm glad I finally do.

What is more difficult to come to terms with is fear of the genetic legacy of mental illness in my family. Part of the distancing and disaffiliation process I mentioned earlier has resulted in excessive fear that I, too, will one day decompensate. Although this is surely irrational given that I am not prone to magical thinking, superstition, or paranoia, which would be expected prior to a schizophrenic illness, fear is not about rationality. Furthermore, even though I am past the expected age of onset for schizophrenia, my mother was a late-onset case. I am also prone to bouts of melancholia. Fortunately, I am less fearful with each passing year, and my depression is under control. Perhaps I will write about that one day, but for now, my thoughts are with my mother.

NOTES

1. The literature addressing the long-term neural effects of maltreatment and abuse has expanded considerably in recent years. Interested readers are referred to the following important contributions: Pollak, S. D., & Sinha, P. (2002). Effects of early experience on children's recognition of facial displays of emotion. *Developmental Psychology, 38*, 784–791; and Cicchetti, D., & Curtis, W. J. (2005). An event-related potential study of the processing of affective facial expressions in young

children who experienced maltreatment during the first year of life. *Development and Psychopathology, 17,* 641–677.

2. Research has indicated that patients who receive antipsychotic medications as an early intervention for schizophrenia suffer from fewer long-term symptoms and fewer relapses compared with nonmedicated controls. See Wyatt, R. J., & Henter, I. D. (1998). The effects of early and sustained intervention on the long-term morbidity of schizophrenia. *Journal of Psychiatric Research, 32,* 169–177. In addition, many of those at high risk for schizophrenia who exhibit incipient but subthreshold signs of the disorder can be prevented from suffering acute psychotic breaks by prophylactic administration of low doses of modern antipsychotics. See McGorry, P. D., Yung, A. R., Phillips, L. J., Yuen, H. P., Francey, S., Cosgrave, E. M., et al. (2002). Randomized controlled trial of interventions designed to reduce the risk of progression to first-episode psychosis in a clinical sample with subthreshold symptoms. *Archives of General Psychiatry, 59,* 921–928.

9   Weeping Mother

Jarralynne Agee

THE TRIBUTE

For an African American woman, the hardest thing to do is to tell a story about your mother and know that not everything that you could share would be perceived as a tribute to the incredible woman that she was. But as a psychologist who is concerned about the prevalence of depression, particularly as related to social factors, I have a greater fear about what would happen if I did not share my mother's story accurately and truthfully. In fact, there were things in my life that wouldn't qualify my mom as "mother of the year." She was severely depressed for much of my childhood; she often threatened to kill herself, her kids, or both. In our home, there was a constant sense of loss and grief that was caused by a spiraling effect of one tragedy followed by another. For me, the work of replacing the cloak of secrecy and shame with a feeling of openness and gratitude is crucial. I appreciate the opportunity to tell my mother's story with compassion for what she endured—even if I did not understand what she was going through at that time. I start with a story of what happened many years ago and then provide an account of her life and mine, including my eventual coming to terms with what she has meant to me.

ACCIDENTS OF BIRTH

It has been said that that which does not kill us makes us stronger. If that's true, I was ensured invincibility before I was even born.

On one August day in 1969 my mother had just come back from working a graveyard shift as an operator at Ohio Bell. She had just begun to lie down in her bed, cradling my 3-year-old sister next to her, when she heard her husband walk in the door. They shared a tiny government-assisted apartment that was just one short block away from her former home. But those few feet measured an even greater distance, representing a downward social spiral away from the respectable middle-class life into which she had been born.

Hearing the door slam, my mother clutched the robe that her own mother had given her as a Christmas gift. The robe was one of her last surviving symbols of respectability and normalcy. Although there wasn't much about my mom's life that was simple or well-put-together at this point, this robe was. The clean white fabric and delicate lace at the collar were special enough, but the robe represented much more than its physical presence: it symbolized my mother's former life. That life had abruptly ended when she got pregnant during her senior year of high school and was forced to give up her scholarship to attend college. Adding to the humiliation, her father made her write a personal note to the school that had accepted her, saying that she "regretted that she would not be able to attend due to her disgraceful decisions."

Bounding up the stairs, two by two, was her husband, who was the biggest of these disgraceful decisions. Another such decision was this junk-laden, tired apartment that sat only one street across from where she had grown up. This street separated the hills that were her former home from the ghetto—and her husband with his glassy red eyes, who stood at the foot of her bed, was a terrorizing reminder of how far she had rolled down that hill.

My mother instinctively drew my sister closer, bringing her into her robe. She prayed silently: If she could just lie still, maybe he would leave—or perhaps he would pass out from being too drunk, high, or probably both.

But this night, my mother had no such luck. He knew exactly what time she would have returned home, and he was looking for money for his next fix. My mom ran to her purse. It had been monogrammed with an oversized *K*, for her name, Karen. It was the last gift from her father in her predisgrace life. But her husband made it to the purse first, and she struggled with him as he clawed at her robe. She took hold of the purse as he yanked at her arm. At 6'6", he easily lifted the purse far over her head. She turned to retreat, but he caught her by the neck and ripped the lace collar of her robe. She fell back screaming and cried out for him to just take the money and leave. He seemed satisfied, quite smug that he now had full control of the purse.

He backed into the hallway, taunting her as he inched toward the stairs. He had the money, but his goal now was to show her who was the boss (after all, she had stood up for herself). He took the purse and tugged at its pockets. The sounds of the purse seams ripping tore through my mother's heart. The cursive, monogrammed *K* was soon destroyed as he yanked it off the purse. Tortured by his attempt to destroy the last tangible connection she had to the protective love of her mother and father, she lunged for it. She got a strong hold of a strap and tugged hard. He was confident as he stood by the steps and tugged back, but the strap finally ripped and he lost his footing. He stumbled back on his own drunken legs. To my mother's horror, he fell halfway down the steps. Things had turned in an instant; her fear became his. She was now standing over him as he lay on the steps in a crumpled heap. He pulled himself up by the stair rail and retreated down the steps, defeated.

Terror still raced through her heart. At this point my sister had awakened, and my mother told her to get back in the room. Soothing my sister, my mother recognized that, because she could not hear a sound from her husband, he must be gone. The calm was instant and soothing; she could now breathe a sigh of relief. It could have been much worse. Tired from the late shift at work and now sore from the struggle, she took my sister back to bed and laid her down. She didn't give herself time to think about the robe, imagining that he was out the front door and into the streets, with enough money to be gone for a while. She marveled at how he had gone so quietly, without even a customary slamming of the front door.

But she hadn't heard the front door shut because he had never left. Instead, he had picked himself up from the steps and retreated to the kitchen. And now he was coming back.

What she heard sounded like a freight train roaring ahead. He seemed to take the steps in one angry leap. Stunned, she jumped out of the bed and slammed the door shut on my sister. My mother had barely turned around when she noticed that he had a knife. He wasn't screaming but was now still, eerily quiet and calm. She tried to run into the bathroom down the hall, but she was an easy target for his expansive reach. She instinctively fell to the ground and covered her stomach. He got to her quickly and with no words pulled the knife up over her head. He blindly swung at her but she had crumpled herself into a fetal position. With each swing of his knife she crumpled into a smaller ball. She gripped her stomach and turned her face to the ground. He only had access to her leg. He brought his knife down hard and tore through the robe. Her thigh split open and she screamed out from the pain; the blood stain grew across her robe and more blood began to pool on the floor.

But my sister had managed to make it out the door to her room. Recognition of what he had done washed over his face as my sister ran to my mother who was covered in blood. He looked at the screaming toddler, dropped his knife, and then fled. It was over. The next time my mother would see him was when a neighbor called to say that he was on the news, about to jump into the Miami River.

On the day of the attack, my sister was barely 3 years old. She had come out to see the torn robe and the blood. My mother told her to run across the street and tell Ms. Murray that mommy has been hurt. But my sister needed to ask first, "What about the baby?" Although my mom's leg was burning and it was excruciating to turn over, she managed to maneuver herself to show my sister that her belly was untouched.

My mother was 9 months pregnant when she was attacked by her husband with a knife. Two weeks later, I was born.

JUSTIFIABLE DEPRESSION

In psychology, when people have gone through an extreme trauma and survived, we are likely to diagnose them as having posttraumatic stress disorder (PTSD). In fact, the definition is that a traumatic stressor of sufficient severity (an act of violence, a wrenching loss, a brush with death) can have lasting effects on any person, leading to numbness, flashbacks of some sort, and a tendency to startle and show high arousal at any sign or memory of the trauma.

But for my mother, there was a season in her life when she experienced not just one major stressor—rather, she had one great tragedy after another. The traumas compounded.

Soon after the assault and delivery, she got pregnant a third time—this time by a man who was even more treacherous and abusive than my biological father. How would she make it through to raise another child?

However, my mother did have one bright light, in the form of her mother's care and support. My grandmother helped my mother to care for us as infants. She would slip my mother money behind my grandfather's back. She disagreed with his stance that my mother had to fend for herself. My grandmother shared my mother's belief that things would right themselves in due time. So for my mother, she could hold out a little while longer, because she knew her life would change and that her mother's love was the key to that transformation.

But, mercilessly, the last shred of hope was ripped from my mother on a fall day where a family party turned from a festive event to one of the most tragic days in our family's history. My grandmother was on her way to Gephard'ts grocery to pick up some last minute items before the party was scheduled to start. She never made it to the store. The whole neighborhood heard the screeching of the tires and the deafening crash of the station wagon slamming into a street light. The car was smoking and the engine was still running, However it was a massive stroke that ended my grandmother's life, taking with it with it my mother's last shred of hope at a better life.

This tragedy occurred after a fight my mother had just had with her mother. My mom thought that she'd apologize to my grandmother later. They always fought and they always made up. Instead, my mother never got the chance to say "sorry" or even "thank you." For my mother it was the most incomprehensibly cruel joke that God could have played on her. She wailed in the street as the neighbors tried to console her. My sister came to her side. She was nearly 5, I was 2, and my brother was 3 weeks old. My mother believed that she had clear flaws but that her mother was the good one in the family. In fact, she cursed God for taking the wrong woman. My mother was joined by other grievers who felt that the death of Dorothy Ross was abrupt and unfair. For my mother, it was a devastating blow from which she would never recover.

Before, my mother had viewed her own fall from grace as only temporary, because one day soon, she believed, she would return home, and her mother would be waiting. But now all hope for a normal life was gone. Her father's reaction was swift and unceremonious. He cut my mother off from the supplemental money that my grandmother had given her and refused to provide her with any child care support. She no longer could afford the tiny apartment that she had hated. She was evicted and had to move. Without her mother's protection, my mother found herself fully at the mercy of the social services agency.

Soon my mother had to move her young family from those government-assisted apartments to Parkside Projects. It felt as though she had moved from purgatory to hell. Even though she hated the apartments across the street from her parents, that place was the Ritz-Carlton compared with the drug-ridden, crime-infested projects to which she was then assigned. In 3 short years, she found herself going from being a college hopeful to an orphaned, poor, single mother in the harsh jungle of the ghetto. She would never get the opportunity to have the life she knew she was entitled to. From then on, she had to play the cards she was dealt.

If she could have obtained some relief from the loss, the grief, the violence, and the pain, she could have possibly made a plan on how to restore her life. But such luck was not available. My mother became severely depressed, and that depression was a feature of my reality growing up. I always thought of depression as a problem with sadness and despair deep within a person. But I now see that these symptoms, for my mother, were symptomatic of her terrible social conditions, of the violence and the poverty that had become stable features in our lives.

So my mother's depression never really lifted. It persisted because, in the ghetto, she kept getting dealt devastating blow after blow. In a less deprived and violent setting, I believe that she would have been more mentally stable. I feel as though she never really got a break.

HELP IS NOT ON THE WAY

A couple years after the stabbing incident, and just months after her mother's death, my mother got called to my sister's school. The authorities were planning to launch an investigation of child neglect because Jackie often didn't have lunch or proper winter clothes. A hearing was scheduled on a school day, although my mother hadn't been told that it was a formal hearing. She showed up late, with socks on my sister's hands because she couldn't afford to replace the mittens we kept losing.

The agency had been explicit: "Come with Jackie but no other children." They did not say how long the meeting would last. Living in the worst projects in the city, Mom couldn't trust anyone to watch us, so she thought she'd leave us and come right back.

My mother didn't drink or smoke, having been an honor student in high school just a few years before. In the projects, she was an easy target for every scam under the sun. Men preyed on her as an easy mark, and women scoffed at her for being uppity and "talking white." She had few friends in the projects, and she tried to keep to herself.

So, when she got called to my sister's school, she had no one to watch her sleeping children. Mom had expected a 10-minute meeting, maybe 15 minutes tops; but it went on for over 2 hours. As it dragged on, she began to worry about the fact that she had left my brother and me asleep and alone in her apartment. I was 3 years old, and my brother was barely 2. At the close of her hearing she ran back to her apartment to find that my brother and I had set the apartment on fire.

My brother and I had awakened hungry, and I decided to make us some pork and beans by putting the can on the gas stove. I managed to pry the can open and start the fire. My brother stood with his face staring at the stove. But, instantly, the generic label that read "beans" went up in flames. Soon after that, the can exploded, sending fiery beans toward the window curtains. Instantly the kitchen was in flames. My brother passed out, and I couldn't wake him. It was the winter, and I went out into the snow in bare feet crying for someone to help us. We were rescued by a postman, who called the fire and police squads. My mother had left the child protection hearing only to find herself in a far worse spotlight.

She managed to get to me before the police got to her. She explained what our story would be and told me that I needed to lie to the cops. She explained that if I said she had left us alone, then I would lose her like she had lost her mother.

So, at 3 years old, I learned to cover for my mom. I lied to the police officer, agreeing with my mother that another irresponsible neighbor left us alone while mom went to the school for just 5 or 10 minutes. The officer wasn't buying it, but, in those days, there wasn't the same strictness about enforcing rules related to children who were in harm's way that there is today. He admonished my mom for being careless and took the time to lecture her on the problems of the welfare mothers in the projects. My brother and I were freezing, still in our pajamas with no coats on. My brother was checked by the fireman and cleared to go into the apartment with my mom.

We walked into the house, and my mother fell on the floor crying from exhaustion. She didn't have much time to gather her thoughts; she had to be back at school on time to pick up my sister. They were watching her. She explained this to us in words that we could understand. She sobbed as she held us both. "They are trying to split us up," she said. "Don't you ever forget that a mother is all that you have."

I learned right then that it was us against the world.

Later, for the follow-up hearing, my mother asked a neighbor to babysit while she went to my sister's school. My mother would regret that she ever knocked on the sitter's door, as we probably would have been better off with an imaginary babysitter or even to have been left sitting outside in the snow. Anything would have been better than having to spend our days with Miss Foster and her own overactive, exploitative boys. The situation was far more dangerous than a kitchen fire.

This family envisioned themselves the kings of a twisted game called "hide and go get it," in which the girls would try to hide and the boys would come find them. A girl would always get trapped in a dark space and forced down into a corner, where more than one adolescent boy would start to grope her, which progressed to their sexually forcing themselves on her. They did this with even the smallest of girls, no more than 4 or 5 years old. "Hide and go get it" went on every day until my mother found another sitter. She never knew what went on; she just had a bad feeling about those people.

NO CRYSTAL STAIR

Despite the continuing trauma, there were a lot of good things that happened in our home and in my hometown of Dayton, Ohio. My mother got past her doomed relationships with my biological dad and my brother's biological dad and fell in love with a wonderful, kindhearted soul who loved us all. In 1974, my mother married Gene Fletcher, and he is the only father I have ever known. Even before that, we were able to move into a nicer set of apartments near my grandfather's house. By the time I was 10 we were living in a regular house.

Despite her depressions, my mother was active in our community centers and the local Boys and Girl Clubs. These community meeting places were the center of the universe for fun and enrichment. Even the libraries were an air-conditioned summer retreat. The teachers in the public schools were fantastic and truly supportive. You could tell most any adult your last name, and they were bound to know your mother and would therefore give you a ride or cover the difference for you at the supermarket if you were a few pennies short. Grocery stores extended you credit for necessities and would let you buy one stick of butter or one cigarette out of the pack if that's all the money you had that day. Nobody had any video games, and MTV hadn't happened yet, but we still we managed to have the best summer fun heading up to Mallory Park to swim in the pool for 25 cents a day, which included a box lunch.

So on the surface we had a normal life. But in fact, my family had to overlook and normalize a number of things that weren't so good at all. For example, our cars hardly worked, and we often had to move to avoid eviction.

We lived paycheck to paycheck. Sometimes Christmas was great, but most times it was a disappointment. Christmas and birthdays shed light on what we didn't have. Still, our house was a place of respite for many a family and child.

Gene handled the pain and uncertainty of our life and our poverty by drinking. And my mother handled it all by continuing to slide into severe depressions. Things weren't as stable as they would have seemed to an outsider.

We kids handled it by trying to pull everyone together and pretending to be unaffected. We were verbal and funny. We got used to telling great, elaborate stories that were completely based in truth, but everyone thought that we must have made up the situations we had experienced to make it more interesting.

I once read a veteran's take on writing about war. He said that in anything you read about war, parts of the story are unbelievable, but other portions are easier to understand. Those more comprehensible things, those that we can stomach, are not always truthful; rather, it is the far-fetched things that are more likely to be the real truth about war. The more palatable but less true aspects are put in to protect the reader.

Our life with my mother was in many ways like that. The parts that everyone assumed we embellished, constituting the completely outrageous stories that we told, were all completely true. The parts of the story that were easier to accept were often the lie. We had to add those in there because it made the rest of the story easier for people to swallow.

The stabbing assault while my mom was pregnant, following her removal from the world of achievement and college, clearly triggered her slide into unwavering depression. Her mother's death, coupled with living in the projects and becoming a single mom, promoted a continuing series of depressions.

In fact, the stabbing incident was a story that I heard only once, from a neighbor who reminded my mother about it. When my mother then told the story, she did so as a joke. She would tell one tragic detail after another, and she and her friends would laugh. They would laugh because she told it in a funny way, and she would laugh to keep from crying. My mother saved her crying for private moments.

Throughout my childhood, my mother would say a prayer: "Lord, please let this be my last night." She would cry when she went to sleep and cry when she awoke. She used to pray in the nighttime for the Lord to please give her a break and let her rest—forever.

So, for as long as I can remember, I said a similar prayer. "Now I lay me down to sleep, I pray the Lord my soul to keep.... Dear Lord, please take momma and take me with her." My mother didn't know I prayed that prayer; she would have been very unhappy about it if she had known. She always intended for things to be better for us, different from the life that she had been given.

At the same time, she was one of the most resourceful people in our community. She could get one family's child into college and another family's son out of jail. The fact that she was (and still very much is) a hero in our community made the shame of her depression and our plight even harder to hide. I was once in school and told my math teacher that I was hungry. She became enraged and said to me, in front of the class, "I know your mother, and how dare you tell such a blatant lie like that on such a fine woman."

The fact is, however, that sometimes there was no food in the house. But my siblings and I learned to worry less about our empty bellies and more about my mother, who would cry and cry. No one really knew how dark her worst days could get. She carried the burden of being a helper to the community, but the deeper burdens remained hidden inside of her.

No one would have believed that she would get in her car, driving at top speeds and threatening to end it all. The worst thing that ever happened to her was the loss of her mother, and she could hardly imagine her children surviving her own death. As a result, during those times when she would become so depressed that she threatened to kill herself, she told us that we were all going together. She would drive down Gettysburg, just past Nicholas Road, zooming down the hill at breakneck speed. "This is it," she would say, telling us that she was going to drive right into the lake. We would all go together, she went on, saying that she was sad and sorry but that she couldn't take it any more. We would cry, beg, scream. We would grab at her back, but we were careful not to jerk her arm and pull us off the road. We would be going so fast that the wheels on the car would literally lift off the ground when we hit the hill that started our descent.

Just as we made it to the base of the hill, my mother would slam on the brakes and make a quick left away from the lake and toward home. The three of us would be sobbing uncontrollably in the back seat. Once home, my mother would slam the car into "park" and begin to wail. She'd cry her apologies at the same time that she'd admonish God for not giving her the strength to go through with it. My mother would hug us later, but right then and there, in the car, we would have to pull ourselves together and soothe her. It would take the three of us to loosen her grip on the steering wheel, wiggle the keys from the ignition, and open the door for her, coaxing her to go inside and lie down.

The trigger for these kinds of events was often something related to one of us. Maybe we had complained that we were hungry. Perhaps one of us was embarrassed that we couldn't go on the field trip at school because we didn't have the money for the activity fee. Or perhaps it just came out of the blue, just some grief that had caught up with her on a day that she felt too weak to keep it at bay. She was driven to incredible sadness, and her children were literal passengers on her dark suicidal ride. Recognizing that she couldn't help us because sometimes she couldn't help herself, I began to plan my escape.

In the spring of my eighth-grade year, I befriended a wealthy girl named Amber, who was the granddaughter of a prominent judge in the city. She lived in a mansion with so many rooms that I literally never got to see them all in the week I spent there. It was a paradise that I just happened on. One day after school, I just got in her grandparents' sedan, rode home with her, and slept over for one night. We didn't have a phone at my home, so I didn't call my parents and say where I was. The one-night sleepover turned into a 7-day spring break vacation during which I avoided going home. Amber would ask her grandfather for money every day, and we'd go downtown and buy me an outfit for the next day. As far as they were concerned, I was a poor girl who had no place to go, because I had let on about the chaos and despair at my home.

When Amber's family finally did take me home and found out that my house was a regular brick house with a garage and a car out front, I knew that something was wrong. Amber was disappointed, saying, "this house looks normal." She felt duped and played on because, to her, clearly things weren't as bad as I intimated. She expected crack addicts sitting on the stoop and gunshots whizzing overhead, with police tape from a recent crime scene. Instead she saw our black-and-white cat scatter up a tree.

I could never convince her that the house was just a shell. Even though we still went to school, mom still went to work, and we managed to make it to church on Sunday, our lives were very much in a state of disrepair. Amber assumed that the house must have been filled with a resilient, normal family. But our life was anything but normal. Even if we could define normal (which we couldn't), we knew that our life experiences were a long way from it. Amber never bought my story, nor did she ever trust me again.

"Normal" was not going to happen for any of us, even in a solid brick house. In that house, we always lived in fear. The brick walls couldn't keep external forces from creeping inside. The city had far too many examples of sadness, fear, violence, and loss. We were not immune, and my mother seemed the most vulnerable. In fact, even though our brick house was sitting in the respectable Madden Hills subdivision, we were still nestled in between low-income housing projects on one side, our high school on another, and the cemetery just behind us.

There were constant threats of something being taken away. If we missed one payment on the house, we'd be back across the street in the projects; if we got into trouble, we could end up in the cemetery. So the high school was the focal point of our lives. My mother stressed education, letting us know that doing well at school was our only way out. And getting out was a recurring theme in our family.

Still, in high school I was a popular cheerleader and honor student who cheered our basketball team on to a state championship. The television interrupted regularly scheduled programming to show the games. I went to three proms, and I even was a debutante when I graduated.

MOM WAS ONLY GOOD AT MIRACLES

Many events influenced how unsafe we felt in our environment. Once on the news, when we were teenagers, there were reports of the Ardmore killings. A jilted lover, enraged, took a gun and shot everyone in the house. He was relentless in gunning down everyone, including his girlfriend, her mother, and all of the children in the house. I remember watching this on the news and thinking of how close Ardmore was to my house and of how it was on our parade route in our upcoming high school homecoming festivities.

But we just went on with our lives. Even when the serial killer Alton Coleman took up residence in our neighborhood, we had to go on with life as usual. Every day in the news they speculated about where he might be. The police combed the area behind our home, as he had been sighted just a few streets over. He had kidnapped a pastor and his wife and stuffed them in the trunk of their car. It was unlikely that he had fled the area, so for several weeks the neighborhood's children all lived in fear.

Even with Alton on *America's Most Wanted*, my mother made us walk through the area where Alton had last been seen. We had to go to Gephardt's corner store to get her a soda. We had to go that way instead of Blank's store, which was in the opposite direction, because she owed money to Blank's. So, if we wanted to eat, we had to go to Gephardt's, which meant walking past the house where the pastor and his wife had been kidnapped and the spot where Alton had murdered his last victim.

On the way to the store we saw a man bloody, laid out on the ground. Certainly he was dead, we assumed. We took note and planned to tell someone when we got home. We kept our pace and headed to the store. We picked up our food and headed back to our home. As we walked back the man was still lying there, but this time he moved. Seeing a dead guy was scary but having to walk past a moving, bloody, drunk guy was positively horrifying. We ran back to the house terrified. We didn't mention it to our parents. We took the food inside and went back out to play on the front porch. We made a pact not to worry about Alton any more. He was our neighbor, and if we could walk to the store and back and not get killed, well, then, we just wouldn't worry about him any more.

Three weeks later, the serial killer Alton Coleman was found low-crawling in the fields directly behind my aunt's apartments. People had collected bets about whether he'd be found dead or alive and what part of town he would be found in. But other than that, life went on as usual.

I don't know why my mother didn't worry about Alton Coleman. In some ways we all just absorbed some of the incomprehensible things in our environment, considering them as normal. Overall, my mother really did try to protect us from things she wanted us to avoid. She tried to care for us, provide a home, and maintain her sanity.

And she was often asked to help others in the community to offset the tragedies that we would see on TV. More than a few of those tragedies hit close to home. My stepfather had been a coach, and my mother a mentor, to a 7-foot basketball wonder named Boone. One day Boone followed his friends into a crack house and was forced into playing a game of Russian roulette that took his life. A few weeks after the Ardmore killings, an 8-year-old boy who had been shot, yet survived, came to live with us. My mother helped him find a good school and a job, and he looked up to my college-bound brother. Another time, the paroled older brother of a kid my brother's age threatened to kill my brother at school. My mother had the gun-wielding brother arrested but soon found that my brother's classmate was now orphaned by his brother's incarceration. She let him live with us until he finished high school, and she personally saw to it that he went from our house to college. So, despite her years-long depression and our often-dire circumstances, she reached out to help others in even worse straits.

There were several other people who came in and out of our lives. Not all of their experiences were marked by tragedy. But in every case there was a way that my mom was able to find a way out of a "no-win" situation, to help and support the people that needed care the most.

This was a rallying point for her, somehow. She found ways to get it together for the toughest situations around, even though at home she was usually sad and distressed. She tried to buy herself moments of hope—for example, the time that she decided to become a Mary Kay saleswoman. We were so happy when she brought home those bright cases of makeup. Our new future was covered in pink. On the day that she got the supplies, she made a stop at a friend's house. She discouraged me from staying in the car for fear I'd get into all the makeup. When we came out she wished she had thought differently. The back window was smashed, and someone had stolen all of the supplies. The value of the items that my mother had to replace was several hundred dollars that we didn't have. Even more, however, my mother was robbed of a dream, a cost that was immeasurable.

Later, when she was able to get funding for a 1976 Ford Grenada, someone broke into our house through my window, went into my mother's room while she was sleeping, got the keys, and stole the car. My mother had only had the car one night, and she didn't have any insurance on the car, so it was never replaced.

All of these instances intensified my mother's belief that she wasn't meant to be on this earth. Except for the times that she helped others, she didn't much see the point to life. Having witnessed her depression for years, I understood completely when she threatened to give us up for adoption. Indeed, I truly felt sorry for my mother. I tried to take care of her when I was young, but as I became a teenager I began to blame her for being so inaccessible to us and making decisions that I thought exacerbated her downward spiral.

But even before adolescence, I was forming strong opinions. At 8 years of age, I told her that I thought she should have only had one child, that three was too many. Later, on a toyless Christmas, after quoting Ben Franklin in saying "we are not poor, we are living poorly," I then admonished her for not planning better for the holidays. My brother and sister found me cold and unrelenting. Up until I was 11 the rule was to work to make mommy not cry. By the time I was 13, I had gotten a job and was helping to feed the family. At 15, I was a tour guide at a park and was paying some of the bills. By 17, riding on the heels of my high school success, I left home for college on a full scholarship. I sent home enough money to pay rent and phone bills and to help my siblings. But for the most part, once I left home, I tried never to look back.

REFLECTIONS

I tried to steer clear of the past, but things would always bring me back. I constantly helped my family, and I still do. In 1999 my mother had a massive stroke that left her paralyzed. Knowing all that she had been through, I began to think of her wheelchair confinement as a physical retirement. My mother had been through enough, seen enough, and done enough good that she deserved a break, however it came. After years of living my new life away from my early years in Dayton, I didn't hesitate to make the space for her in my life when she had the stroke. But that was only the beginning of figuring out who my mother was and what she meant to me as a person and as a mental health professional.

In my reflective process I thought about why I decided to go into this profession. Sometimes I actually think that psychologists who don't recognize their desire to go into this field as a primal need to diagnose their own families should probably get their heads examined!

Over my life, I had gone through years of worry about my mom and her sadness. I understood that my early independence represented a way of surviving. At the same time, I experienced rage at my mother for not doing better. At some points as an adult, I became fearful and depressed that I would turn into her. But all the while I knew that I wanted to understand, help, and teach others. My training as a psychologist was a life calling.

There was a singular professional event that caused me to reevaluate my feelings about my mother and to change my understanding of who she was and what she had been through. At one point during my graduate studies, I had a client who suffered with visits from La Llorona. In other words, my client told me that "La Llorona" was visiting her, telling her to smother or drown her baby. My client was at the same time suicidal, and I felt absolutely certain that I should not let her go home. I called in my supervisors, and we formed an emergency triage team.

The on-call doctor administered a mood stabilizer and explained to me that La Llorona is part of Mexican lore about the "weeping mother" who had killed her own children. The vision of La Llorona haunts and torments new mothers, sometimes persuading them to kill their own children in much the same fashion as she had done. What Mexican traditional culture calls La Llorona we would professionally term severe postpartum depression.

I was able to help my client to avoid having her infant daughter removed from her care by devising a treatment plan that appeased the authorities who planned to monitor the situation through our counseling center. We planned for her sisters to take the baby for the weekend, for her husband to pick her up from the counseling center, and for us all to wait for the psychotropic medication to kick in. With this woman medicated and armed with the information that La Llorona is not real—but that deep, fearful feelings certainly are—I was able to help my client reunite with her daughter soon afterward.

That was the only time that I had needed to call for immediate backup in a counseling situation. There were other times that I perhaps should have—for example, when a psychotic parolee revealed to me that he knew where I lived and what kind of car I drove, as he cornered me in my office, placing himself between me and the door. Another time a client handed me what he said was cyanide while I was 5 months pregnant. We never figured out what was in that vial, and my baby turned out fine, but I didn't feel as panicked in that moment as I felt with my client who was haunted by La Llorona.

On reflection, what made me call in the psychological cavalry at that point was the strong desire to get all the help I could to allow this woman to keep her baby. I wanted desperately to prevent the removal of her infant and, at the same time, to prevent blame from being placed on the mother. With the treatment team, I helped to isolate the factors that were causing her distress and to provide real and immediate relief from the pressures that burdened her. I was empathic, seeing the situation from her side and giving her that unconditional positive regard that we try to extend to all of our clients.

What motivated this burst of powerful intervention? Somewhere deep down, I believe that I was doing for her what I wish someone could have done for my mother many years earlier. Couldn't someone have been there for her, guiding her through her trauma? It is clear to me that deep family roots may underlie some of our most important motivations, interventions, and insights.

This, I realized, was what I had wanted to do all along: to take away her pain and to guide her. At that moment, I stopped blaming my mother for not fixing her problem and began to investigate what might have stopped her from getting the intervention that she needed. I recognized that whereas my client had a place that she could go where she could trust the people on the other side of the table, my mother had not had the same experience. There had been no one there to help her.

There is a scale on one of the most popular personality inventories called "Fake-K." This scale assesses whether a respondent is "faking good"—meaning that he or she is trying to make things seem better than they really are. Parolees are likely to spike a Fake-K scale, as are people who are trying to gain entrance for a job or who would otherwise experience some negative consequence for having pervasive negative emotions. My mother suffered from an undiagnosed mood disorder. She had to mask her depression and mood swings in order to keep our family together. She didn't have any of the psychological interventions that I was able to give to my client. Those limited social services to which she had access were all part of an adversarial system. For example, the child welfare agency wanted to help my sister by removing her from the home. My mother would have been in danger of losing her job if she had shared her dark moods with people at work. Even her reputation in the community would have been marred if people did not see her as mentally fit to assist at-risk youths.

Growing up, we knew better than to rely on social workers, housing authority representatives, caseworkers, or even teachers. After the fire, we realized that if we had told the truth, the police officer on the scene would have arrested my mother for child neglect instead of helping her find a viable, safe child-care alternative. On another occasion, in fact, the police arrested my mother for bouncing an $11 check to a store on the white side of town. They detained her over the weekend and effectively left all three of her children alone in the house, orphaned for the weekend. We learned that authorities were not our friends.

So much was at stake that my mother would not seek help, for fear of finding no one whom she could really trust. Think of the benefit she might have received from a counselor regarding the postpartum depression she experienced after the birth of each successive child. She would have also been a perfect candidate for grief counseling after losing her mother. If she had had a caseworker who was a strong advocate in the child welfare hearings, that person would have suggested and advocated for reliable day care to protect the children. These interventions would have allowed my mother to go back to college and restore the pride in her life that once existed before the long slide of tragic events began.

Our environment of poverty, violence, and crime only made matters worse. My mother began to take on an attitude expressed by the following: "I could complain but who'd listen?" In fact, I think that's where my mother's deadpan act came from, which she called the "sad-ass Karen Fletcher" story, referring to herself. Her defense was to be funny, and it often worked as an inspiration for those around her.

In many ways I want the telling of this story to serve the same effect. Perhaps people will read about my mother, understand her shortcomings and her strengths, and take some of it with humor, despite the pain. My family has found a way to avoid wallowing in pity. If all of us in the mental health professions can understand the real pain that people experience, maybe we can begin to address what might be done to ensure that people like my mother can get the help that is so desperately needed.

Even though she is now permanently physically disabled, her demeanor is completely different from that of the woman I grew up with. She is no longer depressed, and she has optimism about life that wasn't there before. I love my new mother and have come to respect her in this phase of her life, as well. When I was younger, there was a time when my mother broke her leg and still drove a car, even wearing a cast. We marveled at how she could get around when she was visibly impaired.

Now, knowing what I know as a psychologist, I see that she was chronically impaired in terms of depression. She got around despite that impairment, too. Despite all of the things that occurred, on many occasions she psychologically limped around as best she could to make our lives better.

I'm certain that our lives would have been different had my mother had the same level of care that I was able to provide for other people decades later. I also know that the survival and success of her three children are a direct result of what my mother went through for all of us. I owe who I am as a psychologist to her. Without her strength, I couldn't be writing this story of her life now.

I hope that people reading this chapter will see that my story is not one of a broken, wounded family. I see my family as a strong and incredibly resilient group of achievers. We are a group to be studied, not pitied.

Nietzsche said, "That which does not kill us makes us stronger." For me, narrowly avoiding death before I was even born almost made the later hardships in my life a ripple in the pond after a major wave. My mother and I shared that bond of survival. We earned the right to mourn, to be depressed, and to be sullen, mean, or distrustful. My mother chose, instead to laugh. She earned that right because after all, she has survived—and truthfully, she has cried enough.

10 The Game With No Rules: A Sibling Confronts Mental Illness

Jessica L. Borelli

I grip the remote controls to the video game system, fully aware that I have no mastery over them, wary that Daniel is likely to be angered and frustrated by the mistakes I will inevitably make but still hopeful that I will be able to participate in a game that gives him so much joy. "Jess, you're the one on the right, I'm the big guy on the left," Daniel educates me regarding the wrestling characters that now appear on the television screen, poised and ready to fight. I nod as though I understand, trying to convince Daniel and myself of my prowess with the video game. The clock in the ring sounds, and the match has begun. I begin to grapple clumsily with the controls, pressing the A button when I should be pressing B, struggling to combine agile forward and backward movements, upper-cuts and turning kicks, in the way Daniel has previously instructed me. After a few misses, I finally manage to deliver a resounding roundhouse kick to Daniel's character and sit back, pleased with myself. Daniel then turns angrily toward me: "Jess, you're not supposed to be attacking me. We lose points for that—you're supposed to help me attack the other guys." At this point two other wrestling characters, clad in scant and flashy clothing, appear on the screen, and the point of the match suddenly becomes obvious to me. I laugh aloud at myself for my lack of understanding of the game, then turn to focus on delivering punches and kicks to the opposing fighters.

I watch Daniel out of the corner of my eye, noting that he is becoming more and more enraptured with the game, his arm muscles taut and his eyes intent on the screen. He straddles the fine line between diversion and frustration, and I study him closely to prepare myself for whichever side of the line he ends up on. Both in the virtual ring and out of it, I find myself repeatedly sizing him up, looking for subtle hints about when his mood will turn, when I should switch to the defensive, and when I should reach out to connect with him. He turns on a dime, and I realize I have to monitor his every move, staring him in the eyes to determine in which direction he will move next.

On this occasion, when Daniel notices me looking at him, he reprimands me and demands that I turn my attention back onto the match: "Come on, Jess. You have to focus." I return to my fumbling with the control, enjoying the randomness of my button presses and attempting to detect patterns in the movement of my wrestler and my interactions with the control. I suddenly notice that Daniel's character has now begun attacking me. I look away from the screen and questioningly toward Daniel: "Hey, Dan, what are you doing?" He smiles deviously through a closed mouth and replies, "I'm getting you back for what you did to me before. You can't hurt me and get away with it." I watch Daniel incredulously as he disregards the point of the match and beats up his own partner, perplexed by this turn of events. His character continues to punch and kick until my character has lost all of his life support points and fades off the screen. Triumphant, Daniel leans back on his elbows and smiles at me: "That's what you get for trying to hurt me, Jess. Anybody who tries to get me is going to get in big trouble."

With Daniel, I have always felt as though I were playing a game for which I never knew the rules.

RAGE, FEAR

I don't even know what triggered the explosion. I've been upstairs diligently working on my eighth-grade algebra homework for an hour and suddenly, out of the corner of an anxious eye, I see my brother dash past the open door of my bedroom and down the hall. I know that run—within a split second I viscerally sense the frenzied energy, the unleashed rage, the frantic posture of his body. My body springs to action: I'm shaking, scanning the environment for cues of danger, ready to unleash my fight-or-flight response. I have been primed for an event like this one over the past few years, which have been characterized by frequent but unpredictable rages on the part of my brother, episodes that have left me and the other members of my family prisoners to our fear and to his fluctuating moods. Within an instant I've shoved my homework and pencil on the floor and run down the hallway toward the room my brothers share. As I run I hear my mom's fearful voice instructing my brother to calm down and put down whatever it was he was wielding as a weapon against her, repeating his name in a pleading and desperate way.

As I enter the room I see Daniel standing near the doorway with his back to me. He has assumed the defensive stance of a boxer, of someone under tremendous threat—his shoulders are protectively hunched, his eyes and head lowered but watchful, his legs constantly moving back and forth, ready to spring in any direction should a threat emerge. My mother crouches in the corner of the bedroom, arms protectively outstretched, looking at Daniel only to beg him not to hurt her. Her attempt to control the terror in her voice is striking. She doesn't want to communicate to her son that his behavior scares her, that he is frightening and capable of hurting her. She wants to soothe and calm him, but her frozen posture and her fear prohibit her voice from sounding calm or soothing. I can tell by the look of the room that the battle has already begun and that, even though I am only a few seconds late, much damage has already occurred. Chairs are overturned, shredded papers are strewn over the carpet, and toys have been thrown across the room and landed somewhere near my mother's feet. Her face is marred by red scratch marks down her cheeks and her neck, one streak increasingly dotted by crimson blood. She looks up and catches my eye, in one instant communicating her intense fear and helplessness, in the next urging me with a subtle eye movement to leave the room. But I cannot leave—I am glued to the scene, paralyzed by terror, mesmerized by the emotional intensity of what I am witnessing. Rather than fleeing, my impulse is to intervene to protect my mother. If there is one primitive thought in my head during that panicky instant, it is that I must prevent him from hurting the person I depend on most in my life.

This was the usual struggle of these fights—my mom, having "provoked" my brother by not giving in to a demand, was always the victim, Daniel always the aggressor. But my mother's status as victim was the single most overwhelming and terrifying feature of these events. I would typically do everything in my power to redirect his anger and aggression away from my mother toward me. This proved to be an easy task with someone to whom every behavior is an affront and a direct threat. In this situation, I simply say, "Daniel, stop!" He immediately swivels on his agile feet to look me directly in the eyes with a challenging glance. "Jess, stay away. Don't make me hurt you." His voice is deeper than usual, teeming with emotion. I respond with as much calm and power as I can muster: "Daniel, don't hurt Mom." At this point he leaps toward me and begins clawing at anything he can grasp—my arms, my face, my neck. He grabs two fistfuls of my hair, pulling them with a vengeance, all to the background tune of my frantic screams and the warning, now near-hysterical, voice of my mother. After what seems like an eternity, he gives my hair one final tug, releasing his fists and taking chunks of my hair with him. Seething and feeling more provoked and threatened than before, he now returns to the original target of his ferocity, and with renewed force begins to hurl anything he can find at my mother's head.

Often during these battles I remember mentally stepping away from the event and gaining enough perspective to note that my brother had *become an animal, a beast crudely fighting for his survival in a self-perceived threatening situation. The agility of his body movements and the desperate quality of his voice all connoted primitiveness. During these times he honestly seemed more like a ferocious beast rather than my adorable brother, who loved Thomas the Tank Engine and Raffi. At this point my brother pounces on my mother and begins biting her hands, her neck, her breasts, all the while grunting and flinging his fists at her with undeterred vigor. At one point during this chaos, Daniel sinks his teeth into my mother's finger, and, as is usually the case when he bites someone, purposely bites down deeper toward the bone. Next something happens that I have never before heard: my mother loses all semblance of control or restraint and screams, "Daniel, YOU'RE GOING TO BITE MY FINGER OFF!" I see the terror in my mother's eyes and hear the unprecedented pain in her voice and I instantly bolt toward Daniel, pulling him by his hair from my mother's body, also screaming: "You cannot hurt Mommy!" In two seconds flat, Daniel has reversed his position, knocked me onto the floor, grabbed a fistful of the hair behind my ear, and fiercely bit my neck and launched his legs into my side. I welcome the physical pain that comes upon me now, relieved to have stopped him from hurting my mother and ready to accept any kind of treatment rather than witness that scenario again. The physical pain I feel means that he is not inflicting pain on her; it is a freeing sensation and I give myself over to it fully, almost memorizing its every incarnation in order to cling to the security of knowing she is (temporarily) safe.*

I cannot remember how long this particular fight lasted; in fact, I had no real sense of time during any of these events. I know that many more punches were thrown and that it seemed as though I cried and sobbed endlessly from my own fear of my brother, the pain he had wreaked on my heart and my body, and, most important, from my great fear of his seriously hurting my mother. At some point my father came home from work, probably because my other brother had called him and begged for help. Once my father came onto the scene, we were typically able to end the fight by physically restraining my clawing, raging brother. My dad would sit on my brother's back, forcing him to remain locked to the ground, while my mom held his head and arms, preventing him from biting or scratching my dad, and I held his flailing legs from behind. Once in this position, it would typically take 30 minutes to an hour for Daniel to reach a state of pure calm.

At the initial point of restraint, he would become even more vehement and enraged, and if he managed to get away from my father, all hell would break loose, and he would begin raging again with renewed ferocity. But if he remained restrained, he would then begin an alternating

*pattern of begging to be let free, screaming that he was going to call the po-
lice and that my father was hurting him, and sobbing. Finally, he would
fall asleep, often still weeping and convulsing. When he would awaken,
he would not be able to remember the majority of his behavior during the
fight but would still weepily apologize for having hurt us.*

Twelve years after that specific event, Daniel still remembers the fact that
I pulled his hair during the fight. This stands out as the only time I aggressed
against him, the only time I used physical force to thwart his actions. Every other
time that he attacked me, I never so much as pushed him away to protect myself.
My mother had instructed my sister, my other brother, and me not ever to use
any kind of force against Daniel, even if it was in the service of self-protection.
Her fear was that he would interpret the self-protective behaviors of his family
as attacks directed against him. What my mother accurately understood was that
Daniel believed the world to be a frightening, threatening place where everyone
was out to get him and that his only choice was to aggressively defend himself.
In her mind, the worst thing would be for Daniel to feel threatened by his own
family, so we should never behave in a way that could possibly be misconstrued
as aggression. However, in encouraging her other children to accept Daniel's brutality without a fight, she effectively instilled in us a sense of utter helplessness.

What transpired instead was incredibly pathetic: Daniel launching an attack
against me and my passively allowing him to hurt me, holding my breath until
he desisted, left with hot tears flooding down my face and a body that would
not stop trembling for hours. Daniel does not recall the hundreds of times he
attacked me, yet he clearly remembers the one time I retaliated. In fact, he still
mentions it almost every time I see him as something that convinces him that
I could hurt him and that he cannot trust me.

BEGINNINGS: JOY, WORRY

Daniel was born in August of 1989 in a hospital in southern California. His biological mother and his entire beaming adoptive family were there to greet him
as he entered the world. His was an easy birth, and he was a healthy infant, such
that we were able to bring him home from the hospital after only two days.
I will never forget those first few weeks when we had Daniel at home from the
hospital. Because it was August, my sister and brother and I were all home on
summer vacation, so that we could spend every waking second fawning over
the baby. I remember us sitting in the living room, taking timed turns holding
Daniel, delighting in his every move, so in love with him after such a brief time
of knowing him. And he was spectacularly beautiful, with tufts of blondish-
white hair, light blue eyes, and a cherub face. It was amazing how quickly our

lives came to revolve around him, especially during those first few months. My family—Daniel's adoptive family—was thrilled by his presence, wondering in amazement at his charming personality, his curiosity, and his beauty.

Daniel continued to be the focal point of our family life, largely because of the seven-year age spread between the third child, my brother Adam, and him and because my parents and family had wished so long for another child, positively thrilled when this became a possibility. He was so social, his smile so quick and bright; he loved cuddling with everyone, and he had three older adoring siblings who thought the world of him. I remember feeling such intense communion with Daniel throughout this time—I had been the one who chose the name Daniel and, in my 10-year-old mind, felt this meant we were in some way especially connected.

When Daniel was about 2 years old, however, it became clear that something was aberrant in his behavior, although fainter signs had been accumulating. He was highly reactive, easily irritated and frustrated, seemingly unable to resolve his feelings of anger. His biting was qualitatively different from that of most children, both in terms of its frequency and intensity. He began to have regular temper tantrums that were far more severe than one would expect of a child his age. At this time he also began to engage in self-injurious behavior: he would often bang his head against the wall when he was upset and beat his body against the ground. My mom hypothesized that perhaps his behavioral volatility at this age was related to limits in language production. Over the next few years, the speculation underwent a metamorphosis into frantic worry and concern about Daniel's behavior, as he continued to become behaviorally volatile despite the growth in his communicative capacity. He was aggressive, hostile, impulsive, irritable, wild, uncontrolled, furious, strong-willed, and active.

When he was 4½, he began to see a psychologist, who diagnosed him with attention deficit disorder with hyperactivity (the diagnostic category in *DSM-III*) and conducted play therapy with him until he was about 6. At this time he also began his contact with psychiatrists. He began taking clonidine rather than Ritalin because his first physician thought he was too young for stimulants.

Other oddities emerged in Daniel. We began to notice that he almost always walked on his toes, which we later learned can be a sign of neurological impairment. It also became clear that he detested clothing and the feeling of cloth on his skin. He therefore insisted on being naked all day, every day, while he was home, and trying to dress him before leaving the house inevitably entailed a battle. It never seemed to bother him to be naked in front of anyone; in fact, he would vehemently refuse to wear even a diaper or underwear when company was over. This preference for nudity disappeared when Daniel was about 5, rapidly replaced by new, equally rigid preferences for specific types of clothing and extreme fear about exposing his naked body. During this time, he was mortified at the thought of anyone seeing him naked, becoming panicked and livid if anybody ever mentioned his being nude in the past. Years later, Daniel found some baby pictures of himself characteristically naked, and he became so enraged that he burned all of them and made everyone swear that they had never seen him naked.

He soon insisted on multiple layers of tight-fitting clothing. He had strict preferences for the way the collars of his T-shirts fit around his neck and began wearing multiple layers of T-shirts at the same time, a pattern that persisted until he was 13. At this time he also refused to wear underwear and instead wore numerous layers of spandex beneath his boxer shorts and, often, more than one pair of jeans. He would agree to wear only a few items of clothing despite the fact that he owned many more, so that my mother would have to wash his clothing almost every day because he would wear so much of it at the same time but demanded to wear it again the next day. Daniel also refused to integrate new clothing into his wardrobe, even if the proposed items bore a remarkable resemblance to his existing shirts or pants. Not having the right clothes also became a reason for his not wanting to go to school, which would typically result in a tantrum that would either necessitate his staying home (more typical when he was younger) or his going to school an hour or two late (more commonplace later). To questions about his preferences, he has responded by saying that the way one shirt alone fits bothers him around his neck, that he cannot stand having any space between his neck and the shirt, and that he feels safer and more protected in layers of clothes.

It was also around this time that Daniel began to refuse to sleep in the bedroom he shared with my brother, sleeping on a couch in the den downstairs. He began having a difficult time falling asleep and staying asleep during the night, often going to bed very late at night and sleeping until midday. His sleep problems were no doubt aggravated by the stimulant medications and tranquilizers he began to take in middle childhood. As his medications would wear off at night, Daniel would become increasingly intense, giddy, silly, and irritable, unable to calm down or sit still, making it quite difficult for him to be soothed. He has continued to refuse to sleep regularly in his own bedroom, most often sleeping on the couches in the living room with his soft "blankees," almost always begging someone to join him there.

Looking back, I now realize how profoundly Daniel's first therapist influenced my parents' thinking. This psychologist suggested that Daniel be exposed to television programs and video games with violence and be allowed to play with violent action figures in an attempt to allow him to release his aggression in an acceptable form. The current state of research on this topic indicates, on the contrary, a positive association between exposure to violent media and future aggression, with a clear focus on the idea that children who strongly identify with violent characters and who internalize the norms presented by violent media—namely, that aggression is an expected and reasonable reaction to provocation and that the world is a hostile, antagonistic place—are more likely to exhibit aggressive behavior.[1] In hindsight, this recommendation to expose an already aggressive child to violent media seems almost criminal.

Daniel was therefore permitted from quite early on to watch violent television shows, including wrestling matches, and to play extensively with violent video games. He would often spend between 4 and 8 hours a day engaging in violent media. While doing so, his mood would fluctuate dramatically, from pure elation and a soothing state of "flow" to irritation and eventually frustration and fury after having his attempts thwarted (e.g., when trying to win a certain video or computer game). Trying to stop him from watching almost always resulted in a verbal power struggle or a physical fight.

This first psychologist also influenced the way my parents chose to handle Daniel's violent episodes. The opinion was that what frightened Daniel the most was his own belief that he could frighten or hurt people and lose control of himself entirely. The psychologist thus argued that my parents should allow Daniel to feel safe (even from himself) in their presence by providing tremendous reassurance that he was not scary enough to be rejected. The specific suggestion was that they disconfirm Daniel's fear by reassuring him that, in fact, his behavior did not frighten the people around him and that he was not really capable of hurting others. I often remember my mother attempting to persuade Daniel that she was not scared of him, that he was not scary, that he was just a little boy and little boys cannot hurt adults.

In retrospect, I am not sure whether I would agree with this logic. Although Daniel's aggressive episodes must have been tremendously frightening to him, I sense that even more frightening was his perception that the rest of the world was threatening and scary, fostering the belief that reacting with extreme aggression was the only way to guarantee his own safety. In fact, the idea that he could not have really hurt someone was simply not true. Yet I specifically remember my mother attempting to convince Daniel that he was not hurting her when he was fiercely biting her arm.

Regardless of the dubious therapeutic effects of these measures for Daniel, they had clear implications for my siblings and me. I have now learned that in denying Daniel's capacity for destructiveness or danger and in minimizing how much her battle wounds hurt her, my mother was also hoping to reassure her other children that Daniel was not a serious threat and that she was not in imminent danger. Yet, unfortunately, these words felt hollow when compared with the terror I experienced during the episodes. I remember feeling incredibly confused and angered by the statements my mother would make about how Daniel's behavior was not scary or dangerous, when my own subjective experience of these episodes was incredibly frightening and terrifying. Still, we acted in accordance with the myth, and not the reality, in an attempt to convince Daniel that he was not dangerous or frightening. The recommendations of this initial psychologist may well have paved the way for increases in Daniel's aggression toward and fear of others.

EMBARRASSMENT, LOVE, RESENTMENT

I am sitting in my 10th-grade English class discussing Lord of the Flies, *by William Golding, which we have been reading and analyzing for a month or more. We are now discussing the animalistic and brutal behavior of Jack, the character who ends up forming a rebel group, taking control of the clan, and killing one of the other boys on the island. The teacher directs a student to read a particularly detailed description of Jack's vicious behavior. After he finishes reading the passage, this student then adds an editorial: "Just like Jessie's brother." Laughter erupts from a few others in the room.*

Equating my younger brother to the murderous villain in a novel about the nature of evil is obviously something that calls for further questioning. My teacher looks back and forth from the other student to me, with a worried though somewhat amused expression on her face. "No, seriously," the student responds to her probing stare, "he's a monster, a little animal." With a coy smile, he then proceeds to relate an experience he had witnessed while in my home for a chemistry study group. He describes in hideous detail my brother's aggressive behaviors toward my mother and me and his extensive use of sexualized language and profanity. He vilifies my brother as "weird…a freaky devil," intermittently laughing throughout his rendition of the scene.

During this whole discussion I sit frozen to my seat, my temperature rising precipitously, horrified and unable to prevent him from disclosing details of my brother's behavior in such a derogatory, blaming, insensitive, and mocking manner. Afterward, the teacher turns to me for an explanation, one that I have difficulty delivering given my extreme emotional arousal. I feel humiliated, naked, exposed. I feel hurt and betrayed, sad for my brother, whose struggle and turmoil has been put on public display without his consent. I am livid with rage against the student who has chosen to make a disclosure I myself would not make, particularly in such an insensitive and cruel way. I feel frightened that an authority figure is now privy to potentially condemning information about my brother, information that I have been warned by my family could result in Daniel's being "taken away from us."

And so, with a trembling voice, I respond in defense of my brother. My chin quivering but thrust bravely forward, I tell the class that my brother has attention-deficit/hyperactivity disorder, that life is a constant struggle for him because he is unable to control his anger; that his behavior, though terrifying to those who witness or are subjected to it, is probably the most frightening for him. The teacher, the student, and the rest of the class are silenced by my comments, their smiles quickly vanishing, likely because the emotional intensity I am feeling is clearly communicated through my voice and my words. I am marginally able to contain the extent of my reaction until the class period ends, when I run to the bathroom to cry and then to the public phone to call my mother to make sure that my worst fear, that she would die during a fight with Daniel, is not a reality. This fear, that my brother would kill my mother, is a constant backdrop for me, one that I need disconfirmed repeatedly in order to calm myself.

In retrospect, I realize that the student's seemingly insensitive and callous comments were probably his way of coping with the scenes he had witnessed in my home. When I view the student's behavior through this lens, I am able to feel more compassion toward him, but at the time I remember only feeling threatened and hurt by his behavior. In general, from talking with friends about their experiences in witnessing Daniel's violent behavior, I realize that, for most of them, exposure to these scenes ranks as one of the most frightening experiences of their lives.

During that time, these friends served as sounding boards, as litmus tests for the severity of the situation with my brother. When my parents would minimize the events at home, these friends validated my understanding of the fights as overwhelming and immediately frightening. From this perspective, I was also better able to understand their negative reactions to my brother, which at times had been a source of distress for me. Most of my friends often reported hating him, wishing that he would disappear and stop tormenting my family. They, too, often described him in unflattering, insensitive ways. I became hurt, wanting to protect Daniel's reputation and to express my love for him. Yet when I place these comments in the context that my friends, too, were grappling with the difficult experience of witnessing violence against someone they loved, I more readily understand their anger toward my brother and their sometimes insensitive reactions.

My own emotional responses to living with my brother were also tremendously conflicted and complicated. I loved him, and I hated him. I was afraid of him, yet I felt so bad for him regarding his struggles. I resented him for entering my family and so drastically changing the way it operated, creating an environment of fear and threat rather than safety and comfort. My emotions about my brother ebbed and flowed, changing by the hour based on his behavior, my sense of safety, and my family's reaction.

I remember often feeling so angry that I would just mentally scream inside my own head the things I felt I could not safely say to my brother: "How could you do this to us? How could you be so selfish? How could you hurt everyone this way? Why is it impossible for you to comply with anything? Why are you so immature, so selfish, so limited? Why are you like this?" But at other times I was simply overwhelmed by the fear, wanting to identify with my brother so that he would be less likely to hurt me and more likely to be kind to me. I struggled to contain all of these parts of myself, to make sense of them, feeling them intensely and fighting the desire to express them.

I also remember experiencing intense love for him. I would watch him when he had fallen asleep on the couch downstairs, peacefully sucking on his middle and ring fingers, or I would play a game with him and watch his face light up with happiness. I remember feeling intoxicated with the joy of connecting with him in a positive way, sharing a happy time or experience with him. Those moments were priceless and potent. It was impossible not to love Daniel and not to feel compassion and caring for him, despite his great potential to hurt me and my family in so many ways.

After the occasional times when I behaved in an angry way toward Daniel—when, for example, I pulled his hair that one time, or when I yelled, "Daniel, stop!" in a less-than-calm voice—I remember that my mother reprimanded me for behaving in a way that would incite him and make things worse. It was almost as though my "normal" reactions to frightening situations with Daniel were worse than his clearly inappropriate behavior. It was difficult to hear my parents tell me that I should just passively let Daniel hurt me (or worse, to hurt them) without interfering. Could this mean my parents thought it was okay for Daniel to hurt me? Did this mean that I deserved to be physically and emotionally abused by my brother or by people in general?

During these battles, I felt unable to express my anger directly to Daniel because I was afraid of how he would react. I had seen how he responded to relatively benign statements or actions during times of intense emotion, and I could only imagine how he would respond to an expression of anger. Instead, I would redirect my anger toward someone else, the next closest person involved in the fight or anyone who could possibly have had any control over my brother. After a huge fight, I remember blaming my other brother for having the audacity to want my mom to take him to his gymnastics class, which required Daniel getting in the car, the act that instigated the entire fight. I vividly remember thinking that he was so selfish: how could he put my family through this just for a gymnastics class?

Everyone was reacting similarly. My mother would blame my father, for example, for not relinquishing control of the car radio to Daniel immediately when my brother had made an inappropriate, angry demand, or she would blame my other brother or me for interfering in fights. My father was the only one who did not seem to blame anybody except Daniel. Practically everyone was polarized against one another; we would all assert each other's guilt in an attempt to avoiding expressing or feeling anger toward Daniel. We did this, I imagine, because it allowed us to believe that the situation in our family was controllable. Blaming my dad for being selfish enough to want to listen to a news program on the radio was a lot less scary than blaming Daniel for his erratic, oppositional, aggressive behavior. I could blame my dad without worrying that he would hurt me, but I could not do this with Daniel. Acknowledging the true uncontrollability of Daniel's behavior, the volatility and violence and chaos, was a far scarier than believing that one or all of the rest of us were at fault. Being afraid of someone you love is a powerful, tormented experience.

CONFUSION AND SHAME

At 7 years of age, Daniel failed to show substantial improvement with play therapy and medication, so he switched mental health professionals and began receiving treatment at a specialty clinic in southern California. Since then, he has switched psychotherapists two more times and has had contact with two other psychiatrists. He has attended social skills groups for boys with ADHD and has had individual therapy, a neuropsychological assessment, and consultation with a neurologist, all to no avail.

The lack of diagnostic clarity for Daniel's symptoms was disconcerting. When Daniel was 10½, a neuropsychologist first diagnosed him with bipolar disorder, early onset, and this became his primary diagnosis, while the others (ADHD-combined type, conduct disorder, social phobia, intermittent explosive disorder, and features of obsessive-compulsive disorder) became secondary diagnoses. When at first he was diagnosed solely with ADHD, I remember feeling that this diagnosis for Daniel felt hollow when compared with the extent of his difficulties, the force of public censure, and the strength of my private fear and anger about Daniel. When he was a toddler and my mother would still attempt to take him to public places, the typical scenario involved Daniel's creating a scene in the grocery store—throwing cereal boxes, screaming obscenities at my mother, using words even my 13-year-old self was not even aware of. He often bit, hit, or scratched her, as my mother quietly begged Daniel to stop his misbehavior and I stood next to the shopping cart, nervously fiddling with the cuff on my shorts, tears escaping down my face. Behind the rage in Daniel's eyes was the shadow of frantic embarrassment and fear; I saw all of those but even then realized that most observers would see only the rage.

I could not help but notice people's reactions as they walked by. Many would uncomfortably avert their eyes from the scene, some would glare at my mother and me, muttering things about Daniel being a brat or spoiled rotten. I felt the public scrutiny of Daniel and our family as blaming and unforgiving. I remember that when I would offer the term ADHD as an explanation for his behavior, I would visualize the words emerging from my mouth, quickly losing all force of movement, and crashing pitifully to the ground in their inability to express the inexpressible. At this point everyone "knew" what ADHD was, everyone knew several children who technically had ADHD. Few, however, believed that it was a legitimate or serious diagnosis, instead sensing it as a crutch for lazy, overindulgent parents. My brother was far more than a child who had trouble focusing, and it was infuriating to be without a language to convey both the gravity of his difficulties and his blamelessness for them.

In retrospect, I am not certain whether a more "serious" label would have ameliorated these difficulties concerning public perceptions of Daniel's problems. For example, had he been diagnosed earlier with bipolar disorder, which carries a certain force to its name, I am not really sure whether this would have been a panacea for my own desire to explain away Daniel's behavior. In those moments of public exposure, I simply wanted to be understood, and I urgently felt that a label or name could help me attain this acceptance, though as time passes I am more and more certain that what was required was greater compassion from others around us, irrespective of label, and a more forgiving stance on my part for all of us caught up in this situation.

The diagnosis of bipolar disorder drastically changed the pharmacotherapy portion of Daniel's therapy, though it has not substantially altered his psychosocial treatment. Since he was 10½, he has been prescribed lithium. He also began taking an anticonvulsant called Depakote, which is used to treat manic episodes, and over the past 2 years he has also taken Trileptal (an antiseizure medication) and Lexapro (selective serotonin reuptake inhibitor, antidepressant/antianxiety medication). At the same time, he has continued with Dexedrine for his symptoms of inattention and hyperactivity and with the sporadic use of clonidine for difficulty sleeping. Although the effects of the stimulants on Daniel's hyperactivity are readily apparent, the impact of the other medications has been difficult to determine. Even if the medication regimen does not seem to effect significant changes in his functioning, it may actually be preventing the worsening of his symptoms over time.

I have mixed feelings about my brother's current medication cocktail. I worry about what these medications are doing to Daniel's brain, especially because the majority of them have not been extensively tested for their neurodevelopmental effects in children or their long-term effects in general.

A few months ago I had a pedestrian but nonetheless upsetting experience in which a professor was discussing the use of medication to treat severe mental illness. The professor contended that the tendency in industrialized nations is to overmedicate individuals with severe mental illness and that dispensing medication is an "easy fix" for some of the persistent problems of mental illness—yet in many cases the medication only dampens the individual's ability to engage in the world, effectively isolating and imprisoning him or her in an antipsychotic chamber of society's doing. The undergraduate students in the class responded to the professor's arguments with agreement that medicating mental illness is detrimental; others added that they thought that it was inhumane, cruel, and negligent, the decision of uninformed, overburdened, and irresponsible caretakers of the mentally ill.

During the class discussion, I sat silent and alone with my conflicting thoughts and feelings on the issue, bringing my personal experience to bear on and illuminate the complexity of the problem. I do not have the ability to view this issue through any semblance of objectivity, because my own life has been so intimately touched by the effects of severe mental illness. During this discussion I was fully aware of having a brother who ingests 14 psychopharmacological pills each day, a boy who has been taking medication in some form since he was 3 years old. He is a child with a pill-carrying case similar to that of my grandparents.

I sat in shame and sadness and anger. Although I agree that there is inhumanity in overmedicating individuals with mental illness, the inhumanity of serious illness—the personal suffering and the havoc wreaked on others—is overpowering. I sit muddled by the complexity of situations in which mental illness begs or even demands a fix of any kind, even a quick fix that will only cause some of the symptoms to subside for a few hours. Medication should, I believe, be a last resort for the treatment of individuals with mental illness, but I also understand that, for some, medication is the only choice. Try telling a mother who cannot leave her house to go to the grocery store for fear of being publicly assaulted by her 4-year-old that medication is not necessary or optimal for her child. It is hard to comprehend the proselytizing of people who may not know what I know, who may not have experienced what I have experienced, who may not be as intimately acquainted with the utter sense of despair that plagues many of those living in the wake of mental illness. My family chose medication for my brother, for better or for worse. Some aspects of his functioning have improved as a result of medication; some remain constant. With the complexity of decisions surrounding medications for mental illness, I wish that the larger society, and even some advocates for the mentally ill, would exercise caution and sensitivity before righteously proclaiming the use of medication as an irresponsible and neglectful course of action.

FEAR AND COMFORT

The worst of Daniel's symptoms during his early years were his rages. During these, everything was a struggle, and our family evolved to adapt to his volatility. We grew into silent, fearful victims, afraid to challenge or assert our wishes for fear of retribution. Family vacations and restaurant meals were endured and detested, and then largely ceased. Friends and family visited the house less frequently and felt increasingly uncomfortable when present. The rages were predictable in certain situations and erratic in others, so that I was in a state of constant agitation and fear, endlessly anticipating a battle and the threat of Daniel's seriously hurting a family member, fitfully reliving and imagining these cataclysmic events during dreams and while awake.

I vividly remember being in high school and being unable to stop thinking about my brother. There would be times when I would leave for school during the early morning, terrified about how my brother would behave during the course of the day following a particularly brutal fight from the night before, and would call home at various intervals just to check to make sure my mother was able to manage his behavior and that my mother was not seriously hurt. I would either be unable to focus on my schoolwork, friends, and sports activities, or else I would intensely immerse myself in the short-term escape from my own fears that these activities provided.

I recall thinking over and over again that nothing in life could possibly be worse than this pain, that anything in the whole world would be better than feeling this way. I remember praying ritualistically for my mother's safety. I would pray every night before I went to sleep and every day before I left the house and intermittently throughout the bad days. I would ask God to take anything from me or to hurt me in any way imaginable, but to please protect my mother. Perhaps in an attempt to give myself a concrete image to hold in mind, my prayer and wishes became more specific, and I began to articulate within my own head the level of pain I would willingly subject myself to in order to avoid feeling the pain over my real life. Although it is difficult to admit even to myself that I could wish something so negative on myself, at this time I vividly recall deciding that I would willingly accept the worst punishment I could imagine enduring—rape—and then began praying to God that I would gladly subject myself to rape if the torment of Daniel's behavior would end. I began to use this idea of self-abuse as a form of comfort during distressing times; before I would fall asleep at night, I remember routinely directing my attention toward the gory details of an imaginary attack against me and would feel solace from focusing on aspects of aggression targeted against me and not my mother. For many years this idea became my respite, my birthday wish, the final thought I would cling to before falling asleep each night. Reflecting back, I feel extreme sorrow for this girl who was so tormented by intense fear and desperation that she wished to experience brutality and violence rather than endure the reality of her life.

Closely coupled with Daniel's aggression—and potentially as debilitating— was his social anxiety. During the early years of Daniel's life, we all believed that his social anxiety was his saving grace and that this inhibition was a protective factor against his unleashed rage. Although there may have been some truth to this idea, I have also come to believe that the social anxiety may be the crux of his difficulties. That is, were it not for his tremendous fears of other people, he perhaps would not resort to aggression so frequently. One of the most pitiable aspects of my brother's illness is his belief that the world he lives in is extremely hostile, unforgiving, and cruel. He sincerely feels that other people are out to hurt him, destroy him, and mock him and that, in order to survive, he must act with force to silence his fears. It is difficult to determine whether Daniel's intense anxiety preceded his aggression or whether the aggression preceded his anxiety, but it is clear that these two aspects reinforce each other over time. Recent research suggests that children who are both aggressive and anxious have far worse outcomes than children who are aggressive but not anxious, which is a strong argument against the idea that Daniel's anxiety is a blessing.[2]

The anxiety has resulted in unique impediments for Daniel, including the inability to enter new situations, to engage in social interactions with unfamiliar people, and to be a carefree child or adolescent. Rare was the time that Daniel would enter a grocery store, the mall, a movie theater, or even school without complete refusal or intense objection. Recently, he has begun to be able to explore new situations more freely with trusted companions, usually my parents. But for most of Daniel's life, his symptoms of social anxiety have been crippling. In preschool, he would cling to my mother and hit and bite and swear at her, refusing to let her leave his side or attend to other conversations. During the majority of elementary school, he would refuse to go into the school. It would often take 2 or more hours for my mother to forcefully guide him through his morning routine; more often than not he would arrive late to school and then would have to sit in the principal's office for some time before feeling comfortable enough to enter his classroom. Daniel found a friend in this elementary school principal, who made him feel safe and welcome in his large office and would often talk him through his anxiety about going into his class.

When Daniel transitioned to junior high school, he also evidenced serious difficulties in integrating into the class and behaving appropriately. At this point he began attending a severely emotionally disturbed (SED) classroom in a public school. He had the same teacher for 3 years in a row, which enabled him to feel more comfortable, facilitating increased attendance and timeliness. At the same time, this phase of life has also presented unique problems, such as elective classes, which he has intermittently acquiesced to take, and physical education, which requires him to wear an athletic outfit and change in the locker rooms. He has received special permission to wear jeans and to change alone. Daniel has also experienced some of the negative effects of being labeled a "special" student, such as critical comments from peers (and even a teacher), as well as self-criticism related to feeling different and troubled in contrast to other students.

By the end of eighth grade, Daniel's aggressive behaviors had begun to decrease substantially, which is a tremendous gain. Though he is still easily irritated and quick to swear, he uses physical aggression much less frequently, and most often he will not step beyond a certain point even when being physically aggressive. When angry, he will now resort to swearing, kicking, hitting, or throwing things, and these behaviors are done more out of frustration than from vicious intentions.

Daniel has been seeing his current psychotherapist for close to 4 years now. Together they have been working on improving his ability to cope with social anxiety and his fears, to control his aggressive behavior and his outbursts, and to find more prosocial outlets for Daniel's interests and behaviors. In addition, they have worked to build a trusting relationship in which Daniel can feel accepted, understood, and safe, with the hope of disconfirming his fear that the world is a hostile, scary place from which he must constantly defend himself. He has also been seeing a skilled psychiatrist in the community who manages and continually titrates his pharmacological cocktail as he develops and changes.

My family's experience with the mental health care system has been a comedy of errors. We have stumbled and fallen and regained our steps, losing valuable time along the way. In my opinion, allowing Daniel to spend so many years in play therapy without seeking out more proactive, empirically supported treatment options was a mistake. Similarly, although Daniel's social skills group with other antisocial boys, which focused on practical skill building and exposure to challenging situations (e.g., entering a supermarket) seemed a significant improvement from play therapy, I question whether group-based treatment of troubled kids is optimal. I have seen the ways in which Daniel learns about new maladaptive behaviors from his peers in his SED class and imagine that he learned similar lessons from the other boys in his social skills groups. In addition, compelling research on the iatrogenic effects of placing aggressive children in group settings casts doubt on the advisability of group-based treatment for antisocial children.[3]

Perhaps the most troublesome aspect of my family's rocky navigation through the mental health care system is the fact that Daniel comes from an educated, financially stable, and privileged family. In addition to having two professional parents, Daniel has one sister who is a clinical social worker, a brother-in-law who is a special education teacher, and another sister (me) who is completing her doctorate in clinical psychology. What must this process be like for families with few or no resources? How do these families find their way to treatment options that will help their child? I remember my dad telling me recently that Daniel's mental health care alone costs $20,000 a year above and beyond insurance coverage. If it is an extreme challenge for my parents to afford Daniel's care, it must be impossible for families less financially fortunate.

The upcoming adolescent years will be formative ones for Daniel, as he will undoubtedly be confronted with new challenges, as well as new opportunities for growth. As early as age 7 or 8 he demonstrated an inappropriate interest in alcohol use, sexual behavior, and self-harm; what will happen as he matures through the developmental phase typically associated with increases in these behaviors? In addition, if Daniel does actually have early-onset bipolar disorder, it is likely that within the next 10 or so years he will experience his first adult manifestations of the disorder—for example, a full-blown manic episode, which could consist of psychotic symptoms and impulsive behavior and which could potentially wreak significant havoc on his life. These symptoms typically manifest in late adolescence or early adulthood, and it may be that his history is only a foreshadowing of extreme suffering to come.

A major debate in my family surrounds whether Daniel should receive more intensive treatment than he currently obtains—including the possibility of stringent measures such as short-term inpatient treatment or residential care. But others in the family believe that home-based care (i.e., keeping Daniel in a safe and known environment, namely, the family home) is paramount. Decision making in this regard is laden with worry, pain, guilt, and sadness. It is impossible to know whether Daniel would react to hospitalization or institutionalization with deep feelings of abandonment, hurt, and anger, potentially undoing any benefits of the intensive treatment offered at such facilities. The thought of Daniel either deteriorating in an unstructured home environment (and potentially seriously harming someone) or entering a hospital setting and feeling abandoned, alone, and rejected is too painful for me to bear. I hope that my family will continue to struggle with these issues of placement and treatment, eventually forgiving ourselves for the decisions we make.

At this stage, I am unsure of how to arrive at a place of peace and forgiveness about Daniel's lot in life. There will always be people to blame, and there will always be things that could have been better. For example, I could blame Daniel's biological parents for their genetic contributions or his first psychologist for the recommendations he made during the early years. Closer to home, I could blame my parents for having adopted him, for not being satisfied with three children, and for opening up our safe home to such a volatile child. I could blame them, too, for their parenting of Daniel. Or I could turn the blame to myself and my siblings for our ways of interacting with him or to his peers for taunting him and teaching him new ways to be aggressive and deviant. I could blame the social environment more generally for not supporting Daniel in a variety of ways, for not tolerating his impulsivity and inattention, for not constantly reassuring him of his safety. Or I could blame Daniel for being born the way he is, a tormented, sad soul who may never find his way. I find a temporary resting place in the knowledge that Daniel was better off in my family's home than he would have been in the care of his biological parents, who at the time were ill equipped for any child, let alone a child with special needs. I also can comfort myself with the knowledge that most families would have given up long ago, but that we loved him enough, cared for him enough, and fought for him enough to keep him in the home and in a safe environment until the present day.

TOGETHERNESS, SHARING, CONNECTION, CONFUSION

I wait on the curb outside of baggage claim at the Los Angeles Airport as my family's white minivan pulls up, packed full of the people I have traveled so far to see. Daniel opens the sliding door for me, grinning sheepishly and lowering his eyes, both thrilled and somewhat shy at seeing me for the first time in a few months. "Hi, Jess," he says, attempting to hide a smile, " you can give me a hug if you want." This is a triumph of momentous proportions: for years Daniel would never allow me to hug him. He knows that this makes me so happy, and I can tell he loves to see my reaction when he suggests it immediately upon my arrival. "Oh, you know how much I would love to do that," I say as I lean over, hugging him with feeling and kissing him on the top of his head. The ride home from the airport is filled with noisy, boisterous conversation, most of which is led or dominated by Daniel, who insists on playing me his latest favorite Metallica songs and asking for my interpretation of the thematic meaning within the lyrics. He imitates several new characters whose voices and mannerisms he has acquired to perfection over the past few months (among his current favorites are Bill Cosby, Grover, and Donald Duck). If one of my parents tries to ask me a more serious question about my trip, Daniel becomes frustrated because he wants the car ride home exclusively devoted to reintroducing me to his humor and interests.

As we transfer from the 405 to the 101 freeway, Daniel watches me intensely, noticing what I laugh at, both in terms of his ongoing comedy routine and in terms of things my other brother or my parents have said during the ride, and repeatedly asking me why I thought a particular comment was funny. He studies my reactions in order to tailor his humor and his behavior to appeal the most to me, to have the greatest likelihood of captivating my attention. As the van passes over the rolling hills leaving the valley, Daniel offers me blankets and adjusts the heat in the car if he senses I may be cold, and he eagerly asks me if I remember the time when Dad did something funny the last time I was home, all in the hopes of engaging me and showing his caring for me. Sometimes on the ride home he will ask me if I can give him a backrub or play with his hair—these are special rituals only the two of us share, and he calls on them now to reconnect with me after my absence.

As I have mentioned previously, the complexity of my feelings for Daniel and his impact on me have at times been incredibly rich and at other times overwhelming. I experience both my love and anger for him as intense, almost frantic emotions. At times Daniel will do something so loving, tender, or sensitive, or he will say things demonstrating such tremendous insight and compassion, that I will be deeply touched and almost overcome by the strength of my love for him. In the past I remember feeling so much love for him that I would desperately want to show this to him, almost as though a part of me believed that if he could see the naked force of my love, he would be healed. If he could somehow link my love for him to his kindness, to his gentle, nonthreatening self, then maybe this would be enough for him to overcome the rages. There still exists a part of me that really believes that if he felt loved enough and safe enough he would not react so defensively to the behavior of others, and this part of me yearns desperately to give him the gift of safety and trust.

Part of what I think has made the whole situation so difficult to grasp, both intellectually and emotionally, is Daniel's uncanny ability to captivate the crowd, to be engaging and charismatic, to perceive and behave in a way that accommodates the needs of others, and to show love and caring for his family. As Daniel has grown, his ability to employ these skills has increased. The sensitive behavior he used to exhibit only in flashes between the ages of 5 and 12 is now more frequent and more developed.

I remember Daniel's creativity from a very early age. When he was about 4 he was introduced to the charm of Raffi, a well-known children's folk singer who performs such classics as "Baby Beluga." My parents bought Daniel a videotape of Raffi performing these songs to a live audience, and Daniel became mesmerized, fixated on this tape. He could watch the 90-minute tape four times in a row without tiring. After a few days of intense communion with the video, Daniel had memorized all of the words to every song, as well as every gesture Raffi made at each particular point in the tape. He stood next to the television, performing alongside his muse, mimicking his every move and gesture. Daniel committed to memory the times when Raffi looked to his right, dipping his chin and smiling at a girl in the front row, all in time to the slow beat of "The Itsy Bitsy Spider." He remembered the idiosyncratic features of each of Raffi's smiles and to whom they were directed in the audience. He had absorbed every facet of information conveyed in the videotape and then attempted to make it his own by performing it for us on his ukulele. Once my parents were aware of Daniel's fascination with Raffi, they promptly bought more tapes of Raffi in concert, and Daniel soon added these to his performance repertoire. I remember being amazed that my 4-year-old brother could replicate such complicated and nuanced performances to perfection, when I struggled to remember the order of the verses in "Apples and Bananas."

After about 6 months of intensive Raffi training and imitation, Daniel abandoned the children's singer and began moving up in the world of imitation. Always hoping to entertain those around him, he quickly learned how to impersonate everyone other people found funny (political figures, actors, cartoon characters). He also demonstrated a tendency to become hypnotically involved with certain activities, such as learning about Dragon Ball Z cards and playing Nintendo games, juxtaposed with his almost total inability to remain focused on undesirable tasks, such as getting ready for school in the morning or completing homework assignments. Around the age of 10 Daniel became obsessed with the World Wrestling Federation wrestlers, first collecting information about each character—personalities, strengths, and finishing moves—and then memorizing all of the information he could obtain, relating it in excruciating detail to anyone and everyone who would listen. He would then use these facts as conversation pieces, quizzing others on the weight or height of a particular wrestler.

While pining obsessively over these wrestling characters, Daniel would do something else interesting. For example, he would often pit several wrestlers against one another and then ask me which one I liked the best and why. My typical stance was to slide by with some platitude of how I would choose The Rock because his was the only name and finishing move I ever remembered. Yet Daniel was never satisfied with simple answers. He would challenge my response by asking me detailed questions about whether I liked The Rock best because of the way he clenches his fists in the picture or the way the bandana on his head is folded. Daniel's scrutiny about the rationale behind my choice surprised and challenged me. I came to understand that these questions served the function of keeping me involved in his activity for a longer period of time, engaging me in a more personal way (for example, he would often ask me which wrestler I would prefer to date) in order to continue to command my attention and to dominate the conversation and me. Yet they also seemed an indication of Daniel's desire and efforts to know the mind of the other person, to further understand my thought process and my preferences. He would remember almost everything I had expressed in terms of my thoughts about the wrestlers and use this knowledge with agility in future conversations.

His curiosity about the thought processes of others increasingly pertained to other topics as he grew up. He asked me questions about my thoughts about former President Bill Clinton, the war in Iraq, affirmative action, the death penalty, and same-sex marriage. As with his questions about wrestling, he would ask me to elaborate on my thinking, genuinely trying to understand why I thought about things in the way that I did. Then in future conversations he would revisit the topic, reassuring himself that I still felt the same way and asking me new and more nuanced follow-up questions on the same topic. "So, Jess," he would ask me, "everyone should be able to get married if they love each other, right?" "That's what I think," I would respond, smiling at his internalization of my beliefs. Daniel would then continue with his next question: "But what about if they want to have kids, Jess—what then?" "Well, what do you think, Dan?" "Well, maybe it's still okay because it would be better for kids to have parents who love them. That's the most important thing, right, Jess?" I enjoyed watching the development of Daniel's thought processes and engagement with these complex social and political issues, somewhat amazed by his degree of interest in the surrounding world and his desire to discover a way of thinking about these topics. I viewed him as a sort of amateur scientist who was studying an unknown matter—my mind. The process was an effortful one, and I had the sense that Daniel has to mechanically approach the problem and chip away at it through trial and error, deciphering and memorizing a social sense that for most people requires little conscious thought.

I also noticed Daniel's tendency to try to understand how people interpreted the behavior of others. He would try to figure out, for example, which of my friends I liked the best and why, how my feelings toward my friends were influenced by their behavior toward me, and how I would respond to them given my feelings for them. At times like this, when I felt Daniel to be genuinely interested in me, I would share some of my vulnerabilities with him, to gain more intimacy and also to show him that I, too, was afraid of and felt insecure about certain things. I wanted to model for him the ability to openly disclose fears and insecurities rather than to act defensively or aggressively when threatened. For example, I shared with him some insecurities about my appearance and the academic and social stresses of high school. When confronted with this information, Daniel would typically respond with great sensitivity, reassuring me and then trying to get me interested in another game or activity or impersonation in order to make me smile. When Daniel would see me cry in response to events unrelated to his behavior, he would approach me with concern and worry, searching for a solution to my problems and trying to charm me into forgetting my worries.

All this was a striking contrast to his marked lack of sensitivity or perspective taking during times when he was feeling upset, angry, threatened, or afraid. During those times, Daniel will use information gathered during our heart-to-heart discussions to attack me verbally. In addition to the insecurities I had personally revealed to him, he was also insightful enough to pick up on other, subtler vulnerabilities. For example, immediately on becoming angry with me, he would launch into a diatribe about how hideously ugly I was, how nobody would ever love me because they could not even stand to look at me, how I was a worthless, disgusting, whiney slob, and on and on. At this point I was already struggling with my own depression, insecurity, and self-loathing, and the daggers he threw at me resounded with everything I feared the most. It would get to the point that I would use Daniel's hurtful remarks as evidence to confirm my reasons for hating myself; his verbal viciousness became part of maintaining my sadness.

These contrasts strained my empathy for him. Indeed, it did not seem as though he were fundamentally lacking a cognitive perspective-taking skill but rather that he was unable to implement this skill when feeling threatened—or instead would use it against me. It would have been easier if I had felt that he was simply incapable of understanding other people. Was he, rather, a manipulative, cunning monster, playing on my sensitivity and weaknesses to hurt me? Or was he an endearing, inquisitive brother trying to get to know his adored older sister but who simply lost his way when he was angry?

SADNESS, VULNERABILITY, COMMUNION

One night after a fight between Daniel and the world (at least from his perspective), I quietly knock on the door of his bedroom. "Who is it?" Daniel responds suspiciously in a gruff voice to the request for entry into his room. "It's me, sweetie. Can I come in and talk?" "Okay, Jess." I enter the room and find him sitting on his bed, anxiously picking at the skin on his hands and fingers, which are bright pink and raw from so much abuse. I smooth down the bed covers and sit down next to him, reaching out to rub his back in an attempt to soothe him. I can tell he has been crying but the feelings that came forth more readily now are anger and injustice. "Jess, did you see what he did to me? Isn't Dad such a fucking idiot?" I empathize aloud with Daniel for a few moments, commenting on how it seems as though Dad's behavior really hurt his feelings and suggesting some possible reasons for why Dad behaved as he did. I then offer my own interpretation of our dad's and Daniel's behavior, arguing that Daniel's name-calling and aggression toward our dad was what had provoked our dad to take away Daniel's Nintendo privileges, the offending act. At this point Daniel starts sobbing quietly, wiping away his tears as if doing so would erase them from happening in his and my minds. He then confides in me: "Nobody knows how hard it is to be me, Jess. I hate it." He goes on to describe how he feels that everyone always gangs up on him, that he is always the one who is doing things wrong, and that nobody ever believes anything he says, confessing that he always feels like everyone is against him and that nobody ever supports him.

Although I know that these feelings are partially artifacts of the way Daniel perceives the world—with others as the aggressors and him as the threatened reactor, when typically it is the other way around—I recognize that the feelings he is expressing are the feelings he experiences and that whether or not they are grounded in the reality shared by most people, they are his reality. I let myself feel the weight of this reality with him. I have long known that Daniel has many insecurities and negative thoughts about himself, that he feels lonely and wishes he had more friends, but never before has he so openly admitted these negative thoughts to me, and it touches me, bringing a flash of tears into my own eyes. For a moment I just sit there with him, sharing his pain of being misunderstood, and supporting him in that moment. We look at each other, two pairs of shiny light eyes meeting in a moment of understanding and mutual empathy, joining in a shared experience of pain and vulnerability.

When I think about Daniel and his behavior, I most often think about him in the role of aggressor and about myself and my family in the role of victim. This is a falsehood, as the most pitiable victim in this whole situation is Daniel. The saddest thing is that Daniel is just a little boy, now of adolescent age, trying to grow up. Like so many other boys his age, he loves wrestling and video games, action figure cards and jumping on the trampoline, and catching frogs and lizards and creating nests for them in a shoebox. He did not ask to be plagued with his erratic moods, his terrifying aggression and impulsivity, and his crippling social anxiety. He wants to thrive and mature just like everyone else, but he has never been permitted to do so without tremendous pain. I cannot imagine how difficult it must be to be Daniel: to know that his behavior is frightening and alienating to other people but to be unable to control the behavior in the moment; to feel constantly threatened by his surroundings, hypervigilant and ready to protect himself against threats that seem very real to him; to realize that he is different from other children; to feel the sting of peer rejection; to be unable to partake in typical school activities with the other students because of his inhibitions and fears. Daniel feels like an outsider, imprisoned from the world others share by his inappropriate behavior and his fears. Inside the fortress Daniel has built with his aggression is a scared little boy who does not believe that the world is a safe place or that people will be kind to him. For many people, childhood is a time of carefree enjoyment and happiness, a time when parents absorb children's worries, allowing their children to live unburdened. For Daniel, childhood was a time of intense worry. He has had to shoulder concerns and difficulties of a magnitude most adults never have to negotiate. Many people live to some extent at the whim of their moods; most people struggle to manage and control negative feelings. Daniel's mood states are far more intense and consuming and far more cyclical; his existence in large part consists of riding through the moods, enduring and reacting to the intense affect, and then dealing with the repercussions of his behavior. He, too, is simply trying to make his way through this world, but his path is jagged with stumbling blocks.

There are only victims in this situation; there is only loss and sadness. I have escaped by moving away to college and graduate school, my other brother has escaped by going to college, my sister has escaped by marrying and having her own children. My parents in part escape by having other parts of their lives, by working and thinking about their other children and each other. But Daniel rarely escapes. The majority of the time he feels anxious, hurt, sad, alone, depressed, worthless, irritable, and angry. The uncontrollability must be terrifying. During times of intense anger, Daniel feels out of control, powered solely by the rage coursing through his veins. And this sense of uncontrollability is real, for we have not been able to control his symptoms adequately with medication, with behavioral reinforcement, with psychotherapy, or with boundless love. Although I can create my own sense of safety far from home, Daniel cannot escape the danger because the danger is inside of him.

ESCAPE

My own personal and professional life direction has clearly been influenced by my experiences growing up with Daniel. Throughout the years I have turned to psychology in an almost obsessional pursuit of healing for Daniel and as a more removed mode of connection with my feelings about him.

A few years after Daniel began struggling with his aggression, I found solace in reading popular psychology books of all kinds, devouring them with renewed hope of finding solutions to Daniel's problems and my difficulties in managing my own feelings about his behavior. During my college years I again dove head-first into psychological thinking. At Berkeley I was blessed with many wonderful teachers who opened up an expansive world of theory and research that spoke to me and resonated intimately with my experience. Within the larger field of psychology, I found myself especially entranced by the field of developmental psychopathology, which focuses on the interactive dance between normal development and psychopathology in children.

On reflection, I notice that throughout my professional path I have been unable to prevent my experiences with Daniel from guiding and influencing my every move. As I gain maturity within the academic field, I realize that many academics would consider this personal lens a flaw in my objectivity. Yet I find myself believing more strongly in the power of subjectivity as an aid to scientific discovery. I realize that I see children like Daniel through the teary eyes many academics do not have, and these eyes may impel me to ask more personal, and perhaps more profound, questions.

I have also noticed, however, that studying psychology has become a bittersweet escape from thinking about the pain of my brother's situation. I have found a way to keep the subject matter close, but not too close. I bring my own personal experience to bear on empirical, scientific questions, to study academic topics that have become overwhelming in the personal domain. Even as I write this chapter I notice that I straddle the line between presenting the story from an extremely personal and emotional stance and stepping back to evaluate my experiences through a removed, more academic lens. This latter perspective is my crutch, but I am not willing to discard it, as it enables me to confront personal matters in a titrated and manageable way. I suppose my work in this field has indirect therapeutic value for me; working clinically with children like my brother allows me to view problems like his through a more sympathetic light, untinged by my own pain and biases, while keeping my feelings at somewhat of a distance.

My personal goals also include the hope of continuing to seek to understand Daniel's perspective and his world, as well as to delve into my own internal understanding of the impact of these experiences. It is an ongoing process—as Daniel's struggles and strengths and spirit develop, I strive to integrate my experiences in a narrative that is continuously formed and re-formed, colored by my internal experiences and my own growth and development. I also hope to continue to build a meaningful relationship with Daniel, to share the things that I value with him, to continue to express love and care for him, and to support him in whatever capacity I can manage without sacrificing myself. I try to accept Daniel for all of the things he is: my brother, my friend, an aggressor, a victim, and a child. The process continues to be difficult, and because I have the tendency to file away my worries about Daniel in favor of focusing on work or my own social world, I feel perpetually caught off guard when new situations arise, when I am once again forced to acknowledge the painful reality of the situation.

And I still have nightmares about Daniel's violent episodes. At least once a week I'll awaken, sweating and trembling from a dream in which I am being chased by an angry Daniel, or worse, in which I am watching him hurt someone I love, powerless to stop him. At these times I remind my shivering self that I am safe, that my family is safe (at least for the time being), that Daniel is older and more in control than ever before. Scarier than the dreams, however, is the reality, for when I awaken I realize that although the threats are now less imminent, this may only be the beginning of his suffering. The past years of his life may have been his easiest yet, his version of an innocent childhood.

CONTINUATION

Approximately 2 years have elapsed since I wrote this chapter, and I reread it now with mixed sentiments. Many things about Daniel's life have improved dramatically since these words were written—he is notably more controlled, and he is able to enter into public situations with significantly less fear. He sleeps in his own bedroom now and occasionally will join in on family events. As part of his behavioral program, he even goes to the gym once or twice a week with one of my parents. His sensory sensitivity is much reduced, and he now wears a single T-shirt and jeans to school. And, as noted earlier, his aggressive outbursts are subsiding (though not completely).

However, there are other, new worrisome things about Daniel. For the past year he has self-identified as a neo-Nazi skinhead and has made many racial slurs toward Jews and other ethnic minorities. This is especially striking in light of the fact that our family is Jewish. Partly in reaction to his skinhead affiliation, along with several anti-Semitic comments he made in the classroom, he was expelled from his school a little over a year ago. He now attends a nonpublic school for children who have been removed from public school settings.

Daniel currently receives intensive home-care services as part of a program called "Wrap-Around Care," in which he has daily contact with behavior therapists and in which his whole cadre of treatment providers have weekly meetings with my parents and Daniel present. Together this team of professionals has clearly articulated a behavioral plan that involves calling the police if he becomes physically aggressive, a policy that has resulted in more than half a dozen 911 calls in the past year.

One of the most challenging aspects of the past few years for me has been negotiating my own boundaries with respect to Daniel's behavior and the way in which my parents handle it. I have stopped staying at my parents' house when I come home for visits, because previous visits resulted in violent altercations with Daniel, the most recent of which entailed my fleeing the house at 1 A.M. when he was threatening to kill me. Though I have lived 3,000 miles away for the past several years, I soon will be living closer to home and anticipate having to define and establish new limits and reactions to Daniel's behavior as I create my own family.

During a recent visit that I made, Daniel had a huge blowup in which my parents called the police because he had threatened to kill my aunt. After the police arrived and restrained him (my parents did not want him to be arrested), I went back into the house and knocked on his bedroom door. He was lying on the bed and sobbing.

"Daniel, I need to talk to you."

"Jess, she's such a bitch. Did you hear what she said to me?"

"I did, Dan, but I also heard what you said to her. I want to talk to you right now about something else and it's really important. I need to tell you that I am so worried about you—I am so worried about your future. Because I love you so much and I see all of these good parts of you and then sometimes all I can see is your anger. And that angry part could ruin everything else, Daniel. I don't want you to end up hurting someone and I don't want you to end up in jail.

I want you to be my brother and to grow up and be okay. And I'm so, so scared for you. I really, really love you." My voice shook violently and my tears dripped down onto Daniel's shirt. Our eyes locked. "I mean it, Daniel. I really love you." His tears flowed in parallel with mine. I knew that for that one moment Daniel truly felt that love.

Will it ever be enough?

ACKNOWLEDGMENTS

To Daniel for sharing himself and his life with me, to my family members who have their own stories to tell, and to my friends and teachers who have inspired me.

NOTES

1. Huesmann, L. R., Moise-Titus, J., Podolski, C., & Eron, L. D. (2003). Longitudinal relations between children's exposure to TV violence and their aggressive and violent behavior in young adulthood: 1977–1992. *Developmental Psychology, 39,* 201–221.

2. Frick, P. J., & Morris, A. M.(2004). Temperament and developmental pathways to conduct problems. *Journal of Clinical Child and Adolescent Psychology, 33,* 54–68; Moffitt, T. E., & Caspi, A. (2001). Childhood predictors differentiate life-course persistent and adolescence-limited antisocial pathways among males and females. *Development and Psychopathology, 13,* 355–375.

3. Dishion, T. J., & Dodge, K. A. (2005). Peer contagion in interventions for children and adolescents: Moving towards an understanding of the ecology and dynamics of change. *Journal of Abnormal Child Psychology, 33,* 395–400; Dishion, T. J., McCord, J., & Poulin, F. (1999). When interventions harm: Peer groups and problem behavior. *American Psychologist, 54,* 755–764.

11   Reverberations

Peter E. Nathan

THE SUICIDE

I was about a year old when my mother committed suicide. She was 28 at the time, the mother of two children under 6. Her suicide was the terminal event in a lengthy series of episodes of depression that had begun early in her childhood.

Most of what I learned about my mother's suicide came from my brother, who was told a few things about it by our father and some older cousins. In quite a violent act that by its nature has continued to perplex me because it was so out of keeping with her soft and gentle nature, our mother slit her wrists and throat while in the bathtub and bled to death. She was ultimately found by our father and our grandfather's chauffeur, who broke down the door to the bathroom to find her. She was dead when they found her. Until I finally learned, at the age of 11 or 12, how she had died, I had asked my father repeatedly how and why she had died, to which he invariably responded that "she died of natural causes." I don't recall ever challenging that characterization, which was obviously inaccurate even to a child.

I have spent a great deal of time through the years ruminating about my father's inability or unwillingness to talk to me about my mother's death. Ultimately, I have concluded simply that the angry, violent means by which my gentle mother chose to kill herself so heightened the trauma of the suicide for my father that he could not bring himself ever to talk directly and honestly about it to me. It is just as significant that, even after I learned the truth, I never pursued the issue with him, never confronted him with what I knew about the facts of her death, and never asked him why he could not have been honest with me about the suicide.

Although I was too young to remember anything about this act, my brother believes he remembers the chauffeur breaking down the bathroom door with my father to find our mother. My brother also readily recalls how he explained to himself his mother's decision to leave him. First, he assumed he had not been a good enough boy; had he been, his mother wouldn't have chosen to forsake him. Second, he took for granted that my arrival had played an important role in the suicide, so he blamed me for it as well. As I reconstruct the logic of a grieving 5-year-old, I think my brother reasoned that, because his mother's death came so soon after I was born, there must have been a connection between the two. In fact, there was probably more than a little truth to this causal attribution by temporal contiguity, however naively it was conceived by an anguished little boy. Whether my birth was accompanied by an exacerbation of our mother's chronic mood symptoms that qualified for postpartum depression or whether it simply perturbed an already existing chronic mood disorder is unclear. Either could well have played a role in heightening her depression and leading her to end her life.

My brother kept his distance from me through his youth and into his young adulthood. We only began a relationship when we were a good deal older. As a child, I don't recall spending time wondering why I didn't see much of my brother; I guess I assumed that brothers were not supposed to be friends, especially those 5 years apart in age. The fact that, until adolescence, I didn't have any friends who had close relationships with their brothers helped maintain this belief.

The reader will not be surprised to learn that, like my brother, I, too, blamed myself for my mother's death, following a line of reasoning similar to his. Reality notwithstanding, when I was old enough to realize what had happened, I became convinced that I had somehow played a role in her death, perhaps by being a bad baby or by being an unattractive one—projections strikingly similar to those of my brother.

Notwithstanding the profound impact my mother's death had on her sons, its impact was clearly greatest on my father. Like his sons, he could not help putting a large measure of the blame for the suicide on himself, even though, like them, he almost certainly had less to do with her suicide than he believed. The reality was that her death was overwhelmingly a function of her chronic depressive state, perhaps enhanced by the hormonal changes accompanying childbirth. Nonetheless, my father assumed somehow that he could have prevented the death. In a time well before the significant role of genetic factors in depression had begun to be recognized or effective treatments for depression had begun to be developed, my father's conviction that he was responsible was almost certainly unfounded.

Adding to his burden of grief and self-blame, my father now had two small boys to care for. I believe that he worked hard to do so. He could not depend on his own mother, who would have been a natural helper had she not died soon after my mother's death. He hired a governess, changed his lifestyle to spend most of his nonworking hours with his sons, and acquired and practiced the essentials of child rearing he had previously been able to leave to my mother. Within a few years, he had also moved away from most of the longtime friends in his social circle of upper-middle-class German Jews whom he believed had been complicit in my mother's social isolation and deepening depression.

Compounding my father's anguish were the additional losses he suffered within a few months of my mother's death. Shortly after the suicide, my mother's father died from a cancer that had been diagnosed shortly after my birth. Two months later, my mother's mother leapt to her death from the eighth-floor apartment in which she and my grandfather had lived; like her daughter, she had suffered from depression for most of her life. Finally, and constituting by far the greatest of the losses my father suffered in the wake of his wife's suicide, was the painful, protracted death from cancer of his beloved mother. Given the nature of their relationship, even after he became a young adult and married, I can only surmise that this loss must have been almost as difficult for him to bear as the loss of his wife, although it was not additionally burdened by the guilt and self-reproach that accompanied his wife's death.

In little more than a year, then, my father lost four of the people closest to him, two by suicide, two more following drawn-out, painful illnesses. I can only marvel at what it must have taken for my father to hold things together for his motherless boys while mourning his losses. When I reconstruct the events of 1936 and early 1937 for the Nathan family from the perspective that my own lengthening years now provide, I give my father enormous credit for rising to the challenge, despite a pampered youth and few signs up to that time that he would in fact be able to do so. Although I can find a good deal to criticize my father for before and well after those events, I am immensely thankful that he did what he needed to do for his abruptly motherless sons following his devastating losses. Had I the chance now to express a single sentiment to my father, by now dead almost 40 years, it would be to recognize the strength he somehow found to care for his sons during a time in which he must have been feeling unimaginable sorrow and torment.

ANTECEDENTS

I was an infant when my mother died. I remember nothing about her. Hence, nothing of what I know or believe about my mother is firsthand. For that matter, very little of this narrative is built on anyone else's observations of my mother's behavior, either. Included are a few memories of my brother's, some recollections from a second cousin and an aunt, and bits and pieces from my father, who remained reluctant throughout his life to talk about my mother's life or death. Right or wrong, then, what I came to believe about my mother, largely pieced together from the few people who knew and would talk about her, understandably became reality for me as a child and has remained so for me as an adult. I've tried to stay as close as possible to the hard facts about my mother in this narrative, to the extent that I knew them, but the reader will appreciate that some of what I believe is as much my own construction of what happened as what actually happened.

This narrative does not devote a great deal of space to my mother's chronic mood disorder per se or to reactions to it from family members. Instead, it focuses on the principal result of her mental illness: her suicide and consequent permanent removal from my life, the most significant impact of her depression on me and my family. In this way in particular, the chapter differs from most of the others in this book.

The title of this chapter reflects my attempt to capture the pervasive effects of my mother's suicide through time on those she left behind. Although she has now been dead for more than 70 years, the continuing reverberations from my mother's suicide, the thoughts, feelings, memories, and emotions that stem from it and have built one on another through the years, even now ripple through my life. They are a central focus of my story.

My Mother

My mother contracted poliomyelitis when she was a young girl. Although it did not cause paralysis, the disease left her with a slightly withered right leg, which, after intensive therapy, affected neither her appearance nor her ability to walk. She seems nonetheless to have been quite bothered by the disability. In most pictures of her, for example, during both childhood and adulthood, she appears with her good leg in front of her bad one, in an obvious effort to hide the bad leg. Her first episode of depression apparently began shortly after the polio attack. Although research undertaken two decades after her death by Dr. Leon Cytryn reported an association between chronic medical conditions and depression in children, during my mother's lifetime and for 20 years after her death, children were not considered fully capable of experiencing depression.[1] Accordingly, my mother's depressive feelings, thoughts, and behaviors as a girl almost certainly went unrecognized as such. In her late adolescence, my mother was hospitalized at least once for what had by that time been recognized as depression. I don't know whether that hospitalization was prompted by thoughts of suicide or by an actual suicide attempt.

My mother and her younger brother, her only sibling, were very close. I have a picture of the two that epitomizes that relationship, taken when she was 7 or 8 and he was 5 or 6. She has placed her arm protectively over his shoulder and, smiling, she is looking at him with great fondness. Their close bond, which continued to her death, has significance for this narrative. My uncle never forgave my father for his beloved sister's suicide. He blamed my father for his failure to appreciate my mother's extreme sensitivity at times during their marriage or to heed warnings that she might try to harm herself. Others who knew them at the time confirmed that my father was often impatient with his wife's plight as a diffident outsider in the close-knit German-Jewish milieu in which they lived during their few years together. My father found it especially difficult to respond adequately to her abrupt shifts in mood, reactions to what seemed to him to be minor provocations. I believe I know what my uncle saw—that my father wasn't able to give my mother the support and understanding she needed more than most young women of her age—because he didn't support me very adequately, either, at times during my childhood and adolescence. My uncle's reaction was nonetheless unfortunate; it compounded my father's guilt and deprived my brother and me of the support and affection we might have derived from my mother's sole remaining family. In fact, I have had almost nothing to do with those four cousins on my mother's side, although my uncle and I did establish a limited relationship when I was in my teens.

From what little I have gleaned from what I was told about her symptoms, I conclude that my mother probably met *DSM-IV* diagnostic criteria for major depressive disorder during her childhood. If not, she surely did during adolescence and young adulthood. It also seems quite possible that her condition constituted a "double depression." That is, she may well have been sufficiently depressed between episodes of major depression that she met criteria for dysthymic disorder, a chronic condition that is at least as debilitating as major depression itself.

Nonetheless, my brother always recalls our mother's warmth and affection. Although the two of them were together for under 6 years, he has distinct and loving memories of her. A few others have shared memories of my mother with me. Prominent among them was a second cousin who was her confidante during the years immediately preceding her death, perhaps because, like her, he was on the periphery of the close-knit social group of which they were nominally a part. He described my mother as sweet, kind, and gentle but overwhelmed by the activity level and competitive thrust of the social group into which her marriage had dropped her. This cousin, who was not particularly fond of my father, remembered well that my father was known to lose patience with my mother at the bridge table, more than once reducing her to tears when she made a bid he did not agree with. My father's sister confirmed both my mother's sensitivity and my father's inability at times to respond adequately to it. Perhaps the most distinct sense I have of my mother in this social milieu is her apparent failure to keep up the repartee, express the irony, and share in the ubiquitous teasing and joking that marked its most consistent character. I am quite convinced she felt—and was—isolated, because she was naturally reserved, because she was often depressed, and because she did not possess and was not able to acquire the social repertoire that would have enabled her to participate more fully in my father's social world.

My Father

My father was the only boy in a family of four children. The second oldest, he was his mother's favorite. Everyone I have spoken to about my father emphasized this point to make clear that he occupied a special place in his nuclear family. Like his father, he had an engaging personality and lots of friends, both male and female. It also seems clear that, until the death of my mother, my father did not take the world terribly seriously. His more or less charmed, and charming, life to that point must have made his young wife's suicide that much more difficult for my father to bear.

To my enduring regret, my father never talked spontaneously about my mother, and I never pressed him to talk about her. In retrospect, my failure to insist on knowing more about her and their life together makes no sense to me, because I very much wanted answers that were not forthcoming from my father. My father's discomfort at talking about my mother, even long after her death, was palpable. Why didn't I prod him to talk about her? I have pondered that question many, many times. My answer now, many years after any opportunity to do so disappeared with his death, was that I wanted to protect my father from his terrible feelings of responsibility. On the rare occasions when I did ask my father about her, ever so gently, he said little other than to preface his scant remarks with the wholly inadequate phrase, "Your poor mother...."

My father's guilt over what he clearly believed was his responsibility for her death was enduring. As a psychologist, I am convinced he took on much more responsibility for my mother's decision to end her life than was warranted. Her very strong depressive diathesis was almost certainly most important to that decision, much more so than any inattention or insensitivity on my father's part. It is also the case that, as my father himself so often said, his natural inclination was to distance himself from emotional turmoil. That personality trait, not always a felicitous one, may in fact have enabled him to emerge from the terrible 18-month period in the mid-1930s with the fortitude to take care of his two little boys.

In his early 20s, my father had a long-term relationship with a lively young woman who, like him, was a member of the inner circle of their social group. To me, she has always represented my mother's antithesis because, from my father's description, she seemed to have the personality and self-confidence that enabled her to participate quite successfully in the demanding give-and-take of their group of friends. Apparently, though, my grandmother objected to a match between the two because the girl's family did not meet her social status standards. That intervention, which my father accepted, ended the relationship. It came over the years to epitomize for me the role, not always a positive one, that my grandmother played in my father's life.

Thus my mother was not my father's first choice as a marriage partner. She was chosen for my father in substantial part because of her family's social and financial status, even though she was also a beautiful woman and a college graduate during a time when most women from her background were not. Even though my father spoke very fondly of my mother and their brief marriage on those rare occasions when he could bring himself to do so, he also referred a number of times over the years to the woman he had not married. Although I have no doubt that my father loved my mother and grieved for her for many years following her death, I believe he was also fully aware of the irony that his mother's choice for him did not work out in the end, whereas, by contrast, the woman he might have married had a long, happy marriage to someone else. Whether the knowledge that she had not been first in my father's heart deepened my mother's chronic depression and played a role in her suicide is a question I have certainly considered but have never been able to resolve.

Their Families

My parents' nuclear families were both second-generation German-Jewish and solidly middle-class. Although they identified culturally with Judaism, like many other Jews who emigrated from Germany during this time, they had moved away from traditional religious practices and identified with the Reform movement. The men in the family were by and large business people, and the women were generally wives and stay-at-home mothers. All eight of my parents' grandparents immigrated to the United States from Germany in the 1840s and 1850s. My mother's grandparents and my father's maternal grandparents settled in medium-sized Midwestern cities about 400 miles apart; my father's paternal grandparents took up residence in a small city in the rural South, where my grandfather was born. My father and his older sister were born in that Southern city, and his family took considerable pride in the fact that his grandfather was a Confederate soldier who fought for the South at the battle of Shiloh. My great-grandfather's decision to join the Confederate army and risk his life fighting for the South, in the eyes of the family, proved his deep commitment to his new country.

Sometime after the end of the Civil War, that same great-grandfather started a wholesale liquor business that his son, my grandfather, joined when he was old enough to do so. Later, my father and grandfather worked together as liquor wholesalers. Although these businesses did reasonably well through the years, neither was as successful as the department stores my mother's family founded. They were largely built and run by my mother's uncle, that is, my maternal grandfather's older and distinctly more energetic and successful brother. As a result of these business successes, my mother's family was wealthier and of higher status than my father's. I mention this here because it was a factor in my parents' marriage and may also have played some small role in my mother's suicide.

My mother's mother, the unchallenged decision maker in her family, was largely responsible for and primarily concerned with the family's substantial position in the community. She was also said to be disappointed by and critical of her husband's relative lack of ambition and success as compared with his brother, who was the principal architect of the department store business. According to my father, my mother's father was in the business because he was a family member, not because he ever contributed a great deal to the company's success. Nonetheless, it was his family name that was emblazoned on the entrance to the stores, and he was paid well for the work he did do for the company.

The balance of power and influence in my father's nuclear family was similar to that in my mother's. Although my paternal grandfather was a handsome, energetic, charming man with many friends and admirers, he was not successful in the business his father had built. He was known to be particularly susceptible to get-rich-quick schemes offered by promoters of gold and silver mines in the West. In confirmation, I have a devastating letter written by my father to his older sister when they were in their very early 20s, poking brutal fun at their father's efforts at self-promotion, as well as his recent unsuccessful investment in a copper mine in the West that had mostly yielded ground water.

My father's mother was at the center of my father's family. The daughter of the owner of a very successful dry-goods business, she kept the family going, tidied up when my grandfather made bad financial decisions, and made the most important family decisions. My father's family was as much German-American as American; German was spoken at home until he was 10.

Although my father's side of my family seems to have been largely free from serious psychopathology, serious mood disorder was highly prevalent in my mother's nuclear and extended family. The extent of affective psychopathology in her family strengthens the case for a strong genetic diathesis in her chronic depression and ultimate suicide. As I have already noted, shortly after my mother committed suicide, her mother did so, as well. She had apparently suffered from depression through much of her life, exacerbated perhaps by her husband's disappointing career. As well, through the decades following, at least two of her siblings and several of their children were also diagnosed with either major depression or bipolar disorder. More recently, I have learned that two of my mother's brother's children, my first cousins, have also been diagnosed with bipolar disorder. Fortunately, in my (hardly unbiased) clinical judgment, neither my brother nor I have ever met criteria for mood disorder, even though I believe we have experienced a bit more of life's usual affective ups and downs than others. Because of my family history, I have been extremely alert to any signs of mood disorder in my own children.

CONSEQUENCES

A Motherless Boy

Shortly after I started elementary school, I began to realize how fortunate my friends were to have mothers to go home to at the end of the school day and how sad it was that I did not. Although I was fond of our governesses, it wasn't the same. The other children had something important I lacked. I began to appreciate what I did not have whenever my friends talked about the things they did with their mothers and, especially, when I saw how involved their mothers were in their lives. Perhaps most important, although I certainly could not have articulated it at the time, it was clear to me that whatever these children did, their mothers would love them unconditionally. I never had this feeling about my father. He had been raised in a strict old-world atmosphere in which good behavior on the part of children was what merited parental affection. Some of that conditionality colored our relationship when I was young.

Although my father worked hard to fill the void, in other ways, as well, it proved impossible for him to do so. So, at a level I could not express but clearly felt, I experienced my mother's absence early. On another, more prosaic level, I missed the nurturing hand of a mother on my physical being. Looking at school class pictures through the years, I am always the one whose clothes are the least carefully tended, the one who is most in need of a haircut. At summer camp, while my bunkmates usually got letters every day from their mothers, I heard from my father every week or 10 days. (Shortly after writing these last lines, I received an e-mail from my daughter. My 8-year-old granddaughter is going to overnight camp for the first time. My daughter asked her mother and me and her siblings to write her if we were able. I take this e-mail to be proof positive of one of the many benefits of having a mother!)

Still, I don't remember having had a particularly troubled or unhappy childhood, although I did act out more than most of my peers at school and summer camp. Even then I recognized that I did so to attract attention. Of course, whether my attention-seeking behaviors reflected an absent mother and distant father or were simply a developmental phase is impossible to know.

In middle childhood I began to experience the brief episodes of depression that remain a hallmark of my emotional life. Although they never met diagnostic criteria for dysthymic or cyclothymic disorder, and certainly not major depressive disorder or bipolar disorder, they were and are nonetheless troublesome and occasionally debilitating. I assume, in their attenuated form, that they are a legacy of the genetic diathesis that much more heavily burdened my mother and grandmother, as well as cousins, nephews, and nieces. Also, during the same period, I became more and more aware of my special status as the child of a suicide. Although largely unacknowledged to me by anyone, this fact was a muted accompaniment to my growing up. Most of the time, my mother's suicide led my friends' parents, especially their mothers, to be more solicitous of this poor child whose mother had chosen to reject her children so irremediably. One of those parents, the mother of my best friend (a person who continues, after 60 years, to be a good friend), would every now and then touch me or pat me; it is clear in retrospect that she was trying to reassure a little boy who would never have the unconditional emotional support she so readily provided her three boys.

Were my brother and I stigmatized because of the suicide? Did friends and their parents view me and my brother as victims of a hereditary taint and respond to us accordingly? I suspect that may have the case in one or two instances. I remember, for example, some angry talk by an aunt about my mother's family's burden of mental illness, which she hoped my mother had not passed on to us. I can also remember, as a moody adolescent, wondering whether a depressive Mark of Cain had been visited on me.

A few years after my mother's death, my father remarried. His choice of new wife was a troubled, vulnerable woman not unlike my mother. The marriage lasted only a year. I remember little of her, other than that she brought along a son from her first brief marriage, who became a good friend of mine many years later. The two of us shared similar childhoods: his mother could not provide for him any more than mine could, so his father, like my father, had to raise him by himself. For the past few years, he and I have shared a very wide-ranging e-mail correspondence that we both enjoy a great deal.

As I have already observed, although my father worked hard at being an affectionate and dutiful parent, I don't think he ever fully shed the oppressive sense of responsibility for my mother's death. That sense of culpability clearly affected his relationship with his sons. In particular, I believe that much of what he chose to do with us and much of how he related to us were predicated on the realization that he was all we had, because he had been unable to prevent our mother's suicide. Accordingly, I think he felt an even stronger obligation to succeed as a father because, in his own mind, he had obviously failed as a husband. We were quite close to our father from an early age, although emotional intimacy with anyone didn't come easily for him.

Adolescence

Perhaps the most enduring impact of growing up without a mother during adolescence was my great difficulty understanding—and relating to—girls. Many psychologists believe that a boy's model for relationships with girls and, ultimately, a mate is his relationship with his mother. That would certainly help explain my problems, throughout adolescence and into young adulthood, in figuring out how one was supposed to interact with girls. To that point in my life, I hadn't known any girls or women with whom I had had more than a perfunctory relationship. Although there had been female caretakers during most of the early years, including a couple of whom I was quite fond, those relationships didn't provide me much in the way of skills in interacting with women.

Besides, those caretakers disappeared when I was 10, when my father married for a third time. My new stepmother, 18 years younger than my father, was blond and sexy. A high school dropout (although a reasonably successful businesswoman), she was not Jewish and was probably an alcoholic to boot. She arrived complete with a 3-year-old daughter, to whom she was devoted but for whom she provided little actual nurturance or care.

My father's decision to marry this woman ultimately came to represent for me his final renunciation of the people and values he had known and cherished until his wife's suicide. I am convinced that his rejection of what had been so important to him before my mother's death, embodied in his choice of this woman, represented a further effort to put closure to my mother's death. To the extent that his friends' repeated failure to understand, support, or accept my mother played a role in her suicide, turning his back on them by marrying someone who could not have been more different from her helped my father put even further distance between himself and the events of a decade earlier. Unfortunately, the marriage also estranged him from his sisters, whose dislike of my stepmother grew quickly. Consequently, to my great unhappiness, our family spent time with my father's sisters and their spouses and children only once a year, at Thanksgiving.

Three years after the marriage, my father left his job as manager of a wholesale liquor business to start a children's clothing store with his new wife. She had worked for a wholesaler of children's clothing in our city, although she was Canadian by birth and upbringing. They worked together in that store for the rest of their lives together. Unfortunately for my father, who was devoted to her, she died at the age of 43 of a ruptured aorta, after a marriage of only 15 years. By that time, I was out of the house and married.

If the absence of a mother figure during my youth provided me few cues as to how to relate to girls and women later on, my mutually hostile relationship with my stepmother gave me reason to suspect their motives. Very soon after she and my father married, my stepmother got off on the wrong foot by firing a governess of whom I was quite fond. Things went downhill from there. Admittedly, I wasn't easy to live with, especially because my stepmother took personally my moodiness and occasional outbursts of anger. She also resented the fact that my brother and I had some money in trust from our mother's parents, especially when the business she and my father had started began to do poorly a few years later. It was only after I married an exceptionally kind, gentle, and intelligent woman that I was able to modify my views of women.

I didn't apply myself to my work in high school very conscientiously, and I have often puzzled about why I didn't. I knew I was bright and perfectly capable of doing well, but I chose not to do so. I have come to see this unwillingness to apply myself as a product of my low self-esteem, my father's "hands-off" attitude toward much of my behavior (including my schoolwork), and perhaps even an attempt to punish my father for his unfortunate choice of women. Fortunately, my ambivalent attitude toward academic work began to diminish toward the end of high school and into the college years and reversed itself in graduate school. Nonetheless, its early expression remains perplexing. As with other aspects of my behavior about which I have regrets, I have fantasized that a dutiful mother, someone fully involved with her children's lives who considered it her responsibility to encourage them to do their best, would not have let me slide by during high school.

Despite my mediocre grades, I attended a good college, did well in graduate school, and have been a productive academic researcher. And it is also the case, of course, that many adolescents blessed with parents who are very involved in their lives fail to work to their capacity. Nonetheless, I still fantasize on occasion about what might have been had I had a loving mother and a happy father during my childhood. In short, the reverberations of my mother's act continue to surface in intriguing (and difficult) ways.

Adulthood: Marriage, Parenthood, and Career

My response to potential marital partners was certainly influenced by what I believed I knew of my mother's mood disorder. I tended to screen women for possible depression, to the extent that I knew what its signs were. I was especially sensitive to suicide risk, so far as I could judge it. In fact, a long-term, fulfilling relationship that began after college ended, despite many good things about it, because the woman had come to realize that mention of suicide got my attention in ways nothing else would. If someone can be said to be suicide-phobic, I am clearly such a person. Parenthetically, my extreme reaction to the slightest hint of suicide extends beyond my personal life to my role as a therapist. I have at times had considerable difficulty with patients who admitted thinking of or planning suicide; I know that my clinical judgment about such patients is so skewed that I am quite capable of unwise, countertherapeutic decisions in my frantic efforts to solve the problem and prevent the act. I try to avoid taking on such patients.

I also looked for a partner who seemed to possess some of my mother's qualities. Whereas pop psychology would explain this as an effort to bond with the mother I had had for such a short time, it's obviously more complicated than that. I believed my mother to be a kind, gentle, loving person, and that's what I looked for. Who wouldn't want a partner with those characteristics? It is not an accident that the woman I married had parents she was quite close to, with whom I developed an exceptionally good relationship. In fact, my mother-in-law probably came as close as any woman I have ever known to my idealized image of my mother.

We learn how to parent, at least in part, from the parenting we receive. My father was a devoted, if distant, "hands-off" parent. My perception is that, at least with my brother, my mother was devoted and not distant. Unlike many parents-to-be who take it as second nature that they will be able to be good parents, I never assumed that I would necessarily be a good parent without working hard at it. For both reasons, I played a very active role in my children's growing up, much more so than my father had in mine, even though my children also had the advantage of an effective and loving full-time mother at home. Although I don't know that I was engaged in an effort to outdo my father as a parent, I did want to know what my children were doing, to participate in their activities to the extent that they would let me (at least until they reached adolescence), and to be there for them when and as they needed support. Of course, again, whether these behaviors reflected my motherless state, a rational assessment of my father's strengths and weaknesses as a parent, my training as a clinical psychologist, my personality, or some combination of these, I will never know.

On one dimension as a parent, I consciously diverged from my father's example. As I noted earlier, his approval was at times contingent on our behaving as he wanted us to behave; it was not unconditional. He had acquired this parenting behavior from his parents, clearly, as a function of the way their parents had been raised in the old country. But from my training as a psychologist, as well as from natural inclination, I knew that this was not the way my wife and I would raise our children. We tried hard to express an unconditional love, although we did not eschew discipline or the expression of displeasure when they were called for. But I believe our children always knew we loved them, even if we didn't always love everything they did.

Although my career has been quite important to me, I have never wavered in the belief that the ultimate worth of a person is measured best by his or her success as a parent. Holding this value is hardly exceptional, but I attribute its particular personal importance to my parents' experiences as parents. My mother's death deprived her of the opportunity to succeed as a parent. My father's potential as an effective parent was in all likelihood compromised by his emotional response to the trauma of his wife's suicide; it colored his life, including his relationship with his sons, to its end. Hence, in my emphasis on an involved parenthood, I believe I was trying to make up for my parents' inability fully to parent my brother and me. It is also the case that whatever success I have achieved in my career has been, at least in part, an effort to compensate for my father's only modest career success, despite his early promise, and the consequent downward mobility of our nuclear family. To the extent that my father's career was affected by the belief that he had failed profoundly as a husband, both the trajectory of his career and my response to it were consequences of my mother's mental illness.

It is a cliché that mental health professionals choose their careers to confront their own psychological needs and heal their own psychological hurts.

Did I become a clinical psychologist to treat my own depression or to prevent depression in patients from doing to them what my mother's depression did to me and my family? I don't really think so, although it is tempting to make that easy attribution. My career choice was to become an academic, and the field was psychology because of psychology faculty members I got to know and respect as an undergraduate. On the other hand, clinical psychology was much more attractive to me than other kinds of psychology, in large part because of a desire to do some good for people with mental illness. The idea of doing research that might help patients also had a good deal of appeal. It is ironic that I chose to study alcoholism, given that three generations of my father's family had made their living selling whiskey. However, I didn't make this choice for any more complicated reason than that one of my obligations in my first job was to work in an alcoholism clinic one evening a week. I found the work and the patients fascinating. One thing led to another, I wrote a grant to begin some research, and alcoholism became the research focus of a lifetime.

It is possible that the strong interest in diagnostic decision making that also arose early in my career stemmed in part from a need to know for sure what had motivated my mother to end her life—but that possibility can certainly never be finally confirmed or denied. A professional interest that is more clearly a function of family history is my substantial interest in the genetics of mental disorder. As findings on the genetics of mood disorder, schizophrenia, substance abuse, and even suicide became more and more compelling,[2] my interest in them rose, in part because of what those findings told me about the impact of a mood disorder diathesis on my mother and our family. At the same time, I was always aware of the personal relevance to me of the current findings on the genetics of mood disorders that I covered in the undergraduate and graduate psychopathology courses I often taught.

My father was a procrastinator: he never did today what he could reasonably put off until tomorrow or the day after that. He recognized this tendency, kidded about it, but never overcame it. I believe it cost him a great deal in his life, but it may also have helped him deal with his emotional hurts by not dealing with them until he was able to do so, if ever. My father also prided himself on seeing the silver lining in every black cloud; I thought he fooled himself too often.

On these two behavioral dimensions, I am quite the opposite. After procrastinating through high school by putting off assignments, then doing them shoddily, I began to work to rid myself of the habit. As a result, for many years, I have tried very hard to put off nothing that should be done today for tomorrow. Similarly, through much of my life, I have struggled to view myself, my world, and my responsibilities with the clearest possible eye. Whereas the wish to see things, good and bad, as accurately as possible may reflect the enhanced clarity of vision that a dysphoric temperament yields, it also represents an attempt to avoid being surprised when a situation that hasn't been assessed accurately yields an unanticipated negative consequence. I would much rather expect the worst and be pleasantly surprised when it doesn't come about than assume that things will always work out—because they don't.

REVERBERATIONS AS A MENTAL HEALTH PROFESSIONAL

At some points in this narrative, I have expressed skepticism as to whether my being a mental health professional gave me insights into the impact of my mother's death that others would not have had. Bright, thoughtful, emotionally insightful people do not require an advanced degree in psychology to draw valid conclusions about their behavior or that of others. We all marvel at people, often with limited formal educations, who have extraordinary social skills, including the ability to relate to others instinctively and unerringly. All of this notwithstanding, I do believe that my 40-plus years as a clinical psychologist have given me a perspective that others might not have had on certain matters having to do with my mother and father.

My training and experience, for example, have clearly influenced a willingness on my part, which has grown over the years, to empathize with my father for what he must have experienced in the immediate aftermath of my mother's suicide. I no longer experience the anger and disappointment with him that I felt earlier in my life. Knowing now about some of the extraordinary advances in the genetics of mood disorder and appreciating the extremely strong genetic loading for mood disorder in my mother's family, I have also come to believe that my father's seeming insensitivity to my mother's needs during their brief marriage and his harsh or insensitive treatment of her at times when she was in particular need of his support probably played a minor role, if any, in her ultimate decision to end her life.

My perspective on the impact of the suicide also reflects my psychological training and experience. Although I lament my journey through childhood without either a loving mother or a fully engaged father, I also recognize that my mother's chronic illness would have seriously compromised her ability to take care of my brother and me. In fact, it is possible that, had she lived, my childhood would have been more troubled than it was.[3]

Finally, as a clinical psychologist, I am especially sensitive to the frequency and the manner with which even now, so many years after the event, the impact of my mother's suicide reverberates through my life. My understanding of my own moods, as well as those of my children (and, now, grandchildren), my recognition of behaviors that even now are reactions to my father's behavior, my suicide phobia and depression phobia—all are living legacies of that event of 70-plus years ago. How extraordinary!

NOTES

1. In the late 1950s, a pediatrician, Dr. Leon Cytryn, observed that children hospitalized for surgery were often sad and withdrawn and that those with chronic medical problems often experienced depression. He and a colleague subsequently proposed the first classification of childhood depression; see Cytryn, L., & McKnew, D. H., Jr. (1972). Proposed classification of childhood depression. *American Journal of Psychiatry, 129,* 149–155. In this article, the concept of "masked depression" was first put forward. Characterized by sadness, withdrawal, helplessness, hopelessness, and social isolation, it is the most common of the categories of childhood depression; see Miller, J. A. (1999). *The childhood depression sourcebook.* New York: McGraw-Hill Professional. Most children with depression suffer a recurrence; 70% do so by adulthood, as noted in Surgeon General of the U.S. (1999). Children's Mental Health. In *Mental Health: A report of the Surgeon General.* Washington, DC: U.S. Government Printing Office. A recommended sourcebook on childhood depression is Fassler, D. G., & Dumas, L. (1998). *Help me, I'm sad: Recognizing, treating, and preventing childhood and adolescent depression.* New York: Penguin Books.

2. For a thorough overview of the genetics of major depression, see Sullivan, P. F., Neale, M. C., & Kendler, K. S. (2000). Genetic epidemiology of major depression: Review and meta-analysis. *American Journal of Psychiatry, 157,* 1552–1562. Also Tsuang, M. (2000). Schizophrenia: Genes and environment. *Biological Psychiatry, 47,* 210–220, contains an important review of the genetics of schizophrenia, making the important point that environmental factors often interact with genetic predisposition to produce the disorder. Finally, for a summary of a series of twin and adoption studies that suggest that genetic factors also play a role in suicide, see Roy, A., Rylander, T., & Sarchiapone, M. (1997). Genetics of suicides: Family studies and molecular genetics. *Annals of the New York Academy of Sciences, 836,* 135–157.

3. Clinical depression in children has been found to be twice as likely among the offspring of depressed mothers as among those of nondepressed mothers; see Hammen, C., & Brennan, P. A. (2003). Severity, chronicity, and timing of maternal depression and risk for adolescent offspring diagnoses in a community sample. *Archives of General Psychiatry, 60,* 253–258. The children of mothers who suffered from postpartum depression have been reported to be at higher risk of becoming violent than the children of nondepressed mothers, as reported in Allen, C. (2003, November). Do sad moms make angry kids? *Psychology Today,* 79–81. And 41% of children of depressed parents (chiefly mothers) met criteria for at least one psychiatric disorder compared with only 15% of children whose parents were not depressed; see Orvaschel, H., Walsh-Allis, G., & Ye, W. (1988). Psychopathology in children of parents with recurrent depression. *Journal of Abnormal Child Psychology, 16,* 17–28.

12 He Just Can't Help It: My Struggle With My Father's Struggle With Bipolar Disorder

Esme A. Londahl-Shaller

1997

During my second year of college, I went to the university counseling center with what I presumed to be a fairly simple question:

"Am I bipolar?"

The counselor who had been assigned to me, probably a predoctoral clinical psych intern, looked at me askance and asked me to slow down and back up.

I had been having what I considered to be mood swings. Sometimes I was really, really cranky, and sometimes nothing could get me down. I usually needed about 9 or 10 hours of sleep to feel rested, but every once in awhile there was a week or two in which I really only needed 5. I cried more easily than other people. Oh, and I was the youngest child of a father who had bipolar disorder. I had been reading and rereading my introductory psychology text: "The age of onset of bipolar disorder is typically in the late teens or early twenties." I was 19, almost 20. I burned the paragraph about the high heritability of bipolar disorder and its cardinal symptoms into my brain. Would I get "lucky" and only have bipolar type II, without any of the psychosis associated with bipolar I? Or maybe cyclothymia, the low-grade, chronic form of bipolar disorder? Questions such as these peppered my thoughts for weeks.

The counselor asked me a lot of questions, trying to determine some other area of stress in my life. I tried valiantly to convince him that classes weren't stressful (they weren't), that I wasn't pregnant or having unsafe sex (I wasn't), and that I wasn't having a fight with my boyfriend (what boyfriend?). "Isn't there some kind of test?" I asked, still completely naïve to how crude the psychological diagnostic system actually remains. "Can't you just check to see if maybe I have it?" He gave me the Minnesota Multiphasic Personality Inventory, an extremely long personality test used to assess for many areas of psychological functioning, and told me to come back the following week for a consultation.

My MMPI was clean, if you can call it that. I showed no signs of maladjustment, psychosis, or depression. In fact, my counselor told me I was one of the most well-adjusted clients he had seen and that my main problem was prob-ably just worrying about whether or not I would follow in my father's bipolar footsteps. In short, he told me to chill out.

This did not deter me from going in for another "bipolar checkup" the following spring. Clean.

I didn't know that my father had bipolar disorder until I was in my teens, and I didn't really begin to understand it until college. In fact, I retained hundreds of unanswered questions about my father and his life until I began writing this chapter. I still have unanswered questions. And, as is common in families affected by mental illness, I prefer to leave some of them unanswered.

1980–1990

Even as a tiny kid, I knew my dad was different. That sounds so much like a cliché that I can hardly believe I typed it, but it's true. He wasn't different in the way that children of rock stars always talk about on *Behind the Music*. My pop was no Brian Wilson. He wasn't even a Michael Nesmith. Many of the things I thought were different about him weren't even visible to the general public. Even if someone sensed that there was something unusual about my dad, I think the average person would be hard-pressed to verbalize it accurately. If anything,

The author, enchanted by her father, as was typical (October 1980)

most people just enjoy his personality. The main thing that was unique about my dad as far as I could see was that he was...*more*. That's probably the clearest way I can describe it, and I've been thinking about it for more than 20 years. Growing up, I felt as though my father listened more than other fathers, paid more attention to me, read more, thought more, cared more, loved me more. He also fought with my mother more, got his feelings hurt more, made inexplicable decisions more, yelled more, changed his mind more, and drank more. To know the specifics of my father's behaviors, one would need intimate knowledge of my father's private life. However, even without this knowledge, I think my father's "moreness" is evident even to casual acquaintances.

In public, my dad generally comes off as very confident and friendly, if a little intrusive. He knows personal business about everyone in our neighborhood. Physically, he is 6'1" and strong-looking, especially for age 80. He has a booming voice that he uses about equally for joking and admonishing. Overriding all of these imposing characteristics, however, is a softer, almost childlike face, always ready to listen to a story about your life or share one about his. I have the suspicion that even if you were to talk to my father very casually at a cocktail party, you would still be left with this sense of *more*—that perhaps more exciting things happened to Jan Londahl than to most other people, that there is something special about him, and that something more exists behind his bluster (or his soft-spoken demeanor, depending on when you meet him). Perhaps this sense of *more* is why my mother is my father's third wife.[1] I think that it is this very sense of "moreness" that makes bipolar disorder so hard to accept and especially to understand.

When I was growing up and my father would be inconsistent, irrational, or just plain irritating, my mother would often say, "Esme, he just can't help it." I know she was trying to be helpful, but this was a comment I could never, ever comprehend. How could he not help it? Everything my father did was so deliberate, so seemingly self-assured, that I couldn't fathom the idea that he was doing anything against his will, anything that wasn't completely premeditated. His entire persona was one of purpose, of deliberate action. As is the case in many bipolar families (and I choose that term carefully, because when my father is "off," it often feels as though my mother and I are riding along),[2] I was left with this impression of constant *intention*. This sense went uncorrected for several reasons: I was too young to understand; it would confuse and worry me; my father's psychiatrists advised him not to tell me. There were probably other reasons that I can't begin to guess.

Consequently, based on his deeds and mostly his words, I thought my dad was mean, I thought he was unreasonable, I thought he disliked women and girls, I thought he didn't want to stay with us. And yet I could never begin to reconcile these thoughts with the strong belief that my father prized me and loved me beyond all else and the sense that with him, I was safer than can be described.

Because of this lack of explanation, this silence, I didn't know what was wrong. And now, having recently completed my doctoral education in clinical psychology, I'm just beginning to put the pieces together.

1927

My father was born in 1927. This is hard for me to conceive of, not least of all because I didn't come along until 51 years later. It is also very difficult, at least for me, to picture my parents any younger than I am currently. I have always had old parents, and my dad has always been the really old one (my mom is 9 years his junior). To think of him as a small child, no matter how many stories I hear, is difficult. At the same time (and I realize this is quite a contradiction), it's hard for me to think of him as a real adult, because for his whole life he has been a bit of a child. I can recall many arguments during my youth in which my mother would berate my father for acting like a kid or a teenager and the many impulsive and even silly actions on his part that would merit this attribution. As far as I can tell he was never allowed to be young and yet, painfully, he can't grow up.

Still, he *was* born in 1927, to unmarried parents, a fact he didn't learn until he was in his 30s and has never quite gotten over. My father was always sensitive to the slights of youth and remembers most of them to this day. He can tell detail-perfect stories about being left at school for lunch in first grade while all the other kids went home to eat, or about boxing with his younger brother Dickey and hitting him so hard that, terrified, he thought he had killed him. When I ask him about the depression, mania, or general moodiness that have accompanied his life with bipolar disorder, he says that it was always like that. "No matter what name they gave it, kid, it was still my life."

In spite of his clear accounts of problems as a kid, most of the early childhood memories my dad shares are generally pretty happy: eating pies with Dickey, being walked to school by his older half-sister and half-brother, Barbara and Bruce. He describes memories of sadness and fear, but they are generally embedded in a warm appreciation for the trappings of childhood.

My grandfather, Cyrus Londahl, was a high school football coach who wanted to be an author. He fantasized about writing the great American novel and spent most of his time at home thinking about his book or writing short stories or bits of memoir that would presumably lead up to it. Unfortunately, his time spent at the typewriter was, by necessity, time spent away from his sons. His writings were competent, quite good by some standards, but never published.

They provide powerful insight into Londahl family history, however. My father has sent me many of Cy's observations, most of which contain analyses of my great-grandfather Londahl and the family's early years at the Presidio in San Francisco. The family left the Norwegian enclave of Minnesota in 1910 when my great-grandfather took a post as an army chaplain, and Cy, age 10, carved the family's experiences deep into his memory. His depictions shed considerable light on the emotional pedigree of my family. I'll never know whether my ancestors had bipolar disorder or any other mental illness, but in Cy's writing I am able to catch a glimpse of at least the nonconformity and "moreness" that typifies my father and his kin. Take this excerpt by Cy from 1971 (at 70 years old, reflecting on the way he saw his father, my great-grandfather):

> Although I was nine years old and as yet could not read, I almost instantly recognized that we were not a typical army family....Though my love and loyalty never faltered, my father's non-conformity distressed me. I soon observed that his differentness obliged other officers to hurry past our quarters with attention straight on or averted....He was as demoralizingly discordant as a French horn doing Rock of Ages while the rest of the band attempted a stirring Sousa march.

My father never really got over the slight of Cy's hours spent in front of the typewriter. As he lamented, "He could handle the words fine, but he didn't understand life....Maybe if I'd been raised with a father instead of a workaholic, things would have been different." Perhaps as a consequence of feeling ignored by his father, my father has felt lonely his entire life. Lonely to the point that he is sure no one else can understand. He craves my company; he craves my mother's company, too; and he still feels slighted when we want to go somewhere else or do something without him. His childhood was spent wishing for more attention from his father and dreaming of the time when he would be grown up and be able to get attention from his own family.

1945

My dad had a job loading boxcars of grapes in Lodi and started to feel guilty about not being in the army. He went down to San Francisco and got a post as a merchant seaman on a ship heading to New York via the Panama Canal. When he arrived in New York 15 days later, the ship he had sailed on, the *St. John's Victory*, became a dead ship sitting in the harbor. Being a merchant seaman was not the romantic, heroic occupation he had hoped for. After 45 days, the 18-year-old boy was homesick. He called Cy, who talked to the president of the steamship line and got my dad out of his duty. My dad then took a Greyhound bus from New York to Omaha, and another from Omaha to Sacramento, where Cy picked him up. By my dad's recollection, this is where things "get real hazy." He took some courses at Stockton Junior College, and then at West Contra Costa Junior College, before transferring to the University of California, Berkeley for summer school. In the fall of 1947, my father unceremoniously says he "passed some courses and then had a nervous breakdown."

2007

Let me interrupt the narrative for a moment to say that this is the point at which the story seems the most foreign to me. I want to own it as my family and my history, but I am constantly left staring at figurative passport photos of two entirely different men. My father has left the West Coast only four or five times in his life, and the idea of him sailing down the Panama Canal is impossible for me to imagine. Thinking of him at age 18 picking grapes, when all I can picture is him at 60 in front of a classroom, is nearly out of the question. For all the aggravation he has caused me, and for all the times I thought he was "crazy," the idea of his having experienced a "nervous breakdown" is very nearly unfathomable.

I am left with a muddled confusion. I don't understand what my father's life must have been like, and I can't picture his fear as his symptoms first began to show themselves. This is something that I will probably never really understand, but I can't help but spend hours in the attempt. I keep trying to push the separate, far-flung pieces of my father now and 50 years ago closer together in my head. This process is my labored, inadequate attempt to see one whole man.

Thus I have my own personal reasons for not understanding or believing the psychological turmoil my father has gone through. It's hard to understand and difficult to get my head around. In addition, the empirical psychologist in me is constantly wondering what terms such as *hazy* and *nervous breakdown* mean. Psychosis? Mania? Depression? When my father claims he "got lonely," is that all it was? Or was it something bigger, as it seems to be to him? Do his descriptors really mean what I take them to mean? And when I ask for clarification, is it really as impossible for him to describe as it seems to be?

1948

Clinical terminology aside, my father experienced his first "nervous breakdown" during the winter of 1947–1948, and his parents grew concerned. When I ask my dad what he means by a nervous breakdown, he describes himself as being simply "out of touch and depressed." He is unable to give further details. The previous fall he had undergone a brief stint of therapy at the predecessor to the very counseling center at Berkeley where I would fish for my own diagnosis 50 years later. It did little to help, and he still seemed rattled after he discontinued treatment there.

In late January and February of 1948, my dad says he was "having a lot of ideas and feeling really good" (his words), telling his parents that he was going to do all kinds of things: start 10 new businesses, take trips, try to change the world. He wasn't sleeping, his speech was a million words a minute, he was easily distracted, and he was drinking more than usual. In retrospect, he was exhibiting all seven of the modern diagnostic criteria for a manic episode (only three of which are required to make the diagnosis). His parents, though they didn't know what was wrong, were concerned. They told him he couldn't possibly do all those things at once. My dad said yes-I-can. He wouldn't slow down.

Cy and his wife, my grandmother Vernon, committed my father to Stockton State Hospital on March 4, 1948. It was his 21st birthday.

My dad was given seven sets of electroconvulsive therapy (ECT) during his first stay in Stockton State (his memory for what he sees as transgressions is unfailing, despite the fact that his overall description of this time period is fuzzy). Eventually, he was transferred to Langley Porter Clinic, a nicer facility, where my father played cards with a student from Cal Tech. The Cal Tech graduate taught another kid how to pick locks. When the kid perfected his technique, my father followed him outside. The kid got scared and went back, but my father took a bus to Berkeley to see his girlfriend. He was released to his parents and began working at General Mills as a warehouseman, stacking and unloading boxes of Cheerios and Bisquick until they were shipped.

Later that year he took another Greyhound to Reno with his girlfriend to marry her. They lived with Cy and Vernon for a short time and then moved to Berkeley, where they stayed until his new bride became pregnant and left my father. He had gone back to school at UC Berkeley while his wife worked, but he was lost. As he put it, "I tried to make it on my own, but I wasn't doing it." Things began to fall apart again.

1949

My father's Aunt Evie and her brothers convinced him to sign himself back into the hospital. Back at Stockton State, my dad received another 20 sets of ECT. He also received "hydrotherapy," which at Stockton consisted of being covered in tight clothes to promote sweating and then hosed off repeatedly. Although he did not receive insulin shock therapy, many of his friends on the ward did. He says that he feels lucky not to have received a prefrontal lobotomy, as a high school friend of his was given one that same year. During this second stay at State, one of the orderlies pushed my father from behind. My dad answered this insult by breaking the orderly's ribs, which landed him in the criminally insane ward. My dad's reputation preceded him there, and he was beaten up by a new orderly while he was tied down to his bed, about to receive ECT. Cy promptly got him moved back to a regular ward.

When I asked my dad to describe the state mental hospital in 1949, he told me to go watch *One Flew Over the Cuckoo's Nest*. I laughed nervously. He said, "I wish I was joking, kid."

Some context: the late 1940s and early 1950s were a tumultuous time for state mental hospitals in the United States. The 1948 popular film *The Snake Pit* provided America with a glimpse of what might be going on in hospitals across the country, and many became concerned with the practices of these institutions. Psychotropic drugs had yet to be introduced, and the physical techniques that my father described (insulin and electroshock treatment, lobotomies, and hydrotherapy) were indeed commonplace. In fact, Portugal's Egas Moniz won the Nobel Prize for Medicine in 1949 for the development of the prefrontal lobotomy.[3] Given the large number of these operations that were performed during the period in which my father was hospitalized, he rightly considers himself lucky to have avoided this fate. It is thus not surprising that my dad viewed all of the treatments he received as simple punishments, and nothing else.

Although salutary effects of modern ECT have been established,[4] the ECT being done in the 1940s had very little scientific grounding behind it. Lobotomies were even cruder, and the long-term effects of such operations had not been studied systematically, nor were the procedures performed uniformly for specific symptoms or diagnoses.[5] Amid this climate of drastic attempts at "cures" for the mentally ill, my father recalls his experiences with only disdain. To this day he says he gained no benefit from any of his hospitalizations.

The cumulative effect of my father's trips to and from mental institutions was the receipt of countless diagnoses by his early 20s, none of which proved helpful. He had dementia praecox, paranoid schizophrenia, psychotic mania; some said he was simply incorrigible. A psychiatrist or two did mention manic-depressive illness (the original term for bipolar disorder), but none of these categories pointed the way to an adequate treatment. The world of mental health my father recalls is more like a prison or a torture chamber than anything remotely therapeutic. To this day, my dad says that hospitalization is "just a punishment for nonconformity."[6] He took hospitalization for what it was to him: imprisonment.

In spite of his overall negative sentiments toward his hospitalizations, my father offers little in the way of details or specifics. Besides his vague accounts, all I have to help me to better understand his experiences are some very smudgy mimeographed notes that were sent to my father's current psychiatrist in the mid-1980s. In contrast to my dad's descriptions of his hospitalizations ("everyone was overreacting, I wasn't that bad off, I was just lonely"), the short notes from psychiatrists and residents paint a very different picture. The young men described sound like simplified, cartoon abstractions of various parts of my father's personality, none of them capturing him accurately.

March 13, 1948: On entry was combative, profane, assaultive, resistive, and uncooperative. Attacked personnel without provocation.

October 18, 1949: Evasive. Emotionally flattened. Rambling speech and he goes off on tangents becoming irrelevant. No mood swings.

December 14, 1950: Imagines things, constantly on the go, drives recklessly, doesn't sleep. Talkative, restless, says he is bored. Denies mental illness. Combative: refused to go to bed when asked. Irrational.

Although my father's descriptions of himself during this time sound nothing like this, he took many of the labels and the attributions of the medical staff around him to heart. When I was interviewing him for this chapter, my father noted something quite poignant: "I realized that once people know you're bipolar, they think everything you do is because you're bipolar." My dad rambles, sure—but is this because he is a storyteller, or because he is mentally ill? Bipolar disorder, to me, is the most difficult mental illness to separate from one's general personality. Because many of the symptoms can simply seem like interesting personality attributes, it becomes difficult for both the sufferer and their loved ones to separate what is "bipolar" and what is "himself." My dad holds onto his personality for all it is worth, which often makes him reject the labels he was given early on in his life.

Diagnostic jargon was not doing much for my father, and the widespread introduction of antipsychotic drugs in the 1950s did little to alleviate my father's negative sense of the mental health world. Medications such as Thorazine and Stelazine were given to him nonetheless. As soon as he got out of the hospital, he would stop taking anything that was given to him and enjoy his periods of relative normalcy, only to be faced with confusion, euphoria, or depression again at a later time. So goes the life course of a misdiagnosed and misunderstood person with bipolar disorder.

In an essay from the late 1940s titled "My Philosophy of Life," my father wrote in heartbreaking clarity about his experiences with bipolar disorder:

One week I suffer from depression, the next from euphoria, then two weeks of "normalcy" which slowly, over a varying period of time, slip down into depression. Then after a week or so of wondering what life is all about and of evaluating the relative merits of living and of being dead, something happens (what I don't know) and from the depths of blueness I bounce up and become quite euphoric, thusly the cycle starts anew.

My psyche bobbles up and down like a fishing float—I'd like to take the hook off the float so that I wouldn't catch the fish of depression, dejection, degeneration, and pensive meditation. I'd like to be just an ever-constant subeuphoric. Day in and day out I'd like to be just a little "effervescent." But it isn't as easy as keeping your hair cut the way you want.

2007

Nearly 60 years later, my father still wishes for this constant level of "efferves-cence." His writing beautifully captures the struggle he has continued to fight, the one I watch him both win and lose. Luckily, he has managed to grow stronger over the years, and (although he wouldn't say so) he has gained a greater command over his mood episodes in his old age.

You may notice that my descriptions of my father's mood episodes and hospitalizations in the 1940s and 1950s are rather cursory. In part, this is related to the fact that I wasn't there; but more important, it's because my dad prefers to live as if he had not been there, either. When I ask him about his life, he gives quick, matter-of-fact answers to all questions related to his hospitalizations and mood episodes. As he once put it, "Esme, this is all stuff I've superrepressed. I can't live if I think about that stuff." When he's in a bubblier mood, explaining things like why he can't remember to take out the garbage, he simply says, "I forget everything. I'm gifted."

Through seven hospitalizations, four marriages, five stepchildren, an adopted daughter, a first child that he wasn't allowed to know, and a daughter of his own, my father has been searching for freedom from his loneliness. Bipolar disorder has a major genetic component, and the biological origins of my father's rapid cycling (an unusual form of bipolar disorder involving the drastic, quickly paced mood swings he describes in his previous passage) are undeniable. But if one had to examine the more psychodynamic and environmental reasons for (or at least accompaniments of) my father's disorder, loneliness is decidedly the domi-nant theme.

1956

My father was hospitalized again, this time in Redding, California. He had been "lonely" in the middle of the day and went to my sister Peggy's elementary school (he had adopted her when he married her mother, Lanita, 5 years earlier), to pick her up. When the principal tried to stop him from taking Peggy out of school in the middle of the day, my father punched him.

The details of my father's subsequent hospitalization at the county facility in Redding are fuzzy. He doesn't remember how long he was there or what kind of treatments he received. Although there is no specific anecdote to back it up, my father recalls a general lesson learned during his hospitalizations. At age 29, my father had now decided that he could never listen to what doctors told him again. As he put it, "If you believe everything they tell you, it's impossible to survive. You can't be a label, and you can't follow their advice, you just have to be you."

By his account, much of the early psychotherapy my father received centered on his accepting responsibility for having what we now call bipolar disorder—or, rather, coming to terms with being a "manic-depressive," with being demented, or simply with being "ill." His doctors wanted him to come to terms with a label. His description sounds a lot like many of the popular treatments for alcoholism or domestic abuse, in which clients are expected to accept a label of *alcoholic* or *batterer* before treatment can be effective. Recent studies have shown that this approach can actually have negative effects for many of those being treated, particularly because it often causes people to drop out of treatment.[7] My father has never been someone to accept any kind of label, and it is easy to picture this kind of confrontational treatment completely backfiring for him.

My dad's sentiments toward psychological diagnoses and treatment strike me as a product of the times during which my father received the bulk of his treatment. The mental health professionals who have contributed to the book you now hold in your hands have written their chapters in part to combat the "us versus them" mentality so often demonstrated by those involved in treating people with psychological disorders. My father personifies this conflict vehemently, as it is so often expressed from the client's side: the unwillingness of the client or patient to believe in what the therapists and doctors say. This split was reinforced by older models of treatment, which seemed to instill within the therapist special powers, skills, or insight.[8] Medical doctors are seen as people who know a great deal about diseases and their causes; moreover, psychologists and psychiatrists have been (and in some cases, continue to be) seen to have additional, special powers. That is, mental health professionals were viewed as having a special ability to see what is behind your presenting symptoms and *really* understand you. One can imagine that this is not a comforting feeling for someone suffering from paranoia!

This public perception is still widely held, and I feel its presence every time someone finds out I study psychology and asks me, "OK, then, what am I thinking right now?" However, many modern therapies, such as cognitive-behavioral and interpersonal psychotherapy, have endeavored to teach clients to "be their own therapist." Something tells me this would have been a better approach with my dad. As it was, he was expected to accept a label with nearly limitless negative connotations while simultaneously being told that another person could peer into his inner thoughts. This person with special insight thus held the only key to "fixing" my father, a terrifying idea if you stop to think about it long enough. When I've asked him what was recommended to him and what treatments he tried on his own outside of the hospital, my father says simply, "I ignored all of that. Everyone else should ignore it, too."

Ignoring goes a long way. A hearing was scheduled to determine my father's eligibility for release from Redding. It was commonplace in the 1950s that these hearings were held in a patient's hospital room, with lawyers present and the patient lying in the bed ("like the sick person they thought you were," according to my father). My dad had his wife lie in the bed intended for him, so that he could stand during the hearing while he proclaimed his mental health to the judge. He was released, newly cynical and with a revised outlook on mental illness. He has carried this distrust of psychological science with him throughout his life. I can't really blame him.

2007

I can't describe adequately the anguish of thinking of your father in archaic mechanical restraints or in scary, 1940s-style head gear for ECT or any of the number of other things you might hear about when you're finally being told what "he can't help it" really means. My father was a very handsome young man. Seeing him in a football portrait from high school makes it seem unbelievable that he has ever been anything less than perfectly healthy. Though he comes across as confident and tough, there is a quiet, rabbit-like demeanor behind it all. He will tell anyone that it comes from being Norwegian. *Norwegian* is a code word in my family for being prone to moodiness and being perhaps a little too sensitive. Coupled with being dominated by genetic tendencies and overwhelmed by childhood memories, this proneness made it very difficult for my father to tolerate his life during his 20s and 30s. Thinking of my noble-but-skittish father in any of the previously described hospital scenarios completely overwhelms me. It makes me worry, it makes me obsess, and it makes me never want anyone else to have to think of his or her father in such a way. I'm not an anxious person—moody, yes, anxious, no. But I get so freaked out when I think about these things, it's hard to handle. I am now a psychologist myself, and although my father has said much to the contrary, I can't help but feel complicit in the mistreatment he experienced at the hands of the mental health establishment 30 years before I was born. I ask myself: By attempting to utilize the psychology of today, am I not endorsing the psychology of yesterday?

My personal struggles with my feelings about the science of psychology are deeply linked to troubles within the discipline itself. Although it's true that psychotherapy has come a long way, we still know relatively little about the best ways to treat mental disorders. A great deal of sound research has been conducted, but there's still a great deal to do. Despite the advances in treatment for major depression and bipolar disorder, many psychotherapists and psychiatrists still rely more on outdated theories of psychopathology and neurosis than on science. There are biases and infighting within the mental health field that result in defensiveness and even more desperate clinging to antiquated ideas. Misdiagnosis and improper treatment still occur; current diagnostic categories are still in question.[9] Yet, working in my current settings, I feel almost completely powerless to change the broken system around me. What must this look like to my dad? And how did I get into such a messy discipline in the first place?

1996

Many people go into psychology in order to understand their own foibles or secret tendencies. Though I certainly have idiosyncrasies, I've never much wanted to figure them out. Other people go into psychology to learn to help people close to them. Whenever people find out that my dad has bipolar disorder, they assume I'm in this latter category. I would like to own this noble attribution, the idea that I hoped to spend my life understanding and curing bipolar disorder, but it couldn't be further from the truth.

When I started my undergraduate career at Berkeley, I planned to double major in astrophysics and dramatic arts. I lost interest. I tried English, political science, philosophy, sociology. Everything seemed too narrow. I wanted to triple major, quadruple major![10] Then I took Psych I and I was hooked. I read the entire textbook, including the stuff about the way the ear works and the way door handles are engineered, within the first week of class.

I loved psychology. I just thought it was the most fascinating, relevant subject I had ever encountered. In my late teens and early 20s, as I tentatively waited for the onset of my first manic episode, I conceptualized my interest in psychology as completely unrelated to my father's past and problems. I was interested in psychology in spite of my father, not because of him! I threw myself into course work in developmental and personality psychology. Even when I ventured into clinical psychology, I stayed away from mood disorders because "I just wasn't interested." I served as a research assistant on three different projects on attention-deficit/hyperactivity disorder (ADHD). I did a final paper for a class on obsessive-compulsive disorder. Your average freshman psychology student would perceptively note that I was in complete denial.

I wasn't, however, in denial of my own particular suffering. I had a very difficult time adjusting to college, and while I was searching for a major, I was simultaneously having an emotional meltdown. Because I was still completely uncomfortable with my father's drinking habits, I avoided being around anyone who was drinking heavily during my first year of college. Those readers who have spent any time in a college environment will know that this is a very difficult thing to do on most campuses. As a consequence of my rigid moral standards, I was quite isolated. I had two wonderful friends, whom I had met in the first few weeks of school, but when they were busy with their own activities, I was alone. My roommate, a friend from high school, was heavily involved with the sorority-fraternity party scene, and I was too square and uncomfortable to even imagine *going* with her, the presence of kegs and Jell-O shots aside.

The dining hall intimidated me. Everyone seemed very "cool," in the 90210 sort of way, and though I had been elected both student body president and homecoming queen (long story) at my high school, I felt out of my league and scared among all of the jocks and Southern California surfer girls in my dorm community. I took to eating prepackaged cups of soup alone in my room. I cried a great deal and slept late, even though I am a morning person. When my high school boyfriend broke up with me, it was more than I could bear. On top of it all, my close high school friends were often unreachable, wrapped up in adjusting to their own new worlds. I was hopeless.

Using the diagnostic skills I have acquired during graduate school, I now think I had adjustment disorder with depressed features, a diagnosis that is just what it sounds like—a reaction to a whole new set of circumstances, with a time-limited set of symptoms. Within 6 or 8 months, I was OK. I had found psychology, I had found some friends, and the dining hall looked less menacing. I have never forgotten how awful I felt, however, and I often reflect on that time when thinking about my father's problems.

There's a long-standing anecdote about med students, suggesting that they acquire everything from achalasia to Zollinger-Ellison syndrome during their first year as they read about new diseases and examine themselves for symptoms. This same phenomenon occurs in a rather interesting way when you're a psychologist-in-training who never intended to be a psychologist, coming to terms with the fact that you have a genetic pedigree from mental health hell. That is, depression and alcoholism seemed to run rampant through my grandparents and great-grandparents on both sides of my family. My trip to the counseling center was just part of a never-ending saga to second-guess what might be wrong with me and figure out the best way to handle it. The first part of that saga involved reflecting back on my relationship with my father.

1983–1989

My father was hospitalized twice while I was a child. The first time, the cops came, restrained him, and dragged him down the stairs and out the front door. There was screaming and yelling, with my mother crying. My father didn't want to go and wouldn't leave his upstairs room to speak with the cops, so he was dragged outside. I was 5 years old and curled up downstairs, asleep in my bedroom. I didn't learn about this incident until 20 years later. At the time, my father was floridly manic and extremely paranoid. To this day, he still says he was fine and blames my mother for "overreacting." It is a topic that is purposefully not discussed, as both parents refuse to see the other's side of the story.

He was hospitalized again when I was 11 or 12, during the daytime while I was at school. My mother picked me up and told me he was in the hospital with a hernia. In actuality, my father hadn't slept for several days, and he was growing more and more paranoid and belligerent. He was constantly closing the curtains in the front of our house and looking up and down the block suspiciously. He wouldn't stop talking about "men in black suits" whom he saw on the corners, watching our house and waiting for him. My father doesn't appear to remember any of this, and even my mother's description is hazy. She does remember, however, that she dropped me off at school and went to a pay phone from which she called both the hospital and the police and told them to park around the corner from our house. The police came to the door and asked my father to come with them. He pretended that he was going along peacefully, but he took off running down the streets of our tree-lined neighborhood. The cops chased him, caught him in a couple of blocks (he *was* in his early 60s, remember?), and brought him to the hospital in an ambulance, where my mother and his psychiatrist were waiting. I was in math class, probably multiplying binomials.

I wasn't convinced by the hernia story, but I figured my mom had lied for a reason. I knew the truth. I was sure my dad was an alcoholic.

The closest thing America gets to public service announcements about mental illness are commercials from major drug companies. We don't have real public service announcements about major *DSM-IV* disorders now, and we certainly didn't in the 80s. The only constant I could see through my father's confusing behavior was that he liked to drink. And drink he did. Recently, when I asked him when he started drinking, he said as soon as it was legal and he could afford it. Why? Because it made him feel grown up. To my father, drinking wasn't necessarily an escape, but it did prove that he could take care of himself in one area, that he was at least adult enough to hold his liquor. Though it undoubtedly became a crutch later, my dad started on the alcohol train in order to feel less alone and less like a child.

Looking back, there are several incidents from my childhood that I now understand to be products of mania or depression. These incidents are usually separated from other memories, so I mostly have no idea how old I was at the time. I have flashbulb memories of my father shaving his mustache with a bit of a crazed look in his eye while my mother looked on in horror and I cried. One year when we were visiting my Aunt Polly in Oregon City, we left for what seemed like no reason at all and headed for the coast at an unreasonable speed, never to return to visit my cousins again. We spent the 2 weeks we usually spent with the cousins meandering up and down the Oregon coastline, checking in and out of motels and feeding seagulls. My mother cried a lot, and I buried myself in books I had already read, not really understanding what was going on, but pretty sure it was better if I didn't. Sometimes I would get lots of presents for no reason, but when December came, my father wouldn't get out of bed for Christmas. We seemed to collect old cars in our driveway that didn't really work. Sometimes my father needed no sleep, and sometimes he would sleep for days. But questions about emotions and behavior were subtly frowned on in my household, so I didn't ask them. I assumed rather that my dad was (a) an alcoholic and, at times, (b) an asshole. Only *now* do I understand what my mother meant by "he can't help it."

The tendency to hide psychological problems from family members, particularly children, is a common one. The philosophical idea of the separation between the mind and the body is still rampant in Western culture, even though Descartes has been gone for 350 years. The impact of dualism is particularly heavy regarding mental illness. If you have cancer, it's not your fault—your physical body has turned against you. We have a very hard time, however, acknowledging that our minds may turn against us in much the same way. So we hide mental illness to a far greater degree than we do the physical. I don't blame my parents for doing it, particularly my father, as I know he was spending most of the time hiding it from himself as well. Would I have had an easier time with my father if I had understood what was going on? I have no idea, although current research suggests that I probably would have.[11]

At 11, without the blessings of psychological hindsight and with no information from my parents, I figured my dad was an alcoholic. I implored my mother to get him to join AA; maybe we could go to Al-Anon? Why don't we pour out the whiskey, let's distract him! Can't you see he has a problem!?!? Why won't you admit it to yourself? My assessments of our domestic situation became increasingly moralistic and simple. Naturally my dad had been hospitalized for this, his secret problem with demon alcohol.

My mom responded to my demands and questions in confusing ways: "It's not just alcohol. It's more complicated than that." Was she deluded?! At 11, I saw my mother as a confused and naïve person who was snowed by the charismatic drunk. Only years later did I realize the true depth of my mother's character as related to my father. I had no concept that she had (and has) the patience of a saint and an incredibly good handle on my dad's moods.

Thus my pre- and early teen years were colored by the "realization" that my father had a Problem, the kind from which "very special" episodes of sitcoms are made. Fevered confessions to best friends and boyfriends became the norm. I liked having a name for what was going on, I liked having a disorder to blame, but I saw alcohol as a weakness, not a condition, and I increasingly blamed my father for his erratic behavior rather than trying to understand it. A parent having a terrible disorder, coincidentally, was perfect fodder for developing some good old-fashioned teen angst. This was especially useful to me; I was a "good kid" who wasn't really inclined to participate in my own personal cultivation of said angst. Parental disorder was the perfect starting point for me.

I was quickly embarrassed. When Michael Dukakis campaigned for the presidency in 1988, my dad put no fewer than 70 signs in front of our house, every 2 or 3 feet, with several on the roof. My new conceptualization of his

Problem, coupled with the awkward social fears of preadolescence, made this kind of nonconformist behavior intolerable. I was EBB—Embarrassed Beyond Belief—and I turned away from my father to cope. Then I missed him, and I would crave time with him, only to be quick to become aggravated and completely intolerant.

Toward the end of what I now understand to be periods of mania, my father not only would be embarrassing but would also grow increasingly agitated and irritable and would drink even more than usual. Although he never laid a hand on me, my dad often became verbally abusive during these times. Most of his insults had something to do with the fact that I was female: I was a stupid bitch, I was ungrateful, I was terrible like my mother, I was just like every other woman. He would insult my friends if I asked to go over to someone else's house, although he seldom insulted the prettiest ones. After he said any of these things, I wouldn't speak to him for hours, sometimes a whole day. I grew increasingly more indignant, because verbal abuse *was* on after-school specials, and I knew that no one had the right to call me names.

Now, I simply try to rationalize the fact that he said those things because of the sexist time in which he was raised and the sexist world in which we still live. "And hey, misogynistic music plays on major radio stations every day!" she says at 29. At 12, I couldn't rationalize. I could only cry, get angry, wish I were a boy, or wish my parents would divorce, none of which really helped a lot. I continued to try to pull my father closer, only to push him away more forcefully each time.

This pattern continued well into high school. Like many teenagers, I thought I had all the answers. I remained terribly, thoroughly off base.

1992

I thus entered high school with more than your typical amount of "Oh, Dad!" embarrassment. Now that I study adolescence professionally, I find my own adolescent behavior nearly inexplicable. For instance, here's a list of things I didn't do once during high school:

- drink alcohol, smoke cigarettes, or do drugs
- shoplift
- have sex
- sneak out
- stay out past curfew
- talk back to a teacher
- get a B (OK, I did that exactly once)
- break up with any of my boyfriends
- skip school

- borrow the car without asking
- lie about where I was going to be

Why the consistency? Why the reliability? If there's one thing in this world that shouldn't be reliable, it's a 15-year-old girl. And yet I insisted. I think I tried to stay as stable and predictable as humanly possible. This was not a choice at the time. Others would probably look at it as such, but I just saw myself as doing what I wanted to do and thriving in the environment that was given to me. As I analyze it in retrospect, I'm left wondering if there were indeed reasons related to my dad that influenced me to lead the life that I did.

Some things on my list o' repression can be explained away rather easily: I was too optimistic and clingy to break up with anyone; A's weren't very hard for me to get, and I liked school; I was moralistic and thought drugs and alcohol were for the chronically undercreative. I wore really goofy clothes, I dyed my hair magenta, I only wore Converse All Stars.[12] I was obsessed with the aesthetics of the 1940s, '50s, and '60s. I liked to create alternate universes on paper, with alter egos for all of my friends (sort of like Dungeons and Dragons, but more indie and less overtly geeky). My birthday parties were never the average cake-and-punch affairs—I had elaborate themes, I made people dress up and participate in home-grown murder mysteries or talent shows. This rebellion was never against my parents but against what I considered to be the uptight rules of adult society, a hug of conformity I felt I needed to thwart at every turn. This, predictably, only made my father more proud of me, as I was fighting a fight he had attempted to fight in his youth; I was bucking the system and rejecting society's arbitrary ideas of "normal."

And yet I was winning. Teachers adored me, I won awards and student offices, I had friends galore. No one tried to hospitalize me.

An interesting pattern (having NOTHING to do with my dad, I would have assured you) emerged in which I was being different "just because"—a behavior that drew me closer to my father than I perhaps realized, while all the while I was still trying to push him away. I loved my father just as much as I blamed him and despised him, and twice as fiercely. And yet his unpredictability made it impossible to remember these truths in the heat of an argument or a misunderstanding. I was constantly mad at him, and I would cry and slam doors and lament my situation for hours.

Now trained as a psychologist, I have again and again been taught the importance of consistency in raising children—consistency in love, certainly; unconditional positive regard; all that Rogerian stuff. But also consistency in rules: consistent consequences for transgressions, consistent bedtimes, consistent curfews, consistent allowances. My father, bless him, is the god of inconsistency. One of the sayings he takes comfort in is "consistency is the hobgoblin of small minds." Consequently, sometimes he would purposefully try to foster my independence. Usually, though, it was rules-rules-rules, backed by no more logic than the infamous "because I said so." One night my bedtime would be 8 P.M., lights out, at age 17. The next night I could talk on the phone until 11 P.M. without getting in trouble at all. I would be "grounded" for the weekend without provocation. I would be forced to decline party invitations because my father "didn't have a daughter so that she could be at other people's houses all the time!"

Through it all, my dad prized me like no one would think possible. He could be an ogre, a bear, a drunken, slurred fool. But 2 days later he was choking back tears over his Rice Krispies telling me how proud he was of me. That's how my dad works. And even at his worst, when he was yelling at me for literally no reason, I never questioned that I was important.

2002–2004

My emerging identity as a psychotherapist has further expanded and also constrained my relationship with my father. I moved to New York state in the fall of 2001 to pursue my graduate career in clinical psychology. My first year was uneventful, filled with class work and a little IQ testing, but no actual psychotherapy. As soon as I began seeing clients in one-on-one sessions, however, my father began to pound me with questions.

"Who are you counseling? You're directive, aren't you? I bet you're really bossy. Or are you like Carl Rogers? Are you more of a Rogers girl? What do you tell them? Do you tell them what to do? Do you give them advice? How many people have you cured? Do you give them medication? Why isn't the first person you started seeing better yet? Do any of them get ECT? Do they go to the hospital? What do your supervisors think?"

These questions are not usually asked all at once, and they are fine questions. Don't get me wrong—I know that the process of learning how to be a psychotherapist can seem mysterious to many people, not just to those who have encountered mental illness themselves. My main problem with my father was not his honest questions (although they did get repetitive after a while) but his constant assumption that because I was now a THERAPIST I was also *his* therapist.

You're probably thinking that my father came to me for help and advice in an ethically uncomfortable way, given that he was my father. Oh, I wish it were that simple. No, my father instead assumed that I was constantly *trying* to give him help and advice in an ethically uncomfortable way, help and advice that he did not want. Rather than try to get free therapy from me, my dad was on the lookout for unwanted therapy he was sure I was trying to foist on him. Let me give you a few vignettes:

POP: Your mother's driving me crazy again.

ESME: Well, maybe if you'd clean the garage like she asked....

POP: Stop being directive!

POP: Do you think we should sell the Chevy?

ESME: I don't know…what do you think?

POP: Answer my question, Carl Rogers!

POP: I'm just feeling a little nostalgic today.

ESME: I'm sorry…about what?

POP: No need to give me the third degree, Headshrinker!

Get the idea? Some of you may note that I was not responding to my father in any kind of psychobabble mode, but rather as a Thoughtful Daughter involved in a Normal Family Interaction. My husband, who is also a clinical psychologist, jokes that we should post a sign on our door that says "Reminder: Psychologists are not permitted nor encouraged to perform psychotherapy with family members." With both his parents and mine, we have probably uttered the phrase "You can't be a therapist for your family!" about 100 times in the past 5 years.

Although I wish we could stand by this edict 100%, the realities of mental illness make it difficult to follow through. Sure, I wasn't trying to perform any kind of analysis in the preceding examples, but it's still difficult to completely refrain from giving psychological advice to family members. Sometimes this takes more benign forms. Because I study teenagers, my older sister will often call to ask me if my two teenage nieces are behaving acceptably for their age (they always are). My brother occasionally asked me for parenting advice when my nephew was in the throes of the "terrible 2s." Nothing too inappropriate. For me, the most difficult thing has not been dealing with my father directly but helping my mother to cope with my father's mood episodes.

A spouse's mood episodes are extremely disruptive to daily life, and my mother has had considerable difficulty dealing with her emotions regarding my father's episodes over the years. You'd never know this looking at her—my mom comes across as laid-back, stable, poised, and witty. Which she is! But anyone would get a *little* stressed after dealing with the unpredictability of someone like my father for 30 years. When I was a child, she was impeccable at hiding her stress at all times except during my father's most difficult periods (for example, the trip to Oregon I mentioned earlier; times when his drinking was worst; holidays). Recently, with my own increase in "clinical" knowledge, my mother has been more open with me about her own emotional difficulties in dealing with my father's mood disturbances. Sometimes I am helpful, in a simple sort of way. I serve as someone with whom she can be truthful, someone to whom she can complain—probably the role I might have served earlier if I had understood what was going on with my father.

At other times, I am overwhelmed. I can't, of course, be the unbiased family therapist when I am an integral part of said family unit. Sometimes my own feelings about my father drain me, and I feel incapable of helping my mother, which then fills me with guilt. Sometimes I am able to discuss things with her and even with my father with relative calm, only to hang up the telephone and create some ridiculous fight with my poor husband or my best friend. My own emotions and moods interact with my family's needs and scare my mother, who at times feels that she cannot talk to me without my snapping at her. At other times, I'm fine and actually quite helpful. My only hope is that my family is able to separate the mean, moody Esme from the one who only wants to listen and understand.

2007 AND BEYOND

Where am I today in my relationship with my father? Old men in movies make me cry. Old men in commercials, too. Basically any old man that shows any hint of sincerity, vulnerability, or emotionality—and I'm on the floor. I can't watch Spencer Tracy's ice cream scene in *Guess Who's Coming to Dinner?* without collapsing. A psychoanalytic therapist would probably have a field day with that information, but I take it as a simple internal acknowledgment that my dad is a little more fragile than other dads and that I appreciate his Norwegian sensitivity.

I am also able to see the lessons that I have learned from my father over the years, most of them without any direct, planned teaching on his part. This is a fact that I am sure he'll be pleased by (he will often brag that he taught for 40 years without ever using a lesson plan). Beginning in late elementary school, I became somewhat of a champion for the absurd and nonconformist. In fifth grade, I introduced myself to new kids by saying, "My name is Esme, and I'm weird!" Already readily identifiable as a nerd by my peers, I embraced uniqueness early. I endured comments about my unusual name, and I always ended up highlighting what made me different. This is probably why I was teased somewhat unmercifully from fourth through sixth grade. I survived, and I thrived in middle school, where I met other "weird" kids. My father was a champion for these same causes in his life, but in his case, it was by default—he couldn't help advocating nonconformity, as conformity simply did not come to him easily. Did I take the same approach because of my father's previous struggles? I'll never know. But I have continued to be attracted to these themes for my entire life: not only in others, but in books, movies, and music.

The chief example of this is in my favorite movie, *A Thousand Clowns*, which was originally a Broadway play. The central character, Murray Burns, is a dedicated nonconformist in the button-down world of Manhattan in 1961. The play centers on his struggle to keep custody of his nephew, Nick, in the face of inquiries into his nontraditional home environment. Themes of child psychology, the battle to remain unique, and the definition of both family and mental illness are thoroughly explored in this accomplished and poignant comedy. I realize now that both my mother and I were attracted to this play and the 1965 film because of my father. I love that he has contributed to my tastes in this way. Coincidentally, in 2004 and 2005 I lived two blocks from where much of the movie was shot, and when I was frustrated with my father, I walked by the old row of brownstones where Murray "lived," attempting to remind myself of the positive impacts of diversity and uniqueness—all kinds—on our society.

Dealing with my father as a child, an adolescent, and an adult has also given me the patience and empathy that I utilize daily both in my work with clients and in my personal life. My husband has attention-deficit/hyperactivity disorder, another highly heritable mental illness. I think I am able to tolerate (and even love) his forgetfulness and impulsivity because of my own dealings with my father's similar traits when he's "up." This is not to say that I have some superhuman capacity to tolerate the annoying habits of people with disorders—I wish both my father and Gary would pick up their dishes without being asked—but that I can understand them. It is also much easier to understand traits like these in clients. Clients come to you for help, but you don't have to live with them, which is a plus. Yet without having lived with my father, I don't know that I could empathize nearly as well with my clients or even my own husband.

Finally, my father has taught me a considerable amount about loneliness and its power. Since high school and probably before, I have been a uniter. I have brought people from disparate groups together, and I have constantly surrounded myself with friends. I have helped other people through rough times, and I have sought help from my friends for my own difficulties. My friends have always been a surrogate family, always in need of something—phone calls, letters, birthday cards. This wasn't (and isn't) a chore to me. Rather, I think my father instilled in me a very deep understanding of what loneliness could mean, and I have worked to eliminate it in both myself and others, even in others who may not be feeling lonely at all.

Again, this was not a conscious process, but in retrospect the fact that I was doing it was hard to ignore. I didn't (and don't) like to be alone for long periods of time, and I have always worked to be the best friend possible so that loneliness did not present itself. I think this is probably why I had such difficultly adjusting to college. I came from a high school in which I had countless friends around me. If someone was busy, I could call someone else. My early college years offered no such guarantee, and I felt lost and alone, in much the same way (although milder for me, of course) that my father must have felt 50 years earlier.

Did I go into psychology so that I could help even strangers feel less lonely? Is that a piece of my father's legacy? Subconsciously, I must have, and I thank him for this "idea" hidden somewhere deep in my brain. I have watched my father give to others over the years and have been inspired by it: inspired by his 40 years of teaching the most ungrateful population on the planet (middle school students) and his constant giving to my mother and me. He doesn't just give us money or love, but the gift is himself, which is infinitely more complex. It includes jazz trumpet, vintage cars, and cantankerous liberal values, as well as hugs and tears and confusion, all spectacular. I have tried to emulate this spirit, though it is sometimes difficult to do so on a graduate student stipend or an early career salary riddled with credit card debt. I do know, however, that my father would do anything for me. Such as letting me write this chapter, for instance.

The stories of my father's mood episodes don't end here, of course. New situations can often trigger either mania or depression in my father, and his milder episodes continue to cycle as ever. He and my mother visited me in New York for Thanksgiving during my first year of graduate school. He did all right on Long Island, but a rendezvous in Manhattan with my older sister Peggy and her family ended with my father becoming extremely belligerent, over-whelmed, and horribly drunk. Holidays are always hard, and Christmas often brings with it not only family gatherings but also either agitation or depression, depending on the year.

Larger life events tend to have a delayed impact. In 2004, he lost both his younger and older brothers when my uncles Dickey and Bruce died. On the wings of this double loss, my father's dear friend from high school, Eric, also passed away. Then his youngest daughter got married to some New Yorker. Understandably, the compound impact of all of these things made my father nearly impossible to live with and quite manic. My mother called me in a panic several times. He wasn't sleeping, he was working all the time in the garage, making phone calls at all hours, yelling constantly, not eating. Finally, he injured his leg in the garage under mysterious circumstances. When I ask him about it, he says, "I don't remember, or I don't want to tell you. I don't know which one!" He ended up in the hospital, not for his manic behavior but for his ankle, which he couldn't move or walk on. The hospital atmosphere seemed to calm him, however, and he's been better since. But what if it hadn't just been his leg? My mother and I take turns being frightened and creating personal horror stories about where his moods could take him. For now, he's safe at home.

Did his mania go away because his leg was treated? The medical hospitalization probably just served as a change of pace and a forced opportunity for him to slow down, or maybe my father was on his way down from the high anyway. The two aren't necessarily linked. I don't mean to mislead people about the best treatments for bipolar disorder. It has been difficult to write this chapter, given that my father has never followed medical advice. I don't want to give the wrong impression. I am not suggesting that everyone can be as lucky as he is and that treatment for bipolar disorder does not necessarily involve long-term medication management and family or individual psychotherapy. It does, and it should. But many people with bipolar disorder are like my father and resist proper treatment. People don't want to lose the highs, or they don't feel like themselves when they're medicated. They don't want to acknowledge that anything is wrong, or they don't believe in mental illness. Unfortunately, letting bipolar disorder go untreated can often have disastrous consequences. Suicide is common, as are job loss, divorce, and isolation.[13] Despite all of his suffering, my father has been unbelievably lucky that his bravado and stubbornness have not gotten him into more trouble than they have in his lifetime. He is also lucky to be alive.

Back to the recent past. My wedding in the summer of 2004 wasn't the *smoothest* in the dad department. His welcome speech clocked in at 17 minutes, during which he finished his own flute of champagne and lamented his maternal grandfather's lack of a pension in the 1910s. Through the frustrated cries of my siblings (my father's stepchildren), and through the yelling of other wedding guests ("Talk about Esme and Gary!"), my new husband and I laughed and smiled. The speech did seem rambling and irrelevant to the events of the day: 11 minutes into it, he was only up to 1946. But at 16 minutes and 40 seconds, he pulled it all together:

> Esme is a super, super woman…but it's not my fault. It's because of her three sisters, and her brother, and *hundreds* of other people.
> And I don't think I had anything to do with it. I really don't.
> I love you all, thanks for coming. And maybe I can cry now.

The last line, aimed only at me, referred to his inability to properly mourn the death of his brothers. Everyone under the tent teared up, unsuspecting putty in my father's adept hands. As my matron of honor put it, "Best damn wedding speech, ever."

Before the wedding, I was comforting my dad over the phone when he had just lost two brothers inside of 3 weeks. After several minutes, my dad said, "Oh, I just never thought I would be the sole survivor out of a litter of four." My mother laughed in the background, and I told my dad, "Of COURSE you are, how could you NOT be?"

Today, the term *survivor* is overused everywhere, from international politics to the reality show to the Destiny's Child song. If my father could be defined by one term, though, that's it. In fact, that's what most everyone with mental illness is, and that's who the families are that help them fight it. Though I may or may not develop bipolar disorder myself, I have taken that survival instinct and tried to pour it as much as possible into my work. I don't want people to be lonely, and I want those who society thinks have the least chance at survival—at-risk teenagers, families in poverty, the elderly, you name it—to work as hard as possible to have that chance. People like my dad make it possible, and

I hope to carry it on for him. I could never have learned more from anyone about psychology and human beings and life.

In my first year of graduate training, I was required to learn how to administer and interpret the MMPI, the same test I had taken as an undergraduate. I paired off with a classmate, filled out the 500-plus-question instrument for the second time, and held my breath as Anna scored it. Clean. We also practiced the Scheduled Clinical Interview for the *DSM-IV* and several other diagnostic batteries. I have some mood symptoms, sure, but I still don't meet criteria for any major disorders.

I don't have bipolar disorder. But for all the pain it's caused him, there's a part of me that's glad my father has it. I know that in spite of the pain and the loneliness, his perspective on the world is irretrievably linked to his experiences with bipolar disorder. Without the high highs and the horrible lows, my father might not be the amazing, insightful, empathic, surviving man that he is. I, certainly, would be much, much lonelier in this world.

ACKNOWLEDGMENTS

Enormous thanks go to my husband, Gary Shaller, for putting up with my moodiness while I wrote this chapter and always. Huge thanks to my friends Marek Adamo, Michele Fletcher, and Anne Ichikawa for years of support and their nonpsychology insights into earlier drafts and to my labmates, Anna Tverskoy and Alissa Bell, for listening to me bellyache and giving me feedback on everything from papers to pants. Thanks also to my gigantic, sprawling family for living various parts of the preceding narrative with me, especially my siblings. Finally, giant professional and personal thanks go to the psychologists who have advised me and inspired me: Tom D'Zurilla, Steve Hinshaw, Jonathan Samuels, Ori Kochavi, and Dacher Keltner.

Most important, to my father and mother: thank you for all of it—the good, the bad, and the hilarious.

NOTES

1. Actually, his fourth, if you count his marriage that was annulled, which my father does not: "The courts don't count it, neither do I." Multiple marriages are quite common among people with bipolar disorder. See Goodwin, F. K., & Jamison, K. R. (1990). *Manic-depressive illness.* New York: Oxford University Press.

2. Prominent investigators of bipolar disorder have often noted the occurrence of "bipolar families," explaining that many traits are common among them. As Miklowitz and Goldstein noted, "Interaction in bipolar families tends to be fast paced, with much humor, raising of voices, frequent interruption, and excited affect." See

Miklowitz, D. J., & Goldstein, M. J. (1990). Behavioral family treatment for patients with bipolar affective disorder. *Behavior Modification, 14,* 457–489.

3. Valenstein, E. S. (1986). *Great and desperate cures: The rise and decline of psychosurgery and other radical treatments for mental illness.* New York: Basic Books.

4. For a comprehensive review, see Abrams, R. (2002). *Electroconvulsive therapy* (4th ed.). New York: Oxford University Press.

5. Valenstein (1986).

6. His comment, indicating that hospitalization is simply a tool of the powerful, is a common sentiment. As the poet Nathanial Lee remarked of his involuntary hospitalization in the 1600s: "They said I was mad, I said they were mad. Damn them, they outvoted me"; as quoted in Dolnick, E. (1998). *Madness on the couch: Blaming the victim in the heyday of psychoanalysis.* New York: Simon & Schuster.

7. For a review and an alternate client-centered model of treatment, see Miller, W. D., & Rollnick, S. (2002). *Motivational interviewing: Preparing people for change.* New York: Guilford Press.

8. Dolnick (1998).

9. For an analysis of the current diagnostic system and suggestions for further reading, please see Spiegel, A. (2005, January 3). The dictionary of disorder: How one man revolutionized psychiatry. *The New Yorker,* 56–63.

10. Astute readers may notice that my overzealousness seems, well, a little manic. Whether this is a genetic marker or simply an artifact of growing up in a home with my father (or both) is not clear. It is certainly common for first-degree relatives of people with bipolar disorder and other mood disorders to display some subclinical symptoms of the disorder; see Goodwin & Jamison (1990).

11. The American Academy of Child and Adolescent Psychiatry, 2000. http://www.aacap.org/publications/factsfam/parentmi.htm

12. This has not really changed. I still prefer All Stars to all other shoes, but I now like to characterize myself as a "serious collector."

13. Goodwin & Jamison (1990).

13 Performing Human

Janet Lucas

This chapter is part of a larger work, which has as its point of departure the stigmatization of mental illness. The larger piece, as of yet unpublished, deals with the significance of parental dynamics in the context of abuse, and specifically their role in the ontogenesis of the child as a social being. It combines a personal and family narrative situated with an analytical and explanatory discourse. Here, with the assistance of editing by volume editor Steve Hinshaw, I present a shorter, more focused narrative that deals with my own experiences of abuse in shaping a lifetime marked by both success and mental illness, with an ongoing sense of observing the world as an outsider, "performing" social roles but simultaneously carrying a deep stigma.

Indeed, growing up with abuse and neglect, I experienced stigma at the very core of my being. As an adult, I have endeavored to counter the stigma with overcompensation, including corporate success in my 20s, followed by my PhD, for which I studied arguably the most difficult theorist of the twentieth century, Jacques Lacan. I have published articles in international academic journals so theoretically complex that only a handful of scholars can interpret them, and I have presented my work with highly distinguished theorists at conferences. These achievements allowed me to remain in the closet, to minimize my exposure to stigma and to protect myself from the shame involved.

Stigma, in this context, is the loss of personhood and reduced status as a legitimate member of society. As a way of avoiding (or at least minimizing) stigma, people develop certain "passes," akin to a societal identification card. As a case in point, when I go to a new pharmacy, or if a different pharmacist is on staff at my usual one, I always "let it slip" that I have a PhD and teach university courses. My advanced education is my "pass"—allowing me to move unnoticed in society, where I am otherwise deeply stigmatized. Otherwise, because of the nature of my medications (a cocktail of about seven antidepressants and related medicines), every time I go to the pharmacy I am not treated as a professor. As soon as the pharmacist views the prescription, there is a noticeable change: I am treated as a mental patient, with all its lack of dignity. Even more poignantly, on the few occasions that I was hospitalized for depression, I lost all rights given to a member of society. I did not *own* myself, I was not a legitimate societal subject, I was *less than human*.

The deeper issue is that the dynamics of severe abuse are such that the child internalizes the messages of devaluation. Stigma and abuse are inextricably linked in the developing psyche of a child. My intent here is to present some of the story of my childhood, adolescence, and adult life in order to show how deep the internalization can be. At the same time, I show how I have been able to transcend my legacy in some important way, although I still maintain a view of myself as an outsider.

Before starting, I must point out that although this analysis describes actions on the part of my parents—progressively shifting toward my father—that are severely detrimental, I believe that, at least initially, they each found themselves faced with impossible situations that they were unable to otherwise negotiate. For example, I know my mother suffered abuse as a child, and although my father will not admit to any such abuse, there must be *some* source of his rage. As an adult, several times (for example, when I would visit at Christmas as an adult), I tried to better understand him. However, with the exception of the short time after my mother's death, I have never able to get beyond the superficial. Even now, although I am an adult, he must maintain his ongoing role as unassailable authority, and any question about his role and status within his own family of origin is met with anger. Still, abuse is multigenerational, and my parents were themselves victims.

FAMILIES, ABUSE, AND SELF-WORTH

A fundamental premise is that the family must be "open"—that is, parents must be subject to the same collective rules and laws of society as the children. Their role is to teach the children such rules and laws and, in so doing, provide them with an existential place in society. For this to occur, the family unit must be permeable. But if the family unit is closed and impermeable—and if the parents can set their own (arbitrary) laws—then children are required to function as containers and gatekeepers, protecting their parents from societal gaze and allowing the parents to continue the abuse unabated. Because children are too young to understand the nature of the dynamics, they unquestioningly function in their inverted roles. In other words, rather than being protected *by* their parents, they are the *protectors of* their parents. Overall, if the parents establish a closed (and abusive) family unit in which it is implicitly taboo for the children to speak, the children become the very boundaries of the closed family, thus unknowingly facilitating the conditions of their own abuse.

More graphically, if children continue to develop as "containers," they progressively assume the function of family "trash bin." This becomes most strikingly evident at puberty and morphs throughout adulthood. At some point, a crucial question emerges: Can the developing individual truly touch another and feel naturally human, or will he or she have to carry the burden of difference and unworthiness, surviving and "passing" in society through performance and leading a singularly desolate and painful existence? In the latter case, it is as though this individual exists within an invisible yet impenetrable glass bubble. Others can be seen and interacted with, but because of the bubble, these interactions may stay on a superficial level. One of my aims is to show how early abuse dynamics can foster such a sense of fundamental difference and distance.

EARLY CONSCIOUSNESS

Parents are central in filling in the child's earliest years, largely lost to amnesia, by showing baby/toddler pictures and providing various anecdotes, creating the perception of a linear self. But for me, there is no physical evidence of my existence at all for the first 5 years of my life. Although there are pictures and baptism records for my sister and brother (2 and 3 years older, respectively), nothing documents my existence. This is ominous, in and of itself.

So, what memories do I have? In Edmonton, Alberta, Canada, as a child, I woke up one day in a state of intense readiness—alarm, terrible fear, and anxiety—but because this had happened countless times before, I knew the drill. In this moment, the moment of my awakening, my mother, with her skeletal face and body and a sharp knife, is chasing and threatening to kill me.

Another memory: my siblings and I are sitting in the living room. My parents' bedroom was to the left; the door opened directly to the living room. Whenever we heard her footsteps toward the door, or worse, the sound of the door opening, we would scatter, hiding behind a banister, under a table or a chair, anywhere that she might not get us.

My father also knew the drill. He would ostensibly beat my mother in order to "protect" us (I indicate *ostensibly* because, while he was protecting us from her, he was also in a violent rage). He would do so by beating her nearly unconscious and then (literally) dragging her down to the basement. While he was down there with her, we would sit quietly, on alert. We would hear her screaming for a while, and then there would be quiet. The door would be locked and my father would emerge upstairs.

At other times I would hear my mother cry from the basement, or scream and scratch on the door to get out. I never knew what went on there, but the memories will never recede. In fact, one of my sister's strongest sensory recollections is the thudding of my mother's ankles on the wooden steps as my father dragged her (our mother) down to the basement.

One of my clearest memories from this time period occurred when my father was in my room. I heard the slamming of their bedroom door. (As an aside, there was a hole in every wall where there was a door knob; at any time there would be slamming, screaming, dishes crashing against the wall, and extreme physical violence.) I knew my mother had gotten out of the room—she had escaped and was heading down the hall for me (the three bedrooms were in the same hallway). I frantically asked my father why he wasn't doing anything, why he didn't stop my mother from trying to kill me. I had expected "the usual," that he would beat her into submission and then drag her down to the concrete basement. Yet he did nothing. My mother had reached my bedroom door, her face wild and distorted with psychotic rage. She jumped on top of me and starting pounding me, shouting that she was going to kill me. I waited for my father to intervene; it felt like a long time, though it was probably only a few seconds. Finally, he tore her off me, beat her, and took her down to the basement.

I can now fill in the gaps and recognize that my mother's mental illness ranged from a near catatonic depression (at one point her weight dropped to 69 pounds) to homicidal psychosis. Although her refusal of food did make her weak, it did not stop her psychotic outbreaks.

When my mother was violently psychotic, she was always supposed to be somehow restrained in my parents' bedroom. It was like living with a rabid dog on a thin leash. The bedroom was one of the two places she could occupy; the other was the concrete basement beneath the wooden stairs.

The dynamics are alarming, to say the least: I depended on my father to protect me from my mother by beating her (often sadistically), often happening right in front of me. Every day, many times a day, I would rock back and forth (in bed, on a chair, anywhere) incessantly. I desperately needed to shut out my external environment, to "not be there." The rocking facilitated dissociation, my only means of escape.

STRUCTURAL FAMILY DYNAMICS

We existed in a *closed family unit*. My father had absolute power and authority. This dynamic arose from the interplay of my mother's mental illness and what appeared to be his propensity for power. Had my mother not been ill, this propensity might have remained somewhat in check. But with the situation as it was, his law was beyond societal law. Irrational and often contradictory, as absolute authority he could do anything he wanted. When I mustered the courage to point out an inconsistency, he would angrily (and threateningly) reply with the interdiction "Don't talk back!"

Franz Kafka describes this perverse paternal law of absolute power in his famous "Letter to His Father":

From your armchair you ruled the world. Your opinion was correct, every other was mad, wild, *meshugge*, not normal. Your self-confidence indeed was so great that you had no need to be consistent at all and yet never ceased to be in the right.

...[A]s a child everything you called out to me was positively a heavenly commandment, I never forgot it, it remained for me the most important means of forming a judgment of the world.[1]

In a closed, abusive family structure, children become trapped in a secretive environment that precludes societal oversight. In such cases, children are not socialized to be part of a collective community; rather, they must assume the lifetime role of "container," absorbing the abuse within themselves, thereby functioning precisely as impermeable boundaries, unknowingly facilitating and absorbing parental abuse. Moreover, as adults, the (former) children do not simply throw off the shackles of their familial role. Rather, their role in life remains to keep the external world out, to maintain the impenetrable boundaries that can prevent them from experiencing meaningful relationships with others in adult life.

EMERGING SEXUALITY AND EMERGING MEMORIES

As I headed toward adolescence, my sexuality was troubled. To the extent that I was the property of my father, he would not allow me to be an autonomous female. Every effort I made was thwarted—I was reminded that I was an *object*, and not only an object, an object that he owned. Even in midlife, after years of psychoanalysis and psychotherapy, I still do not feel that I own myself. My attempts at suicide have largely been attempts to get him out of me.

There is a particular case in point, when I was approaching adolescence. By that time my mother was "well" (i.e., she was working successfully, but any mention of her illness was absolutely taboo), and I, aspiring to be like my older sister, asked if I could wear a delicate blue underwear set to bed. Seeing no harm in this, my mother agreed. An hour or two later my father came home and came to see me in my bedroom. I didn't want him to see me, and he noticed that I was holding the blankets right up close to my shoulders. Knowing that I was hiding something from him (insofar as his children were his property and, as such, boundaries didn't apply) made him both angry and excited. I struggled hard to hold on to the blanket, all the while my mother saying "leave her alone." However, insofar as my father's rule was absolute, answering to no one and nothing, he tore it off.

I couldn't have been more than 10 years old. There I was in my first (pretend) bra and panties. As the conclusion to his perverse invasion of my privacy—and my earliest identification with femininity—he looked at me with disgust, threw the blanket back, and left the room. I just wanted to feel feminine, grown-up.

In one area of my childhood I was very fortunate: I had a best friend. She lived across the street, and we were inseparable from the second grade to the time we were 18. I will love her always. I could never figure out why she would want to be my best friend; after all, she was pretty and, especially in the early days, popular. She later told me about her own abused childhood. We were inseparable, told each other *everything*, but never spoke of our own abuse at the time.

When we were 12 or 13, we would go out in the evening and wait for some guys (any guys) in a car or a van to pick us up. I had learned this routine from my sister. Once picked up, we would almost immediately make out with the guys. My best friend would go all the way, believing it would make her more desirable.

I still clearly remember the night she lost her virginity. I know because I was there. We were in the basement of a house, both making out with guys. She was 12 years old, and the guy was about 16. I heard her crying "you're hurting me, stop." I did nothing. I could have gone over there (she was about 20 feet away) and told the guy to get off her, but being quiet when terrible things were happening was deeply ingrained in me. I don't know if I would have been her rescuer or if she would have seen my actions as embarrassing and interfering, but I lay there beside this guy I despised—his hands on my body, joking about my best friend's cries.

Because she "went all the way" and I didn't, one night five guys in a van dropped me off and pretended to be dropping her off. But they swung around and sped away from our street. When I talked to her the next day, she told me that they had all had sex with her. Because our sexuality and our self-images were so disturbed, we had no idea she had been gang raped.

My parents were neglectful of my brother, my sister, and me. For example, I went to school with greasy hair and in the unwashed clothes that I wore every day; I didn't even know how to brush my teeth. I was therefore considered to be very ugly in elementary and (particularly) junior high school. Whereas the girls just kept their distance, the boys were outwardly and constantly cruel, calling me names like "mucus" and "pukas" (rhyming with my last name), spitting on me, calling me a slut, and so forth. The latter (slut) was ironic because I was actually inexperienced, but because I equated sex with approval, I dressed in a sexually provocative way. At the same time, my father was reinforcing how despicable I was (again, his rage). Conversely, when drunk (he was a lifelong alcoholic), he would make sexual advances toward me once I had drastically altered my appearance and become attractive.

On reflection I can understand why I was singled out as a scapegoat. It was grade 7, and kids had so much going on in their minds that they didn't understand that projecting it all onto someone else was not a good solution. I was already a garbage canister; my classmates easily understood that. They didn't stop at rhymes and name-calling; they would make guttural sounds of vomiting, or feign the repulsion of being in proximity to a dead and decaying body. Although I desperately needed help, I could not tell my parents. Indeed, by absorbing the emotional refuse they were inflicting, I was fulfilling my role as protector of the closed system.

Another example was my parents' preparation of lunches for class field trips. The "lunch" for me consisted of bag of chips and a Coke. On almost every field trip my teacher would single me out and tell me to bring my lunch to the front of the class. She would take out the chips and the can of Coke, making derogatory remarks that openly invited the students to make fun of me. I was mortified—but like just about everything else, I would just shut it out.

I became truant. Although I enjoyed learning and academic environments—in elementary school, I particularly loved reading and comprehension exercises, even though there was no place for homework in our family—my performance declined in school because the scapegoating became unbearable. One day my sister said, "just don't go to school." It presented me with a no-win situation: I could either keep attending school and learn nothing, as all my energies were used to block out my social environment, or I could not go to school and do very little.

I was a wretched sight, with my greasy hair, dirty clothes, and my mother's heavy makeup all over my face (I tried to cover what I despised). The school's way of dealing with my truancy was to call my parents at work. My father would rage violently at me. Rather than get me help, and not wanting to expose the family secrets (or perhaps better put, to have themselves and their actions exposed), my parents instead punished me for my ill behavior (and, moreover, for how much trouble I was causing them).

I was filled with emotions I couldn't understand and certainly couldn't articulate. I knew no way out except to rock in my bed and escape into fantasy, where none of this was happening. I rocked in my bed until I was a teenager and then switched to rocking in a sitting, legs-crossed position. I continued that practice for at least 20 years, eventually adding marijuana and alcohol to the mix to further facilitate the psychological escape.

But things began to change. By my late teens and early 20s, my appearance had altered. I was (to my disbelief) considered striking, even exotic; I had "grown into" my face. I wore expensive, figure-flattering Italian suits, styled my hair fashionably, and learned how to expertly apply makeup. On the outside, I appeared to have everything going for me, and I had fine-tuned my performance. Yet I still felt I was not part of society.

PERFORMANCE

Abused children learn at an early age how to act normal. Of course, as children, their performances are often flawed. As just indicated, in order to shut out the insanity around me, I used to rock incessantly to place myself into a dissociative state. My brother's response to the chaos was to follow *anything* that was regular—the street cleaner, garbage truck, paperboy, and so forth. He would also sweep the sidewalks and street of our entire block. More disturbingly, he was also cruel to animals—he would boil water on the stove and hold our cat up just over the boiling water to watch its terror and panic. My sister read comic books (and later books) incessantly.

Later in life, my brother's performance is now one of conformity and strict adherence to rules and regulations. My sister's performance was, like mine, initially quite successful—or so it appeared. She married young (at 21) and had two beautiful daughters. I recall her telling me that she married and had children because she wanted to have a "normal" family. However, to the extent that my sister was not parented, she did not know how to parent her children. She needed her children to give *her* love (the love she never had in her family of origin), though of course she found that they were incapable of that—that is, children need to *be loved*, not to fill a gap in a parent's life. Her eldest daughter, now a young adult, is struggling with a serious addiction that is threatening to destroy her young life. Undoubtedly out of a deep sense of guilt and helplessness, my sister now blames her daughter in the same way our father has always blamed us. It poses a very difficult situation: although I love my sister dearly and know all too well the environment she grew up in, I cannot deny my niece's right to be angry.

I never had children because I was deeply concerned that I would repeat the pattern of abuse. Instead of a family—which I would never be able to sustain—I ethically chose a career, a safe arena for performance.

My performance was and is *achievement*—both in what I do and how I look. It is important to reiterate that when one is raised in a closed family, in which one's role is to maintain the borders that keep out the gaze of society, existence is predicated on being *against* society. This does not imply antisocial behavior but, rather, that one is positioned at the outskirts, the borders and edges, of society. Individuals in this role are prone to forever experience themselves outsiders, looking in, as though through plate glass. Although they appear to fit it and may in fact may be very successful, it is a performance with an impossible goal: to perform so well that one doesn't have to perform anymore.

When I was in my 20s, working in a corporate environment, I would convince myself that if I could just get that promotion or that raise, I would no longer feel like dirt, and I would be happy. But after several such promotions and raises, and even after setting several precedents—for instance, being the first person (and a woman, which made it all the more scandalous) to move from teaching word processing to data processing—I still was not happy. This is not to say that there was *no* happiness in my life. While living in Vancouver, I was able to "come out" in my sexuality, and I became part of a community in which

I experienced some sense of belonging (and was no longer under the scrutiny of the male gaze). Yet I still experienced my belonging to the lesbian community as though looking through plate glass.

But I did not experience my first serious depression and my first hospitalization until I was 30 years old. Ironically, this was the event that created a strong bond with my mother.

HOSPITALIZATIONS

My father had once again disowned me—a pattern he repeated throughout my adult life—because I had asked about the early years of my life. At that time, I was living in my first "economical" apartment. I became not only depressed but also extremely paranoid. I sensed that there was something horrible, demonic, outside my bedroom door. And I felt as if I were falling into an abyss—a bottomless pit—in which the demonic entities I sensed outside my bedroom door would torture me for eternity as I fell. So I had to hold on with everything I had in order *not* to fall into the abyss. I literally felt that I was holding on with my fingernails. I turned on the radio to a Christian station (not the type of music I would normally listen to), hoping that it would somehow prevent these demonic forces from engulfing me.

Although I did not realize it at the time, many years of analysis (as well as intellectual and emotional maturation) have helped me realize that the abyss and the demonic entities—particularly my fear of falling without boundaries, endlessly tormented by terrifying forces—was the manifestation of a core fear that I have always known existed but that I did everything to avoid. This abyss represents the complete lack of structure, and indeed the chaos, of my early life. It would be simple to say that the terrifying forces were my parents, particularly my father, but the reality is more complex. I was afraid of *myself*, the contents of my being, and the consequences of their unraveling. My insides were either trash, internalized from an early age, or nothing at all.

Late that night, the fear became overwhelming. Because of my mother's psychiatric illness, I had always feared being admitted into a psychiatric ward. However, I managed to get myself to the hospital (I do not recall by what means) and was admitted.

My experience as a patient in this psychiatric ward and others was replete with disdain and dismissal from the staff. Indeed, by the time I left, I felt profoundly wounded. I felt that they had stripped me of the personhood for which I have struggled all my life. After a few days and in desperation, I went to the pay phone and called my mother. I was terrified to call because I had been disowned, and my father had told everyone in the family that *no one* was to be in contact with me. Yet my mother got on the next flight from Edmonton to

Vancouver. When she arrived, she went directly from the airport to the hospital. We hugged and cried; to this day I cannot recall this moment without tears welling in my eyes.

We proceeded to my room. Because I was menstruating during my stay, it was littered with used pads and other items that indicated that I was not "well adjusted" to my environment. She helped me clean up the room and then took out a hair band and pins. With the room clean (and myself now cleaned up), she then convinced the nurse to allow me to change out of my gown into my own clothes. Wearing my own clothes, accompanied by a "custodian" (my mother), showing a clean room and "positive attitude" (irony intended), I was discharged by the psychiatrist on duty. My mother and I calmly walked to the front door of the hospital and took a cab to my apartment.

Just a few days earlier, my apartment had been the site of demonic entities and a terrifying abyss. It goes without saying that I felt apprehension returning to it. But with my mother, I felt safe. And, most important, I felt truly and genuinely loved. Although my mother and I continued to have periodic difficulties, the bond created that day has never been broken. Losing my mother 3 years ago was by far the most painful loss of my life.

My apartment was in complete disarray. After making me a cup of tea (a Dutch tradition that can be very comforting), I rested in my bed while she cleaned up. When I woke, we went out for groceries, though at a certain point I started to experience the world as existentially strange. My mother stayed with me for the next several days, until I was no longer afraid. To help me back into my routine, she also came with me to my doctor to obtain a (very generic) note for my absence from my university (I was, by this point in my life, getting my undergraduate degree). Mostly, though, she just *stayed* with me so that I would feel safe. I cannot stress how important that was in my recovery. I was able to return to classes and return to my life. Granted, this was only the first of three major depressions that required hospitalization, but through it I established a truly meaningful relation with my mother. I was able to forgive her for the past, but she was never able to forgive herself. Plagued by guilt, she bought countless New Age and self-help books. Yet because my father looked down on them, she hid them in her dresser drawers.

This first hospitalization had stripped me of my very sense of personhood, and I swore I would never admit myself again. But during my third year as an undergraduate, I again became overwhelmed. I was physically ill, and because I was again disowned by my father, I had no real support. I did have a good friend at that time, but she had no way of understanding my illness. She brought me some groceries, but seeing me in that state frightened her. Maybe if she could have sat with me by my bed and held my hand, I would have been able to get through that episode without hospitalization. Living in a very small one-bedroom apartment on the ground floor of a house, I started experiencing paranoia once again. Although it was unnamable, I sensed something malevolent and demonic in the hall outside my bedroom door.

Again encountering the abyss and having nothing with which to support myself, I called the nearest hospital. This time, however, I deliberately admitted myself *not* as a psychiatric patient but as a "regular" patient. Before the staff determined that I needed to be in the psychiatric ward, I was put in a large, above-ground, well-lit, and courteously staffed ward. Yet despite my best efforts to "pass" as normal, I was wheeled into the basement, where the psychiatric ward was located. Being in a place where my existence was bound, I began to recover, but the staff (often treating psychiatric patients as naughty children) did little, if anything, to alleviate my condition.

This time, unfortunately, I didn't have the help of my mother, who was becoming progressively more controlled by my father. I returned to my apartment, demons gone, but still very weak and frightened.

My performance continued, and I earned not only an undergraduate degree but also a doctorate.

DEATH OF MY MOTHER AND THIRD HOSPITALIZATION

My third hospitalization occurred 3 years ago, after my mother's death. Although her death prompted the most profound grief I have ever experienced—and I still miss her terribly—my third hospitalization occurred as a result of the events following her death. It occurred, again, during one of the many times that I had been disowned by my father because I had asked about my early life. Remember that my life, and particularly my early life, was his property.

To set the stage: the last thing I had expected was a call from my father, but I woke up early to a message on my voice mail indicating that my mother was seriously ill and in the intensive care unit of the hospital. She was not expected to live; the doctor had asked my father whether she should be put on a ventilator if it became necessary. My father's response was the most human I have ever seen in him (though short-lived).

Hearing his message, I called immediately and took the next flight out to Edmonton. My brother picked me up at the airport, and we went straight to the hospital. During the ride, he told me what had happened. Because my mother had had a hysterectomy years earlier, her intestines had dropped. This in itself was not unusual or serious; the medical team inserted a routinely used device at her cervix. However, it caused an infection and had to be removed.

Following the removal, my mother left the hospital in good health; but shortly afterward she developed pain and started hemorrhaging. My father took her to the emergency ward of the hospital where the surgery had been performed. They told her it was "nothing" and simply gave her an injection for her pain. But after the medication wore off, the pain and hemorrhaging worsened. This time in an ambulance, she was transported to a highly reputable hospital and immediately admitted.

My brother arrived at the hospital shortly after my mother was admitted. She was in excruciating pain, delirious from the infection, with her eyes bulging. My mother begged her son to help her. He was powerless, however, in the wake of this medical emergency, and I know that this was undoubtedly the most difficult moment of his life.

I arrived 36 hours later to the news that she had significantly improved. I rushed to my mother, alarmed at her appearance yet so glad to be able to see her and hold her. And she clearly recognized me. In my father I saw a man I did not know: he was extraordinarily gentle and compassionate. He was strong for her and cried with us. At the end of the day, it was time for me to leave, and I promised my mother I would be back first thing in the morning.

Even though all the signs pointed to an improvement, I felt it in my heart that I would soon lose her. When I arrived at my parents' home, I went to my room and, without taking off my shoes or jacket, lay face down on the bed and sobbed uncontrollably. She had supported me years before at the time of my greatest need; my relationship with her was the deepest, most meaningful one in my life. I didn't know what I would do without her.

Finally I took a heavy sedative and cried myself to sleep. Still, I woke up at 5:00 A.M. I walked upstairs and found my father sitting in a chair in the kitchen, looking more lost and vulnerable than I had ever seen him. He hadn't slept all night. He told me that my mother had suffered a massive stroke that had destroyed all of her brain function. She was on a ventilator, which was the only thing keeping her alive. We called my brother and sister and a close cousin and his wife. As each of us arrived at the hospital, we were taken to a grieving room with a lock on the door. Following standard protocol, we would go in pairs to see my mother. Keeping my mother artificially alive at this point was only for the benefit of the family, to allow us to say good-bye and tell her we loved her. In the room, we would all break down, though it was made more painful by the fact that I was alone (my sister had her husband to hold her, my brother had his wife to hold him, and my close cousin also had his wife for support). Even if they "hugged" me, no one could *hold* me.

After we had all said our good-byes, we decided, as a family, to take her off the ventilator and allow her to die naturally—to release her. The nurses escorted us out of the room temporarily while they removed the ventilator and then allowed us back in. The doctor on staff gently told us that her vital signs would cease within about 25 minutes. We all sat with her while she died. Feeling the warmth go out of her arms, I felt truly alone.

After her death, we were all to meet at my parents' (or now my father's) home. My brother and his wife arrived immediately, but it took a few hours for my sister and her husband to get there. Soon after, my relatives arrived and out of kindness and support, stayed a week. But when they left, when the funeral was over and everything was supposed to move on, I felt completely lost and vulnerable, and, to my surprise, so did my father.

I returned to Toronto and finished the course I was teaching at the University of Toronto. Yet I was in a deep depression and could not teach the following term at York University. With the help of a very strong labor union and an invitation from a compassionate father I had only recently encountered (who was deeply depressed himself) to stay with him so that we could help each other through our grief, I took a leave of absence. The arrangement was that it could either be a term or a year, whatever I required.

But for me, Edmonton is rife with painful memories. Revisiting my home city as an adult, during holidays, has always given me a sense of suffocation. After subletting my apartment in Toronto, I began my (disastrous) stay in Edmonton.

The first thing I did when I arrived was to unpack and show my father my degrees. It wasn't necessary to bring them, but I still felt a child's need for parental approval. Rather than say a few kind words, however, he cast a disparaging look and remarked on how small they were.

In all fairness, though, other than that incident, my father was as sensitive as I'd ever seen him during the first 2 or 3 weeks. For the first time in his life, he felt vulnerable; he *needed* others. Yet he was not clear in his mind—this was particularly evident when he would drive. In a numbing daze he almost crashed into other cars, missing traffic signals and other cues. I would have to remind him (gently) of a red light or an oncoming vehicle. He would even stray from the lane, which was brightly painted in yellow. Even though I felt enormous grief over the loss of my mother, I also felt a sense of purpose while helping my father.

Every day we would sit at the kitchen table or in the living room and talk about her. The recollections were his, or related directly to his relationship with my mother; there was little room for my relationship with her. But our conversations did, for that short time, create a fragile bond between us.

Within a month, however, he had "gotten over" my mother. On the other hand, I was still deeply in grief but with no outlet or solace. I was supposed to move on with my life, but I wasn't ready.

My father believed strongly in moving on, in putting the past into the past. I saw then how he (psychologically) had put the chaos of his early years behind him. At the same time, like his father before him, he was experiencing a serious hardening of the arteries, resulting in deterioration of memory and the ability for rational thought.

Within a few weeks, he burst into the TV room demanding to know why I was there. He had forgotten that he had invited me, and it was only through checking sent e-mails that he could be convinced. It had become evident that he did not want me there. He would have other outbursts—for instance, he gave me *his* version of the "golden rule": "He who has the gold rules." In other words, *he* was the one with the gold (money), and because I didn't have money, I must cater to him.

At this point, still deeply in grief over the loss of my mother and experiencing the resurgence of my father's typical ways, I became severely depressed. I was alone and frightened—in fact, I've always been frightened of my father; his rage is too much for my sensitive personality. I was in Edmonton, a city that I had to escape in order to live, and in the basement of my father's house. But given the arrangement I had with York, the earliest I could return was in the winter term, still several months off.

Also, because I was on an extended stay in Edmonton, rather than receiving my medications on a weekly basis, I received a bulk amount—the only way it could be handled through the pharmacy. This gave me an opportunity.

Unaware that Xanax (unlike other medications, such as barbiturates), even taken in extremely large amounts, is not lethal, I took approximately 100 mg, fully expecting to die peacefully. Instead, I heard my father knocking loudly on the door, and then paramedics rushing me to the hospital.

When I returned from the hospital, my father told me that my brother had said he (my father) should never forgive me for trying to commit suicide *in his house*. Apparently committing suicide was one thing, but desecrating my father's house was quite another. Whether my brother actually felt this way is questionable, but it does speak to his need for my father's approval. In the aftermath of the death of my mother, it was apparent that there was no love left in my family. I did have a relationship with my sister while I was there, but I haven't been able to contact her since. It may be that she simply doesn't receive my messages.

If I had been depressed before, I was far more depressed after my suicide attempt had failed. I had truly *wanted* to die. After 4 weeks of hospitalization in Edmonton, I returned to my father's home. My weekly visits to the psychiatrist who treated me helped me buttress myself against a constant onslaught of underhanded and hurtful remarks from my father. In early December, my father approached me, indicating that he wanted to "buy me out." In other words, he realized that I could return to teaching at York in the winter term, but there would be expenses. He told me to come up with a list of my expenses (minimal, at best) and present it to him.

Because I needed to leave, I did as he instructed. The cheapest flights were in early December, before Christmas. Of course, when relatives asked why I wasn't staying for the holiday, I couldn't reveal that it was so that my father could save some money on a plane ticket. I returned to teaching at York during the winter term and, with that, returned to a life of "performance normality." In other words, I was again able to perform to the extent that it appeared natural.

But I was deeply unhappy and isolated in my life. The feeling has let go only intermittently in the ensuing years.

DISORDERS OF THE MIND—AND BODY

In my longer work, I address the difference between depression that is linked to situational issues, traumatic events, and life stressors and what could be called "terminal depression"—a form that is so deeply imprinted on the mind and brain that it can be progressive and permanent. Unlike diseases such as cancer and AIDS that *directly* kill the body, terminal depression *indirectly* kills the body by invoking a drive to suicide. Intervention at this point is, in my mind, akin to keeping a person alive using a ventilator.

Furthermore, recent research on the neurobiological consequences of abusive experiences during childhood points to the lasting biological, as well as psychological, sequelae of severe trauma.[2] Too often, there is a dualism, a "binary," between conditions that arise from the body and those that appear to relate to the spirit or the mind, when in fact there are multiple, simultaneous consequences of abuse. I hold that just as a person may have been painfully injured in an accident, the person who was abused as a child was also painfully injured through no fault of his or her own. How to come up with views that transcend the mind-body split with respect to understanding mental disorder and consequences of abuse is a huge concern. Yet it is essential that the general public increasingly understand that depression or mental illness is not a simple matter of "snapping out of it" or of personal weakness. If understanding can emerge that an emotional or mental illness can be correlated to the *body* (such that illness is understood *as illness*), the binary may be progressively eroded.

The true difficulty lies in attempting to communicate the profound existential loneliness, the loneliness of not being able to traverse the *qualitative distance* that separates the depressed person from "reality." Although I have made every attempt to clearly elucidate the dynamics of the closed family and the pain of abuse and neglect, if the reader has not experienced this himself or herself, there is little in the way of a common point of reference. Eroding the distance between observer and sufferer—and between mind and body—is the journey in front of us, bound to be a long and difficult one.

CONCLUSION

I realize that in writing this work, I have broken my family taboo of silence. Yet insofar as victims of abuse and neglect "do their duty" by remaining silent and, in many cases, passing the dynamics on to another generation without understanding these dynamics themselves, the cycle will continue, with disastrous implications. Having said this, as I indicated at the start, I believe that my parents were themselves psychologically if not physically abused. In the case of my mother, I know that this was the case. Still, at that time, one didn't question such things. I was caught in the crossfire of that intergenerational abuse.

As a society, we are now beginning to take seriously the implications of abuse. It is my hope that close analysis of the dynamics that often seem to occur so naturally in families in which intergenerational abuse occurs will result in self-reflection—and that such self-reflection can help to stop the repetition of those very dynamics. Stigma of mental illness is strong, and particularly so when abuse histories are present, as these serve to propel the victim to cover for the parent and deny the reality of the experience. Whether words can bridge the gap and erode the binary—the "split" both within oneself and between those who have and have not suffered from abuse—is the key question.

NOTES

1. Kafka, F. Franz Kafka's letter to his father. http://www.kafka-franz.com/KAFKA-letter.htm

2. See Cicchetti, D., & Valentino, K. (2006). An ecological-transactional perspective on child maltreatment: Failure of the average expectable environment and its influence on child development. In D. Cicchetti & D. J. Cohen (Eds.), *Developmental psychopathology: Vol. 3. Risk, disorder, and adaptation* (pp. 129–201). New York: Wiley.

14   The Legacy of Loss: Depression As a Family Affair

Carolyn Zahn-Waxler

My mother suffered from mood and anxiety disorders for most her life. My father experienced anxiety disorders, depression, and eventually alcoholism. This chapter is about the childhoods of my parents, about life in my family while my sister and I were growing up, and about the implications of that upbringing for my own life as the eldest daughter of a depressed mother. The severity of her depressions limited her ability to care for us and to lead the life she desired. My father's problems seemed minor in comparison because he held a good job, was active in the community, and cared for us when our mother could not. However, his difficulties also had repercussions.

Both my parents lost their mothers early in life. My mother's mother died the day after having given birth to her; my father's mother died from tuberculosis when he was 2. His father burned to death in bed in an alcoholic stupor from a dropped cigarette. These early losses set the stage for my parents' own relationship and the kinds of parents they would become. Early loss and stress are risk factors for depression, facts poignantly played out in my parents' lives.

Depression runs in families. Tracing my family history reveals abundant evidence of alcoholism, as well as mood and anxiety disorders on both sides. Assortative mating also occurred: many relatives selected mates with psychological difficulties, perpetuating problems across generations. Although transmission of depression is partly genetic, the environment plays a powerful role in emotional problems that are passed down to the next generation. Having grown up in such an environment, I well know the impact of severe parental depression on the developing child.

MOTHER'S CHILDHOOD AND ADOLESCENCE

The Formative Years: An Idealized Life With Indulgent Aunts

My maternal grandmother, Ema Willman Johnson, died from childbirth complications in my home town of Sturgeon Bay, Wisconsin. She had given birth to my mother, Emma Jean Johnson, the previous day. Emma Jean thus grew up knowing she was the immediate cause of her mother's death. This legacy of loss and guilt led to a lifelong struggle with depression.

Before going to the hospital for delivery, Ema told her husband Earl that if anything happened to her, she wanted the child to be raised by her sisters. Earl had not seriously envisioned this possibility and agreed. As a single working man, he could not care for his daughter, nor did he have relatives who could step in. But he could, and did, provide financial support.

For her first 5 years three maternal aunts doted on Emma Jean. Aunt Jennie was the primary caregiver and assumed that the child would always be with her. Given wide latitude to do and say as she wished, Emma Jean was a free spirit. In early photographs she appears confident and poised to embrace life. She was beautiful, with a cherubic appearance that belied a mischievous, sometimes stubborn nature.

A few years later Earl started to court a schoolteacher from Ohio, Katharine Kinsey. Throughout the courtship they wrote long letters. Now that he planned to remarry, he wanted his young daughter Emma Jean to be part of the new family. Initially, he had been grateful to Jennie for the care she provided, appreciating her love and devotion to his child. He described his daughter as a very loving youngster; she took after her mother in being affectionate *and* after him in being impudent, saucy, loud, and boisterous. Also like him, she was tender-hearted and sensitive. His daughter enchanted him, and he often wrote about his loneliness for her.

Emma Jean perceptively pegged her indulgent aunt as a pushover, once telling her father that "when Aunt Jennie says *no* she means *yes.*" From an early age my mother had learned that she could get what she wanted if she persisted. Her unwillingness to mind caused her father some consternation, yet he also admired my mother's spark and spunk. Earl had clear ideas about how his daughter should be raised once she was with him and her stepmother. She would be required to mind and obey, with strict discipline. She needed a firm hand that included spankings and clear verbal reprimands. He once said "she will be some girl to get to walk turkey" (stay on the straight and narrow; follow the rules). He also warned that "she dies hard," a harbinger of the anger and opposition to come.

Even as Earl and Katharine made their wedding plans, he could not bring himself to tell Jennie or his daughter about the impending marriage. He did not like to deal with conflict, so he avoided the topic. He became even more concerned about his daughter's upbringing. There was little discipline or structure and he lived too far away to have any influence. Jennie and Emma Jean moved around a lot, living with several different relatives until Jennie settled in to live with her sisters. Earl began to make more negative comments about the aunts, especially Jennie. He emphasized the differences in social class and their lack of ambition, which he felt would hold his daughter back. In pictures Jennie appears somber, perhaps even depressed. She had lost her mother at an early age, raised her sisters, recently lost a sister, and been divorced by her husband.

Earl's anger toward Jennie was mixed with ambivalence because of Jennie's clear love for his daughter. He talked about how wrenching the separation would be for them. He decided to wait a while after the marriage because they would need some time together to get used to the idea. Jennie did her best, given that she had been little more than a child herself when she had assumed the care of her younger sisters. But she fell short in my grandfather's eyes, as he envisioned a more cultured, educated upbringing for his daughter. His fiancée was the daughter of a Moravian minister, from a refined family that valued education, social responsibility, and community involvement. She would be better able to instill appropriate values and behaviors in his young, unruly daughter.

Joining a New Family: Rocky Roads Ahead

Earl's admiration for his daughter's loving *and* forthright personality cooled after he remarried and the realities of their new life together set in. Earl and Katharine never had a honeymoon. They married in Ohio and almost immediately left for Wisconsin, spending just one night in Chicago, before picking up Emma Jean the following day. He did not heed his own advice about the need for a gradual transition between the two homes. Jennie had repeatedly reassured Emma Jean that she would always be with her. Once Emma Jean went to live with her new family, she was not permitted to see the aunts for some time.

My mother was oppositional from the start. Before the wedding, when Katharine told her to do something, she simply refused, saying "You can't tell me what to do. You're not my mother yet!" This opposition and defiance continued, as reflected both in letters and recollections of family members. Earl and Katharine had three children together: two sons were born early in their marriage and later a daughter. Katharine created cultural and educational activities and tried to provide a pleasant home environment for Emma Jean. But she was upset by the child's oppositional nature and curiosity. The daughter's interest in her parents led her to follow them around. Unfortunately, they experienced this as an interruption of their privacy and reprimanded her for wanting to be near them. Katharine's distress increased once she became pregnant and then had an infant to tend. Katharine's mother warned her to keep Emma Jean away from the baby because she might eventually teach him naughty tricks. With the birth of a second son, family life became even more complicated. He had serious medical problems that required a great deal of care and attention from his mother.

Emma Jean had already developed a reputation as a problem child. Children react to negative labels and reactions, which can accentuate their problems. Katharine surely must have felt a sense of failure in getting this loud, stubborn girl to mind. As a schoolteacher she would have maintained control over entire classrooms of children. She also knew her husband believed child rearing was the wife's responsibility and that he wanted a well-disciplined daughter. Katharine's fatigue was evident in letters to her mother, in which she described her household chores and problems with Emma Jean. Once Katharine stated that nothing she did seemed to meet with her mother's approval. This theme of daughters' failing to please their mothers was to echo through the generations. When mothers' own needs are unmet, they may express disapproval toward their daughters, which, in turn, can be experienced as a lack of love.

Emma Jean's conflicts with her stepmother escalated during this time. Psychologists who study the development of rebellious behavior in childhood describe "coercive cycles" whereby the child's defiance and the parent's harsh punishment fuel each other and thus entrench the problem behaviors over time. It was said that Emma Jean made family life miserable, but she was miserable, as well. Her father called her a "street angel" because she behaved perfectly outside the home but made family life hell. In fact, she was well behaved in school (based on report cards) and had many friends. The more distant her father became, the more rejected she felt and the harder she tried to gain his attention.

Overall, she remained oppositional, confrontational, and rejecting, a child who did not appear to appreciate what they had to offer. But she viewed herself as caring, sensitive, and misunderstood and her stepmother as unloving. She no longer had the aunts to hug and kiss her, to provide the physical comfort and warmth she craved. The early trauma of an abrupt, unexplained move into a totally different family environment undoubtedly affected her sense of stability and ability to trust others. There is a reason that there are so many stories and fairy tales about the travails of stepchildren. Fairy tales often have happy endings, and my mother sought these out in her own life. When they failed to materialize, she retreated into the realm of imagination and fantasy.

Literature provided a safe way to create an idealistic, alternative world. She would remain immersed in literature, film, and theater for the rest of her life; boundaries between these worlds and everyday life were blurred. She moved back and forth with an ease that suggested she was not always clear as to where she lived.

Mother enjoyed life outside the family home. She was beautiful, popular, and fun-loving and liked many of her classes. At home, no one wanted to sit next to her at mealtime. She must have been a dominating presence, as she talked a lot, disrupting family meals. Given her perceptiveness, it is likely that she was aware of the differential treatment and felt marginalized, possibly stigmatized.

Early Seeds of Depression: Childhood Mental Illness in a Difficult Environment

When she was an adult, my mother's preoccupations with the past assumed an enormity that would govern her life. The main theme was the rejection that had replaced the unconditional love of her aunts. Depressed adults frequently recall feeling unloved and experiencing harsh punishment. Doubtless, her childhood was unhappy, both because of difficulties she brought to the situation and because of the harshness and rejection she experienced in her new home.

During the 1920s and 1930s the concept of childhood mental illness barely existed, and no real treatment programs were in place. Emma Jean may have had attention deficit disorder, possibly with hyperactivity. She was impulsive, had difficulty paying attention, talked excessively, and often interrupted or intruded on others. Her hyperactive mouth persisted throughout her life. She did not show these characteristics in school, but they were evident in interpersonal relationships, especially with her family. In addition, she would definitely have been diagnosed with oppositional defiant disorder. This is a recurrent pattern of negativistic, defiant, disobedient, and hostile behavior toward authority figures. Hers lasted throughout her childhood. She may also have had a learning disability. Although she excelled in speech, language, and the arts, she fared poorly in the sciences.

Her overt symptoms consisted mainly of what we would now call externalizing problems—behaviors that are distressing to others. Childhood depression sometimes appears as irritable, cranky, and obnoxious behavior. Her parents could not have known of her internalized distress (i.e., anxieties and depressed mood) and the possible beginnings of a mood disorder that remained under wraps until years later. Despite her seeming confidence, Emma Jean undoubtedly felt frightened, abandoned, and insecure.

MARRIAGE

The Man She Married

Mother was just 19 years old when she married my father, who was 11 years her senior. He was college educated (the first in his family) and held a stable job at the Bank of Sturgeon Bay as the comptroller. He later became one of the vice presidents. He had come from poor circumstances and had been raised by relatives. His mother's sister, Aunt Minnie, was his primary caregiver after his mother died, but other aunts also were around a lot. They lived on farms. My father worked in the fields with the farmhands from the age of 6 or so. Women served the lunches, which included beer, and the workers would say, "Give little

Carlie a beer." He also had access to alcohol in a bar owned by one of his relatives. He felt well treated by his relatives and remained close to them as an
adult.

My mother saw my father's relatives as common country folk whose lack of
education, coarse manners, and heavy drinking precluded meaningful conversations. Several relatives committed suicide, including a great-aunt who hanged
herself in the closet and two of my father's male cousins, who shot themselves.
His Aunt Minnie was a gentle person, married to an alcoholic, and she surely
suffered from depression. I remember her sad face and voice even well before
her son's suicide. This son's depression had psychotic features that made Mother
nervous when he visited. He'd stare out the picture window in the living room
at a clump of three birch trees in the neighbor's yard. Instead of trees, he saw
the Trinity—Father, Son, and Holy Ghost were present for him, just across the
street.

Good Times and Harbingers of Bad Times

My parents knew about each other's early histories and at first it was a common bond: two souls orphaned at an early age and raised by maternal aunts. It is
doubtful that either of them had any inkling of how their fractured backgrounds
would come to haunt their relationship. After high school Mother worked for a
year at a women's clothing store and did some modeling. She was the only one
in her family who did not attend college. Whereas she perceived this as discrimination, it also probably reflected the hard financial times of that period. Her
brothers went to college on the G. I. Bill after World War II, and more resources
were available when her sister graduated from high school. All her life, mother
harbored fantasies of a different, better life elsewhere had she gone to college.

She did not foresee marriage as another arena of conflict and control in
which her rebellious nature would face new obstacles. In her marriage ceremony she had the vow of obedience removed—she promised to love and honor,
but not to obey. In refusing to make this vow to her husband, she also may have
been thumbing her nose at her parents, for whom obedience had been such an
important child-rearing goal. She was stunning in her lovely gown and full train
of delicate lace and silk, her face relaxed and serene. Life seemed full of promise
then, but the radiance was to become replaced with regret.

In the beginning she and my father were kindred spirits, which made her
later animosity toward him all the more tragic. Photographs reveal intimacy and
ease as she links her arm in his. Both loved theater, films, music, books, bridge,
dancing, and spending time with friends. They were a striking couple. She was
lovely; he was tall and handsome. In addition to their similar backgrounds (having lost their mothers early in life), they both rebelled against their religious

upbringing, which they viewed as conservative, patriarchal, and authoritarian. They sought a religion that emphasized a loving, compassionate deity and the inherent worth and dignity of human life. They found a spiritual home in the First Congregational Church, which played an important role in our lives.

When Opposites Attract

Their temperaments began to clash as the stresses of marriage and children started to take a toll. They exemplified the problems that can result when opposites attract. Personality differences can and do enhance relationships and marriages, allowing each partner to bring unique qualities and abilities to the relationship, but problems arise when personality traits are in extreme opposition—like trying to mix oil and water. Although oil and water do not mix, people do, often with chaotic and catastrophic consequences.

Our father was compulsive, exacting, and a perfectionist. Mother was fun-loving and flamboyant, with a flair for the dramatic; she appeared to be as carefree as he was careful. One theory is that people with these opposite personality types initially attract each other because each senses in the other qualities that they lack. He would serve as a regulating, stabilizing force for her; she would help him become more easygoing. But the "merging" of these different personalities eventually proved lethal to their relationship. Over time, they began to rub each other the wrong way, as each stirred up unresolved problems in the other.

Although they were both of Northern European heritage, my mother began to see them as vastly different in terms of their ethnicity. His family on both sides had emigrated from Germany in the mid-1800s. My mother's paternal ancestors, with whom she identified most strongly, had emigrated around the same time from Norway and Sweden. She viewed Scandinavians as warm, fun loving, expressive, and creative, valuing independence and freedom; in contrast, Germans were cold, rigid, and controlling, preferring conformity and restriction. She used these contrasts as a way to frame what would eventually become irreconcilable differences.

THE NEXT GENERATION

Early Motherhood

With my birth, mother's life story and mine became intertwined. Her gradual descent into depression probably began shortly after my birth. My sister was born 4 years later. Motherhood agreed with our mother for a while, but she was tired and often slept late. I got my own breakfast and then probably played inside or read or pretended to read. I was an early reader, and I also memorized stories and repeated them verbatim for friends and relatives. For several years she took good care of me in many respects and was an animated presence. She sang lullabies at bedtime. I can still conjure the sweet words, the tender sound of her voice, and the good-night kisses that punctuated the melody.

She also taught us a prayer to say each night, beginning with "Now I lay me down to sleep, I pray the Lord my soul to keep." She used an alternative ending because the more common one—"If I should die before I wake, I pray the Lord my soul to take"—was too morbid. Her version ended with the following: "Guard me through the starry night and wake me in the morning bright." Here, darkness was bright and lovely and not to be feared; waking to the light and cheer of day reflected optimism about life. But her life was increasingly interspersed with periods of sadness and despair. She often reminded us not to use

The author with her mother—the early years (ca. 1943)

the gloomy ending to the prayer, which of course made us all the more likely to ponder it.

She liked to take me to the movies and carefully prepared me for tragic events (my father did the same). The unintended consequence of such protection was that I became primed for sadness. I was a sensitive child, and her actions only enhanced that sensitivity. For instance, before seeing *Bambi*, she explained that Bambi's mother would be killed by a hunter and Bambi would be alone. A lump formed in my throat. I burst into tears in the theater before anything had happened and cried throughout the film. I was quite young when she also took me to adult films such as *All About Eve* and *The Snake Pit* (about a woman in a mental institution with unspeakable living conditions). I became hooked early on films about troubled adult relationships, tragedy, and psychological problems.

Letters between my mother and my uncles, near the end of World War II (when my sister was born), reveal that she perceived her life as good for the most part. She spoke of celebrating the end of the war; playing poker, winning on some occasions and "losing her ass" on others; teaching her stepmother how to play cards so they would have enough players; becoming more domestic as seen by other people; having a houseful of company; and enjoying raising her younger daughter, who was funny (in contrast to me, the more serious older sister). She also said jokingly, however, that "your war is over now and mine will just go on," describing child rearing (and possibly her marriage) as an ongoing battle. She first sought medical help for her fatigue around that time.

My sister Barbara and I did not play together a lot as children, given our differences in age, personalities, and interests. Mine were very feminine, whereas hers were masculine. Barbara was mischievous, and I was a good girl. Mother often tolerated (and even enjoyed) Barbara's naughty behavior; she saw a kindred spirit in Barb's rebellious activities. I was jealous of their close, easy relationship and tried to excel in ways that did not require daring and physical prowess.

Despite my mother's amusement at my sister's antics, raising two children must have created additional stresses, and she was probably relieved when I started kindergarten. She continued to sleep late. I'd arrive at school unkempt and poorly groomed unless a neighbor invited me in to comb the tangles out of my hair.

Kindergarten created a new world of learning and opportunities. Standardized tests confirmed what my parents suspected, that I was quite bright. Both parents were proud, but my mother's feelings became ambivalent, as the excessive praise and attention from my father made her jealous. Only later did I realize how much pressure I had felt from my father to achieve. He kept my report cards in a safe deposit box in the bank vault. My identity quickly became linked to my academic excellence: by early grade school my father told me I would go to college, specifically the University of Wisconsin in Madison.

As a child I played by the rules, even when rules were not explicitly stated. I somehow sensed what they were and how to behave. Both parents were determined to use nonauthoritarian child-rearing approaches. Rules that existed were in the form of values regarding, at least in principle, respect for all life (animals, too, as our pets were loved and well cared for). But there was a lack of structure that sometimes left feelings of uncertainty. We received few spankings, although I recall one occasion when my mother spanked me; I ran upstairs crying, and my father comforted me by reading to me. There undoubtedly were occasions that called for discipline, and this was left to my mother. My father could not bear to hurt my sister or me, and this put them at odds with each other. Sensitive men have their virtues, but firm parenting is not always one of them.

When my sister and I were in grade school we spent the summers in a rustic, primitive cottage on Lake Michigan. It was a place of pristine beauty where life was often carefree. We roamed the beaches and woods, played, and swam in the icy cold lake water. Our friends from town came to stay for the weekend, and there were other friends a little way down the beach. My sister and I both recall these times as happy, almost idyllic. The families were known as "the Lake Crowd," mostly affluent and prominent townspeople who owned their summer homes rather than renting, as we did. Mother was highly sensitive to the difference between owners and renters. The women did not share her intellectual and cultural passions, but she respected them and enjoyed playing bridge and socializing. She had many friends her age in town with interests similar to hers.

She often railed against what she saw as the narrow-mindedness of the townspeople, the conservative politics, the bigotry, and the gossip. Within our home both our mother and father espoused humanitarian and egalitarian world-views. My sister and I felt a fierce loyalty to our parents, who viewed themselves as outside the mainstream. Both parents showed great compassion for outsiders (Indians, Jews, blacks, the physically disabled, the mentally ill). I sometimes wondered whether their values and belief systems stemmed from feeling different from others when they were growing up.

Our parents acted in a community theater when we were young. Old photos reveal their pleasure in these activities. Mother often assumed a theatrical presence around the house. Dressed in black and wearing velvet toreador pants, she spoke as if on stage, smoking Pall Mall cigarettes with a long cigarette holder. She took on a larger-than-life persona, which sometimes had a disturbing quality as she assumed personalities of different characters. She also acted victimized, as the child to be pitied for her difficult childhood or, later, for her suffering as an adult. By blurring reality and placing her life on stage, along with the fictional characters, her illness also sometimes seem less genuine. We would think "she's putting on an act" or "here comes another show." She became fascinated with

the Theatre of the Absurd, and at times it felt as though the themes of alienation and meaninglessness of this genre were reflected in our own family life.

Father's Emotional Problems

Even before our mother's anxiety and depression became part of family life, our
father suffered from debilitating anxiety. Overwhelmed with the responsibility
of supporting a wife and family, he experienced crippling attacks and feared
imminent death. He worried about what would happen to his family if he died.
He had been diagnosed with high blood pressure (which was effectively treated
with medication) and a heart murmur in college. Though these symptoms
were not life threatening, he continued to ruminate about them. The doctors
could not detect any further physical health problems, and he was referred to
a psychiatrist in Milwaukee, nearly 3 hours away. Through psychotherapy of
relatively brief duration, he overcame his problems enough to remain the sole
breadwinner of the family, often holding down several jobs, joining organizations, and assuming leadership roles in the community. However, his residual
chronic worries, his obsessive style, and his unhappy marriage to my mother
eventually led to alcoholism and depression.

The aunts who raised my father were nervous women who often engaged
in communal worry. As a boy my father had hung around them at the kitchen
table, listening to stories of family ailments and problems. He sometimes sat
under the table and looked up their dresses while listening to tales of worry
and woe. I don't know why he told us that he peeked up their skirts. Both parents often crossed parent-child boundaries in conversations with us. He always
described his upbringing in glowing terms, but his specific memories painted
a different picture. A tornado had gone through the area when he was young,
terrifying his entire family. My father repeatedly talked about his aunts' worries
and the trauma of the tornado for the rest of his life. By adulthood, he would
have met criteria for generalized anxiety disorder, obsessive-compulsive disorder, panic disorder, and agoraphobia.

When we went on car trips, about halfway to the destination my father
would start to wonder whether he had turned off the stove burners or the water
faucet. We either had to return to find out or have a labored discussion (often
turning into a fight) to persuade him that someone had checked. Both parents
smoked a lot, and when the car windows were shut, I would feel faint and nauseated. My father was often meek and soft-spoken (except when arguing with
mother), but he was a hostile driver. He sped on the country roads, recklessly
passing other cars, and we narrowly escaped several potentially fatal accidents.
The more my mother told him to slow down, the faster he would drive. My

sister and I felt helpless and anxious. For decades I feared car trips, both as a driver and as a passenger.

Mother's Gradual Descent Into Depression

Mother began to have more depressive episodes while I was in grade school. Initially, she showed signs of fatigue, sleeping late and often fitfully. She lost weight and had little appetite. She still did things with friends, but lack of energy made it more difficult, and she showed less interest in activities she typically enjoyed. It would not take too long to diagnose and treat her problems as depression today, but this was not the case back then. When the physicians could find nothing wrong, she began to see specialists in larger cities, such as Green Bay, an hour away. Still, no cause could be found. She was sensitive to the reactions of others, some of whom may have thought she was malingering.

It is not uncommon for people to think that symptoms without identifiable causes are feigned, that responsibilities are willfully abdicated, and that problems will disappear if the person just tries harder. Mother's theatrical presence may have led some to think that she overdid her distress. She was unhappy more and more of the time. On the outside she appeared to have it all. She was a lovely woman with a handsome husband who had a good job. She used an interior decorator and had a cleaning woman, and a seamstress would come to the house to make clothing. Often babysitters came in so that she could attend cultural events, bridge clubs, book clubs, church activities, or anything else she wanted to do. My parents often went to parties. Yet something was missing, and it affected her health.

Many mysterious and ominous diseases were considered, and we were shielded from none of them. Sleeping sickness was quickly ruled out because it occurs only in Africa. Meningitis was mentioned as a possibility. Mother had a low platelet count, a symptom that could result from many different conditions, some of which are life threatening. Because she bruised easily, the doctors thought she might have idiopathic thrombocytopenic purpura, which was sometimes treated by removing the spleen. My sister recalls being terrified when mother told her about this possibility. Would she be cured? Would she live but become incapacitated? Or would she die? This is one of bits of medical information she shared with us that would have been better kept to herself.

Another possible diagnosis, of pernicious anemia, was perhaps the most frightening. A chronic illness caused by impaired absorption of vitamin B-12, it is probably an autoimmune disorder with a genetic predisposition. At that time there was no known form of treatment, and the disease was fatal. The threat of her early demise therefore hovered over us for many years. We thought that she could bleed to death at any time. She clung to slivers of possibilities of illnesses that might explain just how wretched she felt. She was terribly frustrated that no one could tell her what was wrong; she thought that others, including my father, did not believe her. Such sayings as "all in your mind (or head)" were common misconceptions then and even now. I believe that she had many depressive episodes during this time, along with spontaneous remissions that allowed her to function more normally. This would explain why she could sometimes be rejecting and critical but pleasant and fun on other occasions, even as she eventually became incapacitated.

Life With My Father

Almost imperceptibly, our father became both father and mother, doing more of the house care and child care. A nurturing person, he enjoyed this role. He began to experience more satisfaction in his relationships with his children (particularly me) than with his wife, which my mother resented. Later I would become his social companion at events ordinarily attended by spouses. Mother probably felt excluded from aspects of family life, but she did not have the physical stamina to do things with us. Late in life she began to write poetry. In one transparent poem, a man rushes into a hospital room and brushes by his wife, who has just given birth, to take his "creation" (a firstborn daughter) into his arms.

Our father loved nature and took us into the countryside each spring to a farm to see the newborn lambs and pick sweet-scented wildflowers. Because Barbara was a tomboy, he did things with her that fathers tend to do with sons (fishing, golf, and other rigorous outdoor activities). He and I shared several common interests and personality characteristics, including a tendency toward perfectionism and related "Germanic" traits that mother disliked. I liked working with numbers, which sat well with him as a banker. As mother's medical costs increased—and to support an affluent lifestyle—he had to work other jobs. He did bookkeeping for several businesses, some of which were out of town. I would travel with him and spend time at these different workplaces. I also helped with the book work and billing and had my own little "office" area in the bedroom.

Although loving and accepting, he was overprotective, and his special attentions sometimes discomforted me. As a substitute, in part, for the lack of his wife's affection, boundaries were crossed, not in an overtly sexually abusive manner but in a way that communicated unfulfilled needs. His hugs, kisses, and squeezes sometimes went on for too long and provoked my unease. His worries and pessimism continued. This made my mother angry: as ill as she became, she did not give up hope for a cure that would return her to a fuller life. From each of our parents, but for different reasons, we learned that life was hard.

My sister and I had lots to do to distract ourselves. There was a playhouse in the large backyard, complete with child-size furniture and a front porch. We spent a lot of time playing there with friends. We roamed the town and traveled to nearby lakes, beaches, and countryside on our bicycles. It was safe to do that then. There were many other activities. I enjoyed organizing girls' clubs and being in Brownies and Girl Scouts. I liked to sing and dance and had many hobbies, such as baking, knitting, embroidery, hopscotch, and jacks. I also collected stamps and helped my father in the garden.

Childhood Personality

My personality may have made me likely both to internalize my parents' distress and to develop ultimately beneficial ways of coping. I have already noted my serious, sensitive nature. I was shy in unfamiliar situations but fun loving in more familiar settings. In all, I experienced a broad range and intensity of emotions. There were times I felt disappointed, anxious, and sad, more than circumstances warranted. But I could also be very silly and exuberant, and I enjoyed much of childhood. I was a leader in school and enjoyed performing there, winning spelling bees, diagramming sentences, solving math problems at the blackboard, and playing the lead in class plays. I was both confident and sensitive, but over time this confidence diminished, and my sensitivity to distress increased.

I reacted strongly to others' negative emotions and tense situations: my chest tightened, and I'd feel and hear my heart pounding rapidly, making me even more anxious and breathless. When I was a little older I liked to read an encyclopedia called the *Book of Knowledge* and a book called *You and Heredity*. I learned a lot, but some information was not beneficial. I believed I was afflicted with different fatal diseases and dwelt on the details of the death experience. The thought was unbearable, and I'd burst into tears. These ruminative episodes came and went; they reflected, I believe, early depressive feelings. This may have been my intrinsic nature, but it was also likely nurtured by exposure to my father's morbid, pessimistic thoughts and my mother's developing depression.

I was reflective and a perceptive observer of others' emotions and circumstances. But I also sometimes mistook others' emotions, reading more than was there. If someone didn't smile, especially an authority figure, I thought I'd made them mad. Once in high school I was visiting a friend; her mother was laughing and smiling, and I thought she must be faking it (like my own mother). If laughter and chatter in large groups became too loud, it felt ominous; an overwhelming cacophony of sounds would disorient me, make my heart race, and force my retreat. I came to dislike large group settings.

ADOLESCENCE

I remained busy and absorbed by my interests in junior high school. Mother's problems were not yet severe enough to intrude strongly into my activities. She was often between episodes of depression, able to do things around the house and with her friends. However, my parents argued more, and family tensions increased. Once she asked me how I would feel if they divorced. A lump formed in my throat, and later I cried in private. The idea of living with her—and our father living alone—felt unbearable. No one who treated her considered the possibility of a link between her unhappiness in her marriage and her physical symptoms. Our parents stayed together, and we were relieved.

Mother took a job as a clerk in the main department store in town. She took great pleasure in her work, even though it was hard to be on her feet all day. At her break time my sister and I would join her in the break room for a Coke and snacks, listening to her animated chatter and enjoying her pleasure. She now had her own spending money and got a store discount, making additional purchases possible. Even so, family spending patterns were extravagant enough that my father still had to work his extra jobs. Another time, my mother had a yarn shop in our home, and that, too, gratified her. But opportunities in our small town were few, and her on-and-off fatigue created further limitations.

I started to work at a Laundromat that my relatives owned, making close connections with them. They would become a source of support and refuge in the coming years. By high school, when conflicts between my mother and me intensified, I was able to visit them and relax; tensions would dissipate in their calm, caring presence. I worked hard in school, enjoyed extracurricular activities, became interested in boys, and was popular. By high school, life changed considerably.

Hospitalizations for Depression

Mother was first hospitalized in Milwaukee for her depression near the beginning of my sophomore year. My sister went with my father to admit mother to Columbia Hospital for the first time. For some reason I did not go with them. Maybe mother and I had fought and they thought it would be unwise for me to go. Or maybe I was scheduled to work or study for a test. Each time she returned, she told us about her experiences, taking us through her search, in therapy, for the childhood roots of her depression, often in excruciating detail. She sang the praises of the patients on the psychiatric ward. This, too, took on an aura of drama and glamour: they were sensitive, creative, cultured, intellectual, and compassionate. She often talked about the need to be with people like this, where she felt free to be herself. We came to resent her stories of these wonderful victimized people. We wondered why she preferred their company to ours, but not for long, as she reminded us of our deficiencies, especially mine.

Mother's hospitalizations kept me busy. It was all I could do to help at home, keep up with my schoolwork, spend time with my friends, practice piano, and engage in church activities. I now also prepared evening meals, cared for my younger sister, and did housekeeping, laundry, and ironing. I was less helpful when mother returned. Back then, psychiatric hospitalizations were much longer than they are today. Insight-oriented psychotherapy was the norm, and pharmacological treatments were new. She became even more dissatisfied with my father, escalating her criticisms of his controlling nature and blaming him for her unhappiness. Sometimes she blamed me, as well. Consciously I did not believe this, but underneath I began to feel responsible.

Although mother enjoyed talking about her experiences and the people in the psychiatric ward, another part of her felt some shame about her condition and need for treatment. It was rare in the 1950s for people in a small town to be hospitalized for depression, and the general lack of understanding frustrated her. She worried and became somewhat paranoid that people talked about her. She felt stigmatized. I don't know that all that many people gossiped, but there may have been enough to feed her suspicions.

Stigma is a strain for all members of a family. Mother also went to Milwaukee for outpatient therapy sessions; sometimes the whole family would go to make it a family outing. One time mother and I were at the supermarket, chatting with a relative who asked if we'd been in Milwaukee. She had called that weekend, and no one was home. We responded simultaneously but with opposite answers; I affirmed and she denied having been there. Mother was not a deceitful person, but she probably wanted people to believe that she was fine. I felt guilty for having contradicted her and trapping her in a lie. Despite the conflicts, there was still a strong sense of family loyalty.

Mother received many different kinds of medications over the years. None of the tricyclic antidepressants or monoamine-oxidase (MAO) inhibitors helped her depression. This was well before the advances made when selective serotonin reuptake inhibitors (SSRIs) came into use. Instead, she was mostly treated with antianxiety agents (some of which can contribute to depression) and barbiturates for sleeping. At one point she took lithium, as she showed some symptoms of bipolar illness, but this did not work, either. Major tranquilizers such as Thorazine and Stelazine, often used to treat psychotic disorders such as schizophrenia, were also prescribed. They dulled her anxiety and agitation, but side effects included slow, slurred speech and a stumbling gait. Eventually, more effective antianxiety agents eliminated these side effects, but they did not help the underlying depression. Only after I experienced major depression many years later would I fully understand the depth of her misery and despair. This was a hard lesson in empathy, one better learned another way.

Like Mother, Like Daughter?

In terms of outward appearances and personalities, my mother and I could not have been more different. When she was in high school she was lovely and grace-ful and readily made friends. In contrast, I was awkward and uncertain, strug-gling to fit in while others mostly seemed to know what they were doing. I still enjoyed the academic challenges, and these kept my self-esteem buoyed. Some-times uncertain of my abilities, I'd think I had done poorly in certain areas until I got my grades and could breathe a sigh of relief. My mother quickly tired of the way I would complain and fret about poor performance and then receive an A, saying that I was crying wolf. Her unsympathetic comments hurt.

I began to gain weight and to feel anxious. As long as I was not in the limelight, I could keep my tension at bay. Slowly I withdrew from activities, as she continued to press me to perform. She often talked about the need to lose weight so that I could be a model when I was older. This was her dream, not mine; I did not have the body, the bone structure, or the facial features, much less the desire. She pushed me to take speech and to try out for school plays; her disappointment at my refusal was palpable. The criticism intensified as she saw that I was not interested in doing what she had done. Years later I realized that I had been developing depressive symptoms in high school. There were times when I lacked energy and felt moody, leaden, and quite sad. But then I would rebound.

Often when she was ill, my mother focused on my deficiencies. She viewed me as selfish, uncaring, and indifferent to the needs of others, especially hers. I tried to resist these judgments, but her criticisms trickled inward, sapping en-ergy and creating self-doubt about my potential for meaningful achievements and loving relationships. She also thought I lacked common sense and practical knowledge. As she put it: "I just don't know how someone so smart could be so dumb." Later I understood that her anger and criticism were part of her illness. Her pain was severe, and she needed comfort and reassurance, more than we could provide. But at the time it made me angry, and I tried to create distance.

I also became rebellious and began to talk back and act out. Within my peer group we thought of ourselves as a counterculture and fancied ourselves as being "on the wild side," with a group name of the Swamp Rats. A couple of us got into trouble a few times, but we weren't really all that bad. I continued to have fun with my friends, and my love of learning never waned. I began to hone the art of having two different personas, compliant and people pleasing in some situations but rebellious, defiant, and cynical in others.

Mother's criticisms continued throughout high school. They only served to fuel my opposition, which I now also showed by ignoring her. Some of my adolescent rebellion might have occurred anyway, and I did make life difficult sometimes. One time a date told me I should be nicer to my mother, which suggests that I could be rather nasty. Mother-daughter relationships often involve conflict as daughters strive to become more autonomous and develop their own identities. Normally these conflicts are not extreme and diminish over time. But a mentally ill mother struggling for her own independence may resort to more extreme means to discourage her daughter's attempts at self-expression, especially if that daughter is oppositional. This was the case for me.

Others outside the family were mainly unaware of our conflicts. I could not understand how she switched so fluidly from being cold and critical to me to being warm and compassionate toward others. Now I question whether it was all that easy. Her anger toward me in part reflected her own inner distress. Depressed persons are often good (even masterful) at hiding their distress in public but will break down in private, where they can give way to their emotions. Contrary to earlier views, acutely depressed patients often show more rather than less hostility. The hostility is directed toward intimate family members, spouses, and especially children, but less so to others outside the family. The compliant patient in the office can be quite hostile at home. This, too, was my experience.

My sister's recollections bolster my own. Barbara later said "I can't remember her ever saying anything nice about you. She was always critical." She even viewed it as emotional abuse, describing mother as "intimidating, hurtful, and a beast." It was difficult being the brunt of mother's sarcasm and insults, just as it was hard for my younger sister to witness these incidents. The worse mother felt, the more judgmental and critical she became. Barbara and I viewed many of the family processes similarly (despite her closeness to our mother), and we supported each other. This provided reassurance and reality testing throughout many bizarre and frightening events.

Conversations "by" My Mother

Throughout her life mother talked incessantly when not in a deep state of depression. She could not tolerate silence when in the presence of others. If someone was in the room, she felt a void that needed to be filled with words, most often her own. She told me this in her later years. She did not know the comfort of shared, companionable silence. Conversations were monologues, steady streams of uninterruptible words and sometimes fragmented thoughts. In her letters, sentences ended with dashes; even lengthy letters were devoid of paragraphs. She stayed on a theme for a few sentences and then drifted to another. Narrative researchers would describe them as disjointed and lacking coherence. She signed her letters by her nickname, Emmie, never "mother." Later, she told her three grandchildren to call her "Emmie" rather than any variant of "grandmother."

She had a commanding voice that projected well. Her verbal performances covered the gamut: politics, religion, discrimination, individual rights, theater, film, culture, psychological insights, and mixtures of all of these as she traveled from topic to topic. She did not like to be interrupted and became irritated if someone was unable to follow her trains of thought. She loved to tell jokes and laughed a lot, even when she lacked physical energy and was mostly sedentary, especially as she grew older. Many friends and relatives found her to be engaging and charismatic. They enjoyed her irreverence for the status quo, her ideas on varied topics, and her caustic wit. Some called her a wise woman. At her memorial service her minister called her a saint for having overcome so much adversity in her life. Others admired her ability to swear. It troubled me that she had so much freedom of expression and that we had so little. I also felt entrapped, having to listen to the same stories dozens of times. Once she literally blocked the door to prevent my departure.

She told me repeatedly about her difficult childhood and family mental illness. She often talked, too, about townspeople, mostly women, who ultimately dealt with their shattered lives by committing suicide. There was the riveting story of one woman who strayed into madness years after her best friend and father had drowned in a boating accident while she had swum to safety. Sometimes rambling, these stories also contained penetrating insights into human nature; Mother was a perceptive observer. I learned a lot of psychology "at my mother's knee." But it was oppressive, as well as instructive. Her self-focus pulled us all in, making it difficult for us to pursue our own interests and dreams.

Family Life

Family life now was often controlled by mother's theatrical presence, her constant talking, her difficulty being a wife and caregiver, and the severity of her depressions. My sister and I felt sidelined, passive, and helpless in the face of our parents' problems. Their conflicts and moods deprived us of calming parental influences. My sister and I both assumed caregiving roles. She supported mother while I supported my father, a practice now known as "parentification" of the child. Although I could not give my mother emotional support, I tried to help in other ways. She was very messy, and I would clean up after her, making her bed, dusting her room, and sorting through piles of clothing strewn across the floor. Perhaps I thought if I could create order here, she would become more orderly and organized herself.

Preparations for church services (or any social event) were tense. We never knew whether mother would feel well enough to go. She stayed in bed until the last minute, as my father tried to move her along. She would start yelling, and another fight would ensue, right up to the church steps. Then we would smile and be friendly to the congregants, trying to keep up appearances. I choked back tears, but my heart still raced and my palms sweated. Still, the church played an important role in our lives. I liked singing in the choir, the rituals were reassuring, and the friendships and support were invaluable.

Experiences at home often contrasted sharply with the humanitarian themes and hymn lyrics learned at church. The juxtapositions of caring and cruelty were confusing. My parents bickered and argued during the dinner hour. Most often mother provoked the fights, but sometimes he needled her to get her goat. When mother criticized our lack of manners, she did not offer constructive advice, just negative comments about our uncouth behavior. Sometimes she took her plate into the living room to finish dinner, saying we were too boorish to be around. Other evenings were pleasant, and then we felt like a happy family. There was always a nice tablecloth and candlelight. Appearances remained important, whether or not anyone else was there to view the scene. We began to eat out more often as mother often no longer felt well enough to cook meals. Similarly, we spent holidays at the homes of friends or relatives because of her poor health. Here, too, our parents argued right up to our arrival. Once they fought bitterly about how to get a dime for a pay phone. I said it didn't seem worth arguing over something as trivial as a dime, and mother lambasted me.

Her depressions usually began in the autumn, which she attributed to fact that this was when she had been taken from her aunts to live with her new family. The diagnosis of seasonal affective disorder did not yet exist, but it may well have been applicable. Her Scandinavian heritage and the decreased sunlight in northern Wisconsin would have made her a good candidate. She spent more and more time in bed, and I took over most of the holiday preparations. I enjoyed baking Christmas cookies, shopping, wrapping presents, and decorating the house and tree. But over time I, too, felt a sense of dread as the holidays approached, and joy became suffused with sorrow. Birthdays were difficult, too; on my 21st birthday she basically told me she wished I'd never been born.

I stopped having friends over and spent more time in my friends' homes rather than my own. After dinner I went to my room to study in peace and quiet. I also met friends at the library to study or go to a youth center. It was easier to escape the pain away from home. I still enjoyed life and did not like being dragged down from my pleasures, though this feeling sometimes made me feel guilty. We tried to move quietly through the house and to keep our voices down, and if we played music records or the piano, we did so softly. But it was difficult to remain quiet, and sometimes we forgot. At the piano I could lose myself in melody and reverie and drown out the gloom that pervaded the rooms. My sister and I also played records of romantic music: melancholic, bittersweet ballads of love and loss.

Some of mother's behaviors were very irrational. She began to treat her husband as a father figure, reenacting her earlier perceptions of a rejecting father who favored the younger daughter. Once when the three of us were going out, she climbed into the back seat of the car and told me to sit in front with my father. I first refused, but she insisted, and I complied. After we started out she became enraged and accused me of taking her place. Although I knew this made no sense, it still made me anxious.

I remained captive to confusion and chaos, buffeted by her raw rage and stony retreats. Often I would hold my breath and think "If I can just get through this fight, this period of shunning and silence, these sarcastic and demeaning comments, it will pass, and maybe things will get better." But when you hold your breath too often and for too long, you start to disrupt basic respiration and feel even more anxious. It can become a lifelong habit in stressful situations. Sometimes I was relieved when mother took to her bed and the barrage ended. But her retreats were usually preceded by accusations and blame. Once she didn't speak to me for almost 2 months, though she certainly talked to others during this time.

HIGHER EDUCATION

The Undergraduate Years

I could not wait to get away from home to start school at the University of Wisconsin (UW) in Madison. It was a different world. Many students were from larger cities and other parts of the country, particularly the East Coast. They were articulate in the classroom and self-assured. My mother wanted me to join a sorority, because this was what cultured young women did. But this prospect frightened me, as I did not think I had the poise or social graces. She was disappointed with my decision not to try. The size of the campus and classes intimidated me at first, and I worried about my capabilities. But soon I began to do well in my classes and came to love university life, including the anonymity that large classes afforded. I took mostly liberal arts classes and majored in languages.

I spent spare time with old and new friends, often at parties that typically involved drinking. The UW has always had a reputation as a drinking school, and I quickly fell into that pattern. I clearly was in the company of like-minded others. Female college students in Wisconsin (and women in the state in general) currently have the highest rates of binge drinking in the nation. It may not be coincidence that women in the state of Wisconsin are ranked high in terms of depression, stress, and anxiety when compared with women in most other states. For me, I reveled in the sense of adventure, away from the watchful eyes of my parents. Alcohol released inhibitions, and I behaved in ways that were novel, daring, and potentially dangerous. I also now smoked two to three packs of cigarettes a day.

In my sophomore year I learned I couldn't have children. I was treated for a hormonal imbalance, but dosages of hormones used then were very high, causing water retention and weight gain. I was no longer overweight, but the medical treatment changed that, and I grew several dress sizes. My parents persuaded me to see the same psychiatrist they had seen to deal with my loss of ability to have children. So each Saturday for almost a year I took a bus to Milwaukee for therapy sessions. This took up half my weekend, and it didn't help my social life. I did not care for the psychiatrist and felt uncomfortable when I expressed my anger toward mother. I didn't think he would tell her, but it didn't feel right.

Mostly I talked about my dreams. Inevitably he interpreted them in sexual ways, sometimes indicating that the dream reflected my sexual attraction to him (he was in his 60s at least). In other dreams he saw himself as a wise authority figure. Freudian theory, with its concepts of transference, was in vogue. This was of no help to a 19-year-old with feelings of uncertainty and inadequacy; I needed to know how to solve interpersonal problems, make constructive life choices, and reduce anxiety. His overbearing, narcissistic manner also got in the way, but who was I to question him? Yet my personal experiences paved the way to an intense interest in psychology, which became a lifelong passion.

Once I took the introductory course, I knew immediately that I would major in psychology. One of the first books I read was an autobiography by Clifford Beers titled *A Mind That Found Itself.* As a young man he was hospitalized with schizophrenia, but he found his way back to mental health and started the Mental Hygiene Movement in the United States. This book was pivotal in defining my professional future. I was encouraged that recovery was possible, even in someone who had lost his mind, living in a world of paranoia, delusions, and hallucinations. Perhaps it also gave me some hope for my mother.

Though intrigued by clinical psychology, I sensed that it would not be right for me. My family background and hypersensitivity to conflict and distress in others often left my skin tingling and my heart palpitating in emotional encounters. Others' sorrows weighed me down, and their anger frightened me. When I took abnormal psychology, I kept comparing my symptoms and those of my family with the textbook descriptions. The similarities worried me. Fortunately, I liked experimental psychology. It allowed me to remain in the general area but with a more dispassionate, objective approach to the subject matter. I also worked for a professor, conducting perception and learning studies with college students and mentally retarded children. He encouraged me to go to graduate school at the Institute of Child Development in Minneapolis, at the University of Minnesota. This was in an era when not many women did so. Given my strong interest and academic performance, graduate school was a good option.

Throughout this time my relationship with my mother remained strained and tense. Her depression worsened. Her animosity toward me continued to overshadow my ability to see her pain. I felt guilty but also knew I had to maintain distance for my own emotional well-being. Hospitalizations and suicide threats increased. By then she was on several medications and unable to keep track of what to take and when. My father kept the medications in a black bag and dispensed them, which infuriated her. Sometimes I took the bus to Milwaukee to visit her on the psychiatric ward, which invariably left me shaken. I can still visualize the hallway and the heavy doors by which I waited for someone to come and unlock them. Increasingly, I erected mental barriers, given my fear that I would become like her. I often rehearsed the many ways we differed. I thought as long as I remained logical and level-headed I could dismiss this disordered landscape and maintain my sanity.

But I sometimes felt fragile and anxious, making it difficult to concentrate in classes. I studied the same material over and over again, afraid that I would forget it. I sat in aisle seats so that I could escape if fears became too intense. Sometimes I stared at the ceiling acoustic tiles, counting the little holes or in-dentations to keep my mind off morbid, repetitive thoughts. I continued to experience sudden onsets of fear and impending feelings of doom, shortness of breath, tightness in my chest, smothering sensations, and fear of losing control or "going crazy." I did not know then that these were panic attacks. Alcohol and cigarettes provided momentary relief and remained my medications of choice. My experience with psychotherapy left me with no desire to try it again.

Eventually these feelings subsided, and I continued to enjoy many aspects of my education. My friends and I went to foreign films and other cultural events. I made friends with students of different ethnic or religious origins and felt enriched by the diversity. In the early 1960s the civil rights movement was in full swing, with campus rallies and demonstrations. We heard talks by workers after they returned from the South. We enjoyed the music of the Beatles and various folk singers. I fell in love with a black PhD student in biology. I brought him home to meet my parents, knowing they would welcome him, given their liberal bent and feelings about racial prejudice. As I rebelled against societal in-justices rather than against my mother, she became more positive. My boyfriend wanted me to play a more activist role; my shyness made this difficult. He got me to sell tickets to a Malcolm X talk, which was agonizing, and I was not very successful. After graduation I stayed in Madison briefly to be with him. But it was not working out, so I returned home.

When my father drove me to graduate school later in the summer, mother checked herself into the hospital in Milwaukee. In letters to her stepmother she tried to explain her illness, emphasizing that her depression was second-ary to physical health problems, especially her anemia, which was treated with vitamin B-12 shots. The letters are touching, as she was almost childlike in seeking approval for her good behavior despite the lack of closeness with her stepmother. She said that doctors admired her efforts to help others on the ward, even though she was so terribly sick herself. She discussed future plans to become more independent by working part time in Milwaukee while remaining married. She also confided that she didn't want townspeople to know she was in the hospital. Preoccupied with her own troubles, she did not mention Barbara or me.

Graduate School

I began graduate school in the fall of 1962, focusing on topics related to perception, learning, and cognition and on experimental methods that allowed precise control of variables. I liked developing research designs, conducting studies, and analyzing data. This research was manageable, in contrast to naturalistic approaches and field studies used to study the more intangible processes of life in the real world. I stayed away from classes on abnormal psychology, personality, and social development. By the time I took my doctoral exams, my narrowed focus became evident, and I was required to take course work in these areas. It is ironic that all of the research I have conducted throughout my career has covered topics I had ignored in graduate school. Yet the rigorous training in research designs and methods was valuable, as I applied many of the principles and reasoning processes from this training.

The Institute of Child Development was a receptive environment. It was at once intellectually stimulating and comfortable, and the faculty was supportive. I thrived on their encouragement and recognition of my abilities and interests, working hard and taking pleasure in this new setting. As I grew closer to completing the requirements, I became anxious about preliminary and oral examinations to a point at which I could not sleep. I confided in a faculty member, who suggested a therapist with an office in the Institute. I went hoping no one would see me, ashamed of my problems and the need for help.

The therapist was astute and reassuring. I learned that my symptoms were more than normal anxiety responses to stress. Medications helped to quell some symptoms, and I began to talk about my family life. Her insights allowed me to see that my relationship with my father, as well as my mother, was troubled and that I was enmeshed in his difficulties. My father always cried when we parted, which left me sad and uncomfortable. It felt as though I was responsible for keeping him happy. During visits he told me everything that was going on at home (usually over dinner and drinks), and we would commiserate. Because he seemed so victimized, anxious, and sad, I remained solicitous, but it also dragged me down.

The therapist thought that my father's more "tender" emotions were sometimes manipulative. I began to see how he sometimes pushed my mother's buttons; problems in their relationship were not completely one-sided. Although he did not cause her depression, his pessimism, worries, and rigidity were likely to have interfered with her recovery. She often talked about how he had stifled her independence by not wanting her to work and by controlling the family finances. Because of traditional gender roles at the time, his behavior was not unusual, but mother experienced it as control and deprivation. She also must have been upset to see her daughter doing things she could not, such as driving a car and going to college.

My relationship with my mother remained strained during graduate school. She was in and out of the hospital. As before, she rarely visited, and if she did, conflict would ensue. Often she would pick a fight. Once during a visit with me, friends stopped by to see if I wanted to go out for a drink. I said no, as my mother was visiting. She insisted that I go, and I refused. But she kept it up, and finally I went out for a while. When I returned, she was enraged that I had left her alone and refused to speak to me for the rest of her visit. Again, I knew this was irrational, but I still felt angry and guilty.

PROFESSIONAL DEVELOPMENT

After graduate school I went to the National Institute of Mental Health to work with a prominent developmental psychologist. The postdoctoral position was to have lasted for 2 years, but I obtained a permanent research position. There were few female scientists then, and just two of them were in leadership positions, so I considered myself lucky. However, there was a "gentleman's agreement" that I would never be given resources to conduct independent research. At first I was comfortable in a supportive role. There was much to be mastered given the marked change in my research orientation. I learned how to conduct naturalistic, observational studies and experiments that captured real-life social learning conditions for children.

After a decade in this role, I wanted more autonomy and chafed at the constraints and limitations of the appointment. The hierarchical and patriarchal research culture at NIMH did not favor professional advancement for women. Labs were divided into sections, all were headed by "chiefs" (the term still in use), and only chiefs had their own operating budgets. Behavioral research labs were low on the totem pole compared with biomedical research (e.g., genetics, neuroscience, biochemistry). The dual identity of a female psychologist made professional advancement extremely difficult.

Institutional sex discrimination, cultural constraints, child rearing, and early socialization that discouraged assertion all contributed to my slow professional growth. Still, I began to publish first-authored articles in peer-reviewed journals that received attention in the scientific community. I gave talks, joined editorial boards, and served on committees. The sex discrimination was eventually addressed by the National Institutes of Health in the form of "gender-equity adjustments" that provided equal pay for equal work by female and male scientists. Here was external validation that I had not been alone in being unfairly judged as not quite good enough and that I had not been the cause of my lesser status.

My professional life rapidly changed. I became part of a network outside of the government that involved research collaborations and cross-fertilization of ideas from different subdisciplines of child psychiatry and child psychology. I got grants that led to further autonomy. Within the network I observed a variety of mentoring styles and began to mentor scientists just entering the field. These experiences became a springboard for a personally satisfying, productive career that now included national and international travel. My world had become more enlarged, familiar, and comfortable. I assumed leadership roles in professional organizations. All of these activities provided one pathway to maturity and competency as an adult. The other pathway began after I formed my own family, another journey with its own set of opportunities and challenges.

When I was young and still uncomfortable in my professional role, I sometimes believed I had landed there by mistake. I thought I was unqualified for the roles and responsibilities implied by the title of PhD and that I might be a fraud, and, moreover, that it was wrong to pretend to know things I could not possibly fully understand. Such feelings are not uncommon and even carry a name: the "imposter syndrome." Time and experience assured me that I was not an imposter. I stopped being so sensitive to others' judgments, quelled my "internal critic," and used self-criticism to effect changes in my life.

MARRIAGE AND FAMILY

About a year into my postdoctoral position I met the man I would marry. Morris was a "nice Jewish boy," which pleased both of my parents given their belief systems. We loved to laugh together, explore the countryside, and discuss psychology, and we quickly formed an emotional bond. He had grown up in the Washington, D.C. He was in graduate school at Michigan State University but had come to NIMH to work for the summer. We had a lot in common, even though we came from different backgrounds. His parents had emigrated from Russia. His father, Isadore, was a cabinetmaker and antiques dealer, and his mother, Fannie, was a homemaker; together they raised six children.

Morris and I were married by a justice of the peace. I had not wanted a formal wedding in my hometown given the nature of my relationship with my mother. My parents, however, particularly my mother, were adamant about hosting a reception so that people could meet my husband and they could reciprocate similar social invitations. Although reluctant, I felt unable to refuse.

Morris, my sister Barbara, and I drove there, and I was nauseous for most of the 1,000-mile trip. I was tense at the reception and angry about an event I thought Mother had planned to "look good" in the community. Possibly my own perception was skewed, and she just wanted to do something nice.

When I had first moved to Bethesda to work at NIMH, I had again begun to have panic attacks. I did not recognize them as such because the unsettling physical sensations made me think I had a medical problem. Also, I felt happy and excited about living in a large, cosmopolitan city. A physician asked why I had fled from home; perhaps it was unusual then for a young unmarried woman to be on her own and away from family. I felt insulted, thinking I'd left for positive reasons. But I was, in fact, having panic attacks. Claustrophobic in certain situations, my heart thudded, and I felt a sinking, suffocating sensation. I was ashamed of my weakness and vowed to overcome it through stoicism and willing it away. No treatment was prescribed, and eventually the symptoms subsided.

But after my marriage I experienced physical symptoms again, now mainly abdominal distress. Neither my internist nor my gynecologist could find any physical basis, and the problems were seen as "in my head." Because they were imaginary, there was nothing to treat. I persuaded another doctor to prescribe tranquilizers, and he also gave me vitamin B-12 shots for anemia. Only later did I see the parallels to my mother's early experiences. Once I tried transcendental meditation as a way of reducing stress and had a hallucinatory, out-of-body experience. Needless to say, I did not continue along that path.

With time I felt stronger and more energetic, and we decided to start a family. I had recently been told that I could, in fact, have children, and we looked forward to this prospect. However, just 1 month later my internist detected uterine tumors, and I was immediately scheduled for a complete hysterectomy. I was devastated and fell into a depression. The doctors provided no support or comfort. They expected me to feel grateful that the tumors were not malignant and said there was no reason to be affected physically or emotionally. So I believed something was wrong with me because I was affected psychologically. I returned to work about 6 weeks after the surgery and struggled to function. Later I wondered whether the earlier "psychosomatic" stomach symptoms might have been undetected signs of the developing tumors. My anger and sadness combined to make me moody and undoubtedly difficult to be around. Morris tried in vain to comfort me.

I began psychotherapy with a person I later realized was a Rogerian psychologist. This meant that he mostly listened, said little, and was (supposed to be) supportive or affirming by nodding and saying "um hum." The affirming part was missing, as he was mostly silent and robotic. I became more depressed, had difficulty sleeping and eating, and lost a lot of weight. Finally, I was as thin as a model, which pleased my internist, who saw this as a sign of good health. I did not talk about my anxiety and sadness, for I knew he did not understand mental illness. Few physicians did at the time, and there was little communication between doctors who dealt with physical and with mental health problems.

The psychotherapist referred me to a psychiatrist who prescribed an antidepressant. I experienced side effects and felt even worse. He wanted to hospitalize me, but I refused. I did not want to be defined by the same illness as my mother. Her problems had worsened despite repeated hospitalization and treatment, and I feared the same. Besides, what would people think? Acknowledging the problem might make me even more vulnerable. How could I command respect in the workplace if people knew of this weakness? This fear was not entirely irrational. Although a mental health institution should understand mental health problems, this was not the case.

The research environment was adversarial and competitive; one needed to be strong to compete. There was a mentality that we were different from the people we studied because we did not have problems. This state of denial made it difficult for those in need of treatment to recognize their problems and seek help. I was one of those people, and I did something only when I reached a point of collapse. I remained home for a while, saying that I was physically ill. I was given tranquilizers in order to develop some sense of calm. I went back to work and somehow managed to get through the days. The panic continued and developed into agoraphobia. Although I knew I was unhappy, the fears overrode the sorrow, and I could not fully recognize my depression. I'd developed some strong defenses.

By now I could no longer drive and depended on my husband or on taxis to get around. Once I got to work or returned home, I would begin to relax. But even at work I did not feel completely safe until I approached my office. It was difficult to walk down the long corridors because everything loomed, and the visual distortions made me dizzy. My heart raced, and I felt as though I was going crazy. But once I started to work I felt better. I was unable to shop for groceries, or anything else for that matter, unless my husband was with me. I remained haunted by a sense of loss and the feeling that I was no longer womanly.

I became obsessed with having a child and turned almost immediately to the adoption process. Ideally, it would have been better to wait a while, but I was afraid that if we did not start right away, it would not happen. Few infants were available for adoption, and agencies wanted the available infants to be adopted by young parents. We decided on an international adoption, and the process was speedy. The application was approved in late 1971, and our 4 1/2-month-old daughter arrived the following May. I felt better by then, and there was a tremendous sense of excitement. She was fun loving and sociable from the start, and we fell in love with this charming, exuberant infant.

We lived in a neighborhood of modest homes within walking distance of NIMH, downtown Bethesda, and parks and playgrounds. It was populated

mostly by families like us, with young children. We joined a child-care cooperative that included social events with the families. Because I was the only mother
who worked full time outside the home, I felt like an outsider. I was the main
breadwinner, as my husband was still in graduate school. When our daughter
was in kindergarten, he received his PhD and went to work full time at the
Food and Drug Administration. Because his schedule was more flexible than
mine in the early years, he more often took care of our daughter or took her to
sitters. We both embraced the new world of parenthood and its pleasures and
challenges.

There were many stresses and losses during those first 5 years. Morris's
father died the winter before Rebecca arrived from Korea. His mother died not
long afterward, in a hospital in Philadelphia. Three years later one of Morris's
siblings, who was a drug user, seller, and informer, was murdered. There were
many sad visits to hospitals and tensions between siblings. I remember, in particular, one trip to Philadelphia to see my husband's mother. My father was with
us, unburdening his woes about his marriage, as was his wont. I had a severe
anxiety attack in the hospital and was overcome with the guilt of having to
ask Morris to take care of me when he should have been with his mother. On
the ride back, I sat in the front passenger seat with Rebecca on my lap (in the
days before child car seats). My father was in the back seat. I just wanted to escape it all and started to have uncontrollable thoughts of opening the door and
jumping to my death. It felt as though the only thing stopping me was a sense
of responsibility for my daughter. The problems in my life seemed insurmount-
able; I was relieved when my father returned to Wisconsin.

My parents visited one Christmas when Rebecca was 2 or 3 years old.
Mother became inexplicably angry on Christmas Eve. She withdrew to a chair
in an upstairs bedroom, where she sat sphinx-like for hours, her face both blank
and intimidating, immobilized save for the lighting of cigarettes and the chain
smoking that ensued. A small chimney fire broke out while she was upstairs,
the result of too much gift wrap paper and ribbon stuffed into the downstairs
fireplace. The fire trucks were there within minutes, with their sirens and flash-
ing lights. The firemen raced through the house to clear people out, but when
they went into the bedroom, Mother refused to move. I tried to be cheerful
the next day, hoping my daughter at least would have a happy Christmas. But
here we were again, fighting the gloom and rage of the depression my mother
brought with her.

Mother's hospitalizations continued, as did her addiction to the barbiturates she used in order to sleep. She remained angry and emphasized the role
we played in the perpetuation of her illness. She said her psychiatrist wanted to
see the whole family together. Although there was no question of past and current disturbed family dynamics, I did not view family therapy in Wisconsin as
an option. I lived a thousand miles away, and it was all I could do to manage my

own life. According to her, he would explain what we were doing to prevent her recovery and how we would need to change. These guilt-inducing, manipulative messages angered me. This was one of many times I felt that my own emotional survival depended on my ability to maintain distance. To remain engaged was to remain engulfed; keeping distance, on the other hand, created disconnection, hardening of the self, alienation, and guilt. However, separation was the lesser of two evils at this point.

Because my sister now lived in Madison and had a closer relationship with my mother, she took on more of the burdens of trying to help. Mother wanted to leave my father, but she was not yet well enough. On one visit to my sister, she tried to throw herself down the basement stairs and was hospitalized. There she met a psychiatrist, who was to be of great help. He told her she needed to go off her medications in order for her problems to be better diagnosed and treated. By now she was addicted to the barbiturates and left the hospital against medical advice. But later she returned and went through the process needed to begin her recovery. Not too much later she left my father.

At this time I began to take active steps to make changes in my life. A self-righting instinct came into play: I was now a wife and mother, and I could not be effective in those roles if I continued to live in fear and avoidance. I did not want to repeat the past. As a depressed parent of a young child, I was doing just that, though I did not consciously think of it in those terms then. I just knew there was a need for change. I stopped smoking at the plea of my then 6-year-old daughter, who told me she did not want me to die from cigarettes. I also stopped drinking then because alcohol made me want to smoke. Later, when the urges to smoke had disappeared, I drank again, but more moderately, and no longer used alcohol as a crutch. I began to exercise regularly, practice yoga, enjoy outdoor activities, and take up hobbies. I felt better.

As my depression lifted, I took greater pleasure in family, friendships, and work. I took my daughter to Sunday school at a Unitarian church and attended services. One of the first services moved me deeply. The minister and a physician engaged in a dialogue about the physician's recovery from cancer that had been diagnosed as terminal. His career had just started and he had a young family when he was diagnosed. Tears filled my eyes and streamed down my face, and I felt both the pain and a sense of release. My husband joined us after the death of his brother. Our lives were expanded and enriched through further involvements within this liberal religious community. It provided me with an additional means to move past my own suffering.

When our daughter reached adolescence, issues of loss and abandonment by her biological mother surfaced; she became angry, oppositional, and disruptive. As with my mother, these behaviors undoubtedly masked pain and sadness. My own history had created insecurities that sometimes limited my ability to be understanding and to provide the full complement of nurturance and structure she needed. My daughter does not view it in quite the same way. Rather, she thinks that, feeling abandoned by her biological mother, she did all she could to push my buttons, to repeat the rejection she felt and "invite" more of the same. What I can say is that I felt ill equipped at times to help her, and we had more than our share of mother-daughter conflict. Therapy, time, and efforts by both of us led to a strong, loving, and fulfilling relationship.

I also worked to change the nature of my relationship with my mother. When we were growing up, my sister and I were keenly aware of the lack of warmth between our mother and her stepmother. I did not want my daughter to feel torn between family members as we had, and I wanted her to have a sense of family. So I did not talk to her about my own negative childhood experiences as my mother had done with me. I started to communicate more with my mother, and eventually we developed a better relationship. Our first steps toward each other were tentative and wary and with some miscues.

We went to Wisconsin each summer for a vacation, renting a cottage and dividing time between my parents. Sometimes we would go for Christmas, as well. These visits were often tense, but they improved gradually. Mother still liked to be the center of attention and could be sharp-tongued, especially if she was tense. Rebecca also got to know her relatives, and all of us experienced the gifts of being part of this extended family. Predictably, Rebecca developed a close relationship with my father and a more ambivalent relationship with my mother. Rebecca, too, would come to recall dreadful fights between my mother and father. Even though my parents were separated, they did things together occasionally, especially when we were in town. Sometimes they would take Rebecca out to lunch up north, yelling at each other throughout the car ride and frightening her.

Gradually my mother and I became more open with one another and began to let go of the anger, avoidance, and rejection we'd shown in the past. We had fun together and shared our many common interests and passions. The best times were when I went to visit by myself and we had time alone together. She told me once that she thought I would never want to have much to do with her again given the earlier years. Her gratitude touched me and made me more aware of the intense guilt she felt over some of her earlier actions.

These changes came at a cost. I spent time with both parents but stayed with my mother. My father was used to being my favorite and never fully accepted the fact that I wanted to spend time with her, as well as with him. And, as her mental health improved, his deteriorated. He obsessed over her and drank more and more heavily. Later in life he abruptly stopped drinking but did not seek any help for his problems. He saw his role in life as that of being a helper and typically refused help from others. My mother felt guilty about leaving my father, who was lonely and now increasingly isolated. They had been powerfully drawn to each other and maintained a mutual dependency throughout their lives that was unhealthy for both of them. By now I had established more healthy boundaries that prevented their tragic relationship and needs from usurping my own.

Despite mother's declaration of independence from my father, he still provided all her financial support. She had her own checkbook finally, but he was the one who deposited the money and reviewed her bank statements each month. She viewed this as intrusive, but it was hard to fault him. He knew that she could not balance a checkbook. She would counter by saying that she "just knew" or "could sense" how much was there. But instinct is of no help in balancing a checkbook. She found ways to make a little extra money, even though she was not in good health. In fact, she had several health problems that were likely to have resulted, in part, from many years of untreated, undertreated, and inaccurately treated depression. In addition to cardiac problems and high blood pressure, abdominal problems required a restricted diet and made it difficult for her to eat normally. We now know that depression can have a variety of adverse consequences on physical health.

Mother became licensed to provide day care in her home. She said she did it because she needed the money after the separation. But she also viewed this as an opportunity to nurture young children in a way that she hadn't been able to do with her own. She told me that she felt she had not been a good mother and that here she could help other young children. Much of her deep-seated depression had lifted, but she still felt guilty about her earlier anger and rejection. She had a renewed sense of purpose. She loved to talk about the children under her care, the wonderful things they did together, and how good, sweet, and clever they were. She seemed to like them better than her own grandchildren.

But there was another side. I once ran into a mother of three children who had been in my mother's care. The (now grown) children's recollections differed markedly from my mother's tales. They had been frightened by the way she drove. She also yelled at them a lot: "Quit yer bitchin(g)" was one of her expressions. She could be impatient, impetuous, and locked into her own needs and plans. Even in later life mother continued to give back to children what she perceived her experiences to have been as a child. Hearing this, my heart ached both for these children and for my mother.

PARENTAL DEATH AND DEPRESSION

My mother and father died within 5 days of each other in early April of 1995. He was 89 and she was 78. We left for Wisconsin when we learned he'd had a stroke and was not expected to live. He lingered in a state of unconsciousness for 10 days before he died. By the time we arrived, my mother, too, was in the hospital. I'd spoken to her just a few days earlier, and we'd had a great, relaxed conversation with a lot of joking around and laughter. She still suffered from anxiety (which was treated with tranquilizers), had little energy, and slept a lot. But she remained hopeful. By now, though, her symptoms likely did not reflect depression so much as the ravages of time, stress, illness, and prior depressions. She had lost consciousness at home, and an ambulance brought her to the hospital. She had uncontrollable high blood pressure that led to a stomach aneurysm and death. It happened when she learned that my father was near death.

Despite their separation a strong emotional connection remained. Recently I came across a Father's Day card she'd sent him in the year before he died, telling him he'd been a great father to their children. She'd also bake cookies and bring them to him at the nursing center. She understood that he, too, had experienced major losses and that his upbringing had been saturated with stress. But she could not be around him for long, as his morose nature dragged her down. Only after their deaths did we learn, while going through old papers that they had never divorced or legally separated.

My sister and I had just a little over a day to spend with mother before she died. She was in intense pain and became very angry and agitated. Doctors did not prescribe sufficient pain medication, and she truly suffered. She railed and raged against death, vowing to overcome her illness yet another time. Her father's words about her as a child—"she dies hard"—were reflective of the end of her life. She became extremely angry with me and lashed out as she had when I was in high school. Transported back to the past, the relationship changes we'd worked so hard to achieve unraveled in the brief time we had left together. Intellectually, I understood why, but it was still emotionally devastating.

Even in death my mother assumed center stage. Grief compounded by her final rejection, the steady stream of people in and out of her apartment, and the organization of a memorial service held a few days after her death all left me with little emotional energy for my father. Even though he was unconscious, I felt that I was not spending enough time with him. By then I just felt numb. The flowers from mother's memorial service were still fresh, and we used them again for my father's service. We spent a week there clearing their living quarters and completing paperwork. I returned home to prepare for a review of my scientific work to be held in a few months.

The Laboratory of Developmental Psychology, headed by my former mentor, was about to be closed. It was the last remaining behavioral research laboratory within the NIMH Intramural Research Program. My Section on Developmental Psychopathology was transferred into a more biologically oriented laboratory. The review went well, and I obtained more resources than I had in the past. But I felt under the gun and isolated as one of the last behavioral psychologists there. It was just a question of time before I, too, would leave. But while there my team completed a longitudinal study of risk and resilience in adolescents with psychopathology. As losses and stresses accumulated, I pressed forward, ignoring my feelings. It had worked in the past, and stoicism was part of how I coped.

However, I started to experience symptoms of stress. My arms and legs tingled, but I passed it off as feeling energized, as I was very active professionally. One day I passed out in an aerobics class, and an ambulance took me to the hospital. My blood pressure had soared, and I spent a while in the hospital while they tried to regulate it. They did many other diagnostic tests to rule out other problems, and I was highly anxious throughout this period. A beta blocker lowered the blood pressure but also slowed me down to a leaden state that made it difficult to function. I told doctors that it made me depressed (which can happen with beta blockers), but they waited over a month until they had completed all the other tests before changing the medication.

Meanwhile my mental health deteriorated, and I entered a full-blown episode of severe depression. My body didn't work right. I could not stand for any period of time. I was barely able to walk across the room without support. It felt as though I was walking through cotton batting: foggy, laden down, and disconnected. I could not shop because the bright lights in stores created distortions and afterimages of items that projected onto the next items. Sounds were deafening. Heightened sensations left me feeling nauseated and faint. I lost weight and had difficulty sleeping. Everything was fuzzy and distant, and I could barely form sentences. I tried to keep working, to keep writing, but my brain wouldn't cooperate. I'd start to type a sentence but lose the initial thought midway, so I could not complete it. Concentration was impossible. I was tearful, irritable, and agitated.

My husband was supportive. Our daughter was frightened, stressed, and saddened. It is difficult to convey fully the loss of control and emotional devastation that consumes every aspect of life while in this state. It is as if one's very self becomes lost. My internist referred me to a psychiatrist, who prescribed medication that relieved the symptoms. The psychiatrist was helpful while I was very depressed, but became defensive and argumentative as I began to feel better and no longer accepted his authority on all matters. He sometimes fell asleep in the sessions, so I had no incentive to continue for long. With one exception, the quality of treatment I received for depression over the years was mediocre. I've learned the importance of being proactive. It is hard to advocate for oneself or to find high-quality care when you are very depressed or resistant to the idea that you are depressed. Now I am connected to a better, integrated medical care system if the need should arise again.

INTERWEAVING OUR PERSONAL AND PROFESSIONAL WORLDS

Information about the causes, development, transmission, and treatment of depression has grown remarkably since I was a child and young adult. There is now a large literature on offspring of depressed parents, chiefly mothers. Many of the themes in my own narrative are reflected in this literature, reminding me that I am far from alone in my experiences. My own research focused first on how young children develop empathy for others in distress and on how concern for others may become compromised in unsupportive environments. This led to research on children of depressed parents and on sex differences in depression. My understanding of depression and its transmission derives from both my personal experiences and my professional interests, and they have richly informed each other over the course of time.

We now know that the lifetime risk of depression for children with a depressed parent is roughly 45%. Because depression runs in families and can have a genetic basis, heredity is likely to play some role in children's vulnerability. However, the environments of children of depressed parents also increase the likelihood of later depression. Depressed mothers are less reciprocal, attuned, and engaged with their children than are healthy, nondepressed mothers. Not only are they sadder, but they also express a greater range of other negative emotions, such as anxiety, guilt, irritability, and hostility. Children exposed to a parent's despair and lack of pleasure in daily life can experience these emotions through processes of contagion and imitation. Depressed parents often use helpless, passive coping styles. They use discipline that is either ineffectual or too harsh and coercive or that involves guilt induction.

Family communication is often dysfunctional and includes marital conflict. One cannot easily say which comes first, the parental depression or the conflict. But this is beside the point for the child, who experiences each as part of a larger depressogenic environment. Children's specific experiences will differ markedly because of individual differences both in the parents and children.

Girls are more susceptible to maternal depression than boys. Regardless of parental depression, females are at least two times more likely to be afflicted with depression than males, beginning in adolescence. So it is important to consider aspects of the mother-daughter relationship that heighten risk for depression, particularly in girls. The mother-daughter conflicts I have described in this chapter suggest ways in which loss, rejection, and criticism help to perpetuate depression. Patterns of withdrawal, avoidance, and anger (both expressed and suppressed) escalate and become entrenched as styles of interaction that can repeat across generations. Whether the parent or the child plays the major initiating role, both keep the process going once conflict begins.

There are characteristics more common to girls than boys that make them more vulnerable to depression, again regardless of parental depression: a shy, anxious temperament; empathic overarousal and guilt proneness; a strong interpersonal orientation; submissiveness or lack of assertion; conformity to stereotypic feminine traits; ruminative coping styles (i.e., dwelling on problems); sensitivity to rejection; repression and internalization of anger; and poor self-image.

Oppositional, aggressive girls are also likely later to become depressed. It would seem best to be neither "too good" nor "too bad" if you are a girl, especially if you have a seriously depressed mother. When parent and child risk factors combine, the child is even more likely to develop depression.

It is important to begin to use available information, basic and clinical, to help parents and children in these families. William Beardslee has developed an intervention for families with a depressed caregiver. It is designed to help children understand they are not responsible for their parents' bad moods—that is, they are not the cause of the sadness, anger, and withdrawal. This is essential as feelings of extreme guilt or of being at fault can play a major role in the perpetuation of depression.

Some children with a depressed parent take on the role of caregiver, girls especially, and this stance can increase their own depressive symptoms. This is what my sister did. Others, like me, create distance and try to steel themselves against the parents' pain and rage. The child who tries to become a parent to her parent risks being defined more by others' needs and desires than her own. The child who tries to separate, to establish her own identity and independence, experiences guilt over pulling away from and rejecting the parent. Both are pathways to depression that neither my sister nor I were able to avoid.

It would be an oversimplification to reduce the process of transmission of depression to the transmission of guilt. But it is hardly coincidence that guilt plays a central role in some theories of depression. One theory even defines depression in terms of the tendency to attribute negative events to internal, stable, and global causes: "It's my fault"; "I'm responsible for the bad things that happen"; and "It will always be that way." Narratives such as mine show how these negative patterns become part of the fabric of everyday life, even in childhood. Children of depressed parents tend to have high levels of guilt.

Although extreme environmentalists would view harsh parenting and rejection as a form of emotional abuse that causes children's problems, simplistic mother-blaming theories are no longer accepted. But chemical imbalance theories are equally simplistic. It may be convenient to blame one's problems on either a toxic parent or a chemical imbalance, with advocates of the latter suggesting a minimal role for parenting. But good care must consider that, over and above genetic vulnerability, parents do matter—that maladaptive parenting is common in depressed caregivers and can interfere with children's psychological development. Interventions need to focus not only on treating the depressed parent but also on how she or he can become a more effective caregiver. Treatments must promote these goals in ways that avoid judgment or blame.

My reason for writing and talking about my personal experience is to encourage others to do the same and to recognize that they are not alone. This is important for people going into mental health professions, whether research or clinical. It is often easy to disconnect from our own life circumstances and problems, to ignore our own pain. There are many reasons for avoidance: desire for privacy, a wish to get on with our own lives, fear of exposure, stigma, and so forth. We may worry that our ideas will not be taken as seriously as they would coming from someone from a "normal" background (whatever that might mean). We also may worry that our problems don't deserve attention because we are still relatively well off compared with many others. All of these reasons are unfortunate, as the ability to articulate and draw on these experiences can make us better scientists and clinicians. In fact, we may come to see our family histories and dynamics from a unique, enriched perspective that can facilitate theory, research, and recovery.

It would be a mistake to assume that depression is inevitable in children with a depressed parent or that when depression does occur it becomes the central defining feature of a person. We are all so much more than the sum of our symptoms. An intergenerational narrative about mental illness inevitably focuses more on problems than pleasures in life. But it would be a disservice to my family to ignore the riches in our lives. Every family member also experienced love, joy, beauty, growth, and reverence for life, despite setbacks and tribulations. Heightened sensitivities create vulnerabilities, but they also open passageways to unique possibilities and life-affirming transformations. Telling our stories is part of this process.

ACKNOWLEDGMENTS

The love, support, insights, and remembrances of my husband Morris Waxler, my daughter Rebecca Waxler-Ramsey, my sister Barbara Zahn, and my aunt Marianne Kellman have greatly enriched the quality of my life and made the writing of this family narrative possible. I am also deeply grateful to the following wonderful women from our women writers' group at the First Unitarian Society in Madison, Wisconsin, for their encouragement and feedback on many portions of the chapter: Sherry Brenner, Joyce Carey, Hannah Pinkerton, Marnie Schulenberg, and Bobbi Zehner. Finally, I thank Stephen Hinshaw for his wisdom in creating this volume of narratives and for his excellent editorial advice. For scientific references pertinent to the material and themes of this chapter, please contact me at the following e-mail address: czahnwaxler@wisc.edu.

15   Closing Thoughts: The Power of Narrative

Stephen P. Hinshaw

In light of the intensity, depth, and poignancy of the preceding chapters, my first reaction was that any summaries or impressions I might add could risk being superfluous. On reflection, I do believe that there may be some value in commenting on key issues found in these contributions and in providing my own personal perspective on the value of disclosure of mental illness—and the power of narrative in general. These are therefore my goals for this closing chapter, along with providing a brief overview of future trends regarding mental illness, disclosure, and stigma.

REFLECTIONS ON THE CONTRIBUTIONS

In providing impressionistic reflections on each of the book's chapters, I do not give any kind of exhaustive review but instead offer a paragraph-long "take" on each, including a short set of questions that their contents have raised for me. Because I will undoubtedly be missing essential themes in this brief tour, I invite you to fill in the blanks with your own reactions, impressions, and questions.

In chapter 1 ("My Story Is One of Loss"), Laura Mason tells vividly of her family's disintegration in the wake of the crushing forms of mental illness displayed, in turn, by each of her three older sisters. Except for her own therapy, Laura's pain has been essentially unspeakable for much of her life. That she has now found a voice to express that pain is a gift to all readers. The incredible turns in her own life (college by age 15; multiple marriages, careers, and identities; finding a deep calling in clinical psychology) are undoubtedly related to the fragmentation experienced by her family. Yet her devoted work in psychology and her creation of a new family are a tribute to the deep sensitivity with which she was undoubtedly endowed from an early age—and to the empathy and strength she accrued from witnessing her sisters' experiences. Lingering questions remain: Can one ever really escape the pain of such family tragedy? How did Laura, at age 13, have the presence simply to be with and to sit with her oldest sister, who was disintegrating before her eyes? How did she use her subsequent life experiences to discover ways to assist her many patients and trainees in this phase of her life, as a clinic coordinator, teacher, and supervisor? Although we seldom hear about this perspective, experiences of mental illness may well produce strength and compassion, in addition to deep pain and despair.

Ruth White ("Finding My Mind," chapter 2) provides a densely interwoven narrative that incorporates vivid journal entries that bring alive her deepest thoughts and emotions. She reveals the confusion, denial, and terror accompanying the realization that her life's predominant style—brilliance, lightning-quick turnaround of ideas and projects—signals, at a deeper level, a history of not just ADHD and depression but also manic-depressive illness (bipolar disorder). In brutally honest prose, she depicts agitated, impulsive, and hopeless moments that undoubtedly signaled "mixed states," which combined manic levels of energy with dark, destructive impulses. Particularly vivid is her recounting of the sudden temptations to take her daughter's life, as well as her own. She captures, in addition, the support offered by close friends (once she reached out to them) during her frantic moments of heading downhill, as well as her strong ambivalence about admitting her illness and receiving treatment for it. By the chapter's end, she has come to essential realizations about her life as a professor, activist, and mother, emerging with motivation to communicate her experiences to a wider audience. Among many issues, I raise two questions here: How many individuals with similar symptoms and problems make it through to this important "place" of recognition, motivation for change, and letting go of a lifestyle that is inherently destructive? And in what ways is the devastation related to bipolar disorder counteracted, at least to some extent, by the strengths and energy that may accompany mild to moderate forms or phases of mania? Given that most individuals with this condition do not "stay" in hypomania but instead progress to disorganization and despair, this is a clinically important issue.

In chapter 3 ("A Field Agent in Our Midst"), Tara Peris recounts the painful deterioration of her mother from the time that Tara was quite young until her early teen years, at which time her mother departed suddenly for Japan, the victim of an increasingly obsessive, psychotic, and isolating disorder. Throughout the narrative, Tara expresses a sense that she is not really equipped to come to terms with this crucial aspect of her life—her mother's disappearance—because, in her words, she dealt with the feelings long ago, and she is powerless to capture its lingering effects. Yet despite her self-deprecation related to her ability to express herself, Tara vividly portrays a range of poignant themes: her appreciation of many aspects of her mother during her childhood; the sense that her father's support and her own coping have almost—but not quite—compensated for her loss; and her sudden panic when she realizes, in her late 20s, that her mother has suddenly returned to the United States without warning, which throws asunder the tight "packaging" with which Tara has stored away her mother's 15-year absence. I was also struck by Tara's depiction of her interest in psychology, particularly the research aspects of psychopathology, with the insight that the distance accruing from the scientific process may provide just the right "level" of involvement and detachment for her, keeping deep feelings of vulnerability somewhat removed. I ask the following questions: How can children of parents with severe mental illness fill the gaps and holes left by the absences and confusion they have experienced? How does one ever really come to terms with the permanent loss that can sometimes accompany mental illness? In what ways can caregivers and supports best communicate with the child of a parent with a severe mental disorder, balancing honest disclosure and a need to protect?

Next, in chapter 4 ("Laura's Story: Making Sense of and Deriving Meaning From Her Life With Mental Illness"), Liz Owens writes a heartbreaking narrative about her sister's eventual demise from years of substance and alcohol abuse, eating disorder, and depression. In reading this chapter, I had the sense of watching—from a vantage point high above—an impending, catastrophic train wreck occurring in a valley below, with the realization that inevitable destruction will soon occur but utterly powerless to do anything but observe and sympathize. If I experienced such feelings from simply reading this account, what must Liz have felt herself during the process, especially given the wonderful yet vanishingly rare times in which she and Laura had moments of real, sister-to-sister contact? Laura's promise, skill with children, and deep vulnerability emerge vividly in the passages of this chapter, yet the horror of her demise dominates the text. Liz voices utter frustration and anger with the "partners" who aided and abetted her sister's self-destruction. Even though I share some of this outrage, I sense that Laura somehow felt compelled to go back to her identity as vulnerable, weak, and deserving of utter abuse, attesting to the destructive power of addictions. Like Liz, I note that when mental illness is accompanied by alcohol and substance issues, society's patience and tolerance wear thin quite quickly. How can empathy be fostered for this population? In what ways can we foster greater compassion, support, and guidance for those who are losing their way in such horribly annihilating territory?

In chapter 5's portrayal ("In My Voice: Speaking Out About Mental Health and Stigma"), Jeff Liew takes us vividly into the world of his family's struggles as immigrants, compounded by his mother's increasingly severe depression. When we realize, early on in the chapter, that Jeff is suddenly witnessing his mother's attempt to hang herself in the basement of the apartment—with Jeff just 8 years old and his younger brother at his side—and then rescues her, it is abundantly clear that absence, despair, and shame will follow. Jeff also takes us headlong into the stigma he encountered in his neighborhood, as friends essentially repeated what they had heard at home: Jeff's mother was crazy, taken away by the police. After his mother's return from a 3-year absence, her depressions ultimately begin to alternate with disorganized, impulsive periods of mania. When focusing on his own life, Jeff is brutally honest in letting us know that he internalized much of the shame and silence he encountered as a child, holding on to overly harsh self-expectations and denying himself, for too long, the opportunity for treatment. Questions abound: Why is stigma so pervasive in multiple cultures and ethnic groups? How can one who takes on the role of family caregiver balance responsibility and the need to individuate? In what ways can professionals, neighbors, and communities support families experiencing serious mental illness?

At the beginning of chapter 6 ("Columbus Day, 1994: A New World"), Kay Browne discusses her medical, psychiatric, and pediatric training, which left her unprepared for the wrenching events, several decades later, of her 19-year-old son's plunge into psychosis and depression at the beginning of his sophomore year of college. She conveys vividly the lost, despairing feelings that he (and she) experienced during and after his initial hospitalization, the many years it took to find the right treatment regimen, the false starts of different job attempts, the interplay among various family members in supporting Nathan, and the gradual recovery that he has made. In reading this deeply felt work I sensed the isolation that all too frequently accompanied Nathan's sometimes incomprehensible behavior patterns, along with the family's struggle to support him despite his often-voiced resistance. I also sensed Kay's attempts to hold onto hope despite being overwhelmed, at times, with the task of helping him to reenter the world of family and work. Quite telling is her depiction of the ignorance and insensitivity communicated by several caregivers, which recapitulated key experiences from her early training. Over the years Kay has been increasingly motivated toward activism with respect to educating and supporting other family members. Among my questions: Why do mental health providers show, at times, such a lack of hope for those they treat? Can more enlightened, encouraging, and sensitive attitudes come to the fore? Clinically, how can we better predict long-term outcome in young adults experiencing serious forms of mental illness?

Marc Atkins, in chapter 7—"The Meaning of Mental Health (and Other Lessons Learned)"—opens the door on his own difficult experiences in college, the most frightening of which was his auditory hallucination while on his small-college campus during the turbulent era of Vietnam War protests. With the perspective of many years and many life experiences later, Marc discusses the politically infused nature of his upbringing and his college days; the psychiatric treatment he received following this incident, which gave him the message that he had lifelong schizophrenia; the support of his family; his move West, affording him the opportunity to find an identity in working with children in educational settings; and his eventual understanding, as a clinical/community psychologist, that his unique perspectives as both patient and healer could help him give much back to the field. He maintains, in our biologically dominated era, a belief in the restorative power of supportive environments, while recounting his life's troubling experiences with refreshing humor, perspective, and insight.

His contribution sparks such questions as these: How does identity emerge in the wake of fragmenting, life-changing experiences? What, in fact, are the ways in which biological predisposition, environmental context, and personal characteristics blend to shape resilient functioning? Which types of environments and settings can pull individuals out of risk?

Chapter 8 ("Memories of Parental Decompensation") finds Ted Beauchaine describing his childhood, in which he, his twin sister, and their older brother coped with their mother's descent into chronic schizophrenia. Some of the events are so painful that it is hard to get the images out of one's mind—for instance, the time that their mother forced Ted's sister to eat her own vomit as a punishment. Portrayed with considerable force are the loneliness of each of the family members, the seeming impossibility of forging coherent communication about the events that were serving to destroy the family, and the utter misery of serious mental illness for all involved (in this case, endless arguments and tears, paranoia, and shattered boundaries). Yet, many years later, following another psychotic break in which she injured herself, Ted saw his mother in her hospital bed and immediately began to forgive her. How does one deal with, confront, and attempt to escape the pernicious legacy of serious mental illness in one's family of origin? In what ways can forgiveness and acceptance eventually emerge? And, related to the shaping of identity and career, how has Ted used his intellectual prowess to transform such early experiences into his groundbreaking studies in developmental psychopathology? As with all of the chapters, far more questions are raised than answered.

Chapter 9 ("Weeping Mother") portrays, in terms that are sometimes brutal yet often uplifting, the utter depression of Jarralynne Agee's mother, the stark poverty in which the family found itself for many years, and the impact of these early experiences on Jarralynne's life and career. At one point, I felt as though I were inside the car with Jarralynne, her brother, and her sister, as their mother drove ever faster while screaming, crying, and telling them that she would end her own life and theirs by driving into the lake—only to swerve away at the last minute. Neglect, violence, and despair were close beneath the surface throughout Jarralynne's youth. At the same time, her mother found solace and inspiration in becoming a source of support for other children and families in their bleak neighborhood. Eventually, Jarralynne realized that much of her motivation for work in psychology has emanated from a desire to help others avoid the sometimes-crushing fate of her mother. In her later years, as her mother became physically incapacitated and her depression lifted, Jarralynne (like Ted in Chapter 8) found considerable forgiveness in her heart. We might ask such questions as these: How do poverty and severe life stress fuel depression? How do some children escape such a dual legacy and become strong, compassionate, and concerned individuals? In what ways can effective treatments be delivered to the hardest-to-reach people and families in need?

In chapter 10 Jessie Borelli ("The Game With No Rules: A Sibling Confronts Mental Illness") initially conveys the promise of her family's new baby brother—adopted at the time that she, her sister, and her brother eagerly awaited another sibling—and then documents his chronic struggles with extreme acting-out behavior, shutdown moods, and a range of psychiatric diagnoses (including severe ADHD/ODD and, more recently, bipolar disorder). Full of rage, and violent on many occasions, Daniel can be disarmingly honest and sensitive at other moments. But the rules of engagement with him shift constantly, leading to Jessie's lifelong struggle to learn which rules apply. Rifts within the family, alliances intended to help Daniel that simultaneously exclude the feelings and safety of other children, wave upon wave of help seeking...all of these became part and parcel of Jessie's and her family's existence. She conveys with vivid images how she has been torn by panic, chaos, and divided loyalties. What is the prognosis for a boy, now in late adolescence, with the troubling history exhibited by Daniel? What is the right level of care and intervention needed in such cases, balancing the individual's personalized treatment needs with the family's well-being and even physical safety? How can any member of the family find a safe haven, while at the same time pushing for appropriate services? Such questions emerge from this gripping chapter.

For chapter 11 ("Reverberations") Peter Nathan provides the story of an event that occurred many years ago, before his earliest recollections: his mother's suicide, around the time that he was 1 year old. Without any memories of this occurrence, he must rely on the imprecise recollections of his older brother and the accounts of various family members. This tragedy, reflecting the depression that had permeated his mother's short life, as well as a mismatch in style between her and her husband's family, has reverberated through Peter's life and the lives of his relatives for seven decades. Parts of the legacy include silence and untruth (his father told Peter for many years that his mother had died of "natural causes"), distance (Peter and his brother took years to become close), blame (many relatives blamed Peter's father), and Peter's own difficulty in knowing how to relate to women until adulthood. The balance and wisdom evident in Peter's words show how deeply he has processed and dealt with his early loss. Indeed, although he is grateful for his father's support in the early years following the suicide, he has made a conscious effort to be a more involved father with his own children than his father was with him. Among my questions are the following: How do families persevere in the wake of blame and turmoil surrounding tragedies such as this one? In what ways can service providers encourage discussion, even with young children, following these types of events, to prevent the self-blame and feeling of isolation and stigma that are likely to ensue? How can people emerge with the wisdom and perspective of someone like Peter Nathan?

In chapter 12—"He Just Can't Help It: My Struggle With My Father's Struggle With Bipolar Disorder"—Esme Londahl-Shaller conveys the life history of a tempestuous, troubled, strong, and fascinating man, her father. Through four marriages, a history of psychiatric treatments and hospitalizations, an unorthodox style, a propensity for "too much" in the way of alcohol, negative emotions, and love, he has left an indelible impression on Esme, who relishes her many feelings about him, which include alternating waves of puzzlement, sympathy, embarrassment, and admiration. A key theme is the question of whether her father was responsible for many of his actions: the psychosis, the hospitalizations, the dramatic flair, the near-collapses during family holidays. In other words, could he really help it? Nearly all relatives of individuals with serious mental illness ask the same question, raising not only a major philosophical issue (to what extent does free will exist?) but also a deeply personal one—whose fault *is* it when my relative does things that embarrass, frighten, or harm? The constantly shifting time periods of Esme's narrative remind us of the dense interplay of past and present in recounting the life of an individual with mental illness; they also indicate the intense worry felt by offspring over their own risk for abnormal behavior. Of my impressions from this sometimes humorous but always poignant narrative, I recall vividly the huge distrust of psychological and psychiatric caregivers that Esme's father felt, undoubtedly reflecting the crude treatments he received in the 1940s, 1950s, and 1960s, as well as Esme's tender recounting of the many things she has learned from her father. Overall, how does risk for psychiatric illness transmit across generations, through both genes and contexts? What kinds of personal and family qualities promote the kinds of compassion, wry humor, and dedication shown by Esme in her personal and professional life?

Janet Lucas's chapter (chapter 13, "Performing Human") is almost too unbearable to recount, given her untimely demise just months after completing it. Edited from her longer piece on the dilemmas experienced by victims of severe abuse in "closed" family systems, this chapter provides a searing, even brutal portrayal of the kinds of violence and neglect she experienced during childhood. Indeed, she conveys with power her self-image as "garbage" throughout much of her adolescence, as well as her transformation into a talented business person and brilliant scholar in adulthood, while still carrying the overwhelming sense that through these efforts she was able only to simulate normality and humanity. Indeed, her underlying identity was moored in a conception of flawed, damaged goods. Particularly sobering in her account is the sense of stigma she underwent even at the hands of her pharmacists, who would look askance at the prescriptions for the regimen of antidepressant medications she required. Remarkably poignant are Janet's accounts of her adult hospitalizations, during which her mother reached out to her and comforted her, attempting to undo the years of terror from several decades before. (Her father's retreat into sadism, following a few weeks of humanity after his wife's death, is another story.)

But one cannot escape the fact of Janet's ultimate despair, which suffuses the entire narrative and which culminated in what undoubtedly was her suicide in the late summer of 2006. Questions seem futile, but I must ask the following: For victims and survivors of horrific abuse, what kinds of experiences can restore a sense of wholeness, normality, and generativity? In what ways do medication treatments for depression, particularly when there is such a strong abusive history, need to be supplemented by a range of psychological and family-based interventions? How can we prevent the awful waste of suicide, which continues to be a surprisingly strong source of mortality? Janet, I'm so sorry that you ultimately could not find the hope, stability, and wholeness you so desperately needed and deserved.

Finally, in chapter 14 ("The Legacy of Loss: Depression As a Family Affair"), Carolyn Zahn-Waxler presents a multigenerational account of her family, featuring her mother's descent into severe, agitated depression and her father's drinking and poor coping. In its early stages, the chapter provides vivid histories of her parents; as the narrative emerges, Carolyn deals directly with the effects of such behavior patterns on her own personal and career development. This chapter is deep and rich, graphically depicting the barrage of verbiage, criticism, and somaticizing her mother inflicted on her family and the ramifications of this legacy for Carolyn's own adult tendencies to exhibit panic and depression. Its deepest parts, from my perspective, occur when Carolyn discloses her own vulnerabilities as a wife, scientist, and mother, relating these themes to her disgruntlement over (and resulting distance from) her mother's unrelenting criticism and unhappiness. The lack of responsive intervention for her mother, during the middle of the last century, is a recurring theme. Particularly inspiring is Carolyn's learning from her early experiences, which she used to correct difficult aspects of her relationship with her own daughter. Little wonder that she has pursued studies of intergenerational transmission of empathy and distress as part of her distinguished research portfolio. I ask the following: How can families receive help and experience hope when one or both parents experience major mental illness? In what ways can children receive messages that are realistic and yet encouraging? And what qualities seem to distinguish those offspring in high-risk families who succumb to the risk of mood disorder or other disturbance from those who can overcome their legacy? Although the concept of resilience is controversial, we need to understand far better than we do now which processes promote healthy adaptation in the face of risk.

Once again, I offer my heartfelt gratitude to each contributor. Many readers will now know of your pain, your struggles, your triumphs, and your deep humanity.

AFTER DISCLOSING: WHAT NEXT?

As I noted in the Introduction, the event that jump-started the initiation of this volume was the process of writing and publishing my own narrative about my father (*The Years of Silence Are Past*). In writing this book, I probed his fascinating yet sometimes terrifying life, the silence in which I had grown up with respect to his mental illness, the disclosures he made to me about his life story once I was a young adult, my reactions and responses to this information, my growing interest in psychology, and my attempts to integrate scientific and personal perspectives on mental illness in my life's work.[1] At this point, I discuss briefly some reflections on writing this narrative and provide my own sense of the outcomes of such disclosure.

Disclosing

The most important experience of my entire life was hearing, once I started college, my father tell me about his psychosis, mental hospitalizations, religious and philosophical quests, and lifetime of shame over his history. Such experiences were enshrouded in silence and concealment throughout my youth, until my father decided to go "against medical advice"—his doctors had told him never to tell my sister and me about his mental illness—and open up with his story. Once I began hearing it, I was both fascinated and terrified by his revelations, with the terror related, in large part, to wondering about my own risk for mental illness. At the same time, I welcomed the honesty and disclosure, realizing that he was telling the truth—and beginning the long process of coming to terms with the loneliness that was much a part of my growing up.

Only after getting education and training in clinical psychology, and then having Kay Jamison as a teacher/supervisor at UCLA's Neuropsychiatric Institute during my internship, did I begin to sense that my father's story could prove valuable for others to know about. Indeed, many individuals with psychotic episodes were misdiagnosed during the twentieth century. Still, it took many more years before I began to sense that I could put material together for *The Years of Silence Are Past*. In other words, it was not until my late 30s and early 40s that I became serious about constructing a narrative.

As my father had with me in his discussions, I began slowly, in measured tones, to write down what I had learned about his initial breakdowns and hospitalizations, his triumphs and periods of despair, my life at home as a child, and my growing sense of the need for accurate diagnosis and responsive treatment for all those with mental illness. My initial attempts were articles; but these became, with time, a book-length contribution, given that the story of my father's life, my responses to it, and the clinical lessons that I wished to convey (e.g., the underlying humanity of people with mental illness; the need for family communication) took many pages to tell.

My initial efforts were often constricted, sometimes overly intellectualized. I didn't have a language or a voice for talking about such difficult events and my feelings surrounding them. At the same time, it was hard to hear criticism from friends, colleagues, and editors about my early drafts. It is one thing to have a scientific paper critiqued for clarity and cogency but quite another to have intimate portrayals of one's father and one's own deeply personal experiences edited and criticized. I was vulnerable and sensitive; I began to sense that the story was not worthwhile or important and that I couldn't tell it right in any event.

Perseverance is the ally of every writer, however. I had enough faith in the importance of my father's life, the importance of disclosure in general, and the need to tell the truth about mental illness that I kept at it. How hard it was, at times, to break through the stilted words that I had written or the stuck places within which I had become embedded to try and convey, far more directly and cogently, how frightening it was to have a father disappear for periods of time…or to wonder whether I myself would end up in a mental hospital if I relinquished the tight control under which I existed…or to ask myself how I might have survived being chained to a hospital bed, with voices plaguing me and with fellow inmates sometimes attacking me. Or, too, what it was like to be part of a family that appeared to produce either high achievement or mental illness across many generations.

Over several years, the book took shape, through my wrestling with phrasing, structure, and tone. Yet a major issue arose: how to publish it and at the same time honor my mother's desire not to have intimate details of the family history available to the public. My mother had seen an early draft that I wrote in the mid-1990s, near the time of my father's death, and was taken aback by my initial attempt to portray the hospitalizations, the absences, and the warmth he showed to me (but not always to her) when he returned. "Publish this in a journal, if you must," she said to me, "but not so that I could see it in a bookstore or newsstand."

I felt trapped. Should I accede to my mother's understandable wish for privacy—after all, it was she who had held the family together without any real support during her husband's psychotic bouts and lengthy hospitalizations when my sister and I were young—and fail to tell the story of my father's life? Or do I break the silence and shame that surrounded my father's episodes for so many years but at the same time risk both hurting and alienating my mother?

As usual, my wife, Kelly, was correct. Although she identified strongly with my mother's plight across so many decades (Kelly's own family history is marked by alcoholism and mental disorder), she realized that I simply had to complete my mission and that my mother would sense how deeply important this entire task was to me. Still feeling stuck, I told Kelly, with frustration, that she didn't really get it: publishing the book would betray my mother, but withholding its publication would mean that the most important story of my life would never be revealed. There was no way out.

Against my better judgment, I went ahead. When the book was released, in the fall of 2002 (and with Kelly newly pregnant with Evan, our youngest), we returned to my childhood home in Ohio to see my mother. Giving her the book was a tense situation, as she was clearly uncomfortable. Yet it was not more than a couple of months later that she called me in Berkeley, asking whether I could get a copy to her for her bookreading group. Within a couple of weeks, she called back, saying that some members of the group—including friends from her childhood, who knew something of my father's history and episodes but certainly not all that I revealed in the book—were amazed at her courage, perseverance, and sensitivity in keeping the family together. Soon after, my mother would call to ask me why the book hadn't been reviewed in more outlets!

I believe that it was the validation from some of her oldest friends, who finally understood what she had so courageously done, that turned the tide. Indeed, my mother may well have been the biggest victim of all of the family's silence, and formal acknowledgment of her crucial role in keeping the family together must have been both a relief and a clear validation of her unsung work.

Disclosure may not be what everyone in a family wants. Each family system is unique, but in my case, I now know that Kelly was right: my mother came to terms with my deep conviction about the importance of the material I wished to present to the world, and she herself not only acceded to but gained from the process.

Changed Identity

What has happened in the years since the book's publication? Initially, I was disappointed with the response, or lack thereof, to the book's release, but I soon realized that a book from an academic publisher that blended personal and family disclosure with clinical and scientific background about bipolar disorder was not likely to have large sales. Still, hundreds of responses came via letter and e-mail, from far and wide. To a person, the correspondents voiced relief that a story of family mental illness had been told, with some hugely grateful that a person with severe bipolar disorder had been accurately portrayed as a sensitive father. Many divulged their own, or their family's, long struggles with mental illness. It was clear that I had touched a nerve.

In lectures, community talks, and book readings, I began to speak about families and mental illness and, in addition, about the stigma that still surrounds people with mental disorder. At every talk I gave, people clamored for time afterward to discuss their own stories, their own narratives of pain, concealment, despair, and latent hope. In my teaching of large undergraduate courses at Berkeley, as well as smaller graduate seminars, I felt freer to add segments on the personal and family impact of mental illness, supplementing the usual material on scientific models and evidence-based treatments. Students hunger for such disclosure, for such humanization of mental illness. I have felt more empowered to emphasize the dual goals of rigorous science and meaningful narrative.

At the same time, my research has become richer and more fulfilling. I am still utterly convinced of the need for objective testing of hypotheses, validated measures, rigorous research designs, and other necessary components of sound science. Yet because of my having publicly disclosed some of the most personal roots regarding my interest in the field, I now feel even more committed to developmental psychopathology, clinical trials, longitudinal follow-up, family and peer factors, neuropsychological risk, and all of the other topics I investigate. Understanding one's own powerful motivations can help to focus deepened interest.

Overall, I now have a richer sense of who I am as a clinical scientist, advocate, narrator, teacher, and (more recently) department chair. I sense a deeper "calling" than ever in terms of my work and my commitment to the field, along with a clearer conviction that all aspects of my efforts have an underlying integration.

Picking up on the theme, from my father's life, of the shame and silence that still cling to mental disorder, during the past few years I have published a number of reviews on the stigmatization of mental illness and on the need for personal and family disclosure in pointing scientists in the right direction with respect to important research questions.[2] Recently, I published a major book on the continuing stigmatization of mental illness (*The Mark of Shame*), and a core section of my lab at Berkeley is now devoted to stigma-related research efforts. Along with my other projects, I plan in the near future on rewriting *The Years of Silence Are Past* for a wider audience, focusing this revision on the narrative of my father and our relationship at a deeper and more intimate level, downplaying some of the associated clinical and scientific issues from the original book. The hope is that the act of disclosure and the contents of the narrative can reach more families, clinicians, scientists, and policy makers, as well as the public at large.

Overall, my main wish is for a great many more years to work on all that I would like to accomplish with respect to my expanding scientific, narrative, and advocacy-related efforts. In every way possible, disclosure has invigorated all aspects of my career and life—a signal, perhaps, that the time is ripe for a widening circle of narrative accounts to chip away at concealment and stigma.

THE FUTURE

What kind of a world awaits patients and clients, research participants, and families who are confronting mental illness on a daily basis? I see two distinct avenues.

On the one hand, the increased openness of the past few years could pervade the work and worldviews of a great many scientists and clinicians, as well as large segments of the general public. In this scenario, it will not be considered deviant or especially "brave" to reveal mental illness; indeed, discussing life stories relevant to all categories of mental disorder will be more commonplace. A true humanization will occur, as policy makers, professionals, providers, scientists, and the citizenry at large can come to realize that no one wins when the deep pain of mental illness is concealed and suppressed. Funding for relevant research will increase, treatments will be more responsive and powerful, insurance coverage will attain parity, and—despite the fears that will cling to behavior patterns that are unusual, threatening, and irrational—a general wave of social acceptance will emerge.

The other vision is far more pessimistic. In this scenario, stigma toward mental illness may well increase. As educational success becomes more and more valued, as conformity is more highly sought as a function of industrialization and mass production, as community supports continue to evaporate in a world of fractionated families who are disconnected from their roots, as causal models of mental illness increasingly propose deviant genes as the underlying roots (with the potential for ascriptions to permanence and fundamental, internal flaws), and as media portrayals continue to promote single standards of appearance and behavior, mental illness may become more feared than ever. In addition, as social standards change, with proscriptions against the overt castigation of mental illness, bias and prejudice may increasingly be displayed via internal, implicit, and hidden forms of rejection and distancing.[3] In other words, parallel to current racial and ethnic attitudes, mental illness stigma may head underground and fester.

The reality is likely to fall somewhere in between these two poles. In our pluralistic society, some elements may tilt toward openness and acceptance, whereas others may close their ranks. Much will depend on how mental health workers, professionals, and scientists decide to work and live. If we opt for openness, disclosure, and honesty in important narrative accounts; if we realize that an "us versus them" stance is not only disrespectful but also likely to prevent maximization of treatment benefits; and if we can integrate the best of clinical skill, scientific gains, and policy reform, we will have a fighting chance of making a real dent in the struggle to overcome both mental illness and the stigma that surrounds it. In short, if those in the field can model and promote a different set of attitudes and postures toward mental disorder, they will be sending a meaningful signal to the rest of society.

With all that remains to be done, we need to begin with ourselves as scientists, clinicians, and policy makers, examining our biases and our own tendencies to feel superior to and distanced from those afflicted by mental disorders. Nearly all of us are deeply affected by mental disorder, in terms of ourselves or our family members, and we can change the entire terrain by admitting our weaknesses, our sources of inspiration, and our pain, as well as our hopes and aspirations. The entire effort to promote mental health is at stake, and it will take a new way of integrating utterly personal and utterly scientific efforts to meet the many challenges ahead. What more important battle can there be?

NOTES

1. Hinshaw, S. P. (2002). *The years of silence are past: My father's life with bipolar disorder.* New York: Cambridge University Press.

2. See Hinshaw, S. P. (2004). Parental mental disorder and children's functioning: Silence and communication, stigma, and resilience. *Journal of Clinical Child and Adolescent Psychology, 33,* 400–411; Hinshaw, S. P. (2005). The stigmatization of mental illness in children and parents: Developmental issues, family concerns, and research needs. *Journal of Child Psychology and Psychiatry, 46,* 714–734; and Hinshaw, S. P. (2006). Stigma and mental illness: Developmental issues. In D. Cicchetti & D. Cohen (Eds.), *Developmental psychopathology: Vol. 3. Risk, disorder, and adaptation* (2nd ed., pp. 841–881). New York: Wiley. See also Hinshaw, S. P., & Cicchetti, D. (2000). Stigma and mental disorder: Conceptions of illness, public attitudes, personal disclosure, and social policy. *Development and Psychopathology, 12,* 555–598.

3. Hinshaw, S. P. (2007). *The mark of shame: Stigma of mental illness and an agenda for change.* New York: Oxford University Press.

Index

brother's aggressive outbursts, 226, 228, 234, 238
child's bipolar disorder, 48–50, 57, 61
father's bipolar disorder, 283, 287
parent's depression, 326–327, 331–332, 334, 338–339, 340, 344–345
parent's schizophrenia, 194–198, 201–202, 206
sister's psychotic breakdowns, 29–30, 31, 38
See also abusive family, Lucas's narrative; bipolar disorder, Londahl-Shaller's narrative; depression, Agee's narrative; depression, Zahn-Waxler's narrative; schizophrenia, Peris's narrative
mother-son relationships, mental illness context
brother's aggressive outbursts, 225–228, 234, 235
parent's depression, 123–125, 126–127, 128, 129, 132, 137, 138–139, 141–143, 145, 256
parent's schizophrenia, 196, 198–199, 200, 201
See also schizoaffective disorder, Browne's narrative

Navane, 160, 166
Nathan. *See* schizoaffective disorder, Browne's narrative
Nathan, Peter
chapter by, 252–267
comments on, 4, 13, 18, 19, 22, 352

open *vs.* closed families, 295–296, 297–298, 301
overcompensation. *See* abusive family, Lucas' narrative
Owens, Elizabeth B. "Liz"
chapter by, 102–121
comments on, 4, 12, 19, 20, 21, 349

pain, as narrative theme, 15
See also specific topics, e.g., aggressive outbursts, Borelli's narrative;

depression, Liew's narrative; substance abuse, Owens's narrative
panic attacks, 133, 332, 336, 337
paranoid delusions. *See* schizophrenia *entries*
parent-child relationships. *See specific relationships, e.g.,* mother-son relationship, mental illness context
parenting styles and substance abuse, 108, 116–117
Pauley, Jane, 24n17
People Say I'm Crazy (documentary), 172
Peris, Tara
chapter by, 70–101
comments on, 15, 19, 21, 348–349
posttraumatic stress disorder (PTSD), 211
poverty, 183–184, 351
See also depression, Agee's narrative
prefrontal lobotomies, 275
Prozac, 45, 53, 57, 59
psychiatric training experience, in Browne's narrative, 154–156
psychotic breakdowns, Mason's narrative
college years, 33–35, 38
family life, 26–33, 35–36, 40
personal healing process, 37–39, 43
post-college life, 35–37, 39–43
questions/comments on, 4, 11–12, 15, 18, 19, 21, 347–348
symptom patterns, 28, 29, 30, 31–32, 35, 36
See also schizoaffective disorder, Browne's narrative; schizophrenia *entries*
PTSD (posttraumatic stress disorder), 211

Raffi, 227, 243–244
recognition and realization, mental illness context
mother's depression, 123–124
mother's schizophrenia, 72–73, 78–79, 81, 97–98, 203–204
as narrative theme, 4
personal bipolar disorder, 48, 49, 54–55, 56, 59–64, 66–68, 348